IMMIGRATION STATISTICS

A Story of Neglect

Daniel B. Levine, Kenneth Hill, and Robert Warren, editors

Panel on Immigration Statistics
Committee on National Statistics
Commission on Behavioral and
Social Sciences and Education
National Research Council

NATIONAL ACADEMY PRESS
Washington, D.C. 1985

NATIONAL ACADEMY PRESS 2101 Constitution Ave., NW Washington, DC 20418

This report was prepared for the Immigration and Naturalization Service, U.S. Department of Justice, under contract number COW-2-90530. Points of view or opinions stated in this document are those of the contractor and do not necessarily represent the official position or policies of the Immigration and Naturalization Service or the U.S. Department of Justice.

Library of Congress Catalog Card Number 85-61694

International Standard Book Number 0-309-03589-9

Printed in the United States of America

Panel on Immigration Statistics

BURTON H. SINGER (Chair), Department of Statistics, Columbia University

SAM BERNSEN, Fragomen, Del Rey and Bernsen, Washington, D.C.

GEORGE BORJAS, Department of Economics, University of California, Santa Barbara

NORMAN CHERVANY, Department of Management Sciences, University of Minnesota

CHARLES KEELY, Population Council, New York

ELLEN KRALY, Department of Geography, Colgate University

MILTON MORRIS, Joint Center for Political Studies, Washington, D.C.

ALEJANDRO PORTES, Department of Sociology, Johns Hopkins University

JACK ROSENTHAL, *The New York Times,* New York

MARK ROSENZWEIG, Department of Economics, University of Minnesota

TERESA SULLIVAN, Department of Sociology, University of Texas

MARTA TIENDA, Department of Rural Sociology, University of Wisconsin

JAMES TRUSSELL, Office of Population Research, Princeton University

KENNETH WACHTER, Department of Statistics, University of California, Berkeley

DANIEL B. LEVINE, Study Director
KENNETH HILL, Associate Study Director
ROBERT WARREN, Research Associate
ROBERTA PIROSKO, Administrative Secretary/Research Aide

Committee on National Statistics

Contents

Acknowledgments

Many people contributed time and expertise to make this study possible, and we are most appreciative of their cooperation and help. In particular, staff of the Immigration and Naturalization Service at every level from headquarters through regional, district, and Border Patrol offices to data processing facilities and individual ports of entry cooperated with and contributed to the panel and its deliberations with admirable candor. Lisa Roney deserves special thanks for her tireless efforts in opening doors and directing us to the appropriate people in the service. Her advice, criticism, and suggestions over the past two years have been invaluable. Our work on refugees has depended entirely on the advice, encouragement, and work of Susan Forbes of the Refugee Policy Group and Linda Gordon of the Office of Refugee Resettlement. In particular, Linda Gordon's contributions to the panel's deliberations have been so extensive that she should in every way be viewed as equivalent to a panel member. Our report also benefited from the thoughtful comments of the many reviewers within the Academy and from the reorganization and editing by Eugenia Grohman, associate director for reports, and Christine L. McShane, editor, of the Commission on Behavioral and Social Sciences and Education.

I also wish to express my appreciation to my fellow panel members for their generous contribution of time and expert knowledge and for their insights and ideas, all of which helped to shape and are reflected in this report.

Finally, it is well known that behind every panel of the National Research Council, there is a staff that oversees the preparation of a final report. In this instance, the staff, consisting of Daniel Levine as study director in collaboration with Ken Hill, Bob Warren, and Roberta Pirosko, have done much more than simply oversee the preparation of a report. They have provided an example of excellence in research, writing, politics, and administrative organization that is unsurpassed in my experience. The panel and all those who benefit from this report are deeply indebted to this outstanding team.

Burton H. Singer, Chair
Panel on Immigration
Statistics

1

Overview and Major Recommendations

The minute you walk inside the room, you sense that you've walked into a metaphor, a huge metaphor, for what ails the world of immigration statistics. The room is an immense space inside the district headquarters of the Immigration and Naturalization Service near Wall Street in New York City. It is called the File Room; the simplicity of the name belies the complexity of its contents.

The room is as wide as a tennis court and as long as a football field, with sunlight streaming in along the long 300-foot side and the interior aisles between the files lighted by strings of neon.

To walk around this room is amazing as a spatial experience. Along one wall are endless banks of metal drawers containing cards for immigration files there's no longer room for. They've been sent to purgatory at a Federal Records Center in New Jersey; some 25,000 are called back for use each year. Near the door are stacks of cardboard boxes and rows of shiny shopping carts full of files in transit. A wall of metal bins distinguishes between "JFK," "Seaport," and other origins. But all these trappings of mundane bureaucracy are mere shrubbery compared with the centerpiece of the File Room.

What occupies most of the vast space is the "A-File." This single room contains the immigration records of 2.1 million people and to see them all in one place is to see a startling contradiction. Superficially, the A-File radiates modernity. It is housed in huge wall segments called Electric Compack-to-Files, 24 on one side of the center aisle, 34 on the other. The system looks as up-to-date as the nomenclature. The file segments are metal, handsomely painted in designer pastels of blue, salmon, tangerine, and they move from side to side, with a hum, at the push of a button.

The A-File, alas, only looks modern. Its packaging covers a Dickensian interior, for inside, the system for record-keeping is no better, indeed is clumsier, than that used by clerks of the Cratchit era. Precisely because the file segments do move from side to side, to save space, they block each other. When one clerk uses a seven-shelf segment, she blocks another clerk who needs to consult the adjacent one: mechanical gridlock. Typically, it takes 20 minutes to get traffic moving again.

Even then, for all the electric modernism, the contents, when you can get to them, are still paper, the paper is still sometimes wrong, often incomplete and always clumsy, and it takes three days to put files back; that's what's in those shopping carts up front. Sometimes the files can't be found; they've been misplaced in some bureaucratic limbo.

And even if the paper system were improved, its utility would still be dismally limited. It might work better for enforcement as applied to individuals, but would still be wholly useless for answering larger questions, answers that can and should be available to help manage the Service and, still more important, to create a basis for national immigration policies.

Consider a famous example: How many Iranian students are there in the United States? President Carter asked that question of the Immigration and Naturalization Service (INS) in 1979 after the hostage crisis began. The hostages were released after 444 days and another 1,500 or so days have passed since then and still the INS cannot answer the question. Yet, at least in theory, the Service now has a computer entry in its Nonimmigrant Information System for every foreign student admitted to the United States.

Consider an example more relevant to immigration policy: Do aliens pay more in taxes and unclaimable social security contributions than they use up in social services--and which levels of government come out ahead and behind? If the Service had been able even to offer an informed estimate in October 1984, the Simpson-Mazzoli immigration reform bill might not have died in the closing hours of the 98th Congress from concerns over a proposed ceiling of $1 billion on federal reimbursement to local governments.

Consider a question of still wider public interest: Do immigrants, legal and illegal, take jobs away from unskilled natives, especially minorities and youth? We just don't know, and the underlying reason why we don't know is not that analysis has been inadequate, but that the data needed for a convincing analysis do not exist. It is not just a question of timeliness or of quality, issues that may be resolved by the INS's enthusiastic pursuit of electronic sophistication, but also a conceptual failure to understand what data are for, and what data can do for the Service and the nation. The INS and other government agencies produce masses of data, if not always timely and not always accurate, about immigrants, refugees, and the foreign-born, but the data are not what we need to answer the fundamental policy issues of the day.

THE PROBLEM

As a nation built by waves of immigrants from colonial times to the present, we know remarkably little about the composition and characteristics of the flow of new arrivals in any given year or about how they settle in to their new lives in the United States.

This anomaly is particularly surprising in view of two further considerations. The first is that immigration and immigration policy affect the lives of enormous numbers of people, both in the United States and elsewhere. Residents of the United States may benefit or suffer from immigration: some may receive lower wages or even lose their jobs as a result of immigration; many more may benefit from lower overall prices that may result from immigration. Would-be immigrants unable to migrate legally to the United States under present policies find their aspirations for a better life thwarted and may respond by attempted illegal entry. Past immigrants and their immediate relatives who may be unable to obtain early admission under existing policies may suffer substantial emotional costs, although remittances sent home may improve the economic lot of those left behind at the cost of the United States' balance of payments and any lost multiplier effects. The problem is that we really do not know anything concrete about the costs and benefits involved because the basic statistics are so limited; policy has been made in a data vacuum that should naturally be abhorred by policy makers.

This point leads to the second consideration, namely the substantial effort that goes into the collection of many of the other data series generated by government. Immigration for some reason is the Cinderella of the federal statistical system. In essence a history of neglect has afflicted record-keeping concerning one of the most fundamental processes underlying the development of American society: the arrival and integration of new populations into contemporary American social and economic structures.

In recent years, the expressions of concern over inadequate, incomplete, and often unreliable information available for use in planning, implementing, or evaluating immigration policy have become both more numerous and more strident: for example, the Select Committee on Population of the House of Representatives (1978:1), in attempting to explore the role of immigration in future population growth, concluded that "immigration issues are clouded by faulty data and inflamed passions--not a good combination for rational policymaking." The Interagency Task Force on Immigration (1979:212) reported that "the level and accuracy of available immigration data have been repeatedly criticized as unresponsive to policy issues and inadequate for use in social science research." And even more recently, during the debate over aspects of the Simpson-Mazzoli legislation, a committee in the House (House Report 98-759, 1984) noted that, "The Committee is deeply concerned about the unavailability of accurate and current statistical information on immigration matters. . . . The Committee notes . . . that INS has not devoted sufficient resources and attention to this problem and, to a great extent, has ignored the statistical needs of Congress, as well as, the research needs of demographers and other outside users."

These few examples amply demonstrate that the need for a high-quality, readily accessible data base of timely information on immigrant populations has been manifest for years. This need has been heightened recently by renewed controversy in the Congress and in public debate over both restrictions on the size and composition of new immigrant groups and the perceived threat posed by the supposed onslaught of illegal or undocumented migrants against our borders.

THE CHARGE TO THE PANEL

Responding to the growing chorus of concerns in the late 1970s, the Immigration and Naturalization Service of the U.S. Department of Justice asked the Committee on National Statistics of the National Research Council to convene a conference to assess the feasibility of and need for a review of federal immigration statistics. Held in late 1980, the conference strongly supported the idea of a comprehensive review and, accordingly, in late 1982 the Panel on Immigration Statistics was established by the National Research Council, with the support of the Immigration and Naturalization Service.

The panel's objectives were three:

o To determine the data needs for immigration policy, for administration of immigration law, and for other purposes related to immigration;

o To review existing data sources related to immigration, emigration, and the foreign stock and to assess their statistical adequacy; and

o To identify major shortcomings and recommend appropriate remedies and actions.

The panel's activities have included interviews with appropriate officials and experts, visits to regional, district, and Border Patrol offices of the INS, visits to ports of entry, and meetings at the U.N. and with officials from foreign governments. The panel also examined the "demand" side to determine the current and projected needs for data among the range of users, attempted to quantify the "supply" side of what exists both within and outside government, explored organizational responsibilities, and developed suggestions and recommendations for both change and improvement. The panel sponsored workshops on the measurement of illegal entries and the possible uses of administrative data collected for other purposes, such as social security or internal revenue, in immigration research. Finally, the panel supported the preparation of a number of methodological papers related to immigration data issues.

This report is the culmination of a searching two-year study by the panel of the demand for information on immigrant populations and existing data resources to respond to that demand. The panel has taken a very broad view of the problems of immigrant populations and has included in its deliberations not only the statistical needs and products of the INS but also those of the Office of Refugee Resettlement, a wide variety of other federal offices, and a myriad of nongovernmental sources. The panel's recommendations are sweeping and comprehensive and will require major commitments at several levels in the government if real improvement in the immigration statistics area is to be realized. The purpose of this report is to specify the data requirements and to recommend the practical steps that must be taken to place future debate about immigrant populations on a solid base of statistical information.

PLAN OF THE REPORT

The report is organized as follows. Chapter 1 provides an overview of the panel's work. In this chapter the reader will find a brief account of the background to the panel's work (discussion of the inadequacy of our knowledge of the processes underlying migration flows or of the adjustment of immigrants to life in the United States), the charge that the panel undertook, the way in which the panel carried out its work, and the major conclusions and recommendations that it arrived at. Thus Chapter 1 provides the essentials of the panel's study, though for more detail and justification the reader must consult chapters 2 through 9.

The overall approach of the report is to examine data needs (Chapter 3), data availability (Chapters 4 through 7), and the balance, the areas in which data needs are not met by available data (Chapter 8). Although detailed recommendations appear throughout the report, Chapter 9 presents the panel's major recommendations. First, however, Chapter 2 provides a historical overview of U.S. immigration policy in order to set the problems associated with immigration statistics in their proper perspective. This chapter contains definitions of the populations involved in congressional legislation--past and present--and includes a detailed description of the current visa allocation system. A presentation of immigration law and the role of the INS in implementing it clarifies the minimal information that must be collected to fulfill legislative requirements.

The needs for statistics on immigration go well beyond what is necessary for the INS to fulfill its mandate as a law enforcement agency. Chapter 3 examines the diversity of data needs on immigration. The chapter starts with a description of the data collection required by law, that is, the irreducible minimum information on immigrant populations that should be available according to existing legislation. Given this basic, mandated data foundation, the chapter examines the wider data needs for those who make, execute, and evaluate public policy, including the data requirements, primarily within the INS, for program management purposes. The chapter concludes with a discussion of potential impediments to meeting the various data needs identified.

Chapter 4 presents an in-depth analysis of the INS. Because of its central role in regulating the flow of international migration to the United States, the INS's statistical activities are examined in far greater detail than those of the other federal agencies involved in collecting immigration data. As the recommendations of the panel point out, it is from the core of information within the INS--for instance, in the File Room in New York--that we must build the statistical system that can respond to the diverse array of data needs documented in Chapter 3. Recommendations for improvement from the general (overall organization and attitude) to the specific (statistical procedures) are incorporated in the discussion.

Other official government sources of information on immigration are described and evaluated, with recommendations for improvements, in Chapter 5. Complementary to these sources is a heterogeneous collection of data sources and analytical studies produced outside government. Such nongovernment work is discussed in general terms in Chapter 6 together with recommendations for promoting more effective data collection and analysis on immigrant populations in the private sector in the future.

Chapter 7 examines data production for a "best case," that of refugees, and highlights the deficiencies even of this relatively favored system. Chapter 8 weighs supply against demand, and costs against benefits, to identify the approaches to improvement that should be adopted to ensure an adequate statistical basis for the future. Chapter 9 presents the panel's major recommendations by the agency to which they are directed; the recommendations are keyed to the chapters in which they are discussed.

The report is followed by a glossary of terms and abbreviations and a number of appendices concerned with particular aspects of data collection, data analysis, and the panel's work. Appendix A reproduces a selection of the forms that provide the basic raw information for the INS data system. Appendix B contains several methodological papers on immigration-related issues: (a) some new methods for assessing stocks and flows of migrants; (b) a review of estimates of the size of the illegal alien population; and (c) imputation and the treatment of missing data. Appendix C is a paper written for the panel by Douglas Massey on the settlement process among Mexican migrants. Its relevance to the report stems from the fact that it dramatically illustrates the economic and social dynamics of migrant populations that can be ascertained by a coordinated interplay of good survey data and qualitative ethnographic evidence. Appendix D presents the letter report submitted by the panel to the INS in early 1983 concerning selected statistical aspects of the Senate version of the Simpson-Mazzoli bill. Although the legislation died in the waning hours of the 98th Congress, the wording of the bill illustrates that important provisions regarding statistics on aliens have in fact made their way into contemporary pending legislation. Three final appendices complete the report. Appendix E outlines many of the diverse activities undertaken by panel and staff; Appendix F presents a description of key bibliographic sources and selected bibliographic examples; and Appendix G presents biographical sketches of panel members and staff.

WHAT WE FOUND

The one fact that struck the panel repeatedly was that a statistical system to produce immigration data does exist, but it does so in an atmosphere of almost total neglect. We found an extraordinary lack of concern with the situation on the part of many who are key to the operation of the statistical system, an almost total ignorance of its existence on the part of the top management that most needs its products, and, finally, that this neglect extends throughout almost all levels of responsibility and almost all the agencies most directly involved in the system. Further, the Congress, with its ultimate power of the purse, must share in the blame for having condoned the situation far too long.

In its explorations into data needs and availability, the panel was surprised to find that the Immigration and Nationality Act, the legislative centerpiece in the immigration field, mandates very little statistical compilation. Nonetheless, program needs (more than policy needs) have resulted in the establishment of administrative record-keeping systems that are the source of a variety of information on those entering or applying to enter the United States as immigrants, visitors, students, or in some other category. For the most part, requests for information for policy purposes are met from these record-keeping sources.

The panel approached the issue of defining data needs by identifying layers of data users, starting with officials in the legislative and executive branches of the federal government who make and execute immigration policy. At this level, as the recent debates over immigration reform quickly reveal, the argument revolves largely around the issues of whether and why immigration is beneficial or, in terms of data, who benefits from immigration and who loses. Obviously, the data needs vary widely over time, often determined by legislative initiatives far removed from the immigration area, such as Medicaid use by illegal aliens or attempts to evaluate factors affecting the apportionment of funds.

In the middle, the panel identified the data needs of program managers throughout agencies that deal directly with immigrants, either in a service or a law enforcement role. Their involvement is in attempting to achieve effective management and, for this purpose, information is a tool through which scarce resources are effectively allocated. Finally, there are those whose daily contact is with aliens, and who need access to files about individuals. The dilemma is that many of the statistics used by all three levels are generated initially by this last level, who have little if any stake in their use by the other levels. In fact, such program staff often have little or no knowledge about such use or the need for such use by the agency and thus have little commitment to quality, timeliness, accuracy, or adherence to statistical standards. Thus, irrespective of the ultimate data need, the systems must recognize and deal with the need to inform, educate, and motivate the data collector else, as the wisdom goes (and as experience shows), "garbage in, garbage out."

Recognizing that it is not possible to foresee future needs in detail, nor to define every last piece of information that should be collected from or about a specific alien, the panel dealt with the issue by defining major areas in which data are needed and examining alternative strategies for obtaining them. Furthermore, given the awareness that this is a time of acute concern with government spending, the costs of the different strategies were carefully weighed against the value of the expected improvement in both data quality and quantity. Thus, the least expensive type of improvement is to be found in a more extensive presentation of data already collected and available, either in tabulated form or ready for tabulation. Next in cost is the processing of data that have been collected but not previously used, followed by the merging of existing data files to expand the core of knowledge. Modification of existing data collection mechanisms is more costly still, and superseded only by the institution of wholly new data collection systems. These, then, are the choices to be considered and weighed against the information gains and the importance of the needs.

The examination of data needs versus availability led directly to the agencies and offices that produce or use the data or, in many cases, do both. The INS is, of course, predominant in the collection, if not the dissemination, of data. Unfortunately, the panel also found it the most wanting and is highly critical of its performance in the statistical field. Even recognizing the legal and administrative missions of the agency and that the statistical activities of the Service are directly related to and controlled by the activities involved in carrying out its missions--monitoring entry into and exit from the United States and changes in legal status--the panel noted numerous examples of the agency's inability to meet its own needs, much less those from outside.

Two examples illustrate this inability. The first concerns the G-23 report, which summarizes office workload activities on a monthly basis in a variety of areas and contains some 25,000 potential data entries. When "statistics" are discussed at INS, the point of reference is usually the G-23 report. Why then was the panel told repeatedly by staff at all levels of the agency that data reported on the G-23 are assumed to be inaccurate, invalid, and irrelevant to program evaluation and operational analysis? The second example is a quote from the latest INS Statistical Yearbook, that for 1981, which states, "Data processing problems have resulted in incomplete information on immigrants admitted in fiscal 1980 and 1981, the loss of all nonimmigrant information for fiscal year 1980 and incomplete nonimmigrant information for 1982." In fairness to the INS, it should be noted that a major effort is now under way in the agency to install automated systems that are intended to overcome many of the problems that have plagued it in the past. Planning for these systems was preceded by an extensive study of the information requirements of the agency; unfortunately, the needs for policy information of the executive branch or the Congress, while acknowledged, were considered to be outside the purview of the exercise and were omitted from examination.

In sum, then, it would be naive to assume that automation will solve the problems that have been evident for too long a time in the statistical operations of the INS. Data vary in quality, refinement, consistency, accessibility, and timeliness. The agency's problems are fundamental and pervasive but center on the basic issue of quality. The Statistical Analysis Branch, the key organizational entity as far as statistics are concerned, does not even appear on an organizational chart of the agency and its influence is notable for its absence.

Three factors can be said to characterize the low status of statistical programs in the INS:

o A lack of understanding and commitment throughout the agency to the need for high-quality statistics;
o The lack of emphasis on statistics in the current bureaucratic structure; and
o The absence of standards for performance in the collection, processing, or publication of data.

Taken together, these factors are significant warning signals and clearly demonstrate that immediate and direct action is necessary. What is required is a fundamental change in the outlook of the institution toward statistics, a change that will recognize explicitly and unequivocally the role of statistics and statistical analysis in the mission of the INS and will ensure that this role is nurtured and supported.

Not surprisingly, data on aliens are collected and produced by a variety of federal agencies or offices, either as a result of dealing directly with aliens, as in the case of the Bureau of Consular Affairs of the State Department, or as a by-product of their activities, as in the case of the Social Security Administration. The panel reviewed a total of 11 separate organizations within 8 different cabinet-level agencies; the number of organizations having some information on aliens, or the potential to obtain such information, is undoubtedly much greater.

The overriding impression that emerged from this review was of the need for coordination and direction. Each agency has followed its own institutional priorities in the area of what to collect, how to define it, whether to publish it, or how much to spend on it with little regard for the broader issues involved. Furthermore, there is obvious potential for the establishment of symbiotic relationships between agencies, whereby the use and interpretation of one data set could be greatly enhanced by ready access to others, but in the field of immigration statistics this potential has gone largely unrealized. Someone must bring together all the agencies concerned with immigration data, both those who produce and those who use, in order to ensure the best use of scarce resources, whether money, staff, time, or public tolerance. Progress must be monitored, as must adherence to standards, common definitions, timeliness in publication, and full disclosure of methods, methodology, procedures, and problems. Only through such coordination will significant improvement occur in the data base. Logic dictates that this coordinating role be played by the Office of Management and Budget (OMB), which, by statute and through its review of budget proposals, is ultimately responsible for establishing current statistical agenda and for monitoring progress. It is regrettable that OMB has not adequately exercised its coordinating authority in recent years, but action now is not too late to improve the data base for future policy deliberations.

One segment of the data, emigration from the United States, is totally lacking and is generally ignored in discussions of immigration statistics. Yet estimates made during the past few decades indicate that more than 100,000 persons move out of the United States each year. A strategy should be devised for making accurate and timely estimates of emigration.

Finally, as part of our task, the panel explored the possibilities of developing estimates of the illegal population in the United States. Following a review of existing methodologies and studies, as well as meeting with interested researchers to brainstorm new approaches, the panel concluded, albeit reluctantly, that it could not identify or contribute to any breakthroughs in methodology that would substantially narrow the current uncertainty in the estimates. Nonetheless, the brief review of the methods used to estimate the size of the illegal population, which appears in Appendix B, leads the panel to the view that, although all the studies suffer from uncertainties, the number of illegals currently in the United States is between 2 and 4 million and, further, that the number has not been growing remarkably fast in recent years.

SUMMARY OF MAJOR RECOMMENDATIONS

The concluding objective of the panel's charge was to identify major shortcomings and recommend appropriate remedies and actions. The report documents the efforts of the panel in this regard and provides a wide range of suggestions and recommendations on both change and improvement. These are described in the individual chapters and are summarized in Chapter 9. Since many different organizations are involved in the area of immigration statistics, our comments are directed to many different places. The panel wishes to emphasize strongly, however, the need for these diverse groups to act in concert. The recommendations represent a range of different actions that will be fully successful only if implemented as a whole.

Most of our recommendations are general in nature, concerned with process rather than the particular, and intentionally so. It is the panel's belief, after extensive study of the current situation and how it has arisen, that superficial local patching will not solve the problem. Without major changes in direction from the top policy-making levels and focused interest within the key agencies, the immigration statistics system will never produce reliable, accurate, and timely statistics that permit rational decision making concerning immigration policy.

What follows is a brief listing of those recommendations that, in the panel's view, are of overriding importance, both because they require action and commitment at a high policy level and because each is fundamental to the accomplishment of the key goal--the ready availability of accurate, timely, and useful statistical information on international migration. Failure to implement any of these key recommendations will result in failure to improve the data system fully and cost-effectively.

The panel recommends that Congress:

o Strongly affirm the importance of reliable, accurate, and timely statistical information on immigration to the needs of the Congress and direct the Attorney General to reexamine the organizational structure of the Immigration and Naturalization Service as it relates to statistics, with a view to placing greater priority on this important task;

o Require that the Attorney General prepare and submit by June 30 each year an annual report to the President and the Congress, presenting data on aliens admitted or excluded, naturalizations, asylees, and refugees, describing their characteristics, and containing an analysis of significant developments during the preceding fiscal year in the field of immigration and emigration; and

o Mandate that a study be initiated and conducted among new immigrants over a 5-year period, in order to develop information for policy guidance on the adjustment experience of families and individuals to the labor market, use of educational and health facilities, reliance on social programs, mobility experience, and income history.

The panel recommends that the Attorney General:

o Issue a strong policy directive asserting the importance of reliable, accurate, and timely statistical information on immigration to the mission of the INS and unequivocally committing the INS to improving its existing capabilities.

The panel recommends that the commissioner of the INS:

o Issue an explicit statement clearly setting forth that the collection, cumulation, and tabulation of reliable, accurate, and timely statistical information on immigration is a basic responsibility and inherent in the mission of the INS;

o Establish a Division of Immigration Statistics, reporting directly to an associate commissioner or an equivalent level, with overall responsibility:

--for ensuring the use of appropriate statistical standards and procedures in the collection of data throughout the agency;
--for ensuring the timely publication of a variety of statistical and analytic reports;
--for providing statistical assistance and direction to all parts of the agency to help in carrying out their mission;
--for directing statistical activities throughout the agency;

o Direct and implement the recruitment of a full complement of competent, trained professionals with statistical capabilities and subject-area expertise;

o Establish an advisory committee composed of experts in the use and production of immigration-related data, to advise the associate commissioner and the proposed Division of Immigration Statistics of needs for new or different types of data; to review existing data and data collection methodology; and to provide the Service with independent evaluation of its statistical products, plans, and performance;

o Establish formal liaison with other federal and state agencies involved in the collection or analysis of immigration- and emigration-related data; and

o Initiate a review of all data gathering activities to eliminate duplication, minimize burden and waste, review specific data needs and uses, improve question wording and format design, standardize definitions and concepts, document methodologies, introduce statistical standards and procedures, and promote efficiencies in the use of staff and resources.

The panel recommends that the director, Office of Management and Budget (OMB):

o Ensure that OMB exercise its responsibilities to monitor and review statistical activities and budgets concerning statistics on immigration and emigration, and particularly those of the INS, to minimize duplication and ensure that appropriate procedures are used, standards met, and priorities observed in the collection, production, and publication of such data;

o Require and establish an interagency review group responsible for direction and coordination in the field of immigration and emigration data; the group would examine consistency and comparability in concepts and definitions used by individual organizations in the collection of such information; and oversee the introduction and use of standardized approaches; and

o Actively encourage and support the timely publication and dissemination of data on immigration, emigration, the ready availability of fully documented public-use data tapes, including samples of individual records without identifiers where feasible, and data summaries.

In making its recommendations, the panel has been mindful of costs. Many of its recommendations fall within the scope and margin of administrative discretion, and, if they require additional funds, the amounts are relatively small. Two of the panel's major recommendations will require new funding, but in both cases implementation will be gradual, with expenditures spread over a number of years. The major recommendation for change in administrative structure concerns the establishment of a Division of Immigration Statistics within the INS, which will have increased authority, responsibility, and professional staff. We expect, however, that a period of 3-5 years will be required for the full development of such a division, in order to locate and integrate new staff and to acquire new responsibilities and demonstrate capability on a step-by-step basis. Thus, the initial cost implications are modest and the cost increments can be viewed in the light of some initial accomplishments. The major recommendation for a new data collection initiative, the longitudinal survey of immigrants, also requires new funding but, again, the estimated cost will be spread over a number of years and is amply justified in the view of the panel.

2

Immigration Policy: Past to Present

Current immigration policy rests on the twin pillars of the numerical limitations on admission and the grounds for exclusion. These provisions essentially constitute quantitative and qualitative criteria on which the U.S. immigration system has been based for more than half a century. Around them have been woven an awesome complex of exceptions, exemptions, waivers, conditions, criminal penalties, civil fines, reports, definitions, procedures, and classifications and an extremely broad exercise of discretion, in addition to which there are special provisions for asylees and refugees. The first part of this chapter sketches the legislative road the nation has followed in arriving at its present policy; the second part describes that policy. Legislative mandate and policy are the driving forces behind the need for statistics and the determinants of the kinds of information which, in turn, both program and policy require.

HISTORICAL AND LEGISLATIVE OVERVIEW

Before the Twentieth Century: Unrestricted Entry

When the nation posed for its first "family portrait" in 1790, the picture showed a recorded census population of around 3 1/4 million, all of whom were either immigrants themselves or descendants of relatively recent immigrants (Indians were not included). At that time, immigration to the United States was virtually unrestricted, and it continued in that vein for 85 years. Except for a brief flirtation with control in the Alien Act of 1798, which authorized the President to order the departure of aliens he judged to be dangerous, virtually no laws limiting immigration were enacted until 1875. As to policy, George Washington had proclaimed in 1783 that the "bosom of America is open to receive not only the opulent and respectable stranger, but the oppressed and persecuted of all nations and religions, whom we shall welcome to a participation of all our rights and privileges. . . ." The Alien Act itself was not enforced and expired after its 2-year term.

When the Civil War began in 1860, the population totaled more than 4 million. Between 1860 and 1885, immigration surged to 8 million arrivals, with more than 9 out of 10 of the immigrants coming from

Northern and Western Europe. In the latter part of the period, however, immigrants began to arrive from countries on the southern and eastern rim of Europe and, in a little over 10 years, they represented the majority of immigrants. It was during this period that Congress, by its actions in passing the first exclusion law, assumed responsibility for regulating immigration and has retained to this day complete control of the criteria for admission, exclusion, and deportation of immigrants to the United States.

The law passed in 1875 barred convicts and prostitutes; it brought to an end almost 100 years of open borders. The first racial law was enacted in May 1882 to bar Chinese laborers, and, shortly thereafter, in August of the same year, Congress added idiots, lunatics, and persons likely to become a public charge to the list of those who could be excluded. In short order, in 1885, in an action aimed at protecting the domestic labor market, Congress prohibited the entry of laborers induced to immigrate by job offers and, in 1888, allowed deportation of workers who had entered the country illegally. In 1891, Congress expanded grounds for exclusion, authorizing the deportation of any aliens entering unlawfully. And so it went. Over the years, the list has continued to expand: it now contains 33 specified grounds for exclusion.

The Early Twentieth Century: The Beginning of Restrictions

By the turn of the century, the unprecedented growth in both the number of immigrants and the mix of nationalities had begun to generate opposition to unrestricted entry, and the rush to exclude persons continued to mark the legislative history of immigration. In 1910, for the first time, Congress provided for expulsion on the basis of conduct after entry, supposedly in response to allegations that Oriental women--among others--were engaging in prostitution.

The influx of nearly 13 million people into the United States between 1900 and 1914 generated xenophobic outbursts from a wide spectrum of society. A respected anthropologist wrote of "hordes of immigrants of inferior racial value"; the report of the congressionally mandated Dillingham Commission (1911) supported the popular belief that immigrants from northwestern Europe were more desirable than their counterparts from Southern and Eastern Europe; and The New York Times editorialized against the growing "threat of anarchism" represented by an expanding Russian presence in our midst, stating: "[The United States] should cast out this drove of foreign destructionists who have come here to bring about its ruin" (1919:14). On the western side of the continent, the concern was with the influx of Japanese, who were forbidden to buy or lease land in California and Texas and were subsequently excluded by law from entry as immigrants and found by the Supreme Court to be ineligible for citizenship. During World War I legislation barred Orientals generally. U.S. immigration policy discriminated against Asians until 1965. The crisis of World War I also led to legislation that tightened control of alien seamen, strengthened the law against aliens considered by the government to be subversive, and, after three presidential vetoes, added illiteracy as a ground for exclusion.

The 1920s: The Flow is Stopped

The most important legislation of the early period of the century, which was adopted in 1921 and 1924, was designed both to restrict overall immigration and to limit immigration from certain areas. Although earlier legislative efforts undoubtedly had some effects on restricting flows to the United States, Congress for the most part had resisted efforts to impose quotas. But in 1921 Congress passed its first quota act, limiting the annual number of immigrants from each country to 3 percent of the number of people born in that country and residing in the United States as reported in the 1910 census. The intent of the bill was to limit immigration to people from Northern and Western Europe and stop the "growing hordes" from Southern and Eastern Europe.

This temporary measure was followed by the more restrictive Immigration Act of 1924, which used the "national origin" of each individual in the United States in 1890 as the basis for allocating the flow of immigrants. Despite attacks from many fronts, and change in 1929 to using the 1920 census population as the base, this approach stood as the standard for the next 40 years; the national origins quota system was not abolished until 1965. Since their adoption in 1921, numerical limitations have never been abolished and have been central in U.S. policy debates on immigration for more than 60 years.

Coincident with the passage of the 1924 act, Congress established the Border Patrol, in response to the rising concern with illegal movements across the U.S. borders with Mexico and Canada.

The first "legalization" provision, which acknowledged the need to accommodate long-term resident aliens not legally admitted for residence, was enacted in 1929 and applied to aliens who had entered the country before June 3, 1921. Through the years the qualifying entry date has been advanced; it is now June 30, 1948. Recent proposals for change would advance that date to January 1, 1973.

The worldwide depression that began in 1929 virtually shut down the inflow of immigrants, which fell to the unheard-of level of 23,000 in 1933. Even the smallest quotas were left unfilled, and the number of people leaving the United States exceeded the number entering during each year from 1932 to 1936. As a result, during this period the attention of Congress temporarily turned elsewhere.

World War II and the Postwar Years: Concerns About Security

Reflecting concerns with security and the approach of World War II, the Immigration and Naturalization Service (INS), which in 1891 had come into existence in the Treasury Department as the Bureau of Immigration, was transferred in 1940 from the Department of Labor to the Department of Justice, its present home. In the legislative area, the Alien Registration Act of 1940 introduced the concepts of voluntary departure in lieu of deportation and of suspension of deportation. Under the suspension provision, an alien could obtain permanent residence by showing that deportation would result in extreme hardship to the alien or to a U.S. citizen relative. The 1940 act also required the registration and fingerprinting of aliens and reports of change of address. The economic and political needs of the wartime United States and diminished levels of immigration led to liberalization in immigration policy. For example, in December 1943 the Chinese exclusion laws were repealed--two years after China had become a wartime ally. In 1942 the Bracero Program was begun; through bilateral agreements, agricultural workers were admitted temporarily to the United States from Mexico, Barbados, Jamaica, and British Honduras.

The postwar years saw substantial changes in immigration policy. On the one hand, the policy became more open: war brides, refugees, and temporary workers from Mexico were admitted under a variety of exceptions to existing legislation, and a new law in January 1948 provided for the temporary admission of exchange aliens as students, teachers, and for certain other purposes. The Displaced Persons Act of 1948 authorized the issuance of visas for refugees of World War II. Subsequently, the Refugee Relief Act of 1953 provided for the immigration of refugees and escapees from Iron Curtain countries. On the other hand, concerns with subversion and security began to dominate the national dialogue and were reflected in new, restrictive immigration legislation enacted by Congress in 1950 and 1952. The Internal Security Act in 1950 required that aliens in the United States submit address reports annually, made the exclusion or deportation of "subversives" easier, and proscribed the Communist party by name, so that proof of membership alone made an alien inadmissible.

In 1952, the Immigration and Nationality Act (INA) was passed by Congress over President Truman's veto. It both carried forward many of the existing immigration provisions and introduced important changes, such as excluding drug addicts and those who sought to obtain a visa by fraud; it also established priorities within quotas. Although extensively amended since 1952, it is still the basic U.S. law on immigration. The changes have alleviated hardships at the same time that they have made the law more restrictive. The 1954 changes, for example, spared from exclusion an alien convicted of a single petty offense, and 1957 saw bans dropped on the immigration of illegitimate and adopted children and orphans, and discretionary waivers were permitted for aliens inadmissible on criminal or moral grounds or because of tuberculosis or visa fraud. Yet in 1956 a foreign residence requirement was imposed on exchange visitors so that they could not become lawful permanent residents of the United States unless they went home for 2 years.

From 1965 to 1984: Change and Proposed Change

Despite the urgings of Presidents Eisenhower and Kennedy to revise the national origins quota system, it was not until 1965, during the administration of President Johnson, that Congress adopted the immigration reforms that guide U.S. policy to this day. With wide-ranging civil rights legislation about to be enacted into law and economic activity at a high point, President Johnson was able to enact the extensive reforms in immigration policy that had been introduced during the Kennedy administration. Included in his inaugural address in early 1965, the revisions were enacted by Congress in late 1965. The legislation was both liberalizing and restrictive: it abolished the national origins quota system, ending the harsh limitations on immigration from Asian and Pacific countries and the restrictive treatment of countries in Eastern and Southern Europe; it also led to the first fixed ceiling on immigration from the Western Hemisphere (120,000), which went into effect in 1968. In 1964, the United States had also unilaterally ended the Bracero program, thus bringing to a halt the 22-year temporary worker program, which at its peak in the late 1950s allowed the entry of over 400,000 workers.

Since 1965 additional major changes have been made to the existing legislation. For example, in 1966 Congress authorized the granting of permanent residence status to Cuban refugees, who now represent the largest number of refugees from a single country. In 1976 the annual limitation of 20,000 immigrants per country and the preference system were extended to the Western Hemisphere, and in 1978 separate numerical limitations on immigration for Eastern and Western Hemispheres were combined into a single worldwide annual limit of 290,000 per year. The total was reduced to 270,000 with the passage of the first permanent refugee and asylum legislation in March 1980, which created a separate refugee program and removed the refugee category from the preference system for immigrants. More recently, in December 1981, Congress sought to improve the efficiency of the INS by streamlining certain procedures, eliminating various reports to Congress and discontinuing the annual alien address reports. A selected list of immigration laws for the past 120 years is shown in Table 2-1.

Since early 1976, Congress and the various administrations have been discussing and considering the possibilities of major amendments and modifications to the existing immigration legislation. Following a series of hearings, administration-initiated studies, and abortive legislative initiatives, Congress in late 1978 established the Select Commission on Immigration and Refugee Policy "to study and evaluate . . . existing laws, policies, and procedures governing the admission of immigrants and refugees to the United States and to make such administrative and legislative recommendations to the President and to the Congress as are appropriate" (P.L. 95-412:1978). In March 1981 the commission issued its final report and recommendations, and shortly thereafter legislation to implement various of the recommendations was introduced into both the House and the Senate. In May 1983 the Senate approved its version of the legislation, and the House followed suit with a somewhat different version in June 1984. The legislation, however, known as Simpson-Mazzoli after its Senate and House sponsors, did not become law, because a conference committee was unable to reconcile the differences between the respective bills before Congress adjourned.

The Simpson-Mazzoli bill would have introduced significant changes in the Immigration and Nationality Act by prohibiting the employment of illegal aliens and imposing sanctions on employers of aliens not authorized to work and by authorizing amnesty to selected groups of illegal aliens who entered the United States before a prescribed date. The bill would also have imposed a 2-year foreign residence requirement on all foreign students and would have limited judicial review and thus

TABLE 2-1 Chronology of Selected U.S. Immigration Legislation,
1864-1982

1864	Congress passes law legalizing the importing of contract laborers.
1875	The first federal restriction on immigration prohibits prostitutes and convicts.
1882	Congress curbs Chinese immigration.
1882	Congress excludes persons convicted of political offenses, lunatics, idiots, and persons likely to become public charges and places a head tax on each immigrant.
1885	Legislation prohibits the admission of contract laborers.
1903	List of excluded immigrants expanded to include polygamists and political radicals such as anarchists.
1906	Naturalization Act makes knowledge of English a requirement for naturalization.
1907	Head tax on immigrants is increased; added to the excluded list are people with physical or mental defects that may affect their ability to earn a living, people with tuberculosis, and children unaccompanied by parents. Gentlemen's agreement between U.S. and Japan restricts Japanese immigration.
1917	Congress requires literacy in some language for immigrants over 16 years of age except in cases of religious persecution; bans virtually all immigration from Asia.
1921	Temporary annual quotas are established, limiting the number of immigrants of each nationality to 3 percent of the number of foreign-born persons of that nationality living in the United States in 1910. Limit on Eastern Hemisphere immigration (mostly European) set at about 350,000.
1924	National Origins Law (Johnson-Reed Act) sets temporary annual quotas at 2 percent of a nationality's U.S. population as determined in 1890 census and sets a minimum quota of 100 for each nationality. Border Patrol established.
1929	Annual quotas of 1924 permanently set to be apportioned according to each nationality's percentage of the total U.S. population as determined in the 1920 census and applying that percentage against the total number permitted to enter, set at 150,000. Minimum quota of 100 for each nationality reaffirmed.

TABLE 2-1 (continued)

1942	Bilateral agreements with Mexico, British Honduras, Barbados, and Jamaica cover entry of temporary foreign agricultural laborers to work in the United States--the Bracero Program.
1943	Chinese exclusion laws repealed.
1946	Congress passes War Brides Act, facilitating immigration of foreign-born wives, husbands, and children of U.S. armed forces personnel.
1948	Congress passes Displaced Persons Act (amended in 1950), enabling 400,000 refugees to enter the United States.
1950	Internal Security Act increases grounds for exclusion and deportation of subversives; all aliens required to report their addresses annually.
1952	Immigration and Nationality Act of 1952 (McCarran-Walter Act): o reaffirms national origins system, giving each nation a quota equal to its proportion of the U.S. population in 1920; o limits immigration from Eastern Hemisphere to about 150,000; leaves immigration from Western Hemisphere unrestricted; o establishes preferences for skilled workers and relatives of U.S. citizens and permanent resident aliens; and o tightens security and screening standards and procedures.
1953	Refugee Relief Act admits over 200,000 refugees outside existing quotas.
1957	Laws allow immigration benefits for certain illegitimate and adopted children and orphans and permits waivers of inadmissibility for certain alien relatives otherwise excludable on criminal or moral grounds or because of tuberculosis or visa fraud.
1965	Immigration and Nationality Act Amendments of 1965: o abolish the national origins system; o establish an annual ceiling of 170,000 for the Eastern Hemisphere with a 20,000 per-country limit, distributing immigrant visas according to a seven-category preference system that favors close relatives of U.S. citizens and permanent resident aliens, those with needed occupational skills, and refugees; and o establish an annual ceiling of 120,000 for the Western Hemisphere with no per-country limit or preference system.
1975	Indochinese Refugee Resettlement Program begins.

TABLE 2-1 (continued)

1976   Immigration and Nationality Act Amendments of 1976:
- o extend the 20,000 per-country limit and the seven-category preference system to the Western Hemisphere and
- o maintain separate annual ceilings of 170,000 for the Eastern Hemisphere and 120,000 for the Western Hemisphere.

1978   Immigration and Nationality Act Amendments of 1978 combine the ceilings for both hemispheres into a worldwide total of 290,000, with the same seven-category preference system and 20,000 per-country limit uniformly applied.

1978   Congress passes law providing for the exclusion or deportation of Nazi persecutors.

1980   Refugee Act removes refugees as the seventh preference category and establishes clear criteria and procedures for admission of refugees; reduces the worldwide limit for immigrants from 290,000 to 270,000 to reflect the removal of seventh preference from the total.

1981   INS Efficiency Act provides for certain technical changes in the Immigration and Nationality Act to enable the more efficient application of the law and abolishes annual reporting of addresses for aliens.

1982   Law permits nonimmigrant temporary workers who have lived continuously in the Virgin Islands since June 30, 1975, to obtain permanent residence in the United States.

1982   Law eases restrictions on the immigration to the United States of young Southeast Asians fathered by American servicemen.

1982   Congress reauthorizes for one year the refugee resettlement programs established in 1980.

Source: U.S. Immigration Policy and the National Interest. The Final Report and Recommendations of the Select Commission on Immigration and Refugee Policy to the Congress and President of the United States, March 1, 1981, pp. 88-89, with updating.

expedited the procedures for settling disputes. The legislation also was significant in that it contained mandates for the preparation and submission of a range of statistical products.

Throughout all this history, it is important to note one very important factor, consistent over time and conspicuous by its absence--namely, the lack of any substantive controls on emigration, the "out" movement of the population. Various laws and administrative requirements do limit people's freedom to travel from the United States to certain nations or require visitors to complete and provide certain documents upon leaving the United States, but the freedom to leave the country, with rare exceptions (e.g., criminals, etc.) is very loosely circumscribed and virtually uncontrolled. This policy--which is in conformity with the Universal Declaration on Human Rights--has meant that data on the people leaving the United States, their numbers, reasons, or characteristics, do not exist.

PRESENT LAW

Numerical Limitations

The Immigration and Nationality Act provides that up to 270,000 immigrants may be admitted annually under the preference system. Exemptions from the numerical limitations are accorded to spouses and minor children of U.S. citizens and to parents of adult U.S. citizens. Ministers of religion and certain other persons are also exempt. Legal permanent resident aliens, having been counted under the numerical limitations when they first immigrated, are not counted again under those limitations when they return to the United States after a temporary absence. Refugees are subject to separate limitations.

Under the numerical limitation on immigration, there are six preference categories for visa issuance, four on the basis of relationship and two on the basis of occupation; see Table 2-2 for an outline of the preference system. Each category is allocated a specified percentage of the authorized visa numbers. Relatives are allocated 80 percent, professionals and other workers, 20 percent. If the authorized number of visas is not issued for the preference categories, alien visas can be issued to prospective immigrants in the nonpreference category. To prevent any one country or a few countries from capturing the lion's share of the visa numbers, every foreign country is subject to a 20,000 annual ceiling on visas. Dependent areas and colonies are subject to an annual limitation of 600, chargeable against the mother country.

In general, place of birth determines the country against whose numerical limitation a prospective immigrant is charged. To deal with hardship in special situations, a spouse or child may be charged to the foreign state of the accompanying spouse or parent when necessary to prevent the separation of families.

The procedures for obtaining immigrant visas are prescribed in the INA. Except for nonpreference aliens and special immigrants (and refugees), a petition must be filed with and approved by the INS before an immigrant visa may be issued by a consular officer of the Department

TABLE 2-2 Current Visa Allocation System

_____

NUMERICALLY EXEMPT IMMIGRANTS:

Immediate relatives of U.S. citizens
    Spouses
    Unmarried minor children
    Parents of adult U.S. citizens

Special immigrants
    Certain ministers of religion
    Certain former employees of the U.S. government abroad
    Certain persons who have lost U.S. citizenship

NUMERICALLY LIMITED IMMIGRANTS (270,000):

Preference	Category	Percentage and Number of Visas
First	Unmarried adult children of U.S. citizens and their children	20% or 54,000
Second	Spouses and unmarried sons and daughters of permanent resident aliens	26% or 70,200[a]
Third	Members of professions or persons of exceptional ability in the arts and sciences and their spouses and children	10% or 27,000
Fourth	Married children of U.S. citizens and their spouses and children	10% or 27,000[a]
Fifth	Brothers and sisters of adult U.S. citizens and their spouses and children	24% or 64,800[a]
Sixth	Workers in skilled or unskilled occupations in which laborers are in short supply in the United States, their spouses and children	10% or 27,000
Nonpreference	Other qualified applicants	Any numbers not used above[a]

_____

Note: A minor is under 21 years of age; an adult is 21 or older. Refugees are not included in the visa allocation system.

[a]Numbers not used in higher preferences may be used in these categories.

of State to a prospective immigrant. In the case of a petition on behalf
of a relative, the petitioner must establish status as a U.S. citizen or
as an alien lawfully admitted for permanent residence and his or her
relationship to the beneficiary. In the case of a petition based on a
person's profession or occupation, the petitioner must have a job offer,
and the Secretary of Labor must certify that qualified Americans are not
available and that wages and working conditions would not be adversely
affected by the person's admission.

Refugees and Asylees

The number of refugees that may be admitted is determined annually by the
President after consultation with the Congress. Applicants for refugee
status are first reviewed by an immigration officer to determine if they
are qualified, then permitted to proceed to this country. On arrival
they are admitted as refugees. After they have been in the United States
1 year, they are reinterviewed and permitted to acquire the status of
lawful permanent residents. A person who has firmly resettled in another
country is no longer eligible to enter the United States as a refugee.

Applications for asylum may be submitted by aliens in the United
States or at a port of entry. If granted asylum--which is based on a
finding that a person would face persecution if forced to return to his
or her country of nationality or residence--the alien may apply for
permanent resident status 1 year after the grant. Not more than 5,000
asylees may be adjusted to the status of permanent resident in a fiscal
year.

Exclusion Grounds

There are 33 grounds of inadmissibility, affecting both immigrants and
nonimmigrants such as visitors, students, or temporary workers,
enumerated in the INA. They cover a wide range, including involvement in
criminal, immoral, or subversive activities; the presence of physical or
mental afflictions; and economic factors that result in the exclusion of
paupers, vagrants, and workers who would deprive or compete unfairly with
Americans for jobs. However, the ground under which most aliens are
denied visas and refused admission to the United States is unenumerated.
Over 400,000 nonimmigrant visas are denied annually by consular officers
because they are not "satisfied" that the applicant is a bona fide
nonimmigrant. An additional 128,000 visas (immigrant and nonimmigrant)
are denied because the applicant failed to comply with documentary
requirements.* Over 200,000 aliens who arrive each year at ports of
entry with visas or under visa exemptions are persuaded by immigration
officers to withdraw their applications for admission and return home.
Less than 700 are refused entry in a formal exclusion hearing before an
immigration judge.

Temporary Admissions

Most aliens come to the United States for a temporary purpose rather than for permanent residence. In 1982 some 11.5 million people entered the country as temporary admissions (excluding short-term border crossers from Mexico and Canada). By far the largest group of temporary admissions is visitors. Others included in this category are foreign officials, people here on business, crew members of vessels and aircraft, students, temporary workers, and trainees. Each of these groups is specified in the legislation, which sets forth conditions under which they can be admitted and whether they may work in this country. Nonimmigrants in two groups may not work under any circumstances: visitors for pleasure and transit aliens, i.e., people passing through the country in order to reach another country. People in some groups, such as students and exchange visitors, may be granted permission to work by the INS or the exchange program sponsor.

Deportable Classes

There are 19 deportable classes enumerated in the statute. Inadmissible aliens who manage to gain admission may be deported on the ground that they were excludable at the time of entry. There is no statute of limitations, and this provision operates retroactively to include all prior exclusion acts as well as the 33 grounds in the current law (but see the discussion of exceptions below). An alien may also be deported for acts or omissions after entry. A special deportation provision deals with the problem of sham marriages contracted to circumvent the immigration laws.

The largest number of deportable aliens located are those who entered without inspection, that is, other than at an authorized border crossing point. Of the 970,246 illegal aliens found in 1982 by INS, 822,463 (85%) were in that category. In the same year, the next largest groups were visitors, crew members, and students, most of whom remained beyond the period of their authorized stay and some of whom violated the terms of their temporary admission by unauthorized work.

In most cases deportable aliens located in the United States are given the opportunity to depart voluntarily, at their own expense and without the institution of deportation proceedings. In 1982 about 810,000 aliens were permitted to depart voluntarily; 14,154 were deported.

An alien under deportation proceedings has several avenues of relief. For example, if otherwise eligible, he or she may apply for an adjustment of status to that of permanent resident if an immigrant visa is available or if the person has been residing in the United States continuously since a date prior to June 30, 1948. Permanent residence through suspension of deportation can occur if the person has been physically present in the United States for at least 7 years (10 years in certain cases). An alien may avoid deportation if it is established that

_____

*Total visa denials (immigrant and nonimmigrant) in fiscal 1982 amounted to 877,486.

deportation would subject him or her to persecution on account of race, religion, political opinion, nationality, or membership in a social group. And whether or not the alien is under deportation proceedings, an alien who believes that he or she would be subject to persecution for such reasons may apply for asylum.

The government must establish deportability by clear, convincing, and unequivocal evidence. Any decision of an immigration judge may be appealed to the Board of Immigration Appeals. The board is a component of the Executive Office for Immigration Review, an independent agency within the Department of Justice. An alien may file a petition for judicial review from a final order of deportation in the Circuit Court of Appeals within 6 months of the order. Filing of the petition automatically stays deportation pending determination by the court, unless it directs otherwise.

Powers of Immigration Officers

The enforcement powers needed to apprehend suspected illegal aliens and issue warrants of arrest are expressly spelled out in the law. Immigration officers are authorized, without a warrant, to interrogate persons believed to be aliens as to their right to be in the United States and to arrest any alien who they have reason to believe is in the United States in violation of the law and likely to escape before a warrant can be obtained. In addition, immigration officers are empowered to search, without a warrant, any vehicle within a reasonable distance--defined as 100 air miles--from any external boundary of the United States. For the purpose of patrolling the border to prevent illegal entry, immigration officers are empowered to have access to private lands, but not dwellings, within 25 miles of the border.

CONCLUSION

The foregoing review of U.S. immigration policy and its legislative history illustrates the complexity of the issues and the changing views of immigration. It also highlights the extent to which the laws spell out in great detail the affected groups, the actions to be taken, available enforcement powers, and fines and penalties that compel compliance--and thus define the statistical boundaries. This degree of specificity has another effect: it sets forth both the groups and the activities for which selected statistics are necessary, if for no other purpose than to provide measures of magnitude for administrative and legislative review.

3

Needs for Statistics on Immigration

In this chapter we review why the United States needs accurate and timely statistics on immigration. As a panel of the National Research Council composed in part of academics with a strong empirical interest in migration studies, we could have easily provided lists of data needed for our own work, and those lists would be very long. We could also have attempted the difficult if not impossible task of identifying every person or organization with a real or perceived need for information, and their collective appetite for data would undoubtedly be enormous.

Instead, we confine our attention in this chapter to the data that are necessary to the government's functions. We have grouped these data into three loose categories: (1) those that are required by law; (2) those necessary for the formulation, execution, and evaluation of public policy concerning the admission of aliens to the United States; and (3) those necessary for the management of government agencies, primarily the INS, whose mission is to apply the country's laws concerning the admission and residence of aliens. These categories are not mutually exclusive, but rather indicate the possible justifications for particular record-keeping processes and types of data. We conclude the chapter by discussing both the various obstacles to the collection of the necessary data and the ways in which they might be overcome.

DATA REQUIRED BY LAW

Aliens Other Than Refugees

The population of the United States has its origins largely in immigration, and the present characteristics of the population still reflect these origins. One might expect, therefore, that the legislation controlling the flow of noncitizens across the country's borders and their residence in the country would require the regular collection and production of the information necessary to the policy makers and administrators responsible for the drafting, enactment, or implementation of that legislation. It is thus somewhat surprising to discover that the Immigration and Nationality Act (INA), the centerpiece of immigration law, contains virtually no direct references to the preparation of statistics. The single provision on statistics, as such, is hidden away among the naturalization sections, specifically section 347 (8 USC 1485):

> The Attorney General is authorized and directed to prepare from the records in the custody of the Service a report upon those heretofore seeking citizenship to show by nationalities their relation to the numbers of aliens annually arriving and to the prevailing census populations of the foreign born, their economic, vocational and other classification, in statistical form, with analytical comment thereon and to prepare such report annually hereafter.

A review of past performance (at least since 1952, when the present legislation was enacted), suggests that INS has met some of the requirements of this sentence through the publication, more or less annually, of a statistical yearbook and an annual report. Through 1978, these two reports were combined; since then, they have been issued separately, primarily because of severe difficulties in completing the assembly of the annual statistical data. For example, the statistical yearbook containing data for 1980 was issued in December 1983; that for 1981, in August 1984.

The "analytical comment thereon" referred to in section 347, however, cannot be said to have been met adequately by the annual reports, which, in the words of INS's 1976 report, "depict Service efforts, programs, and achievements" but contain no analysis whatsoever of the status of immigrants or their relationship to the prevailing census populations of the foreign-born. The value of the annual report lies in providing readers (particularly policy makers in Congress) with a very abbreviated description of the diverse organizational units and functions within INS and in highlighting what INS considers to be its annual accomplishments. While this compilation includes some selected statistics concerning its operations, it seems to be a far cry from the intent of section 347.

Given the paucity of statistics required by the INA, it is interesting to note that the immigration reform legislation that was almost, but not quite, passed by Congress late in 1984 (the Simpson-Mazzoli bill) would have mandated a manyfold increase in the number and scope of statistical and analytical reports. Those reports would have included, among other things: an analysis of the impact of implementing controls of the unlawful employment of aliens both on the employment, wages, and working conditions of legal U.S. workers and on the number of aliens entering the United States illegally; a report of the impact of general legal admissions over a 42-month period on the economy of the United States and on the employment of citizens and aliens; and a series of reports over a 5-year period on the alien population whose status would have been legalized, including their geographical origins, manner of entry, demographic characteristics, pattern of employment, and participation in social service programs.

Although not specifically mandated for statistical purposes, the INA does contain language that results in the compilation of extensive record systems about people who, as immigrants, visitors, illegals, foreign students, etc., come into contact with the INS. Thus, section 290(a) of the INA (8 USC; 1360) directs the establishment of a central index containing the names of all aliens admitted or excluded and "such other relevant information as the Attorney General shall require as an aid to enforcement of the immigration law." The law also requires that each person seeking a visa to enter the United States be registered through a State Department office abroad, as well as at the time of entry into the United States. The law further specifies that the following information be obtained: date and place of entry into the United States; activities in which the alien has been and intends to be engaged; length of time to be spent in the United States; and any police or criminal record.

The management records compiled by INS are an essential source of information for the administration of its programs. They also have the potential to be important for planning new programs, evaluating old ones, and studying the impact of immigrants on the economy and social fabric, by providing a unique source of samples for longitudinal or other forms of surveys. To date, however, use of these records for any of these purposes has been very limited and their potential largely unrealized.

Refugees

The statistical and informational requirements contained in the Refugee Act of 1980 (P.L. 96-212) offer a startling contrast to the very limited requirements of the INA for data on immigrants. Whether reflecting a new awareness of the value of information or a legislative whim, the data demands of the Refugee Act of 1980 are much greater than those in the INA. Section 207(e), for example, requires that the President provide members of Congress with the following types of information:

o A description of the nature of the world refugee situation;
o A description of the number and allocation of the refugees to be admitted and an analysis of conditions within the countries from which they come;
o An analysis of the anticipated social, economic, and demographic impact of their admission to the United States; and
o A description of the proposed plans for their movement and resettlement.

Apparently recognizing that properly presented data can contribute to the decision-making process, Section 207 also requires: "to the extent possible, information described in this subsection shall be provided [to members of Congress] at least two weeks in advance of discussions in person by designated representatives of the President." It may be noted in passing that the specified information requirements are much more policy related than management related.

Such detailed specification of information needs within legislation ensures that the task is assigned a high priority and that, invariably, funds and competent staff become available for its accomplishment. Such certainly seems to be true in the case of refugee statistics produced by the Office of Refugee Resettlement (ORR) in the Department of Health and Human Services. Even during the current period of extreme budget stringency, the statistical activities of this office have survived (albeit at less than an optimum level). As a final note, the 1982 amendments to the Refugee Act (P.L. 97-363, Ch. 2, Sec. 412(2)) mandate that the director of the ORR "compile and maintain data on secondary migration of refugees within the United States and, by state of residence and nationality, on the proportion of refugees receiving cash or medical assistance--etc." The value of such information for policy evaluation, by indicating the direct costs of admitting refugees and which states bear them, is obvious. Less obvious but also important is the value of such information for understanding the process of social and economic adjustment of refugees.

DATA NEEDED FOR PUBLIC POLICY

As outlined in the preceding section, the relevant law does not require, except for refugees, extensive data on noncitizens coming to or residing in the United States. Therefore, in this section we start from first principles to ask what data should be required in order to formulate, execute, and evaluate public policy on immigration. At the most simplistic level, the issues of immigration policy can be boiled down to two questions: How many aliens should be admitted for long- or short-term residence, and who, in terms of origins, skills, and ties to the United States, should they be? Even a casual review of recent debates about immigration reform reveals that arguments revolve largely around the pocketbook issue of whether and why immigration is beneficial to the nation. Hence, the first thing policy makers need to know is who benefits from immigration and who is hurt by it.

A common assumption is that immigrants gain and current residents, particularly those who hold low-paying jobs, lose; however, this assumption has so far been addressed only by rhetoric, not by data. In addition to identifying those groups who gain and those who lose, it is necessary to quantify the size of the benefits and costs. Economic benefits and costs (wages, unemployment, taxes) are perhaps the easiest to quantify, but the cost-benefit calculation should not be so narrowly focused. Immigration also has social, psychological, and political effects--for example, the work of foreign-born but U.S.-resident Nobel Prize laureates can be evaluated in terms of the economic value of their contribution, the spin-off benefits on their coresearchers, and the morale-boosting effects of their presence in the country.

Analysis should not be limited solely to nationally aggregated data. Although immigration policy is set at the national level, immigrants live in local communities and contribute to public coffers through taxes at the federal, state, and local level; they may not, however, consume public services provided by these governments in amounts equal to their contributions. Hence, as in the case of military installations, which have benefits (national defense, contributions to local revenues) and costs (support from central government taxation, consumption of local services such as public education) that are both national and local, a federalism issue may arise. A time dimension also is involved: immigrants do not adapt instantly to a new culture, and their costs and contributions to society can be expected to change as the duration of their stay in the country increases. The study of such changes over time, and the process of assimilation of immigrants in general, requires longitudinal rather than cross-sectional data.

U.S. policy for the admission of aliens for long-term residence appears, on the basis of current legislation, to have three main objectives: admitting aliens for the purposes of reunifying families, admitting workers with particular skills that are in short supply domestically, and accepting a share of worldwide refugees consistent with foreign policy objectives, altruistic sentiments, and absorptive capacity. To evaluate whether these objectives are being met, empirical evidence is needed. With adequate data, one could study the extent to which families are united and stay united, and also judge whether immigrants do supply needed labor in areas (occupational and geographical) of shortage. Whether the country accepts its fair share of refugees is an issue that cannot be answered by national statistics alone. To answer this question, one would need as a minimum international data on the number of refugees in need of resettlement and on the refugee resettlement capacity of, and admissions by, other nations.

Data on family structure and on labor market dynamics could therefore indicate whether the apparent objectives of current immigration policy are being met. Even with such data, however, policy makers would still need some way to set immigration levels. Few would dispute the proposition that some immigration is beneficial but that totally unrestricted entry would have unacceptable consequences. Clearly, however, such extremes are of little help in deciding how many aliens should be admitted for long-term residence each year. A more rational approach would use data to determine and compare the benefits and costs of different levels and mixes of immigration.

The debate in Congress in 1984 on revisions to the present immigration law provides a clear example of unmet data needs for policy. The requirements of the legislation, from amnesty provisions and employer sanctions for illegal aliens to visa waivers for temporary visitors, called for empirical evidence to set a common framework for the discussion. Regrettably, the record of the debate is replete with concerns over the lack of factual information. In a most unusual action, Congress noted its concerns by including the following language in its authorization of the fiscal 1985 appropriation for the Justice Department (U.S. Congress, 1984):

The Committee is deeply concerned about the unavailability of accurate and current statistical information on immigration matters. The Committee notes in this regard that INS . . . has ignored the statistical needs of Congress. . . . The Committee frequently has been frustrated in its attempts to obtain the statistics needed to assess the impact of legislation it is considering.

Addressing any of the policy questions posed above is rendered far more difficult by the fact that immigrants in the United States do not consist only of those who are living here legally. Information on both illegal and legal migrants is therefore required. Data on the latter are far easier to obtain than data on the former, since those here illegally have little incentive to cooperate with agencies that gather data.

Two concluding comments are in order here. First, we recognize that immigration is an intensely emotional issue. Immigration policy is set through a political process that requires compromise--as does all policy--and the result may well be a policy that appears to lack rational underpinnings. The availability of better data is unlikely to remove emotional issues from national debates about immigration. Yet we would argue that data are essential to these debates by documenting to some extent what the effects of particular policy alternatives are likely to be. Second, we recognize that the history of the use of statistics in setting immigration policy is not a happy one. On too many occasions, those involved in making policy could not have drawn on statistical data because the necessary data did not exist. But even on those occasions when data were used, the results sometimes have been disappointing, if not disgraceful. One of the most infamous cases occurred in the 1920s. The first numerical ceilings on immigration from outside the Western Hemisphere were set in 1921 on the basis of the origins of the people enumerated in the 1910 census. In 1924, the basis of the national origins law was changed, not to the more recent 1920 census but back to the 1890 census. This change was made to ensure more immigrants from northwestern Europe and fewer from southeastern Europe and was based on misinterpretation of data collected from World War I draftees (Brigham, 1923). Despite these reservations, however, there can be little disagreement with the notion that good-quality, reliable immigration data, objectively and competently analyzed, are likely to enlighten debates about policy and consequently to improve policy outcomes.

DATA NEEDED FOR PROGRAM MANAGEMENT

Effective program management requires timely information about various operational aspects of the program. Continuing series of such information enable managers, policy makers, and others to measure their accomplishments (whether they be positive or negative), as defined either by the policy makers or by the managers. Thus, if a program involves admitting numbers of immigrants specified by Congress, program information must be developed, by category of admission, to enforce the limit. Program managers may also want information on method and place of arrival, in order to ensure the most efficient placement of personnel, and on the time required to process immigrants, in order to measure productivity, develop staffing profiles, or justify funding requests.

Another element of program management for which data are collected is evaluation, to find out whether a program is achieving its objectives. This requirement may be specified by Congress or initiated by a program agency itself, and its scope and form can vary widely. Although in many cases evaluation may draw on regular program information, in other cases an evaluation may require additional data collection. Programs aimed at helping refugees to settle in this country provide a simple example of such evaluation: Does the assistance reach those most in need and does it accomplish its objectives of easing the transition period and speeding up the process of assimilation whereby refugees become self-supporting?

A further area of need for accurate data is for population accounting purposes. The census is taken every 10 years, and the Census Bureau is charged with counting all persons normally resident in the United States, regardless of their legal status. Between censuses, the Bureau prepares estimates of current population by adding births and in-migrants and subtracting deaths and out-migrants from the most recent census count. Births and deaths are counted with considerable accuracy through the national system of registration of vital events, but the population between census dates can change more through net migration than through natural increase (births minus deaths). One would not want to establish an elaborate statistical data collection network merely to know the total number of people living in the country in years between the censuses, but where they live is a matter of great importance, since billions of federal dollars are distributed to states and local areas partly on the basis of population counts or estimates. Hence, the interest of mayors and governors in having their populations estimated accurately is strong. Net international migration can be an even more important component of local area population change than it is of population change at the national level, but it is also even more difficult to measure.

Given the number of different agencies involved in administering programs concerned with international migration, it is not surprising that the information needs vary widely. For example, immigrants come into contact initially with State Department representatives throughout the world; with the INS, whom they encounter at U.S. borders; with the federal, state, and local agencies to whom they may turn when in need; with schools, which attempt to provide language capability and citizenship training; with the Department of Labor and related state agencies, which may provide job training or jobs. Refugees, asylees, visitors, and short-term workers all find themselves involved with government agencies and private voluntary agencies before or during their stay in the country, and each such contact invariably becomes noted in the information systems developed by these respective agencies for managing their operations, assessing their successes and failures, preparing requests for funding, and responding to questions from those at all levels of responsibility or from the public.

In view of such diversity, it is clearly beyond the scope of this report to attempt to delineate all the information needed for program management. Above all, program management should be seen as a continuing, ever-changing activity that generates information needs at all levels, from the national level in Washington to the first-level supervisor or individual Border Patrol officer at a small port of entry on the Canadian border in Maine. All such needs must be considered in designing a program information system. What we wish to emphasize here is that program management requires the maintenance of information systems, the primary function of which is administrative, but which may collect and classify data of use for other, more general purposes.

COORDINATING POLICY AND PROGRAM DATA

There is a range of users of statistical data and the products of information systems in the immigration field. At one end we find officials in the legislative and executive branches of national government who make and execute immigration policy. Their need is for analysis of aggregated, summary information: information that gives insight into and understanding of demographic, economic, or geographic relationships, such as the age-sex-family status of entering immigrants, the occupations and incomes of those entering for temporary work, the current labor force status of recent refugees, and how efficiently program activities are functioning.

In the middle we find those who run the agency offices that deal directly with immigrants, in either service or law enforcement roles; they are largely involved with the effective day-to-day management of services offered and activities performed--using scarce resources to accomplish tasks. At this level, the need also is for aggregated information, but of a somewhat different nature. Generally limited in detail or characteristics, the data consist of summaries--of the number of clients processed in a particular time or similar measures used to measure productivity, accomplishment, adherence to statutory or administrative limitations, and a host of similar managerial controls.

At the other end are the program staff who have daily contact with aliens, whose primary need for information is access to records about individuals. The need at this level is for speedy access to information specific to an individual: officials need information to reach a decision and carry out rapidly the service or enforcement activity in the light of all the information available concerning an individual, and subsequently need to update the individual's record to reflect the action taken. Any other information collected at this level is often viewed as an unnecessary burden and an interference with the primary task.

A conflict of purpose exists because many of the statistics used for policy or management purposes are initially generated by the program staff, who have little if any stake in or understanding of how records of their individual-level transactions, in a more aggregated form, are used by agency heads and policy makers. For aggregated data to be accurate and timely, an optimal information system would be designed so that the statistical operations required of the program staff impose little additional burden and either benefit them directly (e.g., by also providing useful operational information) or are understood as important to the mission of their agency.

An overly simple but nevertheless instructive way to visualize such a system would be to imagine that each employee having contact with aliens has the use of a computer terminal. By accessing a computerized data file that contains relevant information on each alien, the employee retrieves information necessary to making a decision; appropriate additions or changes can be made to the file immediately, thus avoiding endless proliferation of forms containing much duplicated information. Since all files are stored and all transactions are recorded electronically, those in middle- or top-level management positions can simply request and obtain directly from their own terminals the aggregated information they need for effective management or to answer the questions of policy makers. Such a system would clearly require built-in safeguards to ensure confidentiality, to protect identifiers of individuals from unauthorized access, and to avoid illegitimate tampering with the records.

At the aggregate level, the records would serve a number of purposes. An office manager could determine how many aliens agent X served or agent Y arrested in a particular period. Other questions that could be answered at various managerial levels would include: How many Iranian students are studying in the United States and where are they located? How many refugees admitted in April 1983 had active cases of tuberculosis? Where are these persons now? What is the age distribution of persons apprehended this year compared with last? Clearly, not all important questions can be answered with management records alone, but they would be much easier to answer if such a system were a reality. For example, suppose policy makers wanted to know how the cohort of Cuban refugees from the 1980 Mariel boatlift has fared in the United States: a special survey would have to be made since the desired information on current status would not be found in the management files. But if a good data system was in place, a sample for the survey could be drawn and located relatively easily from a master listing, including current or most recent address, of the population.

Having identified the policy and program needs for accurate and timely data on international migration and briefly outlined the characteristics of a suitable information collection system, we turn next in Chapters 4 through 7 to examine what data are actually collected, by whom, and for what purposes.

REFERENCES

Brigham, Carl
    1923   A Study of American Intelligence.   Princeton, N.J.:
            Princeton University Press.
U.S. Congress, House
    1984   Department of Justice Appropriation Authorization Act,
            Fiscal Year 1985. Report to accompany H.R. 5468. Report
            98-759. 98th Congress, 2d session. Available from the
            Superintendent of Documents, U.S. Government Printing Office.

4

The Immigration and Naturalization Service

OVERVIEW: MANDATE AND PERFORMANCE

This chapter describes the programs and operations of the Immigration and Naturalization Service (INS), an agency of the U.S. Department of Justice. It highlights the procedures followed to collect data and the type of data collected. Because of the INS's central role in administering the flow of international migration to the United States, its statistical activities were examined in considerably more detail than were those of the other federal agencies involved in collecting immigration data.

The INS is charged with the administration of the Immigration and Nationality Act as well as of other federal statutes concerning the status of aliens in the United States and of the process of naturalization. The work of the agency in carrying out its legal and administrative missions can be divided into two broad areas, examination and enforcement. Operational programs and services are administered through field offices of the INS throughout the United States and in selected locations in U.S. territories and abroad. Although the legislative history of the INS contains few references to statistics or data (as outlined in Chapter 3), the agency is following a long tradition in collecting and furnishing information on the movements of aliens. The reporting of U.S. immigration statistics was first authorized by the Congress in 1819, and in 1892 that reporting responsibility was given to the Bureau of Immigration, then in the U.S. Department of Labor, the forerunner of the INS. Hence, the gathering of immigration statistics has been an integral part of the mission and activities of the INS or its previous incarnations for close to 100 years.

The statistical activities of the INS are directly related to its administrative and operational structure; consequently, to describe and evaluate the statistical activities requires an understanding of the organizational context of data collection and analysis within the agency, which is shown in Figure 4-1. Each area of operation in INS is concerned with the processing of aliens and, in some cases, citizens: monitoring entry to and exit from the United States and changes in legal status. In carrying out its duties, the INS generates many types of information on alien populations within a range of legal and administrative statuses.

35

36

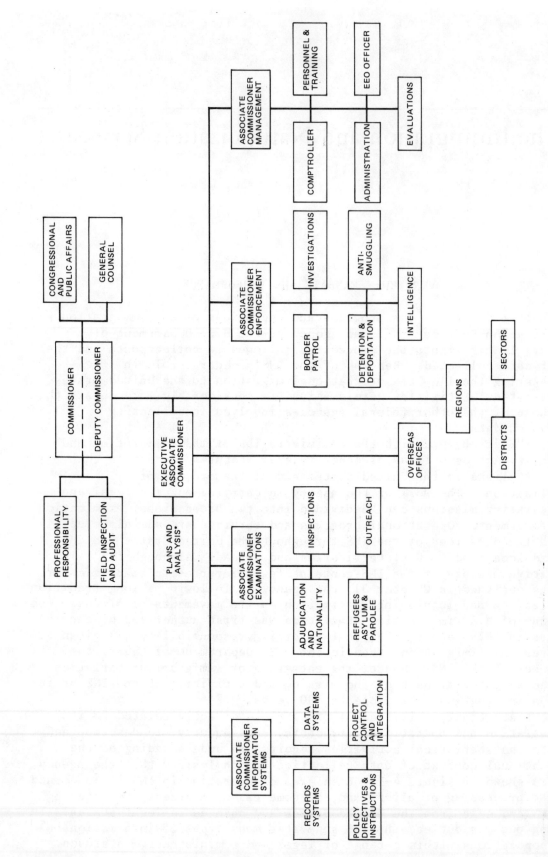

FIGURE 4-1 The Immigration and Naturalization Service

*The Statistical Analysis Branch is a part of this office; however, it does not appear separately on any organizational chart.

The data vary in quality, refinement, accessibility, and timeliness, and the focus of the information is operational rather than statistical.

During the past decade the INS has been criticized by the General Accounting Office and the House Committee on Government Operations for internal problems--such as poor record management, inadequate service to the public, and low employee morale--and for being unable to prevent illegal entry or to maintain adequate control over the nonimmigrant population in the United States. Coincident with these management problems was a sharp increase in the agency's workload. Testifying before the Senate Appropriations Committee in March 1980, the Acting Commissioner of INS noted (U.S. Department of Justice, 1980:11):

> Major changes in the law in 1965 resulted in considerably more paperwork for the agency, and it was not and has not been equipped to cope with it, either through systems or procedures or through automation. At the same time, immigration to this country has been increasing substantially, and we now find ourselves in a hole from which it will not be easy to extricate ourselves.

Table 4-1 shows the steady and in some cases dramatic increases in alien admissions, naturalizations, and apprehensions of deportable aliens since 1966. While immigrant admissions less than doubled, admissions of nonimmigrants (visitors, students, and other nonresident aliens) increased fivefold, from 2.3 million in 1966 to 11.8 million in 1981; apprehensions increased sixfold, from 139,000 in 1966 to more than 1 million during the late 1970s. In addition, nearly 1 million refugees were admitted to the United States during the past decade.

As the workload of INS expanded after 1965, its budget also increased significantly, reaching $351 million in 1980. However, the number of authorized permanent positions increased by a little more than 50 percent, from 7,000 in 1966 to 11,000 in 1980. Only a minuscule portion of its resources were devoted to statistics: 49 permanent positions were allocated to the statistics program in 1980. Most of these positions were held by clerical personnel who manually sorted and compiled statistics. Except for its initiatives in the data-processing area and in spite of increasing national concern about immigration in recent years, INS for many years has not requested any additional funding for the purpose of improving its statistical capabilities or products, nor has it taken significant actions to accomplish such a goal with its existing resources. This budgetary and organizational neglect has been accompanied by a deterioration of its statistical functions. Prior to the late 1950s, the INS statistics program and its staff, although comparatively small, had the reputation of producing quality statistics in a timely fashion, but in recent years both quality and timeliness have deteriorated seriously.

The great expansion of automated data processing (ADP) at the INS during the past few years provides the opportunity for a rapid improvement in its statistical capabilities in meeting both its own information needs and the demands for data by external users. Consequently, this chapter includes a review of the development of automated data processing, a description of the ADP plans that are being

TABLE 4-1 Immigrants and Nonimmigrants Admitted, Persons Naturalized, and Aliens Apprehended: 1966-1981 (in thousands)

Fiscal Year	Immigrants Admitted	Nonimmigrants[a] Admitted	Persons Naturalized	Aliens Apprehended
1981	597	11,757	166	976
1980	531	NA	158	910
1979	460	NA	164	1,076
1978	601	9,344	174	1,058
1977	462	8,037	160	1,042
1976[b]	104	2,674	48	222
1976	399	7,654	143	786
1975	386	7,084	142	767
1974	395	6,909	132	788
1973	400	5,977	121	656
1972	385	5,171	116	506
1971	370	4,404	108	420
1970	373	4,432	110	345
1969	359	3,645	99	284
1968	454	3,200	103	212
1967	362	2,608	105	162
1966	323	2,342	103	139

[a]Includes visitors, students, and other nonresident aliens.
[b]Transition quarter July 1 - September 30, 1976.

Source: INS Annual Reports, 1966-1981.

implemented, and a discussion of their statistical potential. Before turning to these developments, however, and in order to understand those plans within the context of the agency, we first present a summary of the information collected by the INS in carrying out its responsibilities, a summary of its operations, and an examination of its primary work report. Following the ADP review, we consider the agency's resources for statistical analysis and, finally, present our conclusions and recommendations about the INS.

INFORMATION COLLECTED BY THE INS

Categories of Migrants

With regard to data, six broad categories of migrants are incorporated within the complex of legal and administrative boundaries that define the areas of responsibility of the INS:

Permanent resident aliens	Naturalized citizens
Nonimmigrants	Border crossers
Refugees, parolees, and asylees	Deportable aliens

These categories are not mutually exclusive in all cases, nor is the list comprehensive of all movements in or out of the country; they do, however, cover the major categories of movement. With virtually no exception, the information generated for each of these categories derives from program needs; none of the items has a statistical origin. Not all of the data that are collected are processed. The glossary contains more detailed and technical definitions of these categories; all the forms mentioned in the discussion below are shown in Appendix A. The numbers of people given below for each category are for the most recent year for which data are available.

Permanent Resident Aliens

A relatively extensive array of social and demographic data is available for permanent resident aliens, a group that consists of people entering the country with immigrant visas and those already in the country who adjust to permanent resident status. In fiscal 1981, a total of 596,600 people were recorded in this group, with adjustments representing about one-third of the total, primarily because of refugees who adjust to permanent resident status. The data on immigrants admitted for permanent residence are the most widely accessible of the INS data sets, both as published in the annual statistical yearbook and as available on tape in the form of public-use micro record samples. The following information is collected, mainly from immigrant visas (or in the case of adjustment, INS form I-485):

District and port of entry	Sex
District of residence	Occupation
Month and year of admission	Marital Status
Class of admission	Labor certification
Country of last permanent residence	Expected zip code in the United
Country of birth	States
Nationality	Class and year of entry (for
Age	persons adjusting status)

Nonimmigrants

Nonimmigrants are those temporarily in the country as visitors, tourists, students, on business, or as temporary workers. There are more than 9 million admissions with nonimmigrant visas each year. Information on these admissions is generated from the items contained on the I-94 form required for both entering and leaving the country:

Visa issuing place	Class of admission
Date of birth	Country of residence

Date of entry	Mode of travel
Date admitted until	Occupation (obtained for
Citizenship	temporary workers, intercompany
Port and date of departure	transfers, exchange
Port of entry	visitors)
State of destination	

Tabulations for this group are available in the annual statistical yearbook, except for the years 1980 and 1981, when processing was abandoned due to excessive workload.

Naturalizations

This category covers aliens receiving citizenship, either through direct application or by derivative means, such as children born outside the country of at least one parent who is a U.S. citizen. In fiscal 1981, 166,317 persons were naturalized. The data for this group are collected on forms N-400 and N-600:

INS district handling case	Marital status and marital
Country of birth	history
Year of birth	Number of children by sex
Year of admission	and date and country of
Applicable section of law	birth
Type of court--federal/state	Occupation and 5-year work
Former nationality	history
Month and year naturalized	Zip code of residence
Sex	Five-year residence history

Refugees, Parolees, and Asylees

Refugees consist of those persons outside their country of nationality who fear persecution if they return. In fiscal 1984, a total of about 70,000 persons entered the country as refugees. Persons already in the country as nonimmigrants or those at a port of entry who are unable or unwilling to return to their country because of fear of persecution are listed as asylees; in fiscal 1984, this group totaled slightly over 11,500. The final group consists of parolees, who are persons allowed to enter the country temporarily under emergency conditions. Prior to the passage of the Refugee Act of 1980, most refugees were paroled into the country and were included in the count of parolees but are now shown separately. In fiscal 1981, some 15,700 persons were allowed to enter the country for humanitarian and other reasons as parolees. Although the INS collects information on refugees at three different times--before admission to the country, at the time of entry to the country, and when the refugee applies for status as a permanent resident, relatively little of the information is actually made available publicly. The 1981 Statistical Yearbook contains only three tables presenting data for refugees: refugees granted lawful permanent resident status; authorized admissions (that is, ceilings) and approvals of refugees for admission by geographic area of chargeability; and refugees granted lawful permanent resident status by country or region of birth. Additional tables will be included in the 1982 and the 1983 Statistical Yearbook. The Office of Refugee Resettlement also collects and publishes information on refugees, as described in Chapters 5 and 7.

Border Crossers

Border crossers are a heterogeneous group of people entering the United States from Canada or Mexico who are not required to complete form I-94 arrival declarations. Such entries take place predominantly but not exclusively across land borders, and are made up of U.S. citizens, permanent resident aliens, and those nonresident aliens entering the United States for periods of no more than six months (from Canada) or 72 hours (from Mexico). The number of such entries reached almost 290 million in fiscal 1981; however, relatively little information beyond the total is available for this group. The methods used to obtain the information are described later in this chapter.

Deportable Aliens

Close to 1 million deportable aliens were located in fiscal 1981. Information collected about them included:

Citizenship
Residence in the United States
Date and manner of entry
Date and place of birth
Visa status
Social security number

Length of time illegally in country
Last employer and dates of employment
Occupation
Wage earned

The information is collected on form I-213, which is not machine processed; limited data on locations by nationality group, type of entry, broad categories of length of illegal stay, and employment status are manually extracted for form G-23 (see below), and further manual extraction of data on earnings and use of social services is made for internal INS reports. Further data on aliens deported and aliens required to depart, excluding those opting for immediate voluntary departure, are generated by INS enforcement operations, but they cover only 5 percent of all deportable aliens located.

Records Control: The Alien File

Throughout its history, the INS has been a massive producer of administrative records, in paper form, all of which were supposedly filed in case of future need. The heavy emphasis on automated data processing, discussed below, is a response to this proliferating, virtually uncontrollable mass of records. It appears quite certain that the INS will remain, along with the Social Security Administration and the Internal Revenue Service, among the leading government agencies in generating records. Successful record control thus becomes a necessity in the battle to achieve efficient operation of this organization.

The key record in this battle is the alien file, the "A-file," which is a hard-copy folder containing the store of original documentation available for each alien to whom an alien number has been assigned. The criteria for deciding whether an A-number should be assigned to a particular alien, and hence a file established, are not clearly laid down. Essentially, an A-file is created whenever the need arises; the last of the official list of 19 circumstances that warrant the creation of an alien file is "[a]ny other time a case file is needed for an individual" (INS Administrative Manual:2702.02). The major categories of aliens with A-numbers and for whom documentation is maintained, of course, consist of permanent resident aliens, naturalized citizens, refugees, asylees, and parolees. Alien files are physically maintained in the records section of the district offices of the INS; inactive files are retired to federal records centers.

The content of the A-files varies widely. Files may contain virtually any piece of documentation pertaining to the case of an alien, including birth certificate, immigrant visas, petitions, any official or unofficial documentation supporting claims and petitions, correspondence, travel forms, etc. There appears to be little effective policy about which documents should be filed. Files are supposed to be kept in the INS control office having jurisdiction over the area in which the alien currently lives; in fact, they may be located in some other office for a variety of reasons. Because of this situation, the master index (see below) originally was introduced as a file tracking measure.

OPERATIONAL ASPECTS OF THE INS

The data collected by the INS are the by-product of administrative activities carried out by the various operational units of the agency. This section describes briefly the role of each major organizational unit and its contribution to collecting data on international migration.

Inspections

Immigration inspectors are responsible for determining the admissibility of all persons seeking to enter the country and for collecting original documentation from aliens admitted to the country within the range of legal statuses. Examination of U.S. citizens and the inspection of aliens seeking admission occurs at officially designated ports of entry located along international land borders and at air and sea ports. Preinspection occurs in some foreign cities; deferred inspections can be administered at INS offices other than the designated ports of entry. Immigration officers share the responsibility of border control with other federal agencies, including the Customs Bureau (U.S. Department of the Treasury), the U.S. Department of Agriculture, and the Public Health Service (U.S. Department of Health and Human Services).

Admissions

The documentation collected from aliens entering the United States varies with legal or visa status. Aliens entering as permanent residents present their immigrant visas and supporting documentation to inspectors. Nonimmigrant aliens arriving by international air and sea carriers present arrival forms (form I-94), and inspectors also collect passenger manifests (form I-92) from carriers. The I-94 form collects little social and demographic information, and inspectors seldom check the accuracy of what is collected. The coverage and processing of I-94 and I-92 forms is discussed further in Chapter 5.

Flows Into the United States Across Land Borders

Inspectors at land ports process people crossing borders in a variety of legal categories. Most aliens entering the United States over land borders do not require documentation: Canadians may travel for business or pleasure for a period of six months without requiring a nonimmigrant visa; Mexicans crossing the border frequently may present border crossing cards for admission to the United States for business or pleasure within 25 miles of the Southwestern border for a period not to exceed 72 hours. Aliens admitted for permanent residence who work in the United States yet continue to reside in Canada or Mexico are considered commuters and present an immigrant visa upon first admission and a special "green card" thereafter.

Procedures for counting people entering at land border ports vary significantly among ports. Generally, land ports experiencing a large volume of traffic rely on estimates of the number of aliens and U.S. citizens arriving per vehicle or as pedestrians; smaller ports make actual counts of the number of people inspected and admitted, by citizenship status.

By far the largest number of entries into the country each year occur through points of entry on the Mexican and Canadian borders. In 1981, almost 99 million border crossings were recorded across the Canadian border, and 190 million across the Mexican border, compared with some 21 million arrivals by air and sea. (The figures are not quite comparable, since the land border data count number of crossings, while some categories of the air and sea data may count multiple arrivals in a year by the same person only once, but the difference in magnitude is nonetheless clear.)

In order to review the procedures used by the INS to arrive at a count of border crossings, the panel conducted a telephone survey of 20 offices, 11 on the Canadian border and 9 on the Mexican border, selected purposively to give a spread both geographically and by size of reported flow. The individual office responses then were evaluated, if possible, through examination of data produced by the offices and reported on the work measurement form (G-23) and on the semiannual workload report forms G-540-542. It should be noted that primary inspections are shared between the INS and Customs Bureau officers at land borders, and, although reporting is an INS function, Customs officers share in the recording process. Table 4-2 summarizes the findings from the survey.

The most striking feature of the procedures used is their variability from office to office, although this variability is not surprising given the lack of guidance provided by district, regional, and central offices: the only invariant response to the survey was that all the offices reported receiving no guidance from district or regional offices about how to carry out surveys or make estimates. At every port but one, a direct count is made of passenger cars crossing into the United States, although the mechanism used to obtain the count varies. At many smaller ports, direct counts are maintained by hand tallies or hand counters, though some of these ports reported that the accuracy of the count might slip at times of peak traffic. At larger ports, vehicle counts are made by sensors; in the case of bridges, some counts are obtained from toll records. Although there may be a problem of overcounting in some cases, since buses and trucks will trigger sensors, the flow of passenger cars into the United States is probably recorded with reasonable accuracy. This is an example of a statistic important to the INS--since port workload varies closely with numbers of cars--but of little interest to policy makers or the research community.

The method of counting of passengers, which is of importance to a wider audience, also varies, most obviously by size of port and by whether the port is on the Canadian or Mexican border. Many of the small and medium sized ports on the Canadian border make direct counts using hand counters or tallies of the numbers of passengers and whether they are citizens or aliens. The larger Canadian border points, and almost all the Mexican border points, estimate the numbers of total passengers by applying an average occupancy figure to the car count. The number of citizens and of aliens is then estimated by applying citizen/alien ratios to the estimate of total passengers. The sources of these average occupancy figures and citizen/alien ratios also vary from port to port. In some cases, the ports report using results from the semiannual survey (forms G-540-542) typically conducted on three days, including a Saturday and a Sunday, in February and August each year. However, the forms contain no breakdown by citizenship, and the semiannual survey does not always collect a citizenship breakdown. It is not clear from our port survey how the citizenship split reported on the G-23 is arrived at for those ports that make estimates rather than direct counts: some ports report using their own surveys conducted at regular periods; others conduct surveys on the hunch that traffic patterns have changed.

The results of our port survey also do not indicate precisely how average occupancy and citizen/alien ratios, however obtained, are used to estimate total passenger flow by citizenship. For selected ports, the forms and the G-23 returns were examined to determine whether the data obtained were consistent with the procedures reported. This examination suggests that those ports that said they used direct counts did so; that most ports using estimates of occupancy based their estimates on G-540-542 returns, while a few applied nonempirical ratios; and that most ports making estimates of citizens and aliens used ratios that did not change over time and presumably had no recent factual basis.

The returns must be used carefully to avoid bias. Traffic flow, average occupancy, and probably the citizen/alien ratio vary substantially and systematically by time of day, day of week, and month of year. An average occupancy figure based on the three-day semiannual survey, including two weekend days, is likely to overestimate the true value, since occupancy is highest at weekends; the ratio of citizens to total passengers may also be highest at weekends. It is clear that in the absence of careful design and standardized procedures, the numbers on flows by citizenship could be (and probably are) substantially in error.

Passengers by car represent a substantial majority of all entries across land borders, but some persons cross by bus or truck and some walk. Numbers of pedestrians (including bus passengers who generally pass through pedestrian lines), by citizenship, are counted directly at many ports, particularly on the Canadian border, but several ports make estimates on the basis of the semiannual or other survey. The error in these estimates is probably quite high, but since the pedestrian flow is a small proportion of total flow, the effect on estimated totals is probably not large.

Our review of methods used by the INS to estimate the number of border crossings raises serious doubts about the accuracy of the numbers by port and by citizen/alien designation, which are published annually in the INS statistical yearbook, as well as about the accuracy for some ports of the figures laboriously compiled on the G-23 each month and in the G-540-542 report every six months. The importance of these numbers to the agency managers must also be doubtful, given the difficulty of locating reports for some ports, and the fairly obvious deficiencies, including simple arithmetic errors, in some G-23 returns.

A more fundamental question is whether these numbers are important for any purpose at all. Many border crossings are made by commuters, shoppers, or people out for an evening who spend at most a few hours either in or outside the United States and who are of no interest to those concerned about immigration policy or to studies of immigration. Even staff workload seems to depend more on numbers of vehicles processed than on passengers by citizenship. The installation of automatic sensors of vehicle traffic at all points of entry that recorded weekly or even monthly, with no attempt at tallying passengers, would save greatly on inspections and clerical workload at the cost of sacrificing data that are virtually worthless. If INS officials or policy makers decide that some count of passengers by citizenship is desirable, sound statistical procedures using sampling should be introduced, removing the burden from the ports themselves. The INS could establish traveling teams to carry out regular and standardized surveys, at least of the medium- and large-flow ports; these teams could also record departing vehicles by occupancy during the survey period, to provide comparable figures on outgoing border crossings, which do not now exist.

TABLE 4-2 Summary of Procedures Used at Selected Points of Entry to Record Vehicle and Passenger Flow Into the United States

Port of Entry	Total Flow Fiscal 1980 (millions)	Method Used to Count			If Estimates Made, Reported Basis
		Cars	Passengers	Citizens/Aliens	
Canadian Border:					
Skagway, AL	0.1	Direct count	Direct count	Direct count	Not applicable
Sumas, WA	1.9	Sensors	Estimates	Estimates	Semiannual survey and own surveys on hunch that patterns have changed
International Falls, MN	1.4	Tolls	Estimates	Estimates	Direct counts for semiannual survey
Detroit, MI	13.8	Tolls	Estimates	Estimates	Semiannual survey
Peace Bridge, NY	10.9	Tolls	Estimates	Estimates	Own monthly survey, one randomly chosen lane, 15 minutes each hour for one week
Ogdensburg, NY	0.6	Direct count	Direct count	Direct count	Not applicable
Norton, VT	0.3	Direct count	Direct count	Direct count	Not applicable
Derby Line, VT	1.1	Direct count	Direct count	Direct count	Not applicable
Houlton, ME	2.4	Sensors	Direct count	Direct count	Not applicable
Madawaska, ME	2.4	Sensors	Direct count	Direct count	Not applicable
Calais, ME	4.2	Sensors	Direct count	Direct count	Not applicable
Mexican Border:					
El Paso, TX	38.4	Direct count	Estimates	Estimates	Annual survey for occupancy; no data collected on citizenship split

Location					
Hidalgo, TX	12.3	Sensors	Estimates	Estimates	Survey every two years for occupancy; no citizenship data
Los Ebanos, TX	0.1	Direct count (ferry)	Direct count	Estimates	No citizenship data collected
Presidio, TX	1.0	Sensors	Estimates	Estimates	Semiannual survey for occupancy, once a year for citizenship split
Roma, TX	3.1	Sensors[a]	Estimates	Estimates	Survey one week a month for occupancy when enough staff; semiannual survey for citizenship split
Columbus, NM	0.3	Sensors	Estimates	Estimates	Survey of one lane for three days every three months; days selected for heavy, medium and light traffic
Douglas, AZ	4.4	Sensors	Estimates	Estimates	Survey for weekend every three months, and semiannual survey
Naco, AZ	1.3	Sensors	Estimates	Estimates	Semiannual survey for occupancy; no citizenship data--use "percentages established over the years"
Nogales, AZ	10.0	Sensors	Estimates	Estimates	Semiannual survey
Total	110.0[b]				

[a] Estimates made at one very small port.
[b] About 45 percent of yearly land border crossings.

Adjudications and Naturalizations

The adjudication and naturalization programs are concerned generally with processing petitions and granting benefits on behalf of aliens (but see following section). Determinations for some benefits, such as petitions for relative and occupational preferences, applications for various travel documents, and for extentions of stay are sometimes made immediately by INS personnel in district offices through the "up front" adjudications process, although the INS has found it more efficient to use other methods of processing. Other determinations, such as naturalizations, require more studied analysis of the documentation submitted or personal interviews; they, too, may be done in the district offices, but the INS is opting increasingly for remote adjudications in which specific types of petitions are sent to INS personnel assigned to adjudications centers.

The quality of information entered by aliens on the forms and applications is likely to vary. Examiners review closely those items that are very relevant to case determination; often these items are checked against supporting documents. The accuracy of reported information that is less relevant to determining the validity of claims is unknown.

ADP developments will have a major impact on the statistical reporting systems in the adjudications and naturalization program. The case tracking systems in both operational areas will have the capacity to produce major sections of the work measurement report (G-23), so these data should become more timely and accessible for users at all levels within the INS.

The Refugee, Asylum and Parolee Program

The activities of the INS concerning the admission of refugees and the processing of asylees, and the process of paroling aliens into the United States, are coordinated in the central office by the Refugee, Asylum and Parolee Program. However, the program is administered and services are provided in different parts of the examinations sections: for example, personnel in adjudications are concerned with aliens applying for political asylum; immigration inspectors are responsible for processing the requests of refugees for admission as legal permanent residents as well as for paroling aliens into the country; INS officers overseas collect data on individual aliens applying for refugee status. Aggregate data on refugee admissions are submitted monthly on a special supplement to the G-23 report by the ports officially designated to process refugees. Individual-level data on the entry of refugees are generated through the nonimmigrant information system; the quality of these data is dependent on whether refugee status is recorded on the arrival portion of form I-94. The most comprehensive data on refugee admissions and settlement patterns come from the data systems managed by the Office of Refugee Resettlement in the U.S. Department of Health and Human Services (see Chapters 5 and 7).

The INS statistical yearbook now includes tabulations of characteristics of refugees and asylees adjusting to permanent resident status. (Since the passage of the Refugee Act of 1980, parolees are not shown.) Published tables do not include information on the characteristics of refugees at the time of entry nor on the population of aliens in the United States seeking or granted asylum. The implementation of automated case tracking systems is expected to increase the availability and the accessibility of statistical information concerning the entry of refugees and persons seeking political asylum in the United States.

Enforcement

The operational areas classified as enforcement include the Border Patrol, investigations, antismuggling activities, intelligence, and detention and deportation. In general, enforcement programs are concerned with identifying and processing violators of the Immigration and Nationality Act.

The Border Patrol

The Border Patrol is responsible for the security of the borders of the United States with Canada and Mexico. The operations of the Border Patrol generate information on aliens apprehended on grounds of violating immigration law. Most of the data collected by the Border Patrol are maintained in local Border Patrol sector headquarters. The basic record completed for apprehended aliens is the Report of Deportable Alien Located (form I-213). Other local data bases have been developed to serve local needs and requirements. Border Patrol field units also complete relevant sections of the G-23 report.

The I-213 report is completed by a Border Patrol agent for each alien apprehended. The conditions under which an agent completes the form vary widely. For example, the record may be completed in a Border Patrol station for a group of aliens or in the field at the point of apprehension. As noted above, the form includes a substantial number of items including name, age, nationality, physical characteristics, visa status, family information, occupation, date of entry, and circumstances of apprehension. Because of the volume of apprehensions in certain areas, forms with preprinted entries in selected blocks (name of sector, method of entry, nationality, etc.) are used to collect certain items of information. The complexity of the form and the varied conditions under which it is completed cast doubt on the accuracy of the information collected. A study by Davidson (1981) of a sample of forms for 1978 reports high nonresponse rates for certain questions.

Most of the data collected through the activities of the Border Patrol are manually processed and submitted in aggregate form on the G-23 report. For example, the information recorded on form I-213 is available for analysis, for the most part, only in the form of aggregated G-23 report statistics. Greater emphasis on quality and machine processing of

I-213 data would make possible much more detailed and valuable tabulations for a group about which little is known.

The Border Patrol Division in the central office in Washington also has authorized the special collection of data for certain enforcement operations. An example is the survey of apprehended aliens, begun during 1983. Data collected through the survey are intended generally to support program evaluation and planning within the Border Patrol and specifically to provide a basis by which changes in undocumented immigration can be anticipated. The survey questions include age, sex, family and household characteristics, details of entry, and intentions concerning length of stay and activity within the United States. Data are processed by the ADP unit in Washington.

It should be noted that this survey was not discussed with staff of the Statistical Analysis Branch prior to initiation, nor has it been reviewed and approved by the Office of Information and Regulatory Affairs of the U.S. Office of Management and Budget, as federal regulations require. More emphasis on, and minor changes to, form I-213 would make such additional data collection exercises unnecessary.

The INS statistical yearbook includes a few summary tables on the activities of the Border Patrol and on characteristics of deportable aliens located. These published tabulations are the most accessible source of information on Border Patrol activities.

Detention and Deportation

Detention and deportation programs are administered through district offices of the INS. These programs are concerned with any aliens being maintained in INS detention facilities and all aliens awaiting a hearing or trial or awaiting exclusion, required departure, or deportation. Data are maintained on aliens being detained and moving through the various stages of the legal system and aliens exercising available legal or administrative options. Individual-level data on deportations, required departures, crew member desertions, and exclusions are submitted each month by detention and deportation units to the Statistical Analysis Branch in Washington for data processing. Selected items submitted refer to demographic characteristics of the alien as well as information on status at entry, location of processing, and country of destination. However, the vast majority of deportable aliens are apprehended by the Border Patrol and, if given the option, request immediate voluntary return. These persons can be tracked only through data on the G-23 report and are classified by nationality only—as Mexican or other than Mexican.

There is increasing public concern about differences in legal treatment among deportable aliens of different nationality groups. The automated case tracking systems have the potential for generating aggregate data on selected groups of aliens in various statuses in order to study the issues involved. There is also concern about what information is not provided by the data systems that are being developed. For example, the process of immediate voluntary departure (voluntary departure under safeguards) remains undocumented within the

data systems in existence now and those that are being developed for
future use, except for highly summarized results available from the G-23
report.

Investigations

Immigration investigators, like Border Patrol agents, are charged with
the responsibility of locating persons violating the Immigration and
Nationality Act, but they generally operate away from the border areas of
the United States. Most investigators are in cities and concentrate
their activities on economic sectors in which undocumented aliens are
believed to be working.

The data generated in the investigations process are similar to those
collected through Border Patrol activities. Data on investigation
activities and alien violators (from form I-213) are summarized on the
G-23 report, with files and records existing in generally inaccessible
form in the field. Tables in the INS statistical yearbook are based on
the G-23 reports and refer to the activities of district offices,
covering deportable aliens located by nationality, by length of time in
the United States, and by employment status.

Trial Attorneys

Immigration trial attorneys, located in the office of the General Counsel
(Figure 4-1), represent the agency in hearings and cases conducted by the
Executive Office of Immigration Review, U.S. Immigration Court.
Attorneys rely on statistical information generated by various units of
the INS, particularly detention and deportation, for anticipating future
workload. The G-23 report has been the primary source of such
information despite its apparent lack of timeliness and accuracy (see
below). The work of INS attorneys will soon be supported by an automated
case tracking system, which should provide information on backlogs and
produce current statistics on the number and types of cases in progress.

THE WORK MEASUREMENT REPORT: FORM G-23

The statistical data base most familiar to INS personnel is the "Report
of Field Operations," the G-23 report. Introduced in the 1940s, the G-23
report summarizes office workload activities in specific operational
areas within examinations, enforcement, legal counsel, and management.
When statistics are discussed at the INS, the G-23 report is the usual
point of reference. It is the one statistical activity that is
experienced in common among the range of diverse programs, personnel, and
geographic locations. Having expanded dramatically over the years since
its inception, the G-23 report today is a handwritten monthly compilation
of thousands of numbers entered on as many as 43 pages of reporting
forms. The report is used for a wide variety of purposes within the INS;
it is generally inaccessible to those outside the agency.

The G-23 report is relevant to a review of U.S. immigration statistics because it is the sole source of statistical information for certain categories of aliens. For example, the entry of aliens at land border crossings is reported only through G-23 statistics on primary inspections. Aggregate data on refugee admissions are compiled monthly for a special supplement to the G-23 report that is submitted by the ports officially designated to process refugees. This supplement identifies refugees by nationality and class of admission (principal, spouse, child). The number of aliens paroled into the United States is also tracked through G-23 report statistics on inspections. Special supplements to the G-23 report have been developed to document selected characteristics of populations of aliens such as the Cuban and Indochinese parolees. Currently, the G-23 report is the only source of aggregate statistics on the process of seeking political asylum. Most of the data collected through the activities of the Border Patrol, including information on deportable aliens located (form I-213), are manually processed and submitted in aggregate form on the G-23 report. Investigations units submit a consolidated report on the employment characteristics of deportable aliens located, their wage levels cross-classified with sector of employment, and the number of deportable aliens receiving public assistance. The G-23 report is the source of investigations data published in the statistical yearbook.

The G-23 report is used extensively within the agency for administrative purposes; the report is the data base used by personnel in the central, regional, and district offices for analysis of programs and allocation of resources. Analysis of G-23 report data has figured prominently in the evaluation of remote adjudications programs and efforts to reduce backlogs.

Despite the widespread use of data from the G-23 report, there is a pervasive skepticism among program and policy analysts in the INS about the accuracy and comparability of the G-23 reports for support of operational research and analysis. For example, field inspections personnel use G-23 report statistics only as rough indicators of office performance prior to a site visit. The data are considered neither accurate enough nor appropriate for office or employee evaluation. The lack of timeliness of G-23 data has been a serious problem, resulting in delayed responses to inquiries from other agencies of government, policy makers, and the public concerning trends in refugee admissions and applications for political asylum. In summary, there has been critical concern within the INS about the quality of data reported and the possible lack of consistency among the offices submitting the reports.

Much sharper criticism of the G-23 report came from program managers in district offices to panel members and staff in the course of our study: "The data are inappropriate as indicators of performance and productivity"; "The use to be made of many of the data items is unclear"; "The data do not represent the trends in or characteristics of operations being performed locally"; "The data are interpreted by central office personnel out of context"; etc. Because data from the G-23 report cannot serve program needs, many program managers develop their own information systems or bootleg reports that are more appropriate for evaluation and management of local programs.

The G-23 report is a detailed document that requires considerable experience and patience to use. The servicewide G-23 report for fiscal 1980, for example, had approximately 25,000 data entries: 17 columns and an average of 35 lines on 43 pages. In an effort to increase the utility of the information, the INS instituted a crash program in 1983 to keypunch, and thereby "automate," the handwritten G-23 report. At best, the keying of the information from the G-23 report may increase the accessibility of the data and make evaluation of the data easier. However, it does not address the critical issues of quality of data and comparability across organizational units. As the INS proceeds with plans to automate the collection of data in various operational areas, a considerable portion of the information that is now compiled in the G-23 report can be generated and tabulated by machine. A thorough review of the utility and quality of the data and the manner in which they are collected for the G-23 report could greatly reduce the reporting burden within offices and increase the timeliness and accuracy of the data for statistical analysis and program management.

AUTOMATED DATA PROCESSING

The INS depends heavily on the accuracy and accessibility of its records to accomplish its mission. Yet until the early 1970s the INS was dependent on manual systems for filing and retrieving information about millions of aliens. This section gives a brief review of the major automated systems that were introduced between 1972 and 1983 and raises a number of issues concerning automated processing of data on international migration by the INS.

The INS started to automate its recordkeeping in the 1970s as the workload increased and significant backlogs began to develop; the decade was characterized by rather uncoordinated development of automated systems to handle the most pressing current problems. A study (Immigration and Naturalization Service, 1981:executive summary) reported that "there has been little standardization in the development of most of the systems. Automation capabilities simply evolved out of discrete needs. As a result, there are no automated interfaces, formal system documentation is either lacking or inadequate, and the administration of the systems is widely dispersed."

In 1979 and 1980 the Committee on Government Operations of the U.S. House of Representatives conducted a thorough review of INS's automation efforts and put a hold on further procurement of hardware until a detailed strategy for automation was devised (U.S. Congress, 1980a). In reaction and response, the INS created an internal structure to plan and implement automation activities, develop detailed plans, purchase software and hardware, and integrate the new automated processes into the daily activities of its employees.

Early ADP Systems

Two major systems were developed in the early 1970s to keep track of the files maintained by the INS and to maintain a record of the millions of nonimmigrants, such as visitors, students, and others who come to the United States each year. The master index system, operational since 1972, was the first agencywide effort to introduce automation at the INS. The second, the nonimmigrant document control system, was an index of the records of arrival and departure of visitors and other nonimmigrants to and from the United States.

The Master Index System

The master index is a system of records that identifies the field location of files for the more than 12 million aliens who entered or were excluded from the United States since 1959. Documents for those who entered the country earlier are recorded on microfilm. The records in the master index are accessible either by the alien's file number (A-number) or by the alien's name and date of birth. The master index file includes the A-number, name, date of birth, country of birth, file control office in which the A-file is located, and the date of the latest transfer of the file. The master index remote access capability (MIRAC) provides the field offices with access to the master index via remote terminals, which expedites interrogations, adjudications, and investigations and reduces the manual work of the records sections both in the field offices and the central office.

The master index has been a valuable tool for determining the location of A-files and for verifying that a record exists for a particular alien. The system has limitations, however, in its basic design as well as in its operational features. Because it was designed primarily as an index to the location of A-files, the master index is not suitable for generating statistics for policy needs. The system also was not designed to interact with other information systems, such as the nonimmigrant information system. Problems with MIRAC cited during panel visits to district offices include slow response time, inadequate numbers of terminals, and excessive restrictions on district office personnel in updating records. The extent of omission of alien files from the master index is unknown, but one official estimated that up to 30 percent of the files that should be in the system are either missing or have been entered incorrectly. No systematic study has ever been carried out to determine the completeness or accuracy of the master index system. Because of these limitations, the master index is scheduled to be replaced in mid-1985 by the central index (described below), which is the core of the new data base management system in INS's long-range ADP plan.

The Nonimmigrant Document Control System

One of the earliest systems to be automated by the INS was the nonimmigrant document control system (NIDC), a centralized automated index developed in 1972 to automate the processing of records for the millions of nonimmigrants who arrive and depart annually. In 1982 NIDC included roughly 50 million records of the arrival and departure of nonimmigrants.

The development of NIDC illustrates some of the recurrent problems that have been encountered by the INS in its efforts at automation. The system was designed to provide an index to the records of entry into and departure from the United States, derive statistics on types of visitors, and identify those who overstayed their visas. Unfortunately, no useful data were produced because of serious delays in entering records into the system and because of the lack of adequate controls on the collection of departure forms, and the system has been scrapped. In fact, the primary source of nonimmigrant data was the Statistical Analysis Branch, which independently produced data through manual processing of the basic forms. The process of collecting information on nonimmigrants is described more fully in the discussion of the new nonimmigrant information system that replaced NIDC in January 1983.

Mid-Course Corrections

Congressional Investigation

In 1979 congressional concern about delays in processing applications and responding to public inquiries led to hearings by the House Committee on Government Operations. The committee examined the management of records by the INS and made recommendations in a number of areas, including record-keeping, forms, procurement, and ADP planning (U.S. Congress, 1980b). The recommendations of the committee set the framework for the further development of automated systems. The committee recommended that the INS:

    o Continue to pursue plans for automated input into the master index from the field (i.e., continue to develop MIRAC);
    o Postpone all procurement of ADP equipment until a long-range plan was completed and approved by the committee;
    o Work closely with the General Accounting Office, the General Services Administration, the Office of Management and Budget, and the appropriate committees of Congress in formulating its ADP plans; and
    o Develop and implement a plan assigning accountability to its senior executives for completing a satisfactory ADP plan.

The Scope of ADP Planning

In 1980 and 1981 the INS completed a mission plan, a study of its information requirements, and a long-range ADP plan. In addition, an Office of Information Systems was formed to oversee the planning and implementation of information-related programs and automation projects at the INS. The director of the office, the Associate Commissioner for Information Systems, participates in developing information policy and directs all automation activities. The automated systems that are currently being put in place will have a major impact on the daily activities of INS employees and could affect the timing, quality, and availability of statistics produced by the INS for decades.

The INS mission plan (Immigration and Naturalization Service, 1980a) states the major responsibilities of the agency and describes 81 specific strategies for achieving its goals. Unfortunately, more emphasis is placed on eliminating the collection of unnecessary data than on improving the accuracy and completeness of the data that are collected. Information requirements are narrowly defined as being the information needed by INS officers to make decisions about individual cases. This restricted view of what constitutes adequate data on immigrants--and emigrants--underlies INS statistical policy.

In 1980 the INS conducted a study of its information requirements to lay the foundations for the development of automated systems. Although a limited attempt was made to address the statistical needs of other agencies, the study focused almost exclusively on the information considered to be critical to INS officers for making decisions in their daily work. The limited scope of the study was stated clearly (Immigration and Naturalization Service, 1980b:13):

> The need for policy information of the Executive Branch and Congress--while long recognized--fell outside the purview of this report. Finally, the information needs of non-government users were omitted from this exercise. These users include the general public, members of which frequently request general information from INS, and the research community (colleges, universities, research foundations and consulting firms), members of which frequently request detailed information on aliens from INS. The scope of this study reflects the current top priorities of the INS.

This succinct statement clearly indicates the low priority placed on immigration statistics by INS management.

Interim Systems

As work proceeded on a long-range ADP plan, the INS was authorized to develop two interim systems to handle the increasing backlogs and problems in tracking cases being processed in the largest offices.

The naturalization and citizenship casework support system (NCCSS) was designed to monitor the status of naturalization and citizenship cases and to provide support to the clerical staff. As each application is entered in the system, a sequential number is assigned to the case. This ensures that cases are processed in the proper order and that accurate counts of pending cases can be compiled. Prior to implementation of the NCCSS in Los Angeles, the estimated backlog of cases was 30,000; when NCCSS was implemented, with more accurate counting of cases, the backlog was discovered to be more than 50,000.

The deportable alien control system (DACS) was designed to improve the storage and retrieval of information on detention and deportation cases. In addition to monitoring the status of cases, the system is supposed to produce reminders of the next scheduled event and provide data concerning aliens who have been detained.

An evaluation of the two interim case tracking systems by the Justice Department and the INS (U.S. Department of Justice, 1983) concluded that both systems were operating successfully in the offices in which they were initially installed. The evaluation noted, however, that technical problems at the test sites resulted in relatively slow and sometimes erratic response times.

Recent Developments

The Long-Range ADP Plan

In September 1981 the INS completed a long-range plan that is expected to expand its ADP capabilities dramatically. The new initiatives in the area of automation differ significantly from the earlier efforts. Considerably more planning has gone into the development of the new systems, and an effort has been made to include most of the agency's operations in the plans for automation. The plan was developed on the apparently sound assumption that sufficient resources would be available to purchase equipment and software. The budget for automation activities is expected to double from approximately $60 million in 1984 to $120 million in 1986. A new strategy for information management is also being implemented. Rather than automating, and thereby institutionalizing, existing processes, the plan calls for a series of modular data bases in different functional areas. The use of the data-base approach permits flexibility for changing information requirements and is expected to make data available for INS users to generate their own reports.

The long-range plan calls for the data bases to be linked to a central index that is scheduled to replace the master index in mid-1985. In terms of implementation, development of the central index is nearing completion, the nonimmigrant information system and the immigrant data capture system are operational, and the two interim case tracking systems described above are being revised to conform to the specifications of the long-range plan. In 1984 the INS began purchasing ADP equipment to satisfy the future automation requirements of all offices.

The Central Index

The purpose of the central index is to provide a list of the particular
data bases in which more information about an individual can be found.
The central index will contain such identifying data as name, A-number,
date of birth, sex, classification of admission, country of birth, port
of entry, date of admission, files control office, and a list of the data
bases containing information about the person. Statistical information
is expected to be available for reporting and management purposes.

The central index is being created by merging data from the master
index, the nonimmigrant information system (see below) and other INS
computer systems. After the central index is operational, each action by
the agency will provide an opportunity to create or update records for an
individual. In developing the central index, considerable emphasis is
being placed on being able to respond rapidly to field and other
inquiries. Data bases that could be linked to the central index include
those for legal permanent residents, students, other nonimmigrants,
smugglers, exclusions, apprehensions, and refugees, asylees, and parolees.

The Nonimmigrant Information System

The Nonimmigrant Information System (NIIS) is the first operational
system that is consistent with the long-range ADP plan. The purpose of
NIIS is to collect information on the arrival, departure, and status of
visitors, students, and other nonimmigrants. The process begins with a
nonimmigrant completing INS form I-94 at the time of entry into the
United States. The arrival section of the form is collected by the
inspector at entry, and the departure section is stapled to the
passport. The NIIS is supposed to be updated for each change of status,
such as an extension of stay, while the nonimmigrant is in the country.
When an alien leaves the United States, the departure section of the I-94
form should be turned in to an INS official or collected by the carrier.
The data keyed into the NIIS include name, date of birth, address while
in the United States, changes of status, mode of travel, port of entry
and departure, school attended (if applicable), and the city in which the
nonimmigrant visa was issued.

The nonimmigrant information system does not reflect the arrival and
departure of all aliens. For example, resident aliens who are returning
from a visit abroad are not required to complete I-94s, and immigrants
arriving to reside in the United States complete the forms, but they are
not entered into the system. Collection of I-94s for arrivals is more
complete than for departures, reflecting the lack of departure controls.
The absence of such controls may severely limit the ability of the NIIS
system to estimate the number of persons who stay longer than their
period of admission; generally, the numbers of "overstayers" will be
overstated.

The Immigrant Data Capture System

The immigrant data capture (IMDAC) system was designed to process
information from immigrant visas and forms for adjustment of status and
to produce data tapes for the alien identification card facility, for the
Statistical Analysis Branch, and for the Records Branch for updating the
master index. Prior to the establishment of IMDAC, immigrant visas and
adjustment of status forms were processed separately by each of these
three organizations. In addition to eliminating the duplication in
coding and processing visas, the system creates the A-files that are sent
to the appropriate INS district offices. The system appears to be
working as designed.

Issues Raised by Automation

There are important issues and potential problems related to automation
that deserve further consideration. These include the need for
sensitivity to users when redesigning forms or making changes in data
collection, adequate current documentation of systems, increased
attention to the quality of the input to automated systems, and the need
for establishing training and maintaining communication between the
systems designers in the central office and the users in the field.
Finally, adequate safeguards should be established to ensure the
confidentiality of the information INS maintains about individuals.
Optimism about the efficacy of the systems now being developed and
introduced within the INS should be tempered by knowledge of both the
difficulties encountered in earlier efforts at automation and the
difficulty of the tasks that remain to be accomplished.

INS RESOURCES FOR STATISTICAL ANALYSIS

As the preceding discussion has clearly indicated, the different parts of
the INS, in carrying out their diverse missions, produce a large amount
of administrative information, some of which they use internally for
management purposes. The key to unlocking the potential within this
structure for information of use in policy-related analysis, in
evaluating the numbers and movements of immigrants, and in informing
Congress and the public is the presence of a competent, adequately
staffed and funded statistical organization fully supported by management
and charged with the responsibility of producing timely and high-quality
data and analyses and of ensuring the collection of such data throughout
the organization.

The Office of Plans and Analysis

Institutionally, the mandate of immigration policy analysis lies within
the Office of Plans and Analysis (OPA), an executive-level unit under the
executive associate commissioner. This office conducts studies to

evaluate the implications for INS of legislative initiatives as well as analyses of INS programs, organization, and resources; it is also responsible for anticipating the effects of changes in patterns of international migration to the United States and in characteristics of the resident alien population. Since 1982 the Office of Plans and Analysis has been responsible for the agency's statistics and research programs and presently oversees the activities of the Statistical Analysis Branch.

The Statistical Analysis Branch

The Statistical Analysis Branch is the unit within INS that has responsibility for assembling both workload (i.e., management) data and population (i.e., policy) statistics. The branch does not have a major role either in determining what is to be collected and how or in formulating statistical policy for the agency; its responsibilities are simply to compile and disseminate what is produced elsewhere. The branch is responsible for producing an annual statistical report, compiling work measurement statistics, and responding to requests for information from Congress, other federal agencies, and other users of data on aliens and naturalized citizens.

The branch's functions currently are being carried out by a staff of about 30, including 9 analysts and statisticians (in early 1984, the number stood at 5), at an annual operating cost of approximately $1.3 million (fiscal 1983). Prior to 1983, the Statistical Analysis Branch was located within the Office of the Associate Commissioner for Information Systems; since then, the branch has received its day-to-day direction from the Office of Plans and Analysis, although its budget is within the newly organized Office of Information Services.

Discussion of the Statistical Analysis Branch must begin with consideration of the staff available to undertake its assigned tasks. The branch does not have a full-time head, and far from being a one-time or short-term phenomenon, this situation has existed, with rare exceptions, for long periods over the past few years. It is therefore not surprising that high turnover has marked the other professional positions and that the professional staff, however capable, has been unable to achieve the performance that could follow from enlightened and strong professional leadership and agency support. The failures of the Statistical Analysis Branch also can be traced to the extremely inadequate size of its professional staff: even when fully staffed, with only nine professional positions, it is surprising and to their credit that so many of their tasks are carried out.

About half of the 30 staff members have responsibilities related to statistics from the work measurement (G-23) system. Incoming forms are checked for completeness, and compilations are done for the district, regional, and national levels. The other half of the staff oversee the compilation of demographic data, produce the annual statistical report, and respond to requests for information. Statistics are compiled and distributed for immigrants, students, visitors, temporary workers, refugees and asylees, and naturalizations. In addition to compiling and distributing statistics, the branch staff inform field offices of changes in reporting requirements and coding procedures.

It is instructive to compare the INS with a parallel federal agency, the Internal Revenue Service (IRS). Similar in structure and responsibility to INS, the IRS is a constituent part of a larger agency (the Treasury Department); has many field offices and diverse responsibilities; and most of its data derive from a large flood of administrative records. Within IRS, however, the statistical responsibilities are centralized within a division headed by a professional statistician and reporting directly to an assistant commissioner. The division is known and respected throughout the agency, including the IRS service centers; it is similarly known by and involved with sister statistical organizations in the federal government; and its products are extensively used in program planning and evaluation by the Office of Tax Analysis in the Treasury Department as well as by the Congress. As a final point of comparison, the IRS division's direct budget in fiscal 1984 was approximately $7 million and supported almost 170 staff years of effort. In addition, the division received some $8.25 million that it distributed to other parts of the IRS to support statistical activities required for its work. Our purpose in making this comparison is not to suggest that the statistical activities within the INS require or deserve equal treatment; the great disparity between the respective groups, however, whether in organizational status, staffing, budget, or reputation—given their many other similarities—gives a clear indication of the low priority accorded to the statistical program of the INS.

The work of the Statistical Analysis Branch has experienced at least two major setbacks in the last five years. The first of these was the complete loss of statistics for nonimmigrants for the period July 1979 to September 1980. A large backlog had occurred in the processing of I-94 forms for nonimmigrants, partly due to the increased number of visitors to the United States. An unsuccessful effort was made to develop estimates of the flow of nonimmigrants using sampling techniques. As a result, INS has no statistical data on nonimmigrants for the last quarter of fiscal 1979 and for the entire 1980 fiscal year. For fiscal 1981 and 1982, when processing was resumed, only a limited number of characteristics were made available.

The second setback was the loss of records from the immigrant data files for 1980 through 1983. This loss resulted from the physical loss of computer tapes containing immigrants' statistical records. In addition, some adjustment of status cases may not have been coded by the field. The presentation of tables showing data for immigrants in recent years has been made possible only by linking the agency's statistical data file with the data file of immigrants receiving I-551 forms, alien registration receipt cards ("green cards"). However, since the data file on persons receiving I-551 forms does not contain all of the statistical variables that are on the immigrant visa, many of the statistical tables could not be produced from this source. To date, INS has not attempted to recapture the data on these missing records. As a consequence, statistics on immigrants for 1980 and 1981 have not been tabulated for such important variables as sex, marital status, occupation, place of intended residence, country of last residence, and nationality.

It appears that, beginning with fiscal 1984, the problem of missing statistical data has been resolved. The immigrant data capture (IMDAC) system was fully implemented and appears to be working smoothly; however, the best of systems can be rendered useless by a lack of proper storage, control, and protection of data tapes.

The process of automation that is now accelerating at the INS has significant implications for the operations of the Statistical Analysis Branch. For example, the coding of visas and applications for adjustment of status is now done as part of the IMDAC system, rather than by the branch. The new nonimmigrant information system incorporates the processing under contract of the millions of I-94 arrival/departure documents that were formerly coded by the branch. As more data bases are created in accord with the long-range ADP plan, it should be possible for the branch staff to have faster access to information and to allocate relatively more staff positions to professional analysts rather than clerical personnel. More detailed tabulations can be prepared to respond to users of INS data, and it should be possible to release public-use tapes for a wide variety of immigrant and nonimmigrant groups. Increased automation of data systems raises the potential for more detailed analysis and interpretation of data and for more constructive interaction with outside users. Whether this potential is realized remains to be seen; past experience, unfortunately, does not lead to an optimistic forecast.

Automation by itself, however, will not solve the problems that have been evident for some time in the statistical operations of the INS and particularly in the Statistical Analysis Branch. Except for its somewhat limited participation in the ADP planning process, the branch appears generally to have been ignored in the design and implementation of the new systems. Forms are redesigned and specific items are added or deleted without consultation and sometimes without the knowledge of personnel in the branch. Similarly, the branch has no clear responsibility for, or control over, the quality of data collected throughout the INS. In summary, automation is likely to have an increasing impact on the operations of the branch, and the INS should make sure its staff and organization are prepared for the inevitable changes in its role and involved in the evolution of the system to ensure adequate quality control and that statistical needs can be easily and quickly met.

Branch Publications

INS Statistical Yearbook Delay in publishing the agency's statistics has increased considerably in recent years. The narrative section of the 1978 Annual Report was published without its statistical component, approximately 100 pages of statistical tabulations, because the statistical tables were not ready in time. Although annual reports had not included any statistical analysis in the recent past, they did include 30 to 40 pages of description of the agency's activities. As this commentary included occasional definitions, descriptions of new legislation, and changes in INS policy, the text was an aid in interpreting the statistics. Since 1978, however, the statistics of INS have been published without any accompanying text, and only three Statistical Yearbooks, for 1979, 1980, and 1981, have been published. For 1980 there was a 3-year lag between the collection of statistics and their publication, which was reduced to 2 1/2 years for the 1981 data.

How can the Statistical Yearbook of the Immigration and Naturalization Service be improved? Certain basic suggestions are readily apparent from the previous discussion: (1) the report should be released in a timely manner; (2) it should be accompanied by explanatory and analytical text; (3) it should present data on all of the agency's data series (i.e., immigrants, nonimmigrants, naturalizations, etc.); (4) the series in the report should be consistent from year to year, with necessary changes clearly noted and explained; (5) for each data series in the report, the data should be tabulated for all relevant variables; (6) some of the tables currently published, consisting largely of empty cells, should be condensed or dropped; and (7) the treatment of missing data and the number of cases missing or imputed should be fully described (see Appendix B).

Many of the problems indicated by the above list could be corrected if the INS placed higher priority on data collection and tabulation efforts. The prompt dissemination of the agency's statistics is hindered by delays attributable to the low priority given to statistical coding--if not all statistical activities--in its field offices. Since INS's statistical data are generated on a flow basis over the year, it should be possible to publish statistics only months after the close of the fiscal year, not several years as is the case now. In addition, quarterly figures could be published during the year. This is a very basic task--the prompt processing of all statistical data. The fact that it is basic, however, does not diminish its importance, nor does it imply that it is effortless to accomplish. It demands significant amounts of planning, continual attention, and resources on the part of INS. Without this firm foundation, other gains made by improving the agency's data-processing capabilities will be negated.

The reporting of INS's statistics would be improved by returning to the consolidation of the statistical tables of the statistical yearbook with the annual report as was done prior to 1978. As mentioned above, this consolidation would serve two purposes: it would link the agency's statistics with a description of its activities during that year, and it would focus needed attention on the statistics, ensuring their prompt publication. Although the present text of the annual report helps in understanding the agency's statistics, it does not meet this need completely. A descriptive analysis accompanying the statistical tables would assist users in interpreting the statistics. Such analysis should describe the characteristics and trends of the data series, as well as providing a discussion of relevant legislation or INS policy that may have affected the data. As the INS strengthens its statistical capabilities, future annual reports should be expanded to include more in-depth analysis and to inform readers of additional sources of INS data, notably unpublished detailed tables and public-use tapes (discussed in detail below). One major improvement in the 1981 Statistical Yearbook over preceding issues is the inclusion of a glossary defining U.S. immigration terms. The definitions of terms according to immigration law are seldom the same as those in common usage. The trend in recent years toward increased documentation--technical explanations of data and methods--should be accelerated because such documentation is essential to informing users of legislative and policy changes and other qualifications of the meaning of the data.

The individual statistical tables need to be reviewed to increase their usefulness and to eliminate those that are downright misleading or based on data of very poor quality, such as tables 48 and 50 of the 1981 Statistical Yearbook concerning border crossers. New tables have been added in recent years presenting detail and perspective on such topics as refugees (1980 Statistical Yearbook:tables 9 and 10) and immigrant classes of admission (tables 3, 4, and 6); in addition, many existing tables have been expanded to cover all, rather than just selected, countries. These changes need careful evaluation since the result is a series of very long, complicated tables with many empty cells. At the same time, however, such changes improve the usefulness of the statistics and should be actively pursued. Not only do they make it easier for users of the data, but they also reduce INS's workload in the long run by decreasing the number of individual statistical requests coming to the agency. In addition, changes in table format and design are essential; some of the tables are difficult to read without a magnifying glass. Finally, there should be increased attention to detail. Reports should be proofread more carefully so that the number of errors, whether processing or typographical, are reduced.

The present published tables of the INS statistical yearbook are formatted (and correctly so) to reflect U.S. immigration law. Data are tabulated by the Immigration and Nationality Act's definitions of immigrants, nonimmigrants, etc., for U.S. fiscal years and for countries as recognized by the INA. However, the agency should also begin to develop additional tabulations to conform to international definitions. The United Nations (1980) has recommended definitions and tabulations for international migration statistics that will improve international comparability. The United States should begin to move toward this goal, even though it is not possible to carry out all the recommendations at this time. For example, it might be possible to use the nonimmigrant information system to produce tabulations consistent with the international definition of long-term and short-term immigrants.

Several other points regarding the statistical tables should be made. Content should be updated annually, reflecting geopolitical changes and changes in immigration law. For example, until recently, data were tabulated and published for such "countries" as Palestine and the Free City of Danzig--long after they were no longer recognized by the INA and the U.S. State Department. In recent years, the Statistical Analysis Branch has begun to incorporate appropriate changes to the statistical tabulations. This monitoring of changes to the INA should be continued.

All of these comments point in one direction: the INS must place a higher priority on its statistics and their publication; after all, the

Statistical Yearbook is one of the major reports of the agency. Many of the recommended improvements can be accomplished with existing staff although some may require additional resources. The Immigration and Naturalization Service has an extremely difficult mission to accomplish in administering the nation's immigration and naturalization laws. The timely publication of high-quality statistics is also an important responsibility that should be given considerably higher priority by the INS.

INS Public-Use Tape Program   In 1979 the Statistical Analysis Branch began a public-use tape program. At present public-use tapes can be made available for most of the sets of data maintained by the Statistical Analysis Branch. Personal identifiers such as name, A-number, and address are removed from the tapes. The INS should make an even stronger commitment to a public-use tape program. The first step would be to define a staff with clear responsibilities for the tape program. Better documentation and public information about the tapes is also crucial for improving the public-use tape program. Such a program may require additional resources, but would be beneficial to the INS as well as to other users of immigration data.

Statistics on the Resident Alien Population

Since the annual Alien Address Registration Program was discontinued in 1981, the INS has been unable to estimate the size of the alien population residing in the United States or in local areas of the country. Until 1981 all aliens residing in the United States in January of each year were required to complete and submit form I-53, listing current address, category and date of admission, and demographic information such as age, sex, and country of birth. The alien registration program provided detailed geographic information about the alien population that was useful for resource allocation and, potentially, for a variety of statistical purposes. Recommendations for using the I-53 data were made by a wide variety of groups and individual researchers during the 1970s. The data have been used in a number of statistical studies such as estimating the annual level of alien emigration from the country and estimating the number of illegal aliens who were included in the 1980 census.

   Despite the actual and potential value of the alien registration data, the perception grew within INS (and subsequently, within Congress) that the data were grossly underreported--although no tests of completeness were ever attempted--and of little value to the agency. Accordingly, when Congress proposed to discontinue the program as an economy measure, the INS did not object and the program was discontinued after 1981. A valuable source of information about the alien population residing in the United States was lost because users of the data, including analysts in the INS, were unable to convince the management of INS that the data were valuable and should be collected, evaluated, and utilized.

The panel seriously considered recommending the reinstatement of a modified alien address program that, for statistical purposes, would have collected information only at two or three fixed points each decade. However, after much discussion, we concluded that it was not appropriate to single out a unique and specific segment of the population in the United States and require registration solely for statistical information. Instead, we wish to emphasize the need for the development of other approaches to fill this data gap. One such alternative for collecting information about aliens residing in the United States, a longitudinal study of immigrants, is described in Chapter 8.

A Statistical Advisory Committee

The preceding discussion points to the need both for strong leadership and enhanced statistical professionalism within the INS and for an ongoing group of outside expert advisers to assist the INS in establishing and maintaining a coordinated and responsive statistical program. Such a statistical advisory committee could consider specific issues, such as how best to fill the gap left by the cancellation of the alien address program, whether and how to collect information about emigrant aliens, and how to estimate the size and growth of the illegal alien population; it also could address broader issues, such as the role of INS in implementing the U.N. recommendations for collecting data on international migration and provide the commissioner with independent expertise on the quality of the INS statistical program and on user needs.

Evaluation of INS Statistics

Evaluation of data quality should have a high priority throughout the INS. For a variety of reasons, including greater objectivity, it would be useful to contract much of the evaluation of data quality to sources external to the INS, either inside or outside the government. Precedent exists within INS for issuing such contracts (this panel's work, for example, was funded through contract). Moreover, such contracts are regularly used by the Office of Refugee Resettlement (ORR), which devotes a portion of its annual budget to evaluation activities.

Contract research also can take advantage of specialized expertise outside the INS. The U.S. Census Bureau has developed and will continue to elaborate statistical procedures and models for estimating the extent of census coverage (see Chapter 5). A contract (or other interagency agreement) could benefit the INS in applying this expertise to its problems of a similar nature.

To date, however, although precedent exists for using the contract mechanism and although substantial increments in data quality might be achieved through contract research, INS has made relatively little use of contracts. More explicit attention should be given to such research as an integral part of the INS's data quality assurance program.

CONCLUSIONS AND RECOMMENDATIONS

As we noted at the outset of this chapter, the effective mission of the INS is to enforce immigration policy and law. In carrying out this mission, the INS, through its various entities, assembles a multitude of administrative records and information items. Traditionally overburdened in the handling and processing of these records, the agency has taken dramatic strides in recent years in planning, designing, and implementing automated systems to deal with the handling, storage, and retrieval of records. Within the next five years, the agency indeed may be able to point with pride to its ability to locate efficiently and quickly the record of a specific alien.

Unfortunately, the INS has not approached either its statistical system or its statistical organization in the same positive manner. On the contrary, from the Office of the Commissioner down through the organization to the single-employee border crossing station, the INS has failed to understand--and therefore failed to support--the need for timely and high-quality data. Even the information contained in its key management form, the G-23, is considered suspect by its staff. In addition, a number of senior staff question any INS role in producing policy-relevant statistics. This position also is reflected in what can only be described as meager staff and funding resources assigned to statistical compilation and analysis--nine allocated professional positions for the entire agency.

The panel's view of the situation is not unique. Concerns about the inadequacies of the system in meeting data needs can be found in the records of innumerable congressional hearings on the INS, in the reports issued by congressional committees considering legislation dealing with aliens, in academic writings, and in popular articles on the subject. The most recent example of congressional displeasure at the situation is found in a House Judiciary Committee report accompanying the Appropriations Authorization Act for fiscal 1985 (U.S. Congress, 1984); the following excerpts highlight the frustration:

> The Committee amendment for the first time provides statutory language requiring the collection, preparation and distribution of information and data on the number and characteristics of immigrant and nonimmigrant aliens entering and departing the United States.
>
> The Committee is deeply concerned about the unavailability of accurate and current statistical information on immigration matters. The Committee notes in this regard that INS has not devoted sufficient resources and attention to this problem and, to a great extent, has ignored the statistical needs of Congress, as well as the research needs of demographers and other outside users. While the Committee recognizes that INS must place first priority on its own operational requirements, the informational needs of Congress cannot be ignored.

The Committee frequently has been frustrated in its attempts to obtain the statistics needed to assess the impact of legislation it is considering. For example, only very rough estimates were obtainable of the number of investors and foreign medical graduates who would potentially benefit from the status adjustment provisions contained in the Immigration and Nationality Act Amendments of 1981, enacted by the 97th Congress as P.L. 97-116. Additionally, the Committee recently had to make a special request to the General Accounting Office for a study on the use of H and L nonimmigrant visas [for temporary workers and intracompany transferees]. This extraordinary step was taken because of the inability of INS to respond to inquiries by the Committee on admission and adjustment of status figures for temporary workers and intracompany transferees (H and L visas) in various occupations.

The most widely publicized lack of statistics occurred during the Iranian crisis in 1979, when INS was unable to provide a count of Iranian students in this country.

The Committee wishes to stress the need for comprehensive and timely statistics on immigration. Since INS processes the source forms for these statistics, the responsibility for their reporting and content rests logically with that agency.

Congress, of course, must share some of the blame for the very situation about which it complains. Congress, as it did in the case of the Refugee Act of 1980, could have mandated both the collection of the data it desired and the preparation of analytical reports for use in its deliberations; it also could have requested an assessment of needs and provided such funding and staff as it deemed necessary to accomplish the task. The panel urges the Congress to exert its leadership to ensure that the INS and the other organizations concerned with this issue clearly understand and are equipped to deal with what is expected of them.

That the INS is a veritable storehouse of data is beyond question; the quality of the information contained in its many millions of records or in summarized tabulations is another matter. The data indeed are used because in most cases they are the only data available, but use is not synonymous with quality. Our study indicates that the INS does not use even the most rudimentary of the accepted techniques in collecting and processing its data, such as: instituting quality control procedures at each level of operation; using sampling when appropriate; documenting procedures; instituting periodic training of staff to ensure understanding of objectives and testing procedures; and developing feedback mechanisms to identify and solve problems. Further, the INS has failed to assign either responsibility or accountability for its statistical program.

As a final point, it is quite clear that despite its huge inventory of facts, the INS has not assembled its data or gathered the relevant information to address either the kinds of substantive policy questions identified in Chapter 3 or even the more focused issues noted in the House report cited above.

We are not unmindful of the difficulties involved in attempting to overcome many years of accumulated problems in a relatively short time. However, given the importance of the Immigration and Naturalization Service, it is essential that the agency begin immediately to improve drastically its statistical policies, programs, and procedures and to be able to show progress in a relatively short time. To expedite the effort the panel recommends that the INS:

o Seek short-term, temporary assistance from the major federal statistical agencies, including advice on statistical procedures and the temporary assignment of experienced staff;

o Establish an advisory committee of outside experts in the field of immigration analysis to advise on data gaps, priorities, and problems. Such a mechanism is used extensively by other federal agencies and provides an invaluable source of expert advice and objective comment; and

o Establish a program of contract research with the short-run objective of evaluating data production and quality and the long-run objective of stimulating quality analysis of INS data sets. Such a program, which has many precedents, would allow the INS to take immediate advantage of the specialized expertise outside the agency. In the longer run, such a program would encourage the growth of experience in the use of INS data and provide a base of knowledge for policy and program decisions.

Given the present situation, the panel also has little confidence in the ability of the INS to meet the statistical requirements associated with enacting and implementing new immigration legislation. Therefore, we believe it essential, given the central role of the INS in assembling data on aliens, that immediate steps be taken by both the legislative and executive branches of government to address and remedy the situation. Some of these steps have small or insignificant budgetary implications, whereas others will require additional funding. The likely financial and personnel costs of these recommendations that cannot reasonably be absorbed within existing budgets are discussed following the recommendations.

The panel recommends that Congress:

o Strongly affirm the importance of reliable, accurate, and timely statistical information on immigration to the needs of the Congress and direct the Attorney General to reexamine the organizational structure of the Immigration and Naturalization Service as it relates to statistics, with a view to placing greater priority on this important task and

o Require that the Attorney General prepare and submit by June 30 each year an annual report to the President and the Congress, presenting data on aliens admitted or excluded, naturalizations, asylees, and refugees, describing their characteristics, and containing an analysis of significant developments during the preceding year in the field of immigration and emigration.

The panel recommends that the Attorney General:

o Issue a strong policy directive asserting the importance of reliable, accurate, and timely statistical information on immigration to the mission of the INS and unequivocally committing the agency to improving its existing capabilities.

The panel recommends that the commissioner of the INS:

o Issue an explicit statement clearly setting forth that the collection, cumulation, and tabulation of reliable, accurate, and timely statistical information on immigration is a basic responsibility of and inherent in the mission of the agency;

o Establish a Division of Immigration Statistics, reporting directly to an associate commissioner or an equivalent level, with overall responsibility:

--for ensuring the use of appropriate statistical standards and procedures in the collection of data throughout the agency;
--for ensuring the timely publication of a variety of statistical and analytic reports;
--for providing statistical assistance to all parts of the agency in carrying out their mission; and
--for directing statistical activities throughout the agency;

o Direct and implement the recruitment of a full complement of competent, trained professionals with statistical capabilities and subject-area experience;

o Initiate a review of all data-gathering activities to eliminate duplication, minimize burden and waste, assess specific data item needs and uses, improve question wording and form design, standardize definitions and concepts, document methodologies, introduce statistical standards and procedures, and promote efficiencies in the use of staff and resources;

o Establish an advisory committee composed of experts in the use and production of immigration-related data to advise the associate commissioner and the proposed Division of Immigration Statistics of needs for new or different types of data; to review existing data and data collection methodology; to advise on the statistical implications and potential of ADP plans; and to provide the agency with independent evaluation of its statistical products, plans, and performance;

o Establish formal liaison with other federal and state agencies involved in the collection or analysis of immigration-related data;

o Establish both a program to enhance and stimulate research into the various effects of immigration and a fellows program, which would bring to the agency for a period not to exceed 2 years outstanding scholars and experts to undertake original research using published or unpublished data from the INS or other sources;

o Authorize the proposed Division of Immigration Statistics to initiate a program of contract research. This research, which may be either extramural or intramural, should be focused on the evaluation of data production and data quality;

o Strengthen the annual report, presenting data on immigrants, nonimmigrants, naturalizations, asylees, parolees, and refugees, describing their characteristics, and analyzing significant developments during the previous fiscal year. The report should be published annually by June 30;

o Establish a process ensuring adequate discussion and consideration both within and outside the agency of changes in forms and data collection procedures; and

o Institute such other activities as are necessary and desirable to ensure:

--understanding at all levels of the agency of the commissioner's commitment to high-quality, timely statistical data;

--agreement with, and support for, the commissioner's policy directive.

The panel recommends that the Director of the U.S. Office of Management and Budget (OMB):

o Ensure that OMB exercise its responsibilities to monitor and review statistical activities and budgets concerning statistics on immigration and emigration, and particularly those of the INS, to minimize duplication and ensure that appropriate procedures are used, standards met, and priorities observed in the collection, production, and publication of such data;

o Require continuing interagency coordination in the field of immigration data; participate in discussions designed to achieve consistency and comparability in concepts and definitions used by the individual organizations in the collection of such information; and oversee the introduction and use of standardized approaches; and

o Actively encourage and support the timely publication and dissemination of immigration data and the ready availability of fully documented public-use data tapes, including samples of individual records (with identifiers removed) where feasible, and data summaries.

The agenda of required actions reflect lengthy deliberations on the panel's part, particularly concerning the cost-effectiveness of the proposed measures. Clearly, in the present climate of budgetary restraint, it would have been inappropriate and futile to recommend a package of improvements entailing sharply higher expenditure; at the same time, no improvement of the order of magnitude required can be expected with the existing budget solely from improved efficiency and attitude. Many of the recommendations listed above, however, require little or no additional funding. For example, when we ask of the Congress and the Attorney General that, to use the words of Arthur Miller, "attention be paid," the benefit should be great and almost immediate and the dollar cost small. Similarly, the costs to OMB of our recommendations, while not zero, should not exceed $25,000 per year, about a half-year of staff effort, in starting, nurturing, and carrying out the coordination function that by law is the responsibility of OMB.

In several instances, however, despite our self-imposed constraints, the panel has found it necessary to recommend actions that will involve relatively large expenditures. An example is the recommendation to establish a Division of Immigration Statistics, an action the panel believes to be essential. In order, however, to mitigate its funding effect in a single year, and recognizing the start-up problems inherent in such an action, the panel proposes that the development of the division be phased over several years; a period of 3-5 years would appear reasonable. Using as a guide the current $1.3 million budget of the present Statistical Analysis Branch, which supports about 30 persons, of whom 9 are professionals, we propose an ultimate annual budget for the division of $3.75 million, supporting a staff of 40 professionals and 20 support staff, 60 persons in all. As noted earlier, the growth would be accomplished over several years. Using a 3-year period, the present $1.3 million budget would increase to $1.8 million in the first year, to $2.75 million in the second year, and would achieve the $3.75 million level in the third year. The increase over the present budget would require an additional appropriation of $2.5 million. We view this level sufficient to accomplish all the recommendations noted above that are directed to the INS, if accompanied by the essential changes in attitude and priorities also recommended for the agency.

REFERENCES

Davidson, C.
1981 Characteristics of Deportable Aliens Located in the Interior of the United States. Unpublished paper presented at the annual meeting of the Population Association of America, Washington, D.C.

Immigration and Naturalization Service
1980a INS Mission Plan, INS Planning Task Force, Robert A. Kane, Chairman. Unpublished paper.

Immigration and Naturalization Service
1980b Information Requirements Study, Volume 1, INS Planning Task Force, Robert A. Kane, Chairman. p. 13. Unpublished paper.

Immigration and Naturalization Service
1981 Long Range ADP Plan, Volume 1, Office of Operations Support. Unpublished paper.

U.S. Congress, House
1980a Immigration and Naturalization Service Record Management Problems. Committee on Government Operations. 96th Congress, 2nd Session. Washington, D.C.: U.S. Government Printing Office.

U.S. Congress, House
1980b Immigration and Naturalization Service Record Management Problems. Committee on Government Operations. 96th Congress, 2nd Session. Pages 7-9. Washington, D.C.: U.S. Government Printing Office.

U.S. Congress, House
1984 Report to Accompany H.R. 5468, Department of Justice Appropriation Act, Fiscal Year 1985. Committee on the Judiciary. Washington, D.C.: U.S. Government Printing Office.

U.S. Department of Justice
   1980   March 15 Statement of David Crosland before the Senate
           Appropriations Committee, p. 11.
U.S. Department of Justice
   1983   Joint Study, INS Interim ADP Projects. Prepared by Justice
           Management Division, Department of Justice and Evaluation
           Division, U. S. Immigration and Naturalization Service.
           Unpublished.
United Nations
   1980   Recommendations on Statistics of International Migration.
           Series M. No. 58. New York.

5

Other Government Sources of Information on Immigration

It is not surprising that the INS, given its name and notoriety, is often thought of as the one and only source of information on immigration. Certainly, as we have shown in Chapter 4, it is, or could be, the most important--but it is not the only one. This chapter describes the more important of what we have labeled other official sources, those federal agencies and offices which in the performance of their mission come in contact with immigrants or collect information about immigrants. The order of presentation reflects, first, those agencies or offices that have a direct program involvement with immigrants or refugees, followed by those that interact indirectly, those that regularly collect data relevant to immigrants as part of their statistical activities and, finally, those that have the potential for providing useful and important information as a by-product of their activities. As an indication of the pervasive nature of the subject of immigration, this chapter deals with nine separate organizations within six different cabinet-level agencies. We describe briefly both the role of the agency or office and the types of information it collects or produces. (Relevant forms are shown in Appendix A.) In the course of this review, we also comment on weaknesses and makes recommendations for improvements.

BUREAU OF CONSULAR AFFAIRS, U.S. DEPARTMENT OF STATE

Responsibilities and Data

The visa-issuing offices of the State Department abroad are generally the first points of official contact for most aliens wanting either to visit or to migrate to the United States. In fact, the State Department issues two-thirds of all immigrant visas abroad; the remaining one-third go to nonimmigrants and refugees in the United States who adjust to permanent resident status through the INS. Given the current laws and regulations, the Bureau of Consular Affairs exercises enormous discretion in determining who is eligible to receive a visa--as either visitor or immigrant.

More important, the State Department is responsible for controlling the numerical limitation on the number of immigrant visas issued. Its actions, in the aggregate, thus can provide the basis for much valuable information for monitoring patterns of visa demand worldwide and of movement into the country. Furthermore, since much of the information that subsequently enters the INS data systems originates at this stage, the degree of attention given to full and accurate reporting is crucial. As in most areas in which administrative functions predominate, however, the interest in data and care with which they are collected are very limited. Not only would more care produce better data, but more effective use of the data might also actually improve the administrative functioning. For example, linking visa applications to entry and departure records maintained by INS, which identify possible visa abusers, could provide a basis for improved screening of visa applicants.

The statistical programs of the Department of State concerning immigration produce aggregate data on visa applications issued and denied at authorized posts abroad. Reports are prepared at scheduled dates each year showing immigrant visa applications and persons waiting for visas by preference category, foreign state of chargeability, class of visa, and determination (granted or denied) and showing nonimmigrant visa applications by class of visa and outcome. Visas denied are classified by general type of visa and grounds for refusal.

The Department of State and INS are collaborating to integrate the process of visa issuance with the process of immigration to the United States by developing a single automated system for recording immigrant visa issuance and utilization. The goal is to monitor efficiently the availability of visas within existing ceilings and to determine the waiting time for applicants by country of chargeability and preference category.

The unique information on immigration collected by visa offices, however, concerns events surrounding the process of visa application; that is, the demand for immigrant visas and the way decisions are made by consular officials. These officials administer the various required application forms and also are responsible for considering additional evidence concerning visa eligibility. While files on aliens to whom visas are granted and used are transferred to the INS, which then creates A-files (see Chapter 4), the State Department remains the sole source of information on immigrant and nonimmigrant visa refusals, including the reasons for rejection. The current data reporting procedures do not include characteristics of aliens refused visas, not even country of origin; nor do the data processing systems being developed tap the documentary sources of information available in consular files concerning the process of denying visas to aliens.

Traditionally, the Bureau of Consular Affairs has produced data--or program information--primarily for its own use. The data are generally available, although external requests are rare. The bureau has produced annual summaries of data on visa issuance since the early 1920s (although there has been no congressional mandate to do so). Yet it is only now beginning to review what it produces, both in content and format, from the point of view of the administrative uses of the information. The issue of data for analytic or policy use is seldom raised. The State Department clearly has information of immediate and potential value for many analytical purposes, but it lacks interest in informing potential users of what may be obtained or in making the information available in useful form. The first need, in this as in a number of other areas, is

to bring a sense of need and awareness to agency management and to set up
much closer coordination in the area of immigration statistics.

Recommendations

The Panel recommends that the State Department:

o Become an active participant in interagency discussions on
improving immigration statistics, in order to enhance its own
understanding of the need for and uses of such information, and

o Establish its own review group to assess the statistical potential
of its programs, to propose actions to be taken to improve its
statistical performance, and to make recommendations to the department.

U.S. DEPARTMENT OF LABOR

One of the fundamental concerns surrounding immigration is its impact on
the labor force. The U.S. Department of Labor's (DOL) involvement with
immigration extends across three of its agencies: the Employment and
Training Administration, the Bureau of International Labor Affairs, and
the Employment Standards Administration. Within the Employment and
Training Administration, two offices deal with immigration to varying
degrees: the Division of Foreign Labor Certifications in the U.S.
Employment Service and the Office of Research and Evaluation in the
Office of Strategic Planning and Policy Development.

Division of Foreign Labor Certifications

Program and Data

The Division of Foreign Labor Certifications is perhaps the best known of
the four DOL offices dealing with immigration, since it is involved
directly with the actual admission process of certain groups of both
temporary and permanent immigrant workers. However, only a relatively
small number of immigrants require labor certifications to be admitted to
the United States, since current immigration policy is based largely on
family reunification. Immigrants entering as immediate relatives outside
the preference system or under the relative preferences do not need labor
certificates. Only immigrants entering under the occupational
preferences (see Table 2-2) or under the nonpreference category (which
has been unavailable since late 1978) need the approval of the Division
of Foreign Labor Certifications.

A total of 54,000 immigrant visa numbers are allotted for the
occupational preferences: 27,000 for the third preference category,
which includes members of the professions or persons of exceptional
ability in the sciences and arts and their families; and 27,000 for the
sixth preference category, which includes skilled and unskilled workers
in short supply and their families. However, since the numbers allotted
include beneficiaries (spouse and unmarried children of the principal
immigrant), the actual number of immigrants entering each year with labor

certifications is less than half the total number of third and sixth preference visas issued. For example, less than 21,000 immigrants were admitted with labor certifications in fiscal 1980, a year in which third and sixth preference admissions exceeded 44,000 and overall immigration exceeded 530,000.

The current labor certification program for immigrants was created by the 1965 amendments to the Immigration and Nationality Act. In addition to a provision requiring that aliens seeking admission to the United States as workers have a U.S. job offer, Section 212(a)(14) of the INA requires that each alien intending to migrate to the United States for the purpose of employment must first obtain a certification from the Secretary of Labor that: (1) there are not sufficient U.S. workers who are able, willing, qualified, and available at the place of intended employment and (2) the employment of the alien will not adversely affect the wages and working conditions of U.S. workers similarly employed. When the requirements for the program were first established in the late 1960s, the list of qualifying occupations in each preference category was determined by the division through a more or less systematic inquiry of employment services offices throughout the country. Changes to the list since that time have been both infrequent and ad hoc, reflecting in the main both positive and negative comments from employers on the supply of available U.S. resident applicants for specific occupations.

There are two kinds of procedures for securing a labor certification. The more common is for the prospective U.S. employer of the alien to apply for certification directly to DOL. The other, far less common, concerns aliens who have obtained U.S. job offers in an occupation precertified by DOL as meeting the requirements of the INA.

The Division of Foreign Labor Certifications is relatively small, having a national office staff of approximately 15, 11 of whom are manpower development specialists. However, more personnel are involved in the labor certification program, since applications are processed in approximately 1,900 local offices of state employment service agencies. These applications are forwarded to 10 regional offices (or to the national office, in some instances) for determination. In addition, authority is delegated to the INS and consular officers of the Department of State to grant employer petitions for precertified (Schedule A) occupations. More than 50,000 requests for permanent labor certifications are processed annually. Of these, an average of 25,000 to 30,000 certifications are granted.

The Division of Foreign Labor Certifications also has the responsibility for certifying that the admission of temporary agricultural and nonagricultural (H-2 visa) workers will not adversely affect the wages and working conditions of U.S. workers similarly employed and that qualified persons in the U.S. are not available. The determination made by the Department of Labor is advisory; INS makes the final decision regarding the employer's petition for foreign workers. In recent years 15,000 to 20,000 agricultural and logging jobs and an additional 6,000 to 23,000 nonagricultural jobs have been certified annually. However, the number of jobs certified does not indicate the actual number of foreign workers admitted for employment: an employer may use only part, or none, of the certifications granted, and some admitted foreign workers may work in two or more certified jobs.

Some statistics from the Office of Foreign Labor Certifications are published annually in the Employment and Training Report of the President. However, the majority of statistical tabulations on labor certifications are unpublished. From 1976 to 1981 approximately nine different tabulations were prepared on labor certifications for immigrants. These tabulations included certifications by sex, age, country of birth, intended state of residence, etc. However, beginning in 1982, in order to reduce both the reporting burden and the paperwork, only variables relevant to establishing labor certification have been collected and processed: immigrant certification data are available by determination (approval/denial) cross-classified by detailed occupational codes. These tabulations are available at the national, state, and regional office level. Precertified cases that are handled separately by INS and the State Department are included in the national totals.

The variables included in the tabulations of temporary agricultural jobs are number of applications (one application from an employer can cover many jobs), crops or industry (e.g., logging, sheep-raising, etc.), and state of employment. Tabulations by nationality are not possible from DOL records since an employer may import a worker from any nation once the job is certified. Data on temporary nonagricultural jobs are available by determination (approval/denial) and occupational groups.

Although limited information is collected by the department on the characteristics of foreign-born workers seeking occupational preferences or admission as H-2 workers, no detail is obtained for employers petitioning for the admissions. Such information would be an important first step toward understanding the demand factors encouraging immigration. For example, a comparison of information on petitioning employers with census data would permit an analysis of the effects of these preferences on the wage rates of native workers.

Recommendation

The Panel recommends that the U.S. Department of Labor:

o Collect and publish summary information on employers who petition for the admission of foreign workers, including those requested under the H-2 provisions.

Other DOL Programs

The Office of Research and Evaluation in the Office of Strategic Planning and Policy Development is another part of the Employment and Training Administration that has been involved with immigration. Over the past 15 years, this office has funded a considerable number of immigration studies, principally on the labor-market characteristics and effects of various kinds of immigration flows. In recent years, however, such funding of immigration research has slowed considerably.

The third group involved in immigration research is the Immigration Policy Group within the Bureau of International Labor Affairs. The group has a staff of four, three of whom are analysts, and conducts analyses of the economic, social, and political aspects of legal immigration (both permanent and temporary), illegal immigration, and refugee movements, both within the United States and internationally. The bureau has also funded some immigration research, on both U.S. and international labor flows.

A fourth Labor Department office is involved with immigration as a result of its enforcement efforts. The Wage and Hour Division of the Employment Standards Administration is responsible for enforcing the Fair Labor Standards Act and the Migrant and Seasonal Agricultural Worker Protection Act. Since 1978 this office has carried out a special targeted enforcement program of the Fair Labor Standards Act aimed at employers of undocumented workers. Compliance with minimum wage and hour laws reduces the economic incentive for employers to hire illegal aliens. In fiscal 1983, wage and hour compliance officers investigated more than 18,000 establishments reportedly employing illegal aliens and found more than $40 million in back wages owed to almost 175,000 workers. Statistics other than totals are not tabulated.

The Migrant and Seasonal Agricultural Worker Protection Act prohibits farm labor contractors from recruiting, employing, or utilizing with knowledge the services of any alien who is not lawfully admitted for permanent residence or is not authorized by the Attorney General to accept employment. Statistics are available on the total number of farm labor contractors found in violation of the act and the dollar amount of civil money penalty assessments.

BUREAU OF REFUGEE PROGRAMS, U.S. DEPARTMENT OF STATE

The Bureau of Refugee Programs in the Department of State has three major roles in collecting data related to refugee resettlement: (1) collecting information and reporting on the world refugee situation for purposes of determining U.S. refugee admission numbers and their allocation among regions and refugee groups; (2) collecting and reporting data on refugees admitted to the United States; and (3) monitoring the activities of voluntary agencies that provide reception and placement services to arriving refugees.

With respect to the first role, the bureau prepares an annual report on the world refugee situation. This report contains both descriptive and statistical information; the latter was presented in a separate volume for the first time in 1984. The statistics focus on two types of refugees: those who are in need of protection and assistance and those who have been resettled and are no longer in need of assistance. The statistics are drawn primarily from information provided by the U.S. embassies and consulates in the countries covered by the report; international organizations such as the U.N. High Commissioner for Refugees and the U.N. Relief and Works Agency, which assists Palestinian refugees; and foreign governments.

In addition to the annual report, the bureau publishes data on the refugee situation in Southeast Asia, the area from which the largest number of refugees are admitted to the United States. Each month, the U.S. embassies in this region report the number of land and sea arrivals in countries of first asylum, the number resettled by the United States and other countries, the number transferred to refugee processing centers for training prior to resettlement, and the remaining camp populations.

This information is disseminated monthly, by means of summary charts that provide information about each country of first asylum and each refugee group, by nationality, in Southeast Asia.

The second role, the collection of information about refugees admitted to the United States, begins with the prescreening of refugee applications, which are used by voluntary agencies under contract to the State Department to determine eligibility for admission. Biographical data are collected about the applicant and family members, including name, sex, birthdate, country of birth, country of residence, marital status, education, occupation, language, and English language capability. These data are transferred to the INS, to be used in making final decisions on admissibility. They are also sent to the Refugee Data Center (RDC) in New York, which is responsible for matching refugee applicants with U.S. sponsors. Under contract with the State Department, the RDC enters these data in its computer system and, using the data bank, determines whether the refugee has ties to any voluntary resettlement agency or has relatives or other close contacts in the United States. This information is used for determining place of resettlement within the United States (for further information on this process, see Chapter 7). Also under contract with the Bureau of Refugee Programs, the RDC provides monthly reports on expected arrivals of refugees by state and locality. These reports provide biographical information on refugees who have been approved for admission, the agency that will be sponsoring them, and the expected date of their arrival. RDC also collects data on actual arrivals, using statistics from the Intergovernmental Committee for Migration, which arranges transportation for the refugees. Using these data, the Bureau of Refugee Programs publishes monthly reports on arrivals by country of origin.

The Bureau of Refugee Programs uses the data it collects for policy-making and administrative purposes. With regard to policy, the data are used to determine the worldwide need for resettlement, in order to determine the U.S. response to this need. Administratively, the bureau attempts to project numbers of future arrivals and to decide whether admissions will be consistent with the number of refugee admissions agreed on as a result of consultation between the President and Congress. This process requires a variety of information, including the number of refugees in first asylum camps, the number of applications pending, the rate at which they are reviewed and the decision reached, the number in language training in refugee processing centers, and the number of recent arrivals. Monthly data provided by the INS are used to regulate the number of new cases that are reviewed and presented to the INS. The object is to avoid large backlogs of approved cases, since the number of refugees who are allowed to enter the United States often changes from year to year.

In carrying out its third role--monitoring grants to voluntary agencies to provide reception and placement services--the Bureau of Refugee Programs requires that case files be maintained by voluntary agencies on the services they provide to refugees. These files also contain biographical and other information that is needed to determine what services should be provided. The bureau also conducts site visits to monitor these activities and issues reports on them.

OFFICE OF REFUGEE RESETTLEMENT,
U.S. DEPARTMENT OF HEALTH AND HUMAN SERVICES

The focus of federal refugee program activity is the Office of Refugee Resettlement (ORR). Created by the Refugee Act of 1980, it is located organizationally within the Social Security Administration of the Department of Health and Human Services. In response to the relatively detailed and specific requirements for data collection and reporting to Congress contained in its enabling legislation, the ORR conducts and maintains a number of data collection programs. For example, the primary sources of statistics for the domestic refugee program are the ORR refugee data systems, which contain some 900,000 individual records for refugees (and Cuban-Haitian parolees) of an estimated universe of 1.1 million who have arrived since 1975.

At a minimum, each record contains an alien number (assigned by the INS), the year of birth, and the date of arrival. Since 1981 information on country of birth, citizenship, sex, and family and marital status has also been included. These items are obtained from the American Council of Voluntary Agencies, from a form completed during processing in the refugee camp by the sponsoring voluntary agency. Monthly summaries of refugee arrivals are published by the ORR.

To the extent possible, the ORR records are updated as further information becomes available. For example, prior to the termination of the Alien Address Registration Program in 1981, information reported by refugees was obtained from the INS and incorporated into the ORR files. As mandated in 1980, INS now serves as the major source of follow-up information, providing the ORR with data obtained from the refugee at the time of application for adjustment to permanent resident status, which can occur from one year after arrival. In addition to basic identifying information, INS collects data on changes in residence since entry, current household composition, education, work history, English language ability, participation in training programs, and the use of cash assistance programs. Finally, additional data elements, such as current occupation and place of residence, are added if and when application is made for naturalization.

The office also maintains a system of regular reports by state grantor agencies and compiles selected additional information through agreements with other federal agencies. In addition, it has funded surveys of refugees in order to obtain current information on internal migration, labor market involvement, and other related topics concerning refugee adjustment. (A more detailed discussion of refugee admissions to the United States, illustrating the interactions and interrelationships of the range of participating groups in the process, both outside and in the United States, is presented in Chapter 7, along with additional detail on the activities of ORR.)

BUREAU OF THE CENSUS, U.S. DEPARTMENT OF COMMERCE

Although not involved in the administration of programs or the implementation of public policy dealing with immigration, the Census Bureau, in carrying out its mandate to produce high-quality statistical data, has a need for and itself produces a wealth of information on immigration. Its need for such information arises from its ongoing program of producing both current and projected national and local-area estimates of the size and characteristics of the population, which requires knowledge of the size and composition of migrant flows into and out of the country. At the same time, the bureau's regular and special programs--the decennial censuses, ongoing sample surveys such as the Current Population Survey, special surveys such as the 1976 Survey of Income and Education, as well as compilations from external administrative systems--all serve as sources of data on the flow of immigrants and emigrants or on the characteristics of the stock of foreign-born persons.

Before turning to the detail produced by these diverse sources, it is important to note that the Census Bureau defines immigrants differently than does the INS: the INS is concerned with legal status; the Census Bureau with residence in the United States. To the INS, an immigrant is someone who has been admitted for permanent residence in the United States; people in the United States who entered with nonimmigrant visas, such as students and temporary visitors, are not considered immigrants. Refugees are not counted as immigrants until they adjust their status to that of permanent resident, which can occur one year after entry. In contrast, the Census Bureau defines as immigrants all noncitizens resident in the United States, except temporary visitors and foreign embassy employees who live on embassy grounds. The Census Bureau includes foreign students, temporary workers, refugees, and even illegal aliens as usual residents in its censuses and surveys.

In addition to the definitional differences, comparisons between INS data and Census Bureau data are difficult because a census or survey refers to a specific date and registers a status at that time rather than recording the flow of migrants into the country. Death or emigration between a person's entry into the country and the date of a census or survey will preclude counting that person as an immigrant. A census count of immigrants actually represents the balance of persons who immigrated during some prior period less those among them who emigrated or died during the period, rather than all persons who entered the country during the period.

The Decennial Census

Value and Limitations

Information from decennial censuses has two features that make it uniquely valuable in the study of immigrants and immigration. First, the large sample size used to collect detailed data permits statistically precise comparisons of the many different country-of-origin groups at different points in time with respect to a large number of social and economic characteristics, including place of residence, period of entry, citizenship, English language ability, earnings, occupation, labor force status, and home ownership. Second, the historical continuity of the census, and hence relative consistency of census information over time, permit valuable historical comparisons of the status of foreign-born people in the United States.

There are, however, a number of important shortcomings of census data for the study of immigration. Because the census serves many important functions (of which the collection of data on immigrants or the foreign-born is only one), the amount of immigration data that can be collected is limited for reasons of both cost and sensitivity. Furthermore, the collection of information about the foreign-born in past censuses has been marked by inconsistency in both the questions asked and the wording used, thus significantly reducing the value of the census as a basis for historical comparisons. Table 5-1 lists the variables of special relevance collected since 1900 on the foreign-born and immigration. As can be seen, such important information as date of entry to the United States, English language ability, and even citizenship have not always been collected. Year of immigration, or the alternate form, number of years in the United States, was asked in the censuses of 1890 through 1930 but not collected in the censuses of 1940, 1950, or 1960. Indeed, 1980 marks the first time since 1930 that two consecutive censuses have collected information on date of entry, permitting comparisons of date-of-entry cohorts over time and thus some assessment of how length of stay in the United States affects social and economic characteristics. Even for this variable, however, the seemingly arbitrary limitation of collection of information on period of entry to only four 5-year intervals for these censuses, with grouped or an open interval for earlier dates of entry, means that only two cohorts of entry (1965-1969, 1960-1964) can be matched and compared.

Indeed, apart from place of birth, which has been included as a census item since 1850, none of the special questions relevant to immigration and the foreign-born, on date of entry, prior residence, citizenship, English language ability, and parental nativity, has been collected continuously since 1900. The most consistently collected variable--birthplace of parents--was dropped in the 1980 census, although this item is of key importance in the assessment of the longer-term consequences of immigration and of the legacies of different country-of-origin groups. Each census from 1890 through 1950, and from 1970 through 1980, included questions on citizenship, but in 1960 such questions were asked only in New York State.

Nonetheless, the decennial censuses remain one of the most important and valuable sources of data on the foreign-born and their descendants, and particularly so for studies at the regional or state level or for individual cities. As with all such data, those from decennial censuses are subject to various types of errors, including incomplete coverage of the population, errors in reporting, and, in the case of data from a sample of the population, sampling errors. A discussion of the errors and their effects on the results are generally found in the reports presenting the data as well as in separate evaluation reports issued by the Census Bureau.

1980 Census Data

Turning to the most recent census, each person in a sample of the 1980 census was asked, "In what State or foreign country was this person born?" Those persons who reported that they were born in a foreign

TABLE 5-1 Questions Asked of Special Relevance to Immigration in Selected Censuses

Question	1900	1940	1950	1960	1970	1980
Country of birth	Yes	Yes	Yes	Yes	Yes	Yes
Year of immigration	Yes[a]	No	No	No	Yes[b]	Yes[c]
Residence 5 years ago	No	Yes	No	Yes	Yes	Yes
Citizenship	Yes	Yes	Yes	No	Yes	Yes
Ability to speak English	Yes	No	No	No	No	Yes
Nativity of parents	Yes	Yes	Yes	Yes	Yes	No
Current occupation	No	Yes	Yes	Yes	Yes	Yes
Occupation 5 years ago	No	No	No	No	Yes	No
Language spoken at home when child	No	Yes	No	No	Yes	No
Education	No	Yes	Yes	Yes	Yes	Yes
Earnings	No	Yes	Yes	Yes	Yes	Yes

Note: Includes censuses for which public-use sample tapes are available.

[a]By single year.
[b]For intervals: pre-1915, 1915-1924, 1925-1934, 1935-1944, 1945-1949, 1950-1954, 1955-1959, 1960-1964, 1965-1970.
[c]For intervals: pre-1950, 1950-1959, 1960-1964, 1965-1969, 1970-1974, 1975-1980.

country were also asked, "Is this person a naturalized citizen?" and "When did this person come to the United States to stay?"

A question on residence five years earlier also was included in the 1980 census sample and was asked about all persons 5 or more years old. Since this question is directed at all persons in the sample (regardless of nativity), it also serves as an indication of the volume of movement of citizens into the United States from overseas during the previous five years. A similar question was included in the 1970 census.

Published volumes by state from the 1980 census show the foreign-born population classified by country of birth for the 30 or so countries supplying the largest numbers of foreign-born persons. Other characteristics by which the foreign-born population are classified are year of immigration (5-year intervals from 1960 to 1980, the 10-year interval 1950-1959, and the period prior to 1950) and citizenship. More extensive data are published for all foreign-born and for recent immigrants in a table that shows race, Spanish origin, age, and sex as well as more detailed country listings for year of immigration and citizenship. For persons who immigrated between 1970 and 1980, the following information is tabulated for each state by country of birth: household and family characteristics, marital status, fertility, educational attainment, language usage, ability to speak English, employment and occupational characteristics, and income. In addition, the Census Bureau plans to prepare a special report on the foreign-born population, and various computer tape files and special tabulations that provide substantially greater detail will be available. For example, a separate micro-file containing only the records of households containing at least one foreign-born member has been used to produce special tabulations on the characteristics of immigrants, by country of birth. The 1980 census also included a question on ancestry that identified the ethnic origin of all persons regardless of when their ancestors entered the United States.

Current Population Survey

The Current Population Survey (CPS) is a sample survey that has been conducted monthly by the Census Bureau since 1942 in order to provide the official government estimates of national employment and unemployment. Its present sample is about 45,000 interviewed households per month. From time to time, questions dealing with other subjects are added to the survey. Two examples of additions dealing with immigration are provided by the November 1979 and April 1983 surveys.

A supplement to the November 1979 CPS was designed to provide basic data on ethnicity and language, to update detailed data obtained in a similar study conducted in 1969, and to bridge the gaps between different measures of ethnicity and language in the 1970 and 1980 censuses: in 1980 questions on ancestry and current language replaced the 1970 questions on country of birth of parents and mother tongue. Questions on citizenship, year of immigration, and literacy were also included. In addition, since country of birth of parents was dropped from the 1980 census in favor of self-designated ancestry, the 1979 CPS is the only official source of data on persons of foreign parentage for a recent date. The measurement of ethnicity--indeed the concept itself--is still inexact and previous work has shown that substantial response variability occurs (for example, see Bureau of the Census, 1974). The 1979 survey permits the examination of the relationship between objective measures of ethnicity, such as country of birth and country of birth of parents, and the subjective measure of self-designated ancestry. These data provide a basis other than the census for examining the characteristics of immigrants and the only recent basis for studying the extent of assimilation of second-generation immigrants.

Other characteristics are available from the November 1979 CPS survey: household relationship, age, sex, marital status, veteran status (males only), race, educational attainment, ethnic origin, labor force status, occupation, industry, hours worked, family income, current language, ability to speak English, literacy in any language, literacy in English, and mother tongue. A public-use tape, containing individual records for the 45,000 households in the sample--of which about 2,500 (just over 5 percent) include a foreign-born person--has been released.

Although the CPS collects much useful information relevant to studies of immigration, the sample size is too small to support elaborate analysis.

In April 1983 a number of questions were included in the CPS to study fertility among foreign-born women. All respondents were asked their place of birth and that of their parents, citizenship status, and date of entry into the United States. Foreign-born women of childbearing age were asked the number of children ever born, the number born outside the United States, and the number currently living in the household. A public-use tape is available, as are tabular results. Again, it is important to note that the relatively small sample size limits the utility of the data.

These two surveys are illustrative of the types of questions related to immigration that are included in the CPS from time to time.

Other Bureau Sources

Some other Census Bureau activities, in a peripheral fashion, are relevant to immigration statistics. One is the Survey of Income and Education, undertaken by the Census Bureau for the then Department of Health, Education, and Welfare in 1976. Included in its extensive data set is information on place of birth, of both the respondents and their parents, English language facility and use, year of immigration, and citizenship status. Both micro-data files and extensive published analyses of the results are available.

Another source of immigration-related information is the biennial CPS surveys of voting and registration, which are conducted in national election years. The surveys include questions on voting and registration; their value for immigration-related information lies in the ethnic data and in the reasons for noneligibility for registration, which include noncitizenship.

Yet another source of data is the current and post-censal population estimates that are produced by the Census Bureau on a regular basis for a wide variety of geographic and political entities. These estimates include an allowance for net migration (as do official population projections), thus reflecting both immigration and emigration. Although current data on immigration are available from the INS, the movement of people out of the United States is not recorded and, thus, must be estimated by indirect means.

For the past 25 years, the Census Bureau has used, in effect, the same annual level of emigration, approximately 40,000, in preparing its current population estimates and projections. Recent evidence, however, suggests a more appropriate level of emigration of legal residents to be around 100,000 per year (Warren and Kraly, 1985). In light of that evidence, the Census Bureau should reevaluate its use of the smaller number of emigrants per year in its national population estimates program. Until now the Census Bureau has also not included any allowance for net illegal immigration in preparing its population estimates and projections; however, it is currently reviewing its approach (see below).

Finally, the ongoing research activities of the Census Bureau present possibilities for obtaining additional information about immigration. Those activities include experimentation with new approaches to estimating emigration and illegal immigration, as well as new and imaginative approaches to sampling that, through cost efficiencies, may permit additional and much needed data gathering on the subject of immigration.

Estimates of Illegal Immigration

Illegal immigration presents the Census Bureau with a number of problems that are quite different from those faced by the INS. For example, the Census Bureau is charged by law with counting in its censuses every person whose usual residence is in the United States, regardless of the legality of the person's residence. Thus the Census Bureau's primary current need for separate statistics on illegal immigration is to enable it to assess the completeness of coverage of the 1980 census. In addition, such information is an essential element in improving the accuracy of postcensal population estimates. The immigration figures used in the Census Bureau's programs of current population estimates and projections have not included a specific allowance for net illegal immigration, since illegal immigrants are not included in the data compiled by INS, and it has not been possible to get satisfactory estimates elsewhere. The need for estimates of net illegal immigration in connection with the Census Bureau programs of coverage evaluation and the preparation of current population estimates has led it to continue research aimed at developing such estimates. So far, however, the Census Bureau has not been successful in developing reliable estimates of the number of illegal residents who have entered the United States in any recent period.

Some information on the volume of illegal immigration has been developed from the sample portion of the 1980 census. These data proved particularly valuable because many illegal aliens, if not a majority, are believed to have been included in the 1980 census (Warren and Passel, 1983). There are several reasons for this belief. First, major steps were taken to reduce potential underenumeration, and many illegal aliens could not escape the enumeration net. Second, experimental estimates permitted the inference that, nationally, the population represented by the November 1979 CPS included about 1.25 million illegal aliens who entered the United States between 1970 and 1980. This suggests that the 1980 census, using similar procedures with additional safeguards against omission, must also have included many illegal aliens. Third, the 1980 census counted nearly 6 million more people than were expected in 1980 on the basis of the 1970 census and 850,000 more people than were estimated to be residing legally in the United States in 1980.

Using the data from the sample portion of the 1980 census, the Census Bureau estimated that about 2 million illegal aliens were included in the census, of whom approximately half were born in Mexico. The estimates were derived by comparing the census count of aliens with estimates of the legally resident alien population, based on data collected by the INS in January 1980. Although the illegal alien population may not be accurately measurable, these results will assist in placing some reasonable bounds on its size. The panel commends the bureau for its innovative work in this area and strongly urges that it be continued. A brief review of methods used to estimate the size of the illegal alien population, including the Census Bureau's method, appears in Appendix B.

Although all these studies suffer from uncertainties, it seems likely that there were between 2 and 4 million illegal aliens in the United States in 1980, and that the number has not been growing remarkably fast in recent years.

Recommendations

The Panel recommends that the Census Bureau:

    o Restore to the 1990 census a question on place of birth of parents. Collected in each census from 1900 through 1970, this information is key to the study of assimilation by immigrants and their children;

    o Make every effort to maintain consistency in question wording and tabulation detail from one decennial census to the next in areas relating to the foreign-born, so that immigrant cohorts recorded in successive censuses can be linked or compared on a consistent and common basis in order to assess adjustment experience;

    o Initiate a program of research leading to improved estimates of emigration. As one approach, the panel strongly endorses testing, as a supplement to the CPS, an emigration module involving the collection of information on the residence of close relatives.

TRANSPORTATION SYSTEMS CENTER, U.S. DEPARTMENT OF TRANSPORTATION

The Transportation Systems Center (TSC) of the Department of Transportation monitors international arrivals and departures by air through two independent studies, one based on the INS form I-92, which summarizes arrivals and departures by flight, and the other, an in-flight survey of passengers conducted by participating airlines.

International Arrivals and Departures by Air

The TSC established a program for processing information from the INS form I-92 in 1972 under a joint working relationship between the Departments of Transportation, Commerce, and State, the INS, and the Civil Aeronautics Board. The object of the program is to produce statistics on international arrivals and departures by air, excluding those between the United States and Canada. The data are intended for use by transportation policy planners and analysts, primarily in international negotiations over carrier market shares, but they also can be used for balance of payments estimates, estimates of net migration to the United States by air, and studies of tourism. Figures are published in monthly, quarterly, and annual reports, and monthly tape summaries are also available. A complete data base is maintained beginning with 1976. Although the purpose of the program is not the measurement of immigration, but rather all arrivals and departures by air, the program is discussed in some detail here because it represents a clear example of how a lack of interagency cooperation can disrupt a useful statistical system.

The basis of this statistical system is the INS form I-92. The completion of this form is required for each arriving or departing international flight except for direct flights to or from Canada. The form is completed by airline staff and collects the following information: last foreign port for arrivals or first foreign port for departures; airline; flight number; port (arrival or departure); date; type of transport (scheduled commercial, charter commercial, U.S. military, foreign military); and passengers by port of departure (arrivals) or destination (departures) by citizens, noncitizens, and total. Airline personnel provide the count of total passengers by port; the count of noncitizens used to be obtained from summing the INS I-94 forms (for nonimmigrants; see Chapter 4) for the flight, and the count of citizens was obtained as the residual (total passengers less noncitizens). Prior to 1983 the I-92 forms were sent daily to the TSC processing contractor after some verification by INS inspectors against the corresponding I-94 forms; the extent of this quality control apparently varied from airport to airport.

In January 1983 the INS, without consultation and in contravention of a memorandum of understanding with the TSC, changed both the I-94 form and the process for completing and processing the I-92 form. The question on port of embarkation (arrivals) or disembarkation (departures) was dropped from the revised I-94, thus eliminating a consistency check for noncitizens between the I-92 and the corresponding I-94s. At the same time, returning, first arriving, or departing resident aliens were no longer required to complete I-94 forms, thus removing the basis for obtaining the overall citizen-noncitizen breakdown for each flight. The INS also instructed airlines that they need no longer complete the total passenger column for each airport on multistop flights, which represent about 40 percent of international flights serving the United States.

The process was changed so that INS inspectors no longer verify the I-92 form against the corresponding I-94 forms. The I-92 is bundled with the I-94s for the flight and sent to the INS processing center, where some consistency checks are supposed to be carried out between the I-92 and I-94s. However, the number of possible checks is small (for example, the number of aliens on the I-92 cannot be smaller than the number of I-94s, though it can, and often will, be larger). The INS processing contractor is then responsible for sending the I-92s to the TSC contractor.

The changes introduced by INS in January 1983 have reduced the potential for consistency checks, increased the risk of loss of forms, introduced substantial delays into the document flow, and, most important, made it impossible to obtain citizen-noncitizen breakdowns by airport on multistop flights. This last issue deserves some further clarification. Through 1982, I-94 forms for arriving or departing aliens were used to obtain the number of aliens by port of origin or port of destination. The I-92 gave the total number of passengers by port of origin or destination, and the number of U.S. citizens by port of origin or destination was then obtained by subtraction; failure to turn in I-94s on departure would therefore inflate the number of departing citizens and reduce the number of departing aliens. The INS changes affect this procedure in three ways: the I-92 no longer records total passengers by port, the I-94s no longer record port for noncitizens, and I-94s are not required of permanent resident aliens or arriving permanent immigrants.

The first two changes affect only multistop flights, but the third change affects all flights. The INS changes have thus greatly reduced the detail available in the data (the TSC is estimating the breakdowns on the basis of past patterns) and have jeopardized a useful data set covering the period 1976-1982. Negotiations are still continuing between the TSC and the INS about this situation.

There are some doubts about how reliable the information produced by the system has been. Vining (1980) evaluated data quality in a study of net immigration by air, using the balance of arrivals over departures as an indicator of a lower bound for total net immigration. He compared TSC data on arrivals and departures on North Atlantic routes with International Air Transport Association (IATA) data, and he compared data on all arrivals and departures with figures on international air passenger traffic to and from most major international airports in the United States. Though these other data sets are not strictly comparable with the TSC figures--IATA excludes passengers on nonmember airlines and some charters, and the airport data generally include movements to and from Canada--all three show broadly similar trends over time in arrivals, departures, and net arrivals. However, net arrivals as a proportion of total traffic are almost twice as high for the TSC data as for either the IATA or airport data, the differences being accounted for by very high TSC net arrival rates for charter flights. Vining suggests that the discrepancy arises from the failure by some departing charter flights to complete I-92 forms, thus underreporting total departures by air, but argues that the consistency between the three data sources in other respects supports the reliability of the TSC data at least for scheduled flights. A comparison of the TSC and airport data on an airport-by-airport basis (given by Vining in an appendix) is not reassuring, however. Although arrivals and departures from the two sources do follow broadly similar trends, the sizes of the flows are often substantially different. These differences can be partly explained by the fact that the universes are not the same--airport data typically include flows to and from Canada and in some cases other places not included in the TSC data--but not entirely. The most dramatic differences appear for Anchorage: for 1972-1978, TSC annual arrivals average 167,000 and departures 240,000, while the airport data, which include Canadian traffic, average 40,000 for both arrivals and departures. If the elements can include discrepancies of this order of magnitude, one cannot have much confidence in the totals or the net balances.

An examination of the internal detail of the TSC tabulations suggests that Vining is correct about an undercoverage by the I-92 of departing charter flights and also that departing aliens are sometimes reported as departing citizens, inflating the number of the latter at the expense of the number of the former. A plausible explanation for this discrepancy is a failure to collect the departure sections of the I-94 forms from all departing aliens. The TSC data for 1982 for scheduled flights show an excess of citizen departures over citizen arrivals of 1.166 million and an excess of alien arrivals over alien departures of 1.731 million. Both net flows are unreasonably large, probably because 5-10 percent of departing aliens are reported as departing citizens. For charter flights, arriving citizens exceed departing citizens by 198,000, and arriving aliens outnumber departing aliens by 91,000. The net inflow of citizens by charter flights, in contrast to the net outflow by scheduled flights, suggests undercoverage of departing flights, an undercoverage that seems to be more serious for U.S. flag carriers than for foreign flag carriers.

The TSC data for international arrival and departure by air represent valuable information on travel to and from the United States. The data are flawed, however, particularly with respect to coverage and classification by citizenship of departures. No direct checks on arrivals data are possible, but in view of INS procedures these figures are probably reasonably reliable. The data are useful for market share negotiations and studies of tourism, although attempts to estimate net migration flow from them are probably inappropriate. The changes in the I-94 form and procedures introduced by INS in 1983 disrupted the processing system, introducing delays and greatly reducing the amount of detail available for the system. The situation could be improved in at least two ways. If airlines completed the I-92 forms fully--citizens, aliens, and total passengers boarding or alighting at each port--then I-94 forms would not be needed at all. The airlines' computer booking systems could probably provide the I-92 information without difficulty. Alternatively, the I-94 form could be modified to collect information on port of boarding or destination, with airline personnel recording total passengers by port, and the original system could be continued. It might not be necessary to return to requiring permanent residents to complete I-94s, since for most purposes a division of traffic into two categories--citizens plus permanent residents and other aliens--would be closer to what analysts want (a residence classification) than a citizen-noncitizen split. An effort should also be made by the INS to improve the coverage and quality of data on departures, to increase the overall value and applicability of the data.

Survey of International Air Travelers

The Travel and Tourism Administration of the U.S. Department of Commerce is mandated to develop the necessary statistical and market research data on international travel to facilitate and guide planning in the public and private sectors. To meet this requirement, an in-flight survey of international departing travelers was established late in 1982. The survey planning and execution are carried out by the TSC under an interagency agreement; the program is also sponsored by the National Park Service.

Participation in the survey is voluntary for both airlines and passengers. At the end of the first quarter of 1983, 32 of the 53 major international airlines regarded as of special significance for the program were participating, although some major carriers, among them British Airways, were not. A stratified random sample of scheduled flights of participating airlines is drawn from the Official Airline Guide covering the week following the third Monday of each month; the strata are airlines or, for U.S. carriers, airline-route groupings. All passengers on selected flights are included in the sample, and those who respond are assumed to represent all passengers. The four-page questionnaire collects information on place of origin and destination; lifetime air trips to or from the United States; with whom traveling;

purpose of trip; type of ticket; source of information and bookings for trip; age; sex; occupation; household income; citizenship; residence; for visitors to the United States, port of entry, length of stay, places visited, and expenditures by category; and for U.S. residents, length of trip, places to be visited, and expected costs. The questionnaires are distributed by airline personnel at the beginning of the flight and collected before disembarkation.

Statistics are generated from the responses by using additional information from the TSC data on international departures by air derived from I-92 forms. Responses on a particular flight are first weighted to allow for children in the respondent's party, then weighted to allow for nonresponse on the flight, then weighted to represent all travelers on all flights in the stratum, and finally weighted using I-92 data by residence and port of destination to approximate traffic of nonparticipating as well as participating airlines.

The most serious problem with the survey is the response rate, of both airline and traveller. In the first quarter of 1983, only 60 percent of key airlines participated; for these, the flight response rate--flights for which completed questionnaires were returned for processing--was 51 percent (266 of 524); and the average passenger response rate for those flights with responses was about 31 percent. Thus only about 16 percent of the intended sample provided responses, and the intended sample excludes an unspecified number of travelers on the airlines that are not participating in the survey. It is doubtful in these circumstances whether the data can be regarded as better than broadly indicative of the characteristics of departing travelers.

The Survey of International Air Travel is not strictly relevant to a study of migration statistics, since its primary focus is on tourism. It has been discussed here because in theory it covers all departing passengers and uses INS information for data-weighting purposes. The low response rate raises the question of whether the objectives of the survey could be better served by interviews of a smaller sample of departing passengers (who usually have a few spare minutes between check-in and boarding) than by a large sample with a poor response rate depending on self-completion and airline cooperation.

Since we have not had the opportunity to examine all the issues involved, the panel recommends that:

o The Travel and Tourism Administration explore alternatives to the present approach with a view toward obtaining more reliable information.

SOCIAL SECURITY ADMINISTRATION,
U.S. DEPARTMENT OF HEALTH AND HUMAN SERVICES

Programs and Data

The Social Security Administration (SSA) is a largely unexploited yet potentially valuable source of information for analyses of immigration to the United States. On one hand, SSA has a highly professional, well-managed statistical operation that, in supporting the administration of social security programs, has developed data sets covering a substantial proportion of the foreign-born population, both aliens and naturalized citizens, resident in the United States. Social security data thus are potentially useful for analyses of the characteristics of immigrant populations and for studying the impact of immigration on domestic sectors. On the other hand, in seeking access to social security data on migrants, an analyst faces formidable obstacles that derive from policies concerning the availability of federal statistics and from the distribution of resources and ordering of priorities within SSA. The general trend over the past few years has been to impose relatively greater restrictions on the accessibility of SSA data to researchers both from other government agencies and from outside government.

The potential usefulness of SSA data systems for research on international migration derives both from the characteristics of populations covered by social security programs and from the specific items of information that are recorded. Basically, two populations are covered in SSA administrative files: workers whose employment is covered by social security programs and persons receiving benefits from one or more of the social security programs. Approximately 90 percent of U.S. workers, including the self-employed, are covered by the social security system; the major groups excluded are federal employees and persons whose earnings fall below a specified level in a given quarter. Benefits are paid under several social insurance programs, such as Old-Age, Survivors, and Disability Insurance (OASDI) and Supplemental Security Income (SSI).

The administration of social security programs sometimes identifies populations of international migrants. The most obvious example is that of the population of social security beneficiaries residing abroad. Special requirements for awarding benefits outside the country have resulted in an administrative data set for beneficiaries residing in foreign countries, most of whom are foreign-born, both retired workers and elderly dependents. These data have been used by demographers over the years as indicators of the process of emigration from the United States and return migration of former immigrants. Social security program requirements have also generated statistical documentation of the social and economic status of recent refugee groups admitted to the United States. The concern of several of these analyses has been to determine the patterns of use over time of Supplemental Security Income among refugee populations (see Kahn, 1980; Merritt, 1982; Grossman, 1978).

The 1973 exact match study is an illustration of how information on international migration can be generated as a by-product of evaluation of SSA programs and policies. The study was undertaken to document patterns of income distribution among persons and families by matching SSA records on reported earnings and benefits with IRS tax records. However, the final matched files also were used in the application of an estimation technique to produce a measure of the illegal alien population resident in the country (Lancaster and Scheuren, 1977). The exact match study also illustrates the important role of SSA administrative data sets in efforts to link components of the federal statistical system.

Several indicators of migration status are maintained in the micro-data files supporting the administration of social security programs; as a result, these files have substantial inherent potential for analyses of immigrant populations. For example, all applications for a social security number (form SS-5) filed since the initiation of the program have been coded by SSA to create the NUMIDENT file. Country of birth is coded for foreign-born persons (state of birth for the native-born); date of application, age, sex, and race are also coded. Date of application can be used as a proxy for period of arrival in the United States. The file can be linked with other SSA files on earnings and benefits for individual workers and beneficiaries. Analyses of earnings, industry, geographic mobility, disability, and types of benefits can thus be conducted for a range of social and demographic groups, including immigrant cohorts.

The social security application form was revised in 1980 to record the citizenship and visa status of the applicant; thus, for recent applicants the NUMIDENT file now includes four classifications of legal status: U.S. citizen, legal alien allowed to work, legal alien not allowed to work, and other. These categories make possible comparisons of certain economic characteristics between native U.S. citizens, naturalized U.S. citizens (combining information on place of birth with citizenship status), and the alien groups. (The instructions for completing form SS-5 do not identify the specific visa categories for which employment in the United States is authorized. The category "legal alien allowed to work" will include both permanent resident aliens and certain classes of nonimmigrants, such as temporary workers, intracompany transferees, and some foreign students.) District offices of SSA do in fact produce monthly tabulations of applicants for social security numbers by citizenship status, race, and age.

The potential of the SSA system to generate policy-relevant analyses of populations of international migrants has already been demonstrated through the exact match study and the various projects concerning the characteristics of specific refugee groups covered in SSA programs. Unfortunately, obstacles to the use of SSA data on immigrant populations exist throughout the SSA statistical system. The quality of data on immigrant status is one such obstacle, since country of birth is missing from approximately one-fifth of the records. The keying of data from form SS-5 is now more complete for new applicants, but the validity of the information recorded on the application form and accuracy of keying in the SSA district offices has not been assessed. The SSA has made little analytical use of its data on international migration; the agency's program and priorities have not generally required evaluation of the benefit and earnings characteristics of foreign-born groups, although recent refugee admissions are a notable exception.

Releasing data to outside users should result in more extensive use, but two impediments to such release exist. First, SSA currently lacks sufficient resources throughout its data processing and analytic units to support an effective program of user service, even on a cost-reimbursable basis. Furthermore, there is a basis for skepticism concerning the agency's current commitment to user service: procedures for making data available are not standardized; policy is not clear as to what services can be supplied, that is, purchased by outside users; and documentation of data sets is elusive.

The second impediment concerns the issue of confidentiality. Until relatively recently, SSA, through its Office of Research and Statistics, maintained a program of data user service that set an example for the rest of the federal statistical system. The star in the program was the Continuous Work History Sample (CWHS), supported in a manner to ensure data quality, to maintain and update files, to provide documentation and user outreach, and even to provide incentives for outside use through a program of research grants. However, the CWHS has not been available for public use since 1978, at least partly because of constraints on the dissemination of these data resulting from interpretations of the Privacy Act of 1974; SSA no longer disseminates administrative files for outside research.

The restrictions imposed on SSA data have affected many areas of social science research, including research on immigration. It is unfortunate that this change in policy occurred when the potential for analysis actually increased, with the revision of SSA documentary resources and when other data sources on the immigrant population (in particular, the INS's alien address report program) were eliminated. The statistical information maintained by SSA is of considerable potential value for analyses of U.S. immigration.

Recommendations

The panel recommends that the Social Security Administration:

o Incorporate data on country of birth and, when possible, citizenship and visa status into its series of tabulations on workers and beneficiaries;

o Develop a program of special tabulations to be available on a cost-reimbursable basis to support analyses of the economic and social integration of immigrant groups;

o Develop appropriate mechanisms for evaluating and, if necessary, improving the quality of data on country of birth and legal residence status that are captured in its statistical systems;

o Explore with the Statistical Policy Office of the U.S. Office of Management and Budget approaches to permit the sharing of CWHS files with researchers and analysts outside the agency.

NATIONAL CENTER FOR HEALTH STATISTICS, U.S. DEPARTMENT OF HEALTH AND HUMAN SERVICES

The National Center for Health Statistics (NCHS) is responsible for the collection, analysis, and dissemination of statistics on vital events in the United States: that is, births, deaths, marriages, and divorces. The collection of vital statistics in the United States is decentralized. Events are first registered at the local level by state of occurrence; NCHS subsequently also produces tabulations by place of residence of the mother. Certificates for out-of-state-of-residence events are forwarded to the state of residence for processing and tabulation. Under a federal-state cooperative arrangement, the states then forward information to NCHS for processing of national birth and death data. It should be noted that, although all states participate in collecting data on births and deaths, the cooperative arrangement reserves a great deal of flexibility and independent action to the states. Currently, between 44 and 46 states submit vital statistics data to NCHS in the form of computer tapes; the remaining states send microfilm copies of vital statistics certificates.

The standard vital statistics records of birth, death, marriage, and divorce certificates contain information on the place of birth of the person(s) and on place of residence. Thus, there is the potential to tabulate vital events for the foreign-born population.

Although the item on country of birth is coded, the detail, unfortunately, is limited to state in the United States, Puerto Rico, Virgin Islands, Guam, Canada, Cuba, Mexico, remainder of the world, and place not stated. An item on the ethnic origin of the parents of a live birth was included in the 1978 revision of the standard birth certificate and has been incorporated on the birth record of 22 states. The item on place of residence specifies a code for nonresidents of the United States, but the criteria for determining residence are not specified in available documentation.

Vital statistics are published in a variety of NCHS publications. Data on nativity, however, have been included in annual volumes only intermittently. Annual volumes do include a tabulation for births and deaths cross-classified by state of occurrence and state of residence; the residual refers to nonresidents of the U.S. and is an interesting indicator of the utilization of health facilities in southwestern states by aliens. Special reports on the fertility of specific parentage groups have appeared in recent years; however, published analyses and evaluation of trends in marriage and mortality are sorely deficient.

A program of public-use research files is promoted by NCHS. Annual micro-data files are available for births, deaths, marriages, and divorces. However, place of birth is coded as described above in the first three of these files, so use of the information on nativity is quite limited.

The vital registration system of the United States does have the potential of producing annual tallies of most vital events occurring to aliens living in the country, and information on vital events occurring to immigrants has substantial potential for studies and policy on immigration. Data on births occurring to immigrants would provide a direct basis for calculating their fertility rates, useful for studying the impact of immigration on population growth and the pattern of adjustment of immigrant fertility to that of the established population. Similarly, information on deaths of immigrants would permit the direct study of immigrant mortality, would permit the INS to keep its record-keeping systems more current, and could potentially provide a basis for estimating a lower bound for the size of the population of illegal immigrants.

It is evident from this review, however, that the immigration data collected through the vital registration system remain remarkably underexploited. One reason for the low degree of analysis of nativity data is the lack of confidence in its quality, particularly for the foreign-born population. Given the importance of documenting the demographic experience of immigrant groups and the general role of immigration in national population dynamics, the NCHS should improve its data.

Recommendations

The Panel recommends that the National Center for Health Statistics:

o Initiate the coding of the specific country of birth for vital events;

o Routinely prepare analyses and publish tabulations of vital events for immigrant populations;

o Institute a program to evaluate and improve the quality of data on place of birth.

CUSTOMS SERVICE, U.S. DEPARTMENT OF THE TREASURY

Data Collected

Travelers arriving in the United States by air or sea, except those arriving on direct flights from Canada, are required to complete the Customs Service declaration card, form 6059B; one form is completed per arriving family group. Arrivals across land borders are not in general required to complete the form, unless referred to secondary inspection. The information collected is name, date of birth, airline and flight number, U.S. address, citizenship, whether permanently resident in the United States, and if not, expected length of stay, purpose of visit (business or pleasure), and items pertaining specifically to Customs Service activities. The form used until mid-1983 also collected the number of people in the family group, but this question was excluded from the revised form. In addition to a form for each family group, the Customs Service also uses a workload report, form 5905, that summarizes the total number of passengers and crew, the total number of declarations by passengers and crew, and the total number of baggage examinations for each flight. The data collected by form 5905 are thus very similar to those collected by the INS form I-92, though without any citizenship or residence status breakdown.

No statistical use has ever been made of the information collected by the customs forms. The family group forms are packaged by flight number and stored in boxes for a period of two years, after which they are thrown out. The only use ever made of the forms after inspection is in particular investigations, to trace the movements and declarations of individuals over the preceding two years by making a hand search of the forms boxed by flight number and date.

As a potential source of information about immigration, the Customs Service form 6059B has some important similarities and some important dissimilarities to the INS I-94; some are positive features, some negative. Unlike the I-94, the customs form is filled in regardless of citizenship or residence and thus could provide information about numbers of returning citizens. On the negative side, however, only one form is filled in per family group, with no record on the new form of the number of people in the group, so it does not provide directly the total number of people arriving. (The summary form 5905 gives the average number of members in each family group for each flight as the ratio of total passengers to total declarations, but the average might vary systematically by citizenship and thus not give a very accurate expansion factor for obtaining total arriving U.S. citizens from total arriving family groups headed by a U.S. citizen.) On the positive side, the form records permanent residence (in the United States or elsewhere) and could thus distinguish between nonresident and resident U.S. citizens--although that information is never used, and we do not see how it could be used to learn anything about U.S. citizens living outside the country. Neither positive nor negative, relative to the I-94, is the limitation of coverage of the 6059B form to airports and seaports: the vast majority of entries to the United States occur at land ports of entry, across the Canadian and Mexican borders, and only a small fraction of such entries will result in a completed customs form. Thus from the point of view of measuring the gross flow of people into the United States, the customs form does not offer information of sufficient value to justify any data processing for statistical use.

Recommendation

The Panel recommends that:

o The Customs Service and the INS jointly consider merging the two forms currently completed by arriving passengers. The similarities between the Customs Service form 6059B and the INS I-94 are such that the existence of two separate forms is not justified. The only information not common to both forms is, on the I-94, the city in which the alien's visa was issued, country of residence, and the departure record, and on the 6059B, purpose of trip, expected length of stay, and declarations concerning agricultural regulations, currency, and goods obtained abroad. The 6059B is completed by all heads of family groups, the I-94 by all aliens except permanent residents. A single form fulfilling both purposes could be required for all arriving passengers without any great increase in the paperwork burden on passengers, and the machine processing of the information by the new nonimmigrant information system would surely offer advantages to the Customs Service for checking on the movements of individuals under surveillance, as well as offering the potential for recording accurately, with characteristics of statistical interest such as age and country of residence, the numbers of people entering the United States through air and sea ports of entry. The potential gain from such a merger would seem to justify the relatively modest costs involved.

GOVERNMENTWIDE ISSUES

The foregoing sections clearly illustrate the extent of involvement of the federal government, outside the INS, in collecting or producing information relevant to the study and understanding of immigration. Some of the agencies, such as the Bureau of Consular Affairs in the State Department, deal with the process of becoming an immigrant and have data sets offering insight into the selection, numbers, and movements of persons. Others, such as the Social Security Administration, deal with concerns or developments after arrival, which give insight into the processes of adjustment. Together with the INS, they produce or have the potential to produce a broad spectrum of information relevant to policy makers.

Because the nine agencies covered have such different functions and objectives, we chose to present recommendations focused on each agency's operations or activities within the context of our discussion of that agency. In its review, however, the panel noted a number of issues that concern all the agencies, including the INS. This section is therefore addressed to all the government agencies that have a role in providing information on immigration and emigration and to the agency with oversight responsibility for all of them.

The Office of Management and Budget, through its review of budget proposals as well as by statute, plays a key role in establishing the nation's statistical agenda and in monitoring its progress. The panel believes that in recent years these functions have not been exercised appropriately and, consequently, data quality has suffered, coordination among agencies has deteriorated, timeliness has been ignored, and, in general, efforts to improve statistics on emigration and immigration have foundered for lack of leadership and concern. Certainly, each agency must be responsible for its own activities, but OMB, given its position in the executive office of the President, has an overriding ability and responsibility to act as a catalyst and to initiate the process leading to significant improvements in the data base.

The panel thus strongly recommends that the director of the Office of Management and Budget:

o Ensure that OMB exercises its responsibilities to monitor and review statistical activities and budgets concerning immigration statistics, particularly those of the INS, to minimize duplication and make sure that appropriate procedures are used, standards met, and priorities observed in the collection, production, and publication of such data;

o Require and establish the mechanisms for continuing interagency coordination in the field of immigration data; participate in discussions designed to achieve consistency and comparability in concepts and definitions used by the relevant agencies in the collection of such information; and oversee the introduction and use of standardized approaches;

o Actively encourage and monitor the timely publication and dissemination of immigration data; and

o Actively encourage and support the preparation and release of micro-level public-use tapes conforming to the requirements of the Privacy Act and accompanied by adequate documentation, for use by researchers.

A common thread during discussions with virtually everyone concerned with immigration statistics was the obvious lack of coordination between the many agencies involved and their seeming indifference to users, as illustrated by the lack of timeliness in releasing data, failure to address users' needs or apply appropriate quality control standards, and inconsistencies in definitions.

The panel therefore further recommends that the respective agencies undertake a review of their data-gathering efforts in the area of immigration, in order to:

o Minimize duplication and burden and maximize quality and utility of the collected information;
o Develop approaches leading to the timely publication and dissemination of such data, including, as appropriate, the preparation and release of fully documented micro-data, public-use tapes; and
o Establish and maintain formal liaison with other federal agencies involved in the collection or analysis of immigration related data.

REFERENCES

Bureau of the Census
    1974   Consistency of Reporting of Ethnic Origin in the Current
            Population Survey, Technical Paper Number 31, February 1974.
Grossman, H.A.
    1978   OASDHI-Covered Earnings of Indochina Refugees, 1975, Social
            Security Bulletin (41,6) Social Security Bulletin.
Kahn, A.L.
    1980   Indochina Refugee Receiving Supplemental Security Income, July
            1978, Research and Statistics Note (No. 6) Social Security
            Administration.
Keely, C., and Kraly, E.
    1978   Recent Net Alien Immigration to the U. S.: Its Impact on
            Population Growth and Native Fertility. Demography
            15(3):267-284.
Lancaster, C., and Scheuren, F.J.
    1977   Counting the Uncountable Illegals: Some Initial Statistical
            Speculations Employing Capture-Recapture Techniques. Paper
            presented at the Annual Meeting of the American Statistical
            Association.
Merritt, M.G.
    1982   Cuban and Haitian Applicants for SSI Disability Payments.
            Social Security Administration mimeo.
Vining, D.R.
    1980   Net Migration by Air: A Lower Bound on Total Net Migration to
            the United States, Working Papers in Regional Science and
            Transportation, University of Pennsylvania.
Warren, R., and Passel, J.
    1983   Estimates of Illegal Aliens from Mexico Counted in the 1980
            United States Census. Paper presented at the Annual Meeting of
            the Population Association of America, Pittsburgh, Pennsylvania.

6

The Role of Nongovernmental Activities in Immigration Studies

Many government agencies and organizations produce data about immigration, as detailed in the two preceding chapters. These data reflect a large, cumbersome, and poorly coordinated official immigration statistics "system." In addition to the government data, however, many unofficial data sources exist. Moreover, most of the current analysis of immigration data is done outside government, by university researchers, foundations, private firms, and others in the private sector. The immigration statistics system is thus even larger (and less systematic) than our discussion has so far indicated.

"Unofficial" data consist mainly of those collected by individual researchers and not-for-profit institutions or for-profit firms. There are some grey definitional areas in this classification, however. In some cases, government agencies finance the collection of data by nongovernment organizations and individuals: for example, the General Social Survey is conducted by the National Opinion Research Center with support from the National Science Foundation, and its data have been used to compare immigrants with the native-born. Although such programs are funded by the government, the government usually disclaims responsibility for the data, so we classify them as unofficial. There are also data collected by foreign governments or quasi-governmental agencies, such as the United Nations High Commission for Refugees. These data, although official in some contexts, are unofficial as they are used within the United States.

There are large numbers of small-scale data collection activities in the area of immigration carried out by individual researchers, substantial numbers of larger-scale activities carried out by institutions and companies, and large-scale operations carried out by foreign governments and international organizations. It is beyond the scope of this study to attempt to review the quality and relevance of all these unofficial data sets, even for a representative sample of them. Thus in this chapter we do not attempt to review in detail the information collected and the collection processes involved. Instead, we examine what the role of unofficial data should be in an overall system of immigration statistics: what sorts of data collection are best left to nongovernmental bodies, and how needed data collection can be stimulated and financed. A new departure in this chapter is the explicit discussion of data analysis and its implications for data collection.

Good analysis is an essential link in the chain from raw data to policy decision and is a topic suitable for this nongovernmental chapter because, with the exception of the Census Bureau's research activities, most analysis of migration data is conducted outside government.

DATA PRODUCTION AND ANALYSIS

Data production and data analysis are separate activities, although analysis may be constrained by the ways in which data are produced, and collection may be tailored to the intended analysis. Data production refers to the collection, compilation, coding, and storage of basic data concerning immigration. Data are generally produced intentionally, but the intentions of the producer may not coincide with the requirements of the analyst. To take an example, most of the data collected by the INS are collected for programmatic and administrative purposes rather than for policy analysis, but some of them can be used for analytical purposes, sometimes in ways never dreamt of by those establishing the collection process.

The production of immigration statistics is very decentralized. As we have already noted, a number of federal agencies regularly produce data on immigrants or refugees, either as a primary objective or as a by-product of their other activities. Furthermore, the states provide at least some information on vital events occurring to immigrants, refugee program use, bilingual education, and other topics that vary by state.

Outside government, there is, if anything, even greater diversity and decentralization. Unofficial data are produced by intensive ethnographic studies of immigrants and of communities of both origin and destination of migrants, local surveys and compilations of local data, reconstructions of historical series from existing but unsystematized data, and many other collection processes. In addition, as noted, there are also data from foreign governments and international agencies. However, data quantity does not compensate for data quality. Existing nongovernmental data sets are often inadequate in terms of coverage, validity, and reliability of the data they contain, or because they are impossible to compare or to integrate with other official or unofficial data. Analysts have tried to solve some of these problems with more creative uses of the existing data, but the root of the problem lies in the decentralized nature of this nonofficial data production system.

Data analysis includes both primary analysis (that is, to examine the questions for which the data were collected) and secondary analysis (that is, to examine questions for which the data are relevant, though not the purpose for which they were collected). Though data are generally subjected to primary analysis, secondary analysis is even more widespread because of the high costs of data collection.

The agenda for analysis is set by current intellectual issues, policy debates, theoretical developments in one or more of the social sciences, or simply the curiosity of an investigator. Such studies, usually published in professional journals, monographs, or the popular press, may not achieve their full potential impact because their audiences are specialized along political, interest, or disciplinary lines. To the public or the policy maker, the resulting debates and controversies, especially those centering on issues of data adequacy, may seem partisan or merely arcane. Just as diverse motivations underlie the collection of data by unofficial sources, so too the analysis of data by unofficial analysts responds to many goals. A lack of consensus about important issues among analysts may be a sign not of factionalism, but rather of healthy diversity.

Primary analyses of official data may be guided by official or quasi-official perceptions of what is required and of the frequency with which they are required. The Census Bureau is an example of a statistical agency that both produces data and publishes analyses of these data, many at regular intervals, others as occasional papers. Comparisons of official data sources may occasionally be undertaken to provide statistical benchmarks. However, analyses of immigration data under official auspices have been relatively rare. The intellectual division of labor has allocated this task, often by default, to indiviudal researchers outside government.

A considerable volume of recent social science research about immigration has been secondary analysis of official, census-type survey data, most important the 1960 and 1970 census public-use samples and the 1976 Survey of Income and Education. Reliance on such data, however, greatly restricts the range of substantive issues that can be addressed and the analytical approaches that can be pursued. Given the limited social and economic variables available in census files and the virtual absence of cultural indicators, it is not surprising that most immigration studies relying on census data focus on the socioeconomic characteristics of the foreign-born population, usually differentiated by national origin and occasionally by period of arrival. Census micro data encourage the use of individuals or households as units of analysis, but analysis by aggregates such as area of residence could portray the macro dimensions of social phenomena. Multilevel analyses combining person and place variables are less common, but not entirely absent from the literature. The extensive reliance of researchers on official data is evident in the studies noted in the major bibliographies on immigration (see Appendix F), although the coverage of small-scale and ethnographic studies by the bibliographies is not entirely complete.

It can thus be seen that the analysis of immigration data has been profoundly affected by the collection of data. Researchers face the choice of either collecting their own data, which for reasons of cost will be restricted in general to surveys collecting extensive information from small numbers of people, or using official data generally collected for other purposes and thus of limited analytical potential. It should be noted, however, that the dearth of quality research studies in the field of immigration should not be blamed entirely on data deficiencies. Even the limited data available from official sources offer a potential for analytical study that has not been fully exploited. Even the analysis of large data sets is expensive, and funding for immigration research in the recent past has not been sufficient to support extensive analysis or to attract research analysts to the immigration field.

TYPES OF UNOFFICIAL DATA

An important distinction must be made between studies based on statistical data (e.g., social surveys) and those based on nonstatistical data (e.g., ethnographic, archival, and historical material). The data collection processes involved should be viewed as different parts of a continuum, from the quick, extensive (in terms of population coverage) yet limited (in terms of topics covered and questionnaire length) collection process of the traditional survey to the slow, limited (in terms of population coverage) and intensive (in terms of interview length and topics covered) collection process of the ethnographic study. The survey typically collects information about respondent status, either at the time of the survey (age, marriage, income, and education, for example) or at some specified earlier time (place of residence five years before the survey, for example) for a statistically representative sample of the study population. The ethnographic survey, on the other hand, collects a wealth of additional information about opinions, motivations, and community context, often through the use of open-ended questions, but the survey population is generally selected purposively and cannot be taken as representative of any larger population of interest. Each data type has its relative strengths. However, the potential for complementarity among various types of unofficial data is affected by the problems that arise when combining data from different sources and by the analytical approaches that have been used to address specific questions.

Studies based on both ethnographic and survey data have generated useful insights into immigration as a social phenomenon. Both survey and ethnographic data sources can be tailored to specific substantive questions about immigration as a social process whose causes and consequences extend from individuals to communities of origin and destination. Their scope, depth, and the generalizability of the information differ considerably, however, as a result of the qualitative nature of ethnographic data and the quantitative nature of survey data, as well as the manner of soliciting, recording, and coding information. Ethnographic data benefit from greater respondent flexibility but often at the cost of generalizability; survey data often sacrifice the richness of open-ended responses to facilitate coding and to obtain a standardized data set.

Ethnographic Data

The main strengths of ethnographic data lie in their depth and comprehensive coverage of an immigrant community or a specific aspect of the immigration process. Ethnographic data provide a great deal more information about social processes and interactions that structure immigration flows than do conventional survey data. Of course, the comprehensiveness of information produced depends on the amount of time spent in the field and the number of field sites. Ethnographic data are generally not exchangeable between analysts, so they are not easily subjected to secondary analysis, integration with other data sets, or verification except through restudy by different investigators. However, the ethnographic practice of soliciting information from multiple sources--participant observation, key community informants, and respondent interviews--provides some basis for internal data consistency checks and for response validation.

The major drawbacks of ethnographic information are the limits on exchange of information among researchers, the limited generalizability

of the results beyond the population or locality of study, and the
difficulty of subjecting the data to rigorous hypothesis testing using
multivariate statistical techniques. The major advantages of
ethnographic data are the depth of study they permit into the reasons for
and process of migration; survey data on the social and economic
characteristics of immigrants can provide only a partial, and possibly
misleading, view of such reasons and processes.

Survey Data

The strengths of unofficial survey data complement the weaknesses of
ethnographic data and vice versa. The primary strengths of unofficial
surveys relative to official sources are their flexibility in selecting
the number and scope of topics to be included and their ability to ask
sensitive questions; relative to ethnographic studies, their strengths
are that the population universe can be clearly and explicitly defined,
that they adhere to statistical standards permitting the evaluation of
possible sampling errors, and that they are amenable to rigorous
empirical analysis. None of these strengths is absolute, for compromises
in scope, representativeness, population coverage, and quantifiability
are imposed by cost and time considerations. Moreover, some aspects of
immigration are difficult to capture using random sampling survey
techniques. The obvious example to date is that of illegal immigration.
Nonrandom sampling methods, such as network samples, whereby one member
of the study population is asked to provide names and addresses of other
members of the population, who are then in turn interviewed and asked to
provide more names, have been used with limited success, but the process
of statistical inference is seriously impaired. (Such samples are
sometimes also called snowball samples.) Other concerns not easily
pursued with survey--or ethnographic--data are the macro-structural
properties of the immigration process, including the changing nature,
direction, and composition of aggregate flows; fortunately, official data
sources are especially well suited to such issues.

Despite the many virtues of survey data for addressing questions
about immigration, these unofficial data sets suffer from several
drawbacks. Most surveys give a one-time static snapshot of social and
economic status that provides only limited information about the process
of arriving at that status. Thus, most cross-sectional surveys of
immigrants are limited in their ability to address questions about
process or to establish clearly causal relationships. The exceptions are
those few surveys that have collected retrospective histories of the
timing of various events, such as migration, employment, and
childbearing. The dating of changes in social and demographic status
permits a more effective study of process, although events in the more
distant past may not be representative of their time period, since the
sample is representative of the present, and event intervals in the
period shortly before the survey may be affected by censoring and
truncation biases.

An alternative to the use of retrospective questions in sample
surveys involves reinterviewing a sample of respondents several times,
for example every six months or every year. This longitudinal, panel
approach may be preferable to that of repeated cross-sections for making

inferences about process because it permits control for previous events in a sequence without being subject to major event-dating errors that affect life-history reports. However, cost factors have inhibited individual researchers from undertaking truly longitudinal surveys of immigrants. Moreover, immigrants often have a high propensity to move, which usually increases sample attrition and can, over time, impair the representativeness of the sample. Complexity and cost factors aside, it is noteworthy that there does not currently exist a nationally representative longitudinal study of recent immigrants. Longitudinal studies of the general population do not include a sufficient number of immigrants to permit separate analysis even at the aggregate level and still less for nationality or other subgroups.

The strategy used to define a universe and devise a sampling scheme may limit the usefulness of multipurpose surveys for studying immigrants: for example, the General Social Survey includes only the English-speaking population over age 18. Furthermore, even leaving aside the special problem of studying the illegal immigrant population, it is not obvious how to design a survey to study the determinants and consequences of migration for the community and country of both origin and destination. With few exceptions, most sample surveys of immigrants have defined the universe on the basis of those who actually move across international boundaries and settle in a specific locality or who cross at a specific time. Such strategies for limiting the universe are appropriate for addressing questions about the experiences of immigrants in the destination country, but these samples limit interpretations of the causes and consequences of international migration in at least two important ways. First, by excluding those who decide not to emigrate, studies based on samples of individuals who have migrated across international boundaries distort our understanding of the determinants of migration and lead to potentially erroneous conclusions about the nature of migrant selectivity. Second, universes defined by time and locality, especially the latter, exclude an unknown number of immigrants who may have returned to their place of origin or moved on to another destination. This latter problem can be partly resolved by inquiring about past migration history, intended moves, and the existence of friends and relatives in other localities, but it introduces selection problems of unknown magnitude in the statistical analysis of the survey data and may ultimately distort conclusions about the individual, familial, and locational structure of aggregate flows. Survey design may also affect the potential to study impact, since it is clearly necessary in such a case to have information not only on migrants themselves but also on the rest of the community and on other communities.

To summarize, the main advantages of survey data reside in their generalizability, their amenability to rigorous statistical analysis, and their high degree of exchangeability among researchers. In practice, however, the access to and distribution of data from specialized surveys about immigrants is not extensive, and there is no central clearinghouse that receives, classifies, and distributes data sets containing information about immigrants to interested researchers. The generalizability, substantive content, and amenability of unofficial surveys to rigorous secondary analyses of immigration issues varies with the objectives and design of the original data collection. Although cross-sectional surveys can be designed to deal with the timing of events through the use of retrospective questions or through repeated surveys, and longitudinal surveys can be designed to examine processes, each strategy poses different problems of cost, sample attrition, recall error, and analytical limitation.

Immigrant Case Records

One relatively unexplored avenue for immigrant studies is the use of case records collected by private voluntary agencies that assist immigrants or refugees. These files provide a basis for following immigrants for a period of time and for noting their adaptation to life in the United States. Assuming that the necessary standards for confidentiality could be met, such data would offer many of the advantages of a longitudinal survey at a fraction of the cost.

Potential Complementarities Among Unofficial Data Sources

Although there are a number of possible combinations of data types, three particular combinations are promising for research. We term these three combinations multilevel studies, multimethod studies, and multi-data-set validations. A multilevel study uses combinations of data aggregated at different levels to establish a finding: for example, individual or household data might be used to confirm or enhance conclusions based on aggregate data. A multimethod study combines fundamentally different types of data: an example is the way ethnographic and sample survey data are used to complement each other in the study of Mexican migration to California undertaken by Massey (see Appendix C). Such studies frequently combine official and unofficial data, exploiting the relative strengths of each. The third category involves the cross-validation of a finding using different data sets that cover the same population or variable of interest. For example, U.S. estimates of immigration from a country might be compared with that country's estimated emigration to the United States. Such studies also typically require combinations of official and unofficial data. Even given current data production systems, these strategies appear underexploited and offer scope for useful research effort.

OBSTACLES TO DATA ANALYSIS

The bulk of analysis of immigration data, whether collected under official or unofficial auspices, is done by the private sector, but only accessible data can be analyzed. Except for the U.S. Census Bureau, agencies that produce official data either have been largely unaware of or unresponsive to the data needs of the research community. Problems of accessibility and ease of use represent an obstacle to data analysis. Many data sources remain inaccessible for reasons that cannot be explained by privacy or confidentiality concerns alone. Even for the data that are accessible, documentation is often sketchy or unavailable. Coding protocols are not explained, so that the effects of coding practices that differ from one source to another, or even within sources, may be overlooked. With better access to existing data, the research community could produce more relevant and higher-quality analyses. The existence of such analyses is essential to better policy formation, since data per se, in the absence of any examination of implications, give no guidance for policy. The analysis is impossible without the data, but the data, to be useful, must be analyzed.

Greater interaction with the research community would provide a mechanism for improving the policy relevance of officially produced data. Given an understanding of analytical needs, data could be produced in more convenient forms. The expert advisory panel and the fellows program, recommended in Chapter 4, would provide the INS with an important source of expertise and feedback in improving its data collection. Contact with users need not be expensive and does not necessarily require the establishment of a permanent users service. Annual meetings of the professional associations of the research disciplines offer an opportunity to disseminate information about data products and services. The foundations and journals active in the immigration field can serve a similar function. Regular INS publications could also provide information about data availability and changes in data production practices.

A second obstacle to analysis is the shortage of funding for immigration studies. This shortage has been particularly severe for unofficial data collection, which is generally expensive, but has also restricted the analysis of official data and professional interest in the field. Skepticism about data quality may have made immigration studies less attractive to such major grant-giving agencies as the National Science Foundation or the National Institutes of Health, even though data evaluation alone would represent a worthwhile outcome. Once again, the problems of data production haunt data analysis, although indirectly in this case. It should be noted, however, that the National Institutes of Health, through the National Institute of Child Health and Human Development, have been making efforts recently to encourage the submission of research proposals in the immigration field and to increase the funding allotted to it.

The INS also could support a program for immigration studies channeled through the conventional funding agencies, which would apply their usual peer review and grant procedures. This approach would provide a mechanism for the contract research program already recommended in Chapter 4. The Office of Refugee Resettlement and other agencies concerned with refugees might enter into similar agreements to support research on refugees.

SUMMARY AND RECOMMENDATIONS

Unofficial data complement official data in important ways. Furthermore, most studies of immigration are now carried out by nongovernment researchers. However, problems of accessibility and quality of official data, and shortage of funds for unofficial data collection and analysis in general have severely limited the contribution of the nongovernment sector to the policy formation process.

To improve this contribution, the panel recommends:

o   Insofar as is feasible, official government data on immigrants and refugees should be made available to researchers outside the government;

o   The proposed Division of Immigration Statistics in the INS should establish and maintain contacts with the research community and keep it informed about the availability of data and changes in procedures. This recommendation also applies to all other agencies that produce immigration data; and

o   Government agencies that provide funds for research should be encouraged to stimulate the submission of research proposals in the immigration field and to give particular attention to sound proposals for relevant research studies in the area.

7

Collecting Data on Refugees and Asylees: An Illustration of a Complex Process

Chapters 4 through 6 concern the institutional bases for data collection and reporting on immigration and immigration-related matters. As these chapters show, immigration involves activities undertaken in the United States and abroad by a myriad of public and private organizations. To function smoothly, coordination among these various actors is essential.

By describing in this chapter the process of immigration, our focus becomes the data collected at different points in the system as people pass through it, and how the data elements collected at one point find a programmatic use at a subsequent point while yet serving analytic and policy objectives. Our example is the process by which individuals enter the country as refugees (or seek status as asylees if already in the country), settle in communities, and adapt to their new world.

There are several reasons for choosing refugees and asylees for the case study. First, the Refugee Act of 1980 requires that data be collected and reported by a variety of federal, state, and private agencies. Second, several mechanisms for data coordination have been established within the refugee program; although there are still gaps--as we discuss--these too are instructive. Third, the refugee data that are collected by official sources cover a wide range of issues common to immigration in general. (Had the case study focused on undocumented aliens, in contrast, the chapter would have been notably short.) Fourth, the comparison between data collection on refugees and asylees is informative; although both groups must demonstrate that they meet the same definitional standards, different agencies or different arms of the same agency are involved in their processing and, thereby, in data collection activities.

In reviewing the data on refugees and asylees, this chapter follows the process of their admission and resettlement, the organizations that are involved, and the circumstances under which data are requested and generated. The first section describes the process of refugee admissions, including the policies and procedures that apply at each stage and the data that are needed to accomplish the purposes of that stage; reviews the available data; discusses problems with those data and identifies gaps in them. The second section presents similar information for asylees. The third section describes the data collected on refugees and asylees after they have entered (for refugees) or been granted asylum (for asylees), with particular emphasis on data pertaining to adjustment of status.

REFUGEES

Refugees are defined by U.S. law as persons who are outside their countries of origin and who are unable or unwilling to return because of persecution or the well-founded fear of persecution on account of race, religion, nationality, membership in a particular social group, or political opinion. The process of refugee resettlement begins with the flight of refugees into countries of first asylum, where they seek protection. If the prospects for repatriation or settlement in the country of first asylum are unlikely or that country is unable or unwilling to provide them sufficient protection, resettlement--i.e., movement to a third country--may be a necessary solution to their plight.

Setting Admission Numbers and Allocations

Under the Refugee Act of 1980, the United States determines annually the number and allocation of refugees that are of special humanitarian concern to the United States and should therefore be admitted to this country. The President first proposes an admissions level, based on an assessment of the need for resettlement and the domestic capacity of the country to respond. The President then consults with members of the judiciary committees of the House and the Senate regarding the proposed number and allocation of refugee admissions during the next year. However, prior to the formal consultations, the President is required by law to provide the following information:

(1) A description of the nature of the refugee situation;
(2) A description of the number and allocation of the refugees to be admitted and an analysis of conditions within the countries from which they came;
(3) A description of the proposed plans for their movement and resettlement and the estimated cost;
(4) An analysis of the anticipated social, economic, and demographic impact of their admission to the United States;
(5) A description of the extent to which other countries will admit and assist in the resettlement of such refugees;
(6) An analysis of the impact of the participation of the United States in the resettlement of such refugees on the foreign policy interests of the United States; and
(7) Such additional information as may be appropriate or requested by such members.

Following the formal consultation, the two judiciary committees respond to the President's proposal, sometimes suggesting alternative levels or allocations of refugee admissions. Then, having reviewed the congressional recommendations, the President sets the admissions numbers and allocations for the year. For fiscal 1984, for example, the numbers were as follows:

Total refugee admissions	72,000
East Asia	50,000
Eastern Europe/Soviet Union	12,000
Near East/South Asia	6,000
Africa	3,000
Latin America/Caribbean	1,000

The President also prepares a report on the proposed refugee admissions and allocations for the year, providing the information detailed above.

Four federal agencies with major responsibilities for refugee resettlement are involved in preparation of the consultation proposal and the report: the Office of the U.S. Coordinator for Refugee Affairs and the Bureau of Refugee Programs in the State Department; the Office of Refugee Resettlement in the Department of Health and Human Services; and the Immigration and Naturalization Service in the Justice Department.

The Office of the U.S. Coordinator for Refugee Affairs in the State Department encourages coordination between the government and private-sector agencies concerned with refugees and between various levels of government with regard to both domestic and overseas resettlement activities. This office oversees activities related to the consultation process, but it is not involved in the admission or resettlement of refugees.

The Bureau of Refugee Programs, which administers the State Department's refugee programs, is responsible for the development and implementation of U.S. policies related to refugee relief and assistance overseas, for setting priorities for admission of refugees to the United States, for providing resources for their processing and training overseas, and for reception and placement of refugees in U.S. communities. In the formal consultation process, this office is responsible for reporting on the worldwide refugee situation.

In the Department of Health and Human Services, the Office of Refugee Resettlement (ORR) operates the domestic assistance program and carries out the informational requirements of the refugee legislation. During the consultations, ORR provides information on the U.S. domestic assistance program and its capacity to resettle refugees who are admitted. Finally, the Immigration and Naturalization Service is responsible for determining if an individual meets the statutory requirements for admission to the United States as a refugee. The Refugee Act gives responsibility to the Attorney General for developing procedures for making those determinations.

At the heart of the consultation report are descriptions of the conditions in countries that generate refugees, in countries of first asylum, and in countries that resettle refugees. These country reports on the world refugee situation, which are prepared by the State Department using annual reports from U.S. embassies, are meant to provide as comprehensive a picture as possible of the international refugee scene.

The State Department also prepares statistics (presented in a separate volume for the first time in 1984) on the number of refugees who have left countries of persecution and sought asylum elsewhere, on those who are in need of protection and relief assistance, on those who have been resettled, on internally and externally displaced persons, and on the voluntary return of refugees to their home country. The statistics are drawn primarily from information provided to the Bureau for Refugee

Programs by U.S. embassies and consulates in the countries covered by the report, by international organizations such as the U.N. High Commissioner for Refugees and the U.N. Relief and Works Agency (which assists Palestinian refugees), and by foreign governments. The international organizations themselves publish periodic reviews of their assistance programs, including the numbers of refugees receiving assistance, and they have the capacity through their field offices to request specific additional information if it is needed.

Counting Refugees

Reliable data on the number of refugees worldwide are limited by two factors: differences of opinion as to definitions and difficulties in counting refugees, particularly during the height of a crisis. To quote from the Report to the Congress for Fiscal Year 1985 prepared by the Bureau of Refugee Programs (U.S. Department of State, 1984): "In most instances, the statistics in this report should be regarded as orders of magnitude."

The problem of counting is logistically the more difficult of the two to overcome, for several reasons. Refugee flows are, by definition, episodic, crisis-oriented phenomena, during which conditions and numbers can change often and quickly. In addition, the flows often occur in areas in which the statistical infrastructure is primitive or has broken down, as a result either of the flow of refugees or of the political events surrounding the flow. Trying to keep an accurate count of refugees under these circumstances is difficult, if not impossible.

Beyond the logistical problems of counting, there are political factors that undermine attempts to reach an accurate count. For example, in order to get what they consider to be an appropriate level of international assistance, host countries sometimes overestimate the number of refugees living within their borders and resist efforts by others to take a census. Since the permission of the host country is needed to operate within its borders, international organizations are sometimes unable or unwilling to do their own censuses of refugee populations.

Definitional problems are easier, but agreement is by no means readily at hand. The U.S. State Department defines a refugee, for the purpose of its report, as one who is in need of international protection, relief, and assistance. Given the use to which the country reports are put--i.e., to justify U.S. assessments of the need for relief and resettlement--this definition makes sense. The U.N. High Commissioner for Refugees (UNHCR) defines a refugee as a person who does not yet have the protection of a government by virtue of citizenship, a definition that includes resettled refugees who have permanent status but have not yet become citizens.

The UNHCR is the principal source for all other international organizations reporting data on refugees. The major U.S. nongovernmental reporter of data is the U.S. Committee for Refugees, which publishes a World Refugee Survey, containing data drawn from both the U.S. government and the UNHCR.

On occasion, the numbers reported by the different organizations differ. Although the UNHCR and the State Department came to the same general conclusion regarding the number of refugees worldwide in 1983--about 8 million in total--they showed markedly different numbers for specific countries. For example, the UNHCR estimated that there were 234,000 refugees in Burundi; the State Department estimated less than 60,000. No explanation for the discrepancy, or for the figure itself, was given in either source. In the 1984 reports the differences were reconciled, with both sources reporting about 60,000 refugees. Again, no explanation for the reconciliation was provided.

Since counts can differ, even when definitions are the same, depending on how and when the data are collected, it is not surprising that there are discrepancies. What is troubling, though, is the lack of explanation offered by the various organizations as to how specific figures were formulated and from whom the data were collected or received. Without such explanations (at least in statistical appendices that can be made available on request), the reasons for the differences are unclear. In addition, none of the organizations provides much guidance in their reports as to why numbers change from year to year: whether new flows have occurred, permanent solutions have been found, or new censuses have been taken. In sum, then, it is difficult for an outside user of these refugee reports to make informed judgments about the comparability or accuracy of the data in them.

Processing Refugees for Admission

Since there are generally more refugees who are in need of resettlement than the United States and other resettlement countries are able or willing to accept, criteria have been established to determine if a given individual will qualify for the U.S. program. The application of these criteria requires data collection. Refugee processing varies from area to area, depending on the number and concentration of people who may be eligible for resettlement. This section describes how the process usually works.

Prescreening by Voluntary Agencies

Applicants for admission are referred to the U.S. program by the UNHCR or other internationally based organizations, which collect data on the ties that refugees have to the various resettlement nations. They are prescreened by the staff of U.S. voluntary agencies under contract to the State Department to determine if they are eligible for resettlement. Biographical data are collected about refugee applicants and members of their family, including name, sex, birth date, country of birth, country of residence, and marital status.

In Southeast Asia the prescreening is conducted by the joint voluntary agencies (JVAs), which operate under cooperative agreements with the Bureau for Refugee Programs. The JVAs coordinate data collection for all the voluntary agencies that assist in resettling refugees. Almost all the JVAs use the same form for recording biographical data. Elsewhere in the world, however, there is no consistency in the reporting format, although standard questions are asked. Each voluntary agency uses its own biographical data form.

Agencies differ also in the amount of additional information about employment and educational background or previous experiences that is collected from refugee applicants. During the interview, a case number (one per family) is assigned; that number is used in later phases of the admissions process. The first letter of the case number indicates where the refugee is being processed; if a refugee moves prior to admission, additional letters are added to the case number to show the subsequent locations.

INS Screening

Upon completion of the prescreening, the applications of refugees who meet U.S. admission priorities are reviewed by a State Department refugee coordinator and then presented to INS officers. The INS officers interview applicants to determine whether they are admissible under U.S. law. At this point, INS form I-590 is used to collect information similar to the information collected by the voluntary agency representative. At a later point in the process, information on the medical condition of the refugee is collected and added to the refugee's official file. If approved for admission as refugees to the United States, all family members are issued alien numbers (A-numbers). These numbers, and the case numbers assigned by the voluntary agency staff, are the two major means of identifying refugees.

The INS collects statistics on the approvals and denials of refugee applications as part of its management reporting system (form G-23). The information includes the number of applications pending at the beginning of the month; the number of new applications filed; the number approved; the number denied, by reason; the number otherwise closed; and the number pending at the end of the month.

The data on approvals and denials are used by the INS and the State Department for both monitoring and planning purposes. Their use for monitoring is difficult, however, because there are no clear standards against which approvals and denials can be measured, that is, no basis for determining how many of the refugees presented to the INS should be approved or disapproved. Generally, therefore, people concerned with refugee admissions look at fluctuations in the rate of approvals and denials rather than at absolute numbers: for example, inconsistencies from month to month and from post to post in Southeast Asia have provoked considerable criticism of INS practices, leading to the development of new guidelines for the processing of refugees.

Sponsorship Assurances

After the INS approves an application but before permission to travel to the United States is given, a sponsor, which can be an individual, a church group, or a resettlement agency, must be identified for each refugee.

The data collected at the time of the initial screening of the applicant are used for determining sponsorship. The data, generally stamped with information about the refugee's current location (i.e., whether he or she is at a refugee processing center), are sent to the

Refugee Data Center (RDC), which is funded by the Bureau for Refugee Programs. The RDC began operations in October 1979 as a temporary center within the American Council of Voluntary Agencies (ACVA), with responsibility for maintaining information on the relatively small number of refugees entering the United States at that time. By 1979, as the rate of admissions rose to 14,000 per month, the RDC became the main data center with information about the vast majority of refugees sponsored by U.S. agencies.

Once a sponsor is confirmed, an assurance form (I-591) is completed and returned to the RDC for processing. The information is entered into the RDC computer and sent to the overseas voluntary agency in the country in which the refugee is located. The information is recorded on an ACVAFS form #1, which includes: name of the principal applicant and family members; A-number; date of birth; place of birth; nationality; sponsoring voluntary agency; local sponsor; local relative, if applicable; airport of final destination; and a statement that the agency "agrees to assist the principal refugee named above to obtain employment and housing for him/herself and family, if any." The overseas agency then notifies the INS that an assurance has been obtained and the refugee can be admitted to the United States.

The RDC also uses the information to prepare a computer printout of refugee assurances by city and state of local sponsors. This report, which is sent to the national voluntary agencies and state refugee coordinators, provides detailed information about each refugee case. The information includes: names; sponsoring voluntary agency; case number; case size (number of individuals in the family unit); estimated date of arrival; country of birth; sex; date of birth; English-language level; occupation (using Department of Labor 3-digit codes); and highest level of education completed.

The printouts are distributed to the voluntary agencies and state refugee offices for dissemination to service providers within their areas. Because each refugee is listed by name, issues of confidentiality arise in the use of these printouts. Furthermore, no summary tables are published, and it is difficult to construct, from the printouts, an overall picture of the characteristics of refugees who have been sponsored by U.S. agencies. Since the RDC has information that is not yet available in other refugee data systems (see below regarding the ORR system), it would be useful to have these data summarized in a more easily used format.

Travel and Entry to the United States

Most refugees travel on flights arranged by the Intergovernmental Committee on Migration (ICM), a nonprofit group established to function as the "travel agency" of the refugee program. Working with the State Department to spread arrivals over time, ICM develops travel manifests that specify when individual refugees and their families will travel to the United States. These travel manifests, called nominal rolls, are transferred to the RDC where the information is entered into the master computer so that local sponsors and others can be informed of a refugee's arrival. The information constitutes official confirmation of a refugee's arrival as far as RDC is concerned.

Refugees travel with the ACVAFS form #1, described above, or a letter from a U.S. embassy that specifies that their admission has been approved. They are also issued INS form I-94 (arrival/departure record), which becomes their major form of identification after entry. Use of the I-94 has presented difficulties for the refugee program since its primary use is for nonimmigrants (visitors, etc.), and items that make sense for that group may not make sense for refugees. For example, when a new I-94 form was introduced in January 1983, it initially caused problems for the refugee program because it did not contain space for some of the information that was routinely used by refugee service providers in identifying and serving clients: the A-number, English-language level, and sponsoring agency. Negotiations between the State Department and the INS led to changes in filling out the forms, and agreement was reached on how and where to insert the additional data.

The Center for Disease Control (CDC) has maintained a computer system for identifying and tracking arriving refugees since 1980, when minicomputers were installed at the four West Coast ports of entry and in New York. Information is also kept at the CDC headquarters in Atlanta regarding refugees who enter elsewhere. These data are used to notify local health departments about the arrival of refugees with major health problems.

Statistics on refugee arrivals are kept by three separate U.S. government agencies: the Bureau for Refugee Programs in the State Department, the INS, and the Office of Refugee Resettlement (ORR) in the Department of Health and Human Services. These agencies do not agree as to the number of refugees entering the United States. In fiscal 1983, the discrepancies were large: the INS reported 57,064 refugees, the Bureau for Refugee Programs reported 61,681, and ORR reported 60,622. During the first quarter of fiscal 1984, the discrepancies remained but the direction of the differences changed, with INS reporting more arrivals than the State Department.

In part the discrepancies occur because each agency counts refugee admissions at a different point in the process. The Bureau for Refugee Programs uses the ICM nominal rolls as the basis of its statistics, adjusting its data to account for refugees who do not travel as scheduled or who travel on their own. In other words, the State Department counts refugees at their point of departure for the United States. The INS and the ORR count refugees at ports of entry, when they actually enter the country, but the two agencies use different sources of data: the INS uses data collected from its own officers; the ORR uses information transferred to it from the quarantine officers who stamp and keep a copy of the ACVAFS form #1.

All these agencies are believed to miss some arrivals. The Bureau for Refugee Programs may miss refugees who do not travel under ICM arrangements since they will not appear on the ICM nominal rolls (although it may still overestimate the number of arrivals since some refugees may make travel arrangements with ICM and then not use them during the fiscal year in which they are counted). The INS and the ORR may also miss refugees who make their own travel arrangements, particularly if they enter at one of the smaller ports of entry or one that is not a usual point of arrival for refugees. The categories of refugees who are most likely to be undercounted are the spouses and minor children of refugees who have already entered the United States, because they are the people most likely to travel under their own travel arrangements. Also likely to be missed are the few refugees who do not require sponsorship assurances because they have sufficient resources to support themselves in the United States.

The official reports on refugee admissions, like the official statistics on worldwide numbers of refugees, provide little explanation as to the discrepancies among them. With the exception of the ORR, the reports that are disseminated to people outside the authoring agencies have few notes explaining the sources of the data. On occasion, changes have been made in the statistical reports without any explanations.

Agency Coordination

At present there is little formal consultation or coordination among the agencies that count refugee arrivals. Nor is there a single agency with responsibility for monitoring the accuracy of the data issued by each agency as "official" statistics. The lack of coordination and absence of a single agency designated as responsible for preparing an accurate and official data set presents problems, particularly in duplication of effort in the collection of data and differences in basic identifying data from system to system that make the transfer of records difficult. For example, separate forms asking for the same basic information (name, birth date, country of birth, etc.) are filled out by the voluntary agencies and the INS, but currently there is no check on the accuracy of the information that is recorded. Refugees also are identified in some of the systems (e.g., RDC) by case number and in others (e.g., ORR) by A-number.

The State Department's Office of the U.S. Coordinator for Refugee Affairs has proposed a new approach to the issue of identification. A Name Check System (AVLOS), which is operated by the State Department foreign service posts, would be used for recording basic data. After the INS approves a refugee for admission and an A-number is assigned, a copy of the INS biographical information would be given to the State Department for entry into the AVLOS computer system. This system currently has the capability to record name, date of birth, and place of birth. Four other data elements would be added: sex, country of citizenship, alien number, and entry status/classification. The AVLOS file would be available to the other agencies that collect data on refugees to be used as the basis for opening, updating, or validating refugee records.

The INS also plans to include these basic identifying data on the I-94 form, to be collected at ports of entry to record a refugee's entry. Once plans for installing computer terminals at ports of entry are implemented, the I-94 data would be entered into the computer system and made available to all the appropriate agencies. These data would become the official U.S. data on refugee admissions.

While this plan may ultimately help eliminate discrepancies, it is recognized by all parties that the installation of computer terminals at the ports of entry will take some time and is not a short-term solution to the problem. The plan also does not address the issue of duplication of effort in data collection. As a first step, the development of a working group in refugee statistics should be considered. With regular meetings of those who are concerned with this issue, perhaps more immediate improvements in the statistical system can be implemented.

ASYLEES

People seeking political asylum in the United States must meet the same criteria as those seeking to enter as refugees; the definitions (see above) are the same. Unlike refugees, who are selected from overseas, asylum seekers are self-selected from aliens already in the United States. They present themselves to U.S. authorities and request political asylum, whether they are legally in the country on a temporary visa or have entered the country illegally. Valid asylum claims cannot be denied on the basis of numbers, national preferences, illegal entry status, or other selection criteria. When a person who has entered the country illegally or overstayed a visa presents an asylum request that is determined to be without merit, that person must depart or be subject to deportation or exclusion, just like any other illegal entrant.

The volume of asylum applicants has increased dramatically since the passage of the 1980 Refugee Act. While the INS received only 3,000 applications in 1979, there were 40,000 in 1981, and the present INS backlog is about 160,000 cases.

The Political Asylum Process

Requests for political asylum are filed either with INS district directors or with immigration judges. People who make themselves known to the INS have their cases heard by the district director, and they may raise their requests a second time in immigration court. Requests for political asylum that are made by people who have been apprehended by the INS can only be brought before immigration judges.

When a request for political asylum is filed, the local INS district office opens a file on the applicant, containing the A-number, asylum application (form I-589), and other pertinent information relating to the asylum claim. Because asylum determinations are handled within the INS and because they affect alien residence status, much of the information collected by the INS on asylum applicants is aggregated with the information collected on aliens generally. For example, data on deportations and voluntary departures include but do not record separately persons who have applied for political asylum.

The INS forwards all asylum requests to the Department of State for advisory opinions, which are prepared by the Bureau of Human Rights and Humanitarian Affairs (BHRHA). Most advisory opinions are form letters, recommending either approval or denial. As such they do not give any of the data on the basis of which the approval or denial was decided or the source of any of the information used. When applications are filed by people from countries acknowledged by U.S. authorities to have a high level of human rights violations, such as South Africa or Iran, or when applicants come from countries whose governments the United States opposes, such as the Soviet Union, denial letters usually state the reasons for the negative decision.

The BHRHA does not keep a formal count of the advisory opinions it writes. At the end of each month, the staff members inform the office director how many cases they have completed, for which nationalities, and whether their determinations were favorable or unfavorable. This permits the Asylum Affairs Section to answer public inquiries, but this office does not turn the information into a formal record.

Successful asylum applicants initially are allowed to remain for one year in the United States, and at that point they may become permanent resident aliens by completing the standard application (form I-485).

Numbers of asylum applications by country of origin are reported on the G-23 form. Information is publicly available, on a monthly basis, on pending cases, new cases, cases approved, and cases denied. In addition, the INS collects data on the number of requests sent to the State Department for advisory opinions, the number of advisory opinions received, the cases pending for which there are letters, and the cases decided and awaiting a response from the applicant.

Immigration Court and the Board of Immigration Appeals

Immigration judges, appointed by the Attorney General, are located in the office of the Chief Immigration Judge, part of the Department of Justice but independent of the INS. Hearings before immigration judges represent the first level of administrative judicial review. The decisions of immigration judges can be appealed to the Board of Immigration Appeals (BIA). Immigration judges hear asylum cases filed by people who have either been denied asylum status by an INS district director or not presented their claims to a district director. The latter usually arise in exclusion or deportation proceedings. While the INS asylum interviews are confidential, immigration court proceedings are relatively open and adversarial in character, with the applicant frequently represented by legal counsel and the INS always represented by a trial attorney.

In January 1983 immigration judges and the Board of Immigration Appeals (BIA) were placed together in a new unit, separate from the INS, called the Executive Office for Immigration Review. The separation was effected, in large part, in response to criticism about the apparent lack of independence of the review and appeals agencies from the INS itself.

An important change resulting from the reorganization was in the record-keeping procedures: prior to the change, the INS kept monthly consolidated case records that combined the cases heard by the district directors and the immigration judges; now the two categories are reported separately. After the reorganization, the immigration judges adopted the counting procedures of the BIA, keeping track of the total number of cases according to whether they involved exclusion or deportation proceedings; however, the judges ceased to record the nationality of the applicants so that immigration court statistics of asylum grants and denials by nationality can no longer be compiled.

Fortunately, this situation is due to be remedied in early 1985, at which time data collection will be more comprehensive than it was prior to the reorganization.

Data Insufficiencies and Gaps

There are several major problems with the data on applicants for asylum. Perhaps the most obvious is the lack of an accurate count of those seeking asylum.

Although the INS has improved its data-keeping mechanisms and introduced greater uniformity into reporting procedures throughout its operations, there is still little confidence in statistical information generated from the INS district offices, which are the source of information about aliens seeking asylum. A need exists, therefore, for the development and controlled implementation of a standardized record-keeping procedure, incorporating necessary quality control, for asylum seekers as well as other categories of aliens.

Wittingly or unwittingly, asylum applicants also contribute to inaccurate counts by filing more than one application, by filing incomplete applications, and by failing to appear for hearings. Applicants often fail to appear for their second INS interviews or for their hearings, sometimes because they have not received the notices of their appearances, but at other times because they expect negative rulings. Officials claim, for example, that when the New York district office began to rule negatively on many Polish cases, the applicants simply went across the river to Newark, where the reception was more sympathetic, and applied again, presumably under different names. Some districts apparently treat a nonappearance as a voluntary departure, assume the person is no longer in the country, and close the case. Other districts maintain active files for hundreds of applicants who have, in effect, disappeared.

A second problem involves the application form. In June 1981 a revised 45-item form replaced the existing 30-item form. On the old form, the application itself contained primarily biographical and immigration data. Many questions relevant to asylum evaluations, e.g., ethnic and religious affiliations and reasons for leaving the country of origin, appeared on a supplemental form, which applicants frequently left incomplete. The new form incorporates the questions previously on the supplemental forms and requires more specificity on the questions related to an applicant's "well-founded fear." Unfortunately, many of the pre-1981 forms are still in use, because the backlog, particularly in immigration court, is extremely heavy.

There are several gaps in information about applicants for asylum. As noted, INS statistics do not distinguish nationality in certain areas such as cases before immigration judges in which such information is needed. Furthermore, the data specify neither the number of asylum applicants among those who are subsequently deported or accept voluntary departure nor the countries to which asylum applicants from particular countries are deported.

The Department of State and the INS may determine that the members of a certain nationality group merit "extended voluntary departure." This status entitles those who make themselves known to INS officials to remain in the United States until conditions in their countries of origin are safe enough to ensure their physical safety. According to the State Department and the INS, national groups granted extended voluntary departure in the past have remained in the United States after the special status was removed. There is no statistical evidence to support this position, nor to support arguments that people do return to their countries of origin when conditions improve. At a minimum, data are needed both on the number who come forward to request extended voluntary departure status and on those applicants who subsequently leave the country. Such issues and those raised above are appropriate for review by an interagency task force that should be established to deal with data needs for refugees and asylees.

THE U.S. DOMESTIC ASSISTANCE PROGRAM

Upon admission to the United States (or approval of application, for asylees), refugees and asylees are eligible for a range of programs that are aimed at promoting their self-sufficiency. The State Department's Bureau for Refugee Programs is responsible for administering a reception and placement grant program, using cooperative agreements with private voluntary agencies. Under the cooperative agreements, agencies are required to establish case files on each arriving refugee family unit. These files are to record biographical data, health information, English-language level, and other pertinent information to assist in developing plans for employment and meeting the service needs of the refugees. The files are also to detail the services that are provided to the refugee during, at least, the first 90 days. Most other assistance programs for refugees are funded by the Office of Refugee Resettlement in the Department of Health and Human Services and administered by the states. The programs include cash medical assistance, social services, health assessments, educational programs for children, and targeted assistance programs for areas of high impact.

Data Collection and Reporting

The Refugee Act of 1980, as noted earlier, contains relatively detailed and specific requirements for data collection and reporting, and these requirements were continued and expanded when the act was reauthorized in October 1982. All the requirements cover both refugees and asylees. In addition, public interest in refugees, as a highly visible component of the nation's immigration, has been strong. In this context, the collection and dissemination of statistics on refugees has become institutionalized. The Refugee Act of 1980 requires an annual report to Congress on the progress of refugees who have arrived in the United States since 1975; the retroactive mandate is noteworthy. Specific language in the act provides for "an updated profile of the employment and labor force statistics for refugees," "a description of the extent to which refugees received . . . assistance or services, . . . a description of the geographic location of refugees, . . . evaluations of the extent to which the services provided . . . are assisting refugees in achieving economic self-sufficiency, achieving ability in English, and achieving employment commensurate with their skills and abilities," and a summary of the information collected at the time refugees become permanent resident aliens. The Refugee Assistance Amendments of 1982 contained additional data collection requirements on two topics: refugee receipt of cash or medical assistance by state of residence and nationality and the secondary migration (away from the initial resettlement site) of refugees in the United States.

The ORR has been assigned the responsibility of carrying out the reporting requirements of the act. Accordingly, an automated data system for compiling and storing records on individual refugees has been established, and a system of regular reports by state grantee agencies to the ORR exists. An annual survey of Southeast Asian refugees provides a regular picture of their progress, focusing on employment and the use of services. Through agreements with other federal agencies, certain additional statistics on refugees are being compiled. Finally, an evaluation research program has produced several studies of topics related to refugee adjustment, and other studies are being done.

Reports by State Agencies to the ORR

Since the first quarter of fiscal 1983, state refugee program agencies have been required to report certain of their program activities to the ORR on form ORR-6. This Quarterly Performance Report is the basis of program statistics on refugee use of cash and medical assistance funded by the ORR and on the number of refugee clients being served in other types of ORR-funded programs. When completed fully and accurately and combined nationwide, these quarterly reports can yield a useful picture of the refugee cash, medical assistance, and social services caseloads supported by the ORR.

ORR Reports

Several regularly scheduled reports are generated from the ORR data system and the state reports submitted to the ORR, others are being developed, and ad hoc reports are produced to meet management needs. Each month, following preparation by the Center for Disease Control of its tape file of arriving refugees, the ORR prepares a set of monthly report tables, which provides current monthly and fiscal-year-to-date arrival figures. This set, which is the basis of the ORR monthly data report, normally contains five standard tables: estimated total state populations of Southeast Asian refugees; arrival numbers by state of resettlement; arrival numbers by country of birth and country of citizenship; age-sex distribution of arrivals; and arrival numbers by sponsoring agency. This report is distributed by the ORR to all state refugee program agencies, the national headquarters of the voluntary agencies, other federal agencies, and congressional offices. Further distribution by these recipients is encouraged, and state refugee program coordinators have agreed to serve as distribution centers for their own local agencies and service providers.

The ORR also produces state-specific tables covering the same subjects as the national tables, with each state's arrivals broken down further by county of resettlement. These monthly reports are distributed to the state refugee program coordinators in the mailing with the national report. The county-level tables also are used by ORR officials for detailed analysis of resettlement patterns and to assist them in deciding where to place special projects and direct special funding.

At the close of each fiscal year, a number of special tables are produced from the ORR data system for the annual Report to the Congress. Some of these tables essentially summarize the information presented in the monthly tables. In addition, information from the state reports on public assistance utilization and secondary migration are presented. The statistics represent the ORR's official program statistics for the year just ended. A narrative discussion accompanies the tables. Other statistical reports are not presented in tabular form in the Report to the Congress but are summarized in the narrative.

The permanent resident alien file is also a major source of follow-up information on refugees. The data are collected by the INS on form I-643 and given to the ORR for presentation in its Report to the Congress. In use since 1982, the I-643 form is completed at the time a refugee applies for adjustment of status to permanent resident alien; it includes items on changes in residence since entry, household composition, work history, and the use of cash assistance programs.

The ORR also carries out an annual survey of Southeast Asian refugees, which represents the continuation of a series of nationwide telephone surveys that were begun in 1975. The survey is done in October. Sample sizes in recent years have ranged from 1,000 to 1,300. Its major purpose is to fulfill a requirement in the Refugee Act of 1980 to report to Congress annually on "an updated profile of the employment and labor force statistics for refugees who have entered under this Act since May 1975, as well as a description of the extent to which refugees received the forms of assistance or services under this chapter during that period." Questions in the survey focus on labor force participation, employment, participation in educational and training programs, and the use of public assistance. Major findings appear in the annual Report to the Congress.

Information From Other Federal Agencies Through interagency agreements, ORR is currently funding studies on refugees based on data from two existing federal sources: the Medicaid system and the Internal Revenue Service. The Medicaid study, which is limited to three states, will obtain information on the patterns of refugee use of public medical assistance, including type of service, frequency, cost, and the condition for which assistance is sought. The IRS study, based on aggregate data for 1980, 1981, and 1982, covers numbers of tax returns filed, aggregate income reported (by source), and total federal income taxes paid by the cohort of Southeast Asian refugees who entered the United States in the 1975-1979 period. This cohort of refugees is identifiable because its members were assigned special social security numbers during entry processing; similar information for this cohort will be obtained for subsequent tax years.

The ORR Evaluation Research Program Since fiscal 1981 ORR has funded a number of research contracts to assess refugee adjustment to life in the United States and to evaluate ORR-supported projects to facilitate adjustment. Among the issues covered in those studies are economic self-sufficiency, the role of the refugee community, the effectiveness of language training programs, and residency patterns and secondary migration.

At present, the ORR data collection system is well-established and capable of generating information on a wide range of issues. The major weakness in the system is the lack of in-house analytic capacity or adequate funding either to allow for timely distribution of the data for analysis or to permit contracting for analytic resources outside the agency.

CONCLUSIONS AND RECOMMENDATIONS

It is quite clear that the processes involved in determining those refugees eligible for entry into the United States and in effecting the long journey from refugee camp to resettlement in this country are both complex and involve a variety of participants here and abroad. They require and generate many different kinds of data for use in administrative control, program management, program evaluation, policy review, and policy development. However, the utility of the data is compromised by uncertain quality that is a reflection, in large measure, of an absence of concern with consistency, coordination, and purpose. For example, different series purport to measure the same thing but use different definitions; efforts are needlessly duplicated; one group revises a form without consulting a second group whose data needs are based on the same form. Yet the picture is mixed. The legislation establishing the refugee program in the United States sets an example well worth noting in specifying data requirements and analytical products; the agency charged with meeting these requirements, the Office of Refugee Resettlement, has struggled to meet the mandate and, on the whole, has set an example that others would do well to emulate. But the effort cannot be left to rest there.

Therefore, the Panel recommends that the U.S. Coordinator for Refugee Affairs:

o Establish an interagency task force, representing all federal offices responsible for or concerned with refugee issues. The task force, supplemented by persons with appropriate statistical and data processing competence, would undertake to review the statistical program and provide recommendations:

   --on maximizing the utility of data currently being collected;
   --on establishing standard definitions and resolving existing contradictions in the data;
   --on a priority ranking of data needs and where responsibility for each should be placed;
   --on which data items or series should be deleted;
   --for institutionalizing coordination among the participants in the area of data compilation; and
   --on resources and time required to implement quality control and other appropriate statistical methods designed to ensure the maintenance of an adequate data base for policy and program needs.

8

Data Gaps and Ways to Fill Them

INTRODUCTION

In Chapter 3 we reviewed the kinds of data that are needed for legislators, program managers, and program staff to design and implement immigration policy. Chapters 4 through 7 described the data that are actually available, and the processes by which they are collected. In this chapter we compare the two in order to determine major data gaps--that is, areas in which data are needed by policy makers or by analysts examining the consequences of immigration policies but are not currently available. The treatment inevitably must be rather general. It is not possible to foresee future needs in full detail, nor to define every last piece of information that should be collected from a particular alien, because the exact nature of future policy issues cannot be predicted with precision. Such details must be left to the design stage of a data collection initiative. The planning of such an initiative should aim to incorporate the demographic, social, and economic information likely to be of general relevance to policy issues in a format sufficiently flexible to accommodate future needs as they arise. It is possible, however, to identify both major areas for which data are currently needed and general approaches by which such data can be obtained. This chapter has two major sections, the first discussing data gaps and the second discussing approaches to filling the gaps. We start, however, with a brief discussion of the costs and benefits of data improvements to set the stage for the lengthier discussion of the gaps and ways to plug them.

COSTS AND BENEFITS OF DATA IMPROVEMENTS

All improvements have some cost attached to them, and at a time of acute concern with government spending it is important to weigh the costs of different improvements against the value of the expected improvement in data quality or quantity. In this context, approaches can be listed in ascending order of their likely cost. All the approaches listed require, of course, that the basic data are of good quality. The first essential for any improvement of immigration statistics is thus the implementation of quality-control processes at the data generation stage; in the absence

126

of such quality control, the returns to implementing any of the further approaches listed, however sophisticated they may be, will be disappointing. Given this overriding need for emphasis on data quality, the least expensive way to improve immigration statistics is to improve the presentation of data already collected and available in machine-readable form; costs are limited to initial computer programming time and recurrent marginal computer execution time. The next least expensive way is to process data that are collected but not used; the costs are higher because of the inclusion of recurrent data entry. The third way is to integrate existing data sets; even if the data sets are already in machine-readable form, system planning, interagency coordination, data set preparation, and final execution all have substantial and, except for planning, recurrent costs attached to them. The fourth way is to modify existing data collection procedures; planning, testing, and processing design are the one-time costs, while data collection, preparation, and tabulation are recurrent costs. Finally, the most expensive way to improve immigration statistics is to undertake new data collection initiatives; this approach requires major additional costs, including questionnaire, sample, and data processing design, testing, and implementation.

Evaluating the Benefits of Better Data

The information gains from each approach must be weighed against the relative costs of putting them into effect, to facilitate selecting those that offer the best value. Unfortunately, it is much more difficult to determine the value of a data improvement, or even rank order the values of such improvements, than it is to estimate their likely costs. The best we can do is to indicate the nature of the improvement that would result from a particular strategy and to state that in our collective judgment the potential benefits of our recommendations more than justify their modest costs. The judgment of those to whom we direct our recommendations--the Congress and several executive agencies--must be based on their assessment of the benefits to them of the improved data that our strategies offer.

The Costs of Data Improvements

Costs here should not be interpreted narrowly as merely dollars and cents of government expenditure. Data collection exercises involve costs to those providing the data both in terms of the time spent answering questions or filling in forms and in terms of concerns regarding confidentiality of sensitive information. Public goodwill toward data collection activities will wear thin very rapidly, with adverse effects on data quality, if demands for data are perceived as excessive. Immigrants may be more tolerant than other groups of the time costs of data collection activities, although possibly more suspicious of motivation and official interference, but goodwill toward the INS has already worn thin because of the number, complexity, and repetitiveness of the forms to be filled in and because of the excessive waiting time people spend when dealing with the agency.

Issues of confidentiality and civil liberties are still more thorny. The INS already imposes conditions on the alien population that would be unacceptable to the public at large: permanent residents are required to carry "green cards" at all times, and the INS maintains both machine-readable and hard-copy files on aliens with very limited restrictions on accessibility. Public concern with privacy is probably the major barrier to the linkage of data files between agencies. Ultimately it does not matter whether such concerns are well founded or not (experience over the last decade or so suggests they may be): if a majority of the public regards the construction of "super files" on individuals as an unwarranted intrusion on their civil liberties, the construction of such files will be politically unacceptable. Furthermore, if the development of such a system is opposed by the population at large, it is highly questionable whether a similar system should be imposed on the politically underprivileged population of aliens. This conclusion does not mean that no data set linkages can or should be attempted, but rather that they should be made with due regard for legitimate concerns, with adequate safeguards of privacy, and with adequate protection against use for other than statistical purposes.

Data Generation

The vast majority of the data available about aliens is generated when they come into contact with U.S. officials. Thus information about a permanent immigrant is obtained either at the time of applying for a visa and at first entry to the United States or when a nonimmigrant applies for adjustment to permanent resident status. Further information is obtained at subsequent contacts: in theory at every address change (although in practice such changes probably go unreported quite frequently); when applying for naturalization or other immigration benefits; through income tax returns and social security benefits or contributions; at census enumerations or survey interviews; and when registering births or deaths. The number of observations depends on the number of contacts, which may be with a wide range of government agencies, including the INS, the Internal Revenue Service, the Social Security Administration, the Bureau of the Census, and the National Center for Health Statistics. Some of these contacts will happen for all immigrants (application for status, first entry to the United States, census enumeration); some will happen for a large majority (income tax filing, social security contributions); and the remainder (address change, application for naturalization or other benefit, social security benefit, registration of births or death) will depend on events in the immigrant's life in the United States.

Data Linkages

If it were possible to link together the information from all these contacts, our knowledge of what happens to immigrants would be greatly expanded (but there would still be gaps and uncertainties arising from noncoverage of departures from the United States, from the less-than-universal coverage of other systems, and from the inability to collect all the desirable information for each contact; the census, for example, cannot reasonably ask about the visa status of noncitizens). In practice, it is often not possible to link records across agencies, either because of confidentiality restrictions or because of a lack of suitable and accurate identifiers. Even within agencies, notably the INS, opportunities for record linkage--for example between immigrant and naturalization applications or between entries and annual address reports--have not been exploited. However, since not all unmet data needs could be met even by complete linkage, and since complete linkage is not a politically acceptable proposition, we must examine carefully what the most pressing unmet data needs are and how they can be met acceptably.

The next section discusses the major unmet data needs of policy makers in the area of immigration. This discussion provides the framework for the third section, which explores what can be obtained by implementing different improvements.

UNMET DATA NEEDS

There are five groups of aliens that are of major importance for policy formation: permanent resident aliens, refugees, asylees, temporary workers, and illegal residents. Minor policy issues arise for some other groups (such as the Simpson-Mazzoli bill's visa waiver scheme to make it easier for visitors to enter the country), but by and large there is no dispute about either the principle (whether they should be admitted) or the magnitude (how many should be admitted) of entries of temporary visitors, employees of international organizations, crew members, treaty traders, intracompany transfers, full-time students in higher education, and the like. The information needed for the five important groups shares common elements but also differs in key respects, reflecting the different policy questions relevant to each group.

Immigrants

For immigrants, the most obvious issues are how many should be admitted each year and what criteria should be used to decide which applicants to admit. Both issues involve judgments that are not immediately amenable to quantitative assessment--for instance, to answer the question of whether a higher level of immigration, though beneficial overall, would impose unacceptable costs on the poor requires not only data to estimate the possible effects but also a definition of what is unacceptable--and are also too broad for determining information needs. What are needed are enough data to evaluate current policy rather than all possible policies and to answer specific questions. For example: do new immigrants put legal residents out of work or do they create additional jobs? To answer this question, data are needed on where immigrants first settle and on their initial labor market experience (activity, type of employment, wage rate or earnings, type of employer, nature of work), and parallel data are needed for the existing resident population (both citizen and noncitizen). Many such data exist, at least with regard to participation in the formal economy, in IRS, Social Security

Administration, or Bureau of the Census records; however, there is insufficient detail, particularly to distinguish between new permanent residents, existing permanent immigrants, nonimmigrants, and illegal residents. Given the lack of INS data on settlement and secondary migration patterns of immigrants, the necessary data would be difficult to construct even if perfect interagency data linkage were possible. Are immigrants net contributors to, or recipients from, public revenues? Again, many relevant data exist, but it is not possible to link records for a particular individual or even group, such as all nonimmigrants. Whatever the question, the data gaps are similar--detail, individual identifiers for record linkages, visa history, history of life in the United States, and history of life before coming to the United States.

Turning to admission criteria, the policy questions are rather more concrete. Since 80 percent of immigrants are admitted under family reunification preferences, one can examine the underlying rationale for such a policy by examining the results in terms of the family structure of such admissions. Do the families remain united? One could find out whether emigration rates of principal aliens whose spouses or children are admitted under the second preference are higher or lower than those of other aliens; whether emigration or secondary migration rates are higher or lower for those admitted under the family reunification preferences than for other immigrants and how they vary by preference category; whether naturalization rates are higher or lower for some preference admissions than for others. One could also determine whether immigrants admitted under the various family reunification preferences perform better or worse than other immigrant groups in terms of income, assimilation, naturalization, and the like. For immigrants admitted with occupational preferences, policy makers would probably like to know whether the immigrants so admitted actually alleviate labor market shortages, whether they continue to work in the same field after admission, how well they perform relative to native-born workers in that field and to earlier cohorts of immigrants, and what proportions become naturalized or emigrate. What are needed are data on the history of life in the United States by the preference category of entry and country of origin of the immigrant; existing sources provide very little, since it is not possible to link data across data sets and agencies for given individuals.

Refugees

Data needs for refugees are somewhat different, since the admissions policy is at least partly altruistic, numbers of admissions are set by the perceived world refugee pressure, and refugee admissions have an immediate cash cost in terms of resettlement assistance. Selection, however, is based only partly on need and partly on family ties or other connections in the United States. Data on the world refugee situation come largely from the U.N. High Commissioner for Refugees; although the data are of limited scope, covering mainly refugees living in camps, and of limited accuracy (as detailed in Chapter 7), they provide a broad indication of the numbers and geographical concentrations of refugees throughout the world. Improvement of that data system, though useful, is not essential for U.S. policy purposes and would require an international cooperative program that the United States could stimulate but could not run.

Given that the number of refugees who need resettlement is known with adequate accuracy, the question of how many the United States should admit depends in part on how much they cost in terms of cash and program assistance; how quickly they become self-supporting; how well they assimilate; whether on a lifetime (and suitably discounted) basis their contributions to public revenues exceed their receipts; whether they displace domestic workers; how much impact they have on local communities in which they settle; and so on--much the same subquestions, with a few additions about cash assistance, as for permanent immigrants. Data availability is substantially higher, however, for refugees than for immigrants, with a tracking system for the 3-year period during which they are eligible for benefits and a regular though small follow-up survey by telephone. After the 3-year eligibility period, responsibility for refugees passes from the Office of Refugee Resettlement to the INS, and data availability declines drastically; it ceases to be possible to track individual performance or to distinguish refugees from other foreign-born residents. Thus, the most important unmet data needs relate to the long-term performance in the United States of those admitted as refugees and the impact on future immigration of refugees who become permanent residents or naturalized citizens and apply for family reunification benefits. Reasonable data, though lacking depth of detail, already exist for most policy and program purposes for the early stages of the resettlement process thanks to the efforts of the Office of Refugee Resettlement.

Asylees

The data needs for establishing policy concerning the granting of asylum share some common elements with the data needs concerning the admission of refugees, since the justification for asylum is largely altruistic, although the issue of cash benefits, to which asylees are not entitled, does not arise. Asylum is granted on the grounds of well-founded fear of persecution or discrimination in the country of origin, so information is needed to establish how well-founded such fears are in particular cases. However, asylees have a social and economic impact on the United States, so the question of how many applications to grant depends not only on the numbers meeting the formal requirements but also on their costs and benefits to society, implying data needs similar to those for immigrants.

Temporary Workers

Temporary workers are admitted to the United States for short, specified periods to meet temporary labor shortages or for such special purposes as musical or sporting events. The number of people thus admitted is small, about 40,000 in fiscal 1981, and their long-term economic and social impact probably is also small. The policy issues involved are whether labor shortages really justify the admission of such workers or the workers thus admitted are taking jobs that legal residents would otherwise take. This question is not as simple as it sounds: residents may not be willing to take such jobs for the minimum wages offered, but might take them at the higher wage levels that would have to be offered if temporary workers were not available, thus increasing costs and prices, but also increasing domestic employment and reducing losses from remittances abroad. There is also the question of whether the workers actually leave the country when their work is completed (or the admission period runs out) or stay on illegally.

The first issue requires estimates of the wage elasticity of the supply of domestic labor and of the wages paid to the temporary workers, as well as information on the potential for substituting capital for labor; such information is best provided by micro-level studies of particular industries rather than by a national immigration statistics system. The second issue, of compliance with terms of entry, requires the sort of linkage within the INS of arrival, departure, and location of deportable alien records that will become available when the INS long-range ADP plan is fully implemented. Thus, apart from a need for small-scale industry studies and a need for more complete coverage of departing aliens, the data needs for this group are in the process of being met.

Illegal Aliens

Illegal aliens are important for a number of policy reasons. First, they attract more political attention and generate more political passion than any other group of noncitizens. The presumed ill effects, both social and economic, of the presence of illegal aliens in the United States also affects public attitudes to, and debate about, broader issues of immigration and refugee policy. The policy questions related to illegal aliens are very similar to those about legal immigrants. Do they take jobs that legal residents would otherwise fill, or do they take jobs that legal residents do not want at the going wage rates? Do they hold down wage rates for menial jobs and slow productive investment? Do they take more in services than they contribute to revenue, and at which levels of government? Do heavy concentrations of illegal aliens increase crime rates, either as perpetrators or as victims? Do they overburden education and health services? Do they come to work temporarily or to settle permanently? Since it costs money to keep illegal aliens out and would cost a very large amount of money to reduce illegal immigration to a trickle, policy makers have to decide how much should be spent on the Border Patrol and other INS activities in trying to keep illegal aliens out: if a steady stream of illegal migrants is beneficial overall, then legal immigration limits could be increased and enforcement activities could be cut back.

Although the data needs for illegal aliens are much the same as those for legal immigrants, virtually no large-scale data sets are available about illegal aliens, and the official collection of such data, with illegal aliens voluntarily identifying themselves as such, is impossible. Some data are collected involuntarily, for instance by the INS from located deportable aliens, but there is no information about either how representative located aliens are of all illegal aliens or what the location rate is. Some illegal aliens are included in official statistics--for example, in the 1980 census results and in birth and death registration--but are not directly identifiable as such.

So-called informed guesses of the number of illegal aliens in the country made in the early 1970s have given way in recent years to estimates derived from a variety of empirical bases; these estimates, reviewed in more detail in Appendix B, are all indirect and rely on numerous assumptions; in general, however, they suggest a range of between 2 and 4 million illegal immigrants in the United States around 1980. Furthermore, there is no evidence to support the view that the illegal population has grown rapidly since 1980, and INS locations data by duration of illegal stay suggest little general change. These estimates of the number of illegal aliens include their distribution by age, sex, and country of origin (though the estimates may be wrong by a factor of two), but little else is known about this 1 to 2 percent of the U.S. population. What is known comes from small-scale, often ethnographic studies carried out by nongovernment researchers, and it is of uncertain generalizability to the total illegal population. An ethnographic study of Mexican immigrants described by Massey in Appendix C illustrates the information that can be obtained from such an approach.

Program Needs

There are also program, as opposed to policy, needs for immigration data. The Bureau of the Census, for instance, is a major user as well as a producer of data on immigration. Current data on international migration are needed to derive postcensal population estimates that are used, among other purposes: as independent controls for the monthly Current Population Survey; for evaluating the coverage of decennial censuses; for the distribution of revenue-sharing funds; and in the computation of widely used and important ratios, ranging from birth and death rates to life insurance survival probabilities. The immigration data used to derive population estimates for the United States have serious deficiencies in addition to the lack of timeliness already mentioned. No reliable information is available on the flow of illegal immigrants to the United States or on emigration from the country. Furthermore, estimates of the migration between the United States and Puerto Rico are computed annually as the residual between the arrival and departure of millions of people to and from Puerto Rico. Finally, the estimates of international migration used by the Census Bureau to derive population estimates exclude any allowance for migration of civilian citizens who are not affiliated with the U.S. government (e.g., employees of international corporations, university personnel, students, retirees, etc.). These needs are for information on the international migration of all U.S. residents, rather than just immigrants or the foreign-born.

APPROACHES TO DATA IMPROVEMENTS

Unmet data needs of immigration policy and program management can be seen to range from a lack of timeliness and quality of data that are produced to data that are not, and never have been, available or even collected. Approaches to improvement, ranked in cost from improved tabulation

134

through improved quality control and broadened scope to new data
collection processes, have already been outlined above. We now turn to a
consideration of what each of these approaches can be expected to
contribute to meeting unmet needs for data.

Improved Data Tabulation

The cheapest and quickest way of increasing the usefulness of data is by
improving the tabulation of machine-readable data sets or by preparing
public-use data tapes. However, the potential for this method of
improvement is limited by what exists; one cannot tabulate what is not
there. The most important improvement that can be made is speed, since
the more up-to-date the information, the more useful it is. The INS
statistical yearbook for fiscal 1980 was issued in early 1984 and that
for fiscal 1981 was issued in mid-1984; these time lags compromise the
value of the data. The ADP systems now being implemented make an
improvement in timeliness readily attainable. No obvious improvements in
data tabulation are necessary, but some tables in the statistical
yearbook could be simplified to reduce both detail and the number of
empty cells by grouping countries, could have revised layouts to improve
readability, and could make use of fuller, more comprehensible
footnotes. The addition of a glossary to the 1981 yearbook represented a
major improvement. Public-use tapes of samples of both immigrants and
nonimmigrants admitted should be prepared each year as a matter of
routine.

The panel therefore recommends that the INS:

o Maintain its efforts to bring the statistical yearbook up to date;
o Reinstate the publication of figures on temporary entrants;
o Review the content of each table;
o Publish the statistical yearbook no later than 6 months after the
end of the fiscal year; and
o Prepare and release public-use samples covering both immigrants
and nonimmigrants.

The Bureau of the Census is to be commended for meeting United
Nations recommendations for tabulations of data on the foreign-born and
on households including foreign-born members from the 1980 census.
However, the gain has been eroded by the excessive time lag involved; the
tables were not available until mid-1984. The Bureau should ensure that
comparable tables are prepared more quickly from the 1990 census. Given
the data collected and the form in which it was collected, there are no
clear ways to improve the tabulation program. However, the collection
method could be improved by, for example, using precoded periods of entry
for the foreign-born that correspond to the periods used for the 1970
census.

The panel therefore recommends that the Bureau of the Census:

o Ensure speedier tabulation of data on the foreign born from the
1990 census; and

o Ensure the maximum comparability with data from earlier censuses, particularly concerning period of entry.

The Office for Refugee Resettlement collects considerable amounts of cross-sectional and longitudinal data concerning refugees, but staff time constraints have limited the amount of data published or made available for outside analysis. Substantially better use could be made of the data through more extensive tabulation or through the release of public-use tapes, to permit analysis of the data beyond the bare reporting requirements specified by Congress. Such improvements cannot be achieved given current ORR staffing levels and would thus require either some increase in staff or collaborative arrangements with outside organizations, either of which could be readily justified given the relative costs of data collection on the one hand and of data processing on the other.

The panel therefore recommends that the Office of Refugee Resettlement:

o Allocate the additional resources necessary to ensure the adequate dissemination of existing data in both tabular and machine-readable form.

The Social Security Administration is an agency that offers some potential for improved data tabulation. It is not primarily interested in statistics--and still less in statistics about immigrants--but it collects information that could be useful for statistical studies of immigration. Systematic tabulation of data from the NUMIDENT file (new applications for social security numbers) for foreign-born people could provide revealing information about patterns of first settlement. We note that tabulations of beneficiaries receiving payments abroad have been used to study the extent of return migration of elderly immigrants.

The Internal Revenue Service also processes some data of potential value for estimating flows of U.S. citizens out of, and back into, the country. Citizens living abroad can, under certain conditions, claim tax allowances for foreign residence. A minimum figure for gross outflow in a year can be obtained as the number of new claims for foreign residence allowances, weighted by number of dependents claimed, while a minimum figure for gross inflow in a year can be obtained as the number of returning residents, with no claims to foreign residence allowances when such a claim had been made the year before (again weighted by number of dependents). Though the policy value of data on inflows and outflows of citizens is low, and the estimates would be affected by changes in tax law, by filing delays, or by citizens not filing at all, the costs of producing suitable tabulations, by country of residence, would not be high, and the program value of the information would be substantial.

Processing of Data Already Collected

Some data collected for administrative purposes may have a statistical value that goes unrealized. Processing and tabulation of such data may be a cost-effective way of increasing data availability. A case in point is the INS form I-213, record of a deportable alien located. While very little is known about the population of deportable or illegal aliens, a considerable amount of information of uncertain quality is collected, supposedly for administrative purposes, for each such person located by the INS. With somewhat more emphasis on data quality and with regular processing, insights into the structure, economic activity, and even size of the illegal alien population could be obtained with very little increase in workload. Indeed, workload might not be increased at all, since the regular processing of I-213 forms would eliminate the need for hand tallies of locations of deportable aliens for summarized reporting on form G-23 (see Chapter 4).

The panel therefore recommends that the INS:

o Process and tabulate data on a regular basis from at least a substantial sample of I-213 forms, and put more emphasis on the quality of the basic data collected.

Improved Record Linkage

Record linkages across and within agencies offer tremendous potential for improving the statistical base for studies of migration. Linkages across agencies would be most valuable. If it were possible to link INS records on immigrant admissions with decennial census data on residence, current and past occupation, income, and recent internal migration, and with Social Security Administration or IRS data on income (or covered earnings) and residence, much of what policy makers need to know about immigrants, nonimmigrants, and even illegal immigrants would become available at modest cost. Unfortunately, such linkages have never been made; the INS has never participated in such an interagency data linkage project, perhaps because of an understandable modesty about its own data sets.

One stumbling block to attempts to link files across agencies is the rules concerning the confidentiality of the respective files. Each agency that collects and maintains data from or about individuals or business establishments, whether for administrative, program, or statistical purposes, strictly limits its release of information to ensure that the persons (or firms) cannot be identified. In many instances, release of individual information beyond the collecting agency is prohibited by statute (as in the case of the Census Bureau); in others, it reflects an administrative decision consistent with maintaining credibility for the program. As a general rule, adherence to confidentiality has been accomplished by deleting the name and specific address of individuals from any publicly released files, by limiting geographic detail to a sufficiently high level (such as a city with 250,000 or more people) to eliminate any possibility of individuals' being identifiable or, in some instances, deleting what might be perceived as unique information from the file (such as exact dollar amounts for people with incomes in excess of $100,000).

The confidentiality issue, and the responses to it in terms of the record file structures of various agencies, raise a number of problems related to the linking of files produced by two or more agencies. The necessity for a high degree of accuracy in the matching process requires the presence of a common, unique characteristic in each file; name, for example, is insufficient, since there may be many John Smiths in any file. Adding other characteristics, such as address, date of birth, wife's maiden name, number of children, will improve matching precision but at the same time will inevitably increase the risk that a particular record in the file can be identified subsequently as that of a particular individual. Thus files that in themselves do not violate confidentiality become suspect in the matching process as the number of characteristics expands. The use of unique identifiers such as social security number, by their very nature, permit the unique identification of an individual.

In recent years, serious discussion has taken place about the issues of privacy and confidentiality. Studies have been undertaken to explore public perception of the meaning of confidentiality and public concerns with the issues (see for example National Research Council, 1979). Debate also has taken place on how confidentiality can be maintained and individual privacy protected while, at the same time, data are provided for important policy purposes. One approach that has been proposed would recognize the major federal statistical agencies as a single entity within which data files could be exchanged for linkage or other statistical use while still honoring the requirements for confidentiality. Research also is under way on methods by which individual data can be modified sufficiently to ensure the confidentiality of the individual, without harming the data for analytic or linkage purposes.

Given the ever-growing resource of administrative data, the large savings to be had in terms of cost and respondent burden, and the gains to be made in analytic terms from linking files, it is essential that efforts continue to develop acceptable solutions to the problem.

The potential of interagency linkage may at present be limited by a lack of suitable identifiers. Although the Social Security Administration, the Internal Revenue Service, and some Census Bureau surveys all collect social security number, all machine-readable data sets suffer from some nonresponse, reporting error, or keying error, which reduces match rates and increases mismatches. The INS data sets do not include social security number in general, more commonly using the A-file number, so linking INS files with records from other agencies would not in practice be easy. Thus, although the potential benefits of interagency linkage are obvious, the practical obstacles make its implementation doubtful. However, intra-agency linkages are feasible and offer solid though less spectacular benefits.

In the past, INS data systems have been designed and operated as discrete entities, not surprisingly given their administrative rather than statistical origins. The new ADP systems being implemented now represent a major change of direction, with data sets generated by each INS process being viewed as modules of a grand, integrated system linked through the Central Index. Once operational, the new systems will make it straightforward to link records of immigration or adjustment of status with subsequent naturalizations; to link apparent overstayers from the I-94 form (arrival records with no matching departure record) with I-213 records of deportable aliens located; to link petitions for immigration benefits with characteristics of the principal alien; and to link notifications of change of address to other records of an alien. It is important that the INS recognize not only the statistical but also the program value of such linkages, and implement regular, routine data tabulation across functionally independent data sets.

The panel thus recommends that the INS:

o Examine and implement procedures to exploit the potential of linking data sets for statistical and program management purposes as an integral part of the long-range ADP plan.

The Social Security Administration is another agency with data sets that could usefully be linked. Current records of contributions and benefits provide information on area of residence, employment, and earnings, while records of initial applications for social security numbers provide background information on age, sex, year of application (a potential surrogate for year of admission), and country of birth. Though gaps in the record would be impossible to interpret (such gaps might result from absence from the United States, low income, or employment not covered by the system), the linkage of data sets internal to the agency would still provide a substantial amount of information about the economic activity of foreign-born residents, and make possible a direct assessment of contributions paid in against benefits paid out.

Modification of Existing Data Collection Procedures

Existing data collection procedures can be improved by raising data quality and by collecting additional pieces of useful information. Data that fail to meet minimum quality standards waste resources devoted to their collection, processing, and analysis and, worse, can result in misleading analytical conclusions and poor policy decisions. As detailed in Chapter 4, many of the INS data collection activities suffer from shortcomings of design, standardization, adequate supervision, and quality control. These shortcomings are particularly serious for data provided by INS administrative data sets--for example, data for border crossers--but have also affected the timeliness and quality of data on immigrants, temporary admissions, and naturalizations. The highest priority must be given to instituting sound collection and processing procedures incorporating step-by-step quality control, without which the collection of additional data would be pointless. Specific recommendations for necessary improvements are presented in Chapter 4 (and repeated in Chapter 9), and in fairness to the INS, some progress has already been made through the introduction of new ADP systems.

At the level of particular data elements, emphasis must be put on the quality of occupational data for immigrants, by ensuring that INS interviewing officers probe the type of work performed by the applicant; at present, these data are virtually useless. There are also some items that could usefully be added to existing collection processes; applications for immigrant status should include a question on formal education; the I-94 arrival and departure form should reinstate questions on gender and port of embarkation or disembarkation; petitions to naturalize should also include questions on formal education. This list is meant to be illustrative rather than exhaustive; a thorough review of the content of all INS forms is overdue and recommended in Chapter 4.

Other agencies have traditionally paid more attention to data quality than has the INS, but they could still improve the usefulness of their data for purposes of U.S. immigration policy by modifying or adding to questions included in existing collection systems. As recommended in Chapter 5, the Bureau of the Census should continue to include questions relevant to the foreign-born consistent with earlier censuses--in particular, should reinstate questions on birthplace of parents in the 1990 census--and to clarify the question on date of entry to the United States to refer clearly to date of entry to take up residence, coding the responses to be consistent with periods used in previous censuses. A module to measure emigration of both immigrants and native-born citizens should also be included in the Current Population Survey, since little is known about emigration levels or patterns and the cost would be modest.

New Data Collection Initiatives

The modifications to data tabulation, processing, linkage, and collection procedures outlined in the previous four sections represent cost-effective improvements of the statistical base available for policy formation, but they cannot fill the largest single lack: good-quality longitudinal data on the process of settlement in the United States by immigrants and refugees, and on the social and economic impact of such settlement on the existing resident population. Even an automated system of record linkage, in which each contact of an immigrant with any official agency would be added to a historical file for the individual, would go only part of the way toward meeting the longitudinal data need, since the individual records would include gaps for periods without official contact and omit important occurrences such as further education, short- or long-term absence from the country, and changes in family and household relationships.

To meet such needs, the panel strongly recommends that Congress mandate that the INS be the lead agency in:

o The establishment of a longitudinal panel survey of a sample of aliens entering the United States or changing visa status during a 1-year period. This sample of an entry cohort would be followed up for a minimum period of 5 years. The survey should be repeated by drawing a new sample of entrants every 5 years thereafter. The sample would consist of:

   (a) Those admitted to permanent resident status, both new immigrants and those changing status;
   (b) Those admitted as temporary residents under educational, training, and short-term work visas; and
   (c) Illegal aliens given legal status under amnesty provisions included in any future amendments to the INA.

For each participant, data would be collected on:

(a) Initial characteristics: sex, age, country of birth, education, occupational history, year of entry, marital status, visa status and admission preference, family ties in the United States, place of initial settlement, and household structure;

(b) Demographic changes, including: marital status, births, death, internal migration, temporary absence from the United States, emigration, formal or vocational education, and household characteristics;

(c) Income and labor force experience in the United States; and

(d) Program participation and service use, including educational and health costs of children; local, state, and federal taxes paid, and social security benefits and contributions.

We recommend that the survey be funded by the INS but conducted under contract by a recognized survey research organization, either public or private, experienced in longitudinal panel design and execution. The sample should be selected from a 1-year cohort of entrants or those changing status, to ensure that the sampling frame is complete and that potential respondents can be located (at time of entry or change of status). Every effort, including the collection of social security numbers and names and addresses of close relatives or friends and the provision of incentives to respondents, should be incorporated as part of the survey approach in order to minimize the dropout rate and to help to locate those who migrate during the life of the study. The study design should incorporate the use of administrative data sets, partly to obtain data and partly for mutual evaluation. To obtain broad support for the study, as well as to identify key data items and to ensure sound design, an advisory panel of representatives of key agencies and experts in the field of immigration research and immigration policy should be established. Implementing this survey will not be inexpensive--we estimate a cost of around $5.5 million over 5 years for a sample of about 6,000 cases--although this cost is small relative to the $58 million budgeted by the INS for fiscal 1984 alone on ADP development and data processing. Such a survey is overdue and data needs are pressing, so work on the survey should start as soon as possible.

A longitudinal sample survey such as that outlined above will meet many data needs, but it cannot be expected to meet all data needs, particularly for small-area or small-group data for which the sample would be too small. There will remain a need for continued analysis of other data and for in-depth studies of particular areas, issues, or groups; such work is best left to universities and other nongovernment research organizations. It should also be stressed that the proposed survey is complementary to other administrative data collection activities. It cannot tell policy makers how many entries of particular categories of aliens there are in a year, but it will provide a basis for predicting what the effects of such entries will be, and of what the effects of changing the numbers in each category would be.

IMPLEMENTATION OF RECOMMENDATIONS

Immigration is an important and emotional area of public policy, yet as we have seen in this report the statistics on which informed debate and policy formation are based are woefully inadequate. Two of the major reasons for this inadequacy have been a lack of interest in or commitment to the production of relevant, high-quality statistics by the agencies having contact with aliens, and the failure of any one agency to take the lead in fostering a governmentwide coordinated system for collecting, processing, and analyzing the necessary data. This leadership role belongs by right to the INS as the agency primarily concerned with immigration policy and process. However, the INS has consistently failed to look beyond its immediate management needs for information, an attitude clearly expressed in its mission plan and in the assumptions underlying its ADP program, and it has on occasion actually impeded existing collaborative interagency agreements by introducing process changes without consultation or regard for outside needs. Blame for the lack of enthusiasm for producing immigration statistics shown by the agencies involved lies partly with the agencies themselves, but some part of the blame must also be borne by the executive branch and Congress: the agencies have not been told clearly enough to produce useful data.

Two courses of action are necessary to improve the present unsatisfactory situation. One is a congressional initiative to mandate specific reporting requirements, particularly for the INS. The Refugee Act of 1980 shows what Congress can do in the area of data production by legislation, and the Simpson-Mazzoli bill also was a clear movement in the right direction.

The panel therefore recommends to Congress that:

o Specific language covering data collection, analysis, and reporting requirements be incorporated into an amendment to the INA and into all other legislation dealing with immigrants, refugees, and other aliens.

The second is for the executive branch to establish an interagency review group to ensure coordination between agencies, action on necessary new initiatives, and due regard for quality control within agencies. Accordingly, the panel recommends:

o That an interagency review group for immigration statistics be established under the aegis of the Statistical Policy Office of the Office of Management and Budget.

This group would be charged with ensuring the coordination across agencies of data collection and processing in the area of migration and refugees and with overseeing the implementation of improvements within agencies, particularly with reference to timeliness, quality control, and responsiveness to changing data needs. An early task for the group would be to examine the recommendations on statistics of international migration of the United Nations (1980), with a view to proposing changes leading to greater conformity with the recommendations. The group would thus provide the leadership that has been so lacking in the past.

Improved coordination alone will go some way toward remedying the past neglect of immigration statistics, but the interagency review group must go further, to bear responsibility for the testing and implementation of the panel's specific, agency-directed recommendations.

With the exception of the proposed longitudinal survey, we have not provided detailed cost estimates for the recommendations given in this chapter. The reason for this omission is that we believe that the cost of the proposed measures, again with the exception of the longitudinal survey and the reorganization within the INS, are small enough to be met within existing budgets, at least in the initial stages of implementation. Some reallocation with current appropriations will be necessary to effect these actions, but such changes fall well within the scope of normal managerial discretion. Estimates of the cost of reorganizing statistical activities in the INS are given in Chapter 4; as noted, we estimate additional recurrent expenditures of some $2.5 million per year once the proposed system is fully operational. This money must be spent to reverse past neglect, but the returns in terms of improved policy making and program monitoring fully justify the additional expenditure.

REFERENCES

National Research Council
  1979   Privacy and Confidentiality as Factors in Survey Response.
          Committee on National Statistics, Assembly of Behavioral and
          Social Sciences. Washington, D.C.: National Academy of
          Sciences.
United Nations
  1980   Recommendations on Statistics of International Migration.
          Department of International Economic and Social Affairs.
          Statistical Office. Statistical Papers Series M No. 58
          (ST/ESA/STAT/SER.M/58) New York: United Nations.

9

Recommendations

This chapter brings together the recommendations made by the panel throughout the report. They are organized here by the body or agency to which they are directed. The discussion of and justification for each recommendation is included in the chapter indicated in parentheses beside the recommendation.

Most of our recommendations are general in nature, concerned with process rather than the particular, and intentionally so. It is the panel's belief, after extensive study of the present situation and how it has arisen, that superficial local patching will not solve the problem. Without major changes in direction from the top policy-making levels and focused interest within the key agencies, the immigration statistics system will never produce reliable, accurate, and timely statistics that permit rational decision making concerning immigration policy. Even the few specific recommendations made by the panel in order to fill particularly important gaps in the statistical picture require that they be implemented in a new context in order to be effective, one in which quality and timely statistics are seen as priority functions of agencies involved with aliens and foreign-born residents. Establishing this new context requires profound and basic changes of attitude in both the legislative and executive branches of government.

The panel recommends that Congress:

o Strongly affirm the importance of reliable, accurate, and timely statistical information on immigration to the needs of the Congress and direct the Attorney General to reexamine the organizational structure of the Immigration and Naturalization Service as it relates to statistics, with a view to placing greater priority on this important task;   (4)

o Require that the Attorney General prepare and submit by June 30 each year an annual report to the President and the Congress, presenting data on aliens admitted or excluded, naturalizations, asylees, and refugees, describing their characteristics, and containing an analysis of significant developments during the preceding year in the field of immigration and emigration; and   (4)

o Mandate that a study be initiated and conducted among new immigrants over a 5-year period, in order to develop information for policy guidance on the adjustment experience of families and individuals to the labor market, use of educational and health facilities, reliance on social programs, mobility experience, and income history. (8)

The panel recommends that the Attorney General:

o Issue a strong policy directive asserting the importance of reliable, accurate, and timely statistical information on immigration to the mission of the INS and unequivocally committing the agency to improving its existing capabilities. (4)

The panel recommends that the commissioner of the INS:

o Issue an explicit statement clearly setting forth that the collection, cumulation, and tabulation of reliable, accurate, and timely statistical information on immigration is a basic responsibility of and inherent in the mission of the agency; (4)
o Establish a Division of Immigration Statistics, reporting directly to an associate commissioner or an equivalent level, with overall responsibility:

--for ensuring the use of appropriate statistical standards and procedures in the collection of data throughout the agency;
--for ensuring the timely publication of a variety of statistical and analytic reports;
--for providing statistical assistance to all parts of the Service to help in carrying out their mission;
--for directing statistical activities throughout the agency; (4)

o Direct and implement the recruitment of a full complement of competent, trained professionals with statistical capabilities and subject-area expertise; (4)
o Initiate a review of all data-gathering activities to eliminate duplication, minimize burden and waste, review specific data item needs and uses, improve question wording and format design, standardize definitions and concepts, document methodologies, introduce statistical standards and procedures, and promote efficiencies in the use of staff and resources; (4)
o Establish an advisory committee composed of experts in the use and production of immigration-related data to advise the associate commissioner and the proposed Division of Immigration Statistics of needs for new or different types of data; to review existing data and data collection methodology; to advise on the statistical implications and potential of ADP plans; and to provide the agency with independent evaluation of its statistical products, plans, and performance; (4)
o Establish formal liaison with other federal and state agencies involved in the collection or analysis of immigration-related data; (4)
o Establish both a program to enhance and stimulate research into the various effects of immigration and a fellows program, which would bring to the agency for a period not to exceed 2 years outstanding scholars and experts to undertake original research using published or unpublished data from the INS or other sources; (4)

o Authorize the proposed Division of Immigration Statistics to initiate a program of contract research. This research, which may be either extramural or intramural, should be focused on the evaluation of data production and data quality; (4)

o Strengthen the annual report, presenting data on immigrants, nonimmigrants, naturalizations, asylees, parolees, and refugees, describing their characteristics, and analyzing significant developments during the previous fiscal year. The report should be published annually by June 30; (4)

o Establish a process ensuring adequate discussion and consideration both within and outside the agency of changes in forms and data collection procedures; (4)

o Institute such other activities as are necessary and desirable to ensure:

--understanding at all levels of the agency of the commissioner's commitment to high-quality, timely statistical data;
--agreement with, and support for, the commissioner's policy directive; and (4)

o Initiate the planning for and establish a longitudinal study of aliens to be conducted for a minimum 5-year period, to guide and assist future amendment of legislation and for continuing administration of programs. Data would be collected from a sample of:

--persons admitted legally under the regular immigrant preferences
--persons granted entry visas as nonimmigrants
--aliens given legal status under any amnesty program

and would focus on:

--the geographical dispersion and subsequent migration
--income and labor market experience
--program participation and service use. (8)

The panel recommends that the director, Office of Management and Budget (OMB):

o Ensure that OMB exercise its responsibilities to monitor and review statistical activities and budgets concerning statistics on immigration and emigration, and particularly those of the INS, to minimize duplication and ensure that appropriate procedures are used, standards met, and priorities observed in the collection, production, and publication of such data; (4,5,8)

o Require and establish an interagency review group responsible for direction and coordination in the field of immigration and emigration data; the group would examine consistency and comparability in concepts and definitions used by individual organizations in the collection of such information including due regard for the recommendations of the United Nations in this field; and oversee the introduction and use of standardized approaches; and (4,5,8) o Actively encourage and support the timely publication and dissemination of data on immigration, emigration, and refugees, the ready availability of fully documented public-use data tapes, including, when feasible, samples of individual records (with identifiers removed) conforming to the requirements of the Privacy Act, and data summaries.   (4,5,8

The panel recommends that the U.S. Coordinator for Refugee Affairs:

o Establish an interagency task force, representing all federal offices responsible for or concerned with refugee issues. The task force, supplemented by persons with appropriate statistical and data processing competence, would undertake to review the statistical program for refugees and asylees and provide recommendations:

--on maximizing the utility of data currently being collected;
--on establishing standard definitions and resolving existing contradictions on the data;
--on a priority ranking of data needs and where responsibility for each should be placed;
--on which data items or series should be deleted;
--for institutionalizing coordination among the participants in the area of data compilation; and
--on resources and time required to implement control and other appropriate statistical methods designed to ensure the maintenance of a data base of adequate quality.   (7)

Regarding other government and nongovernment sources of immigration data, the panel recommends that:

o The State Department become an active participant in interagency discussions on improving immigration statistics, in order to enhance its own understanding of the need for and uses of such information;   (5,7)
o The State Department establish its own review group to assess the statistical potential of its programs, to review such actions as it might take to improve its statistical performance, and to make appropriate recommendations to the department;   (5,7)
o The Department of Labor collect and publish summary information for employers who petition for the admission of foreign workers, including those requested under the H-2 provisions;   (5)
o The Census Bureau restore a question on place of birth of parents to the 1990 census form;   (5)
o The Census Bureau make every effort to maintain consistency in question wording and tabulation detail from one decennial census to the next in areas relating to the foreign-born, so that immigrant cohorts recorded in successive censuses can be linked or compared on a consistent and common basis in order to assess adjustment experience;   (5)
o The Census Bureau initiate a program of research leading to improved estimates of emigration. As one approach, the panel strongly endorses the testing of an emigration module involving the collection of information on the residence of close relatives, as a supplement to the Current Population Survey;   (5)

o The U.S. Travel and Tourism Administration explore alternative data collection approaches for the measurement of tourism in order to obtain more reliable information;   (5)

o The Social Security Administration (SSA) incorporate data on nativity, country of birth, and, when possible, citizenship and visa status into its series of tabulations on workers and beneficiaries;   (5)

o SSA develop a program of special tabulations to be available on a cost-reimbursable basis to support analyses of the integration of immigrant groups into domestic economic and social sectors;   (5)

o SSA develop appropriate mechanisms for evaluating and, if necessary, improving the quality of data on country of birth and legal residence status that are captured in its statistical system;   (5)

o SSA explore with the Statistical Policy Office of OMB approaches to permit the sharing of Continuous Work History Sample files with researchers and analysts outside SSA;   (5)

o The National Center for Health Statistics (NCHS) initiate the coding of the country of birth for vital events;   (5)

o NCHS routinely prepare analyses and publish tabulations of vital events for immigrant populations;   (5)

o NCHS institute a program to evaluate and improve the quality of data on place of birth; and   (5)

o All the agencies and organizations involved with statistics on immigration undertake a review of their data-gathering efforts in order to:

--minimize duplication and burden and maximize quality and utility of the collected information;

--develop approaches leading to timely publication and dissemination of such data including, where appropriate, the preparation and release of fully documented micro-data public-use tapes; and

--establish and maintain formal liaison with other federal agencies involved in the collection or analyses of immigration related data;   (5)

o Insofar as is feasible, official government data on immigrants and refugees should be made available to researchers outside the government;   (6)

o The proposed Division of Immigration Statistics in the INS identify and consult with the user community and keep it informed about the availability of data and changes in procedures. This recommendation also applies to all other agencies that produce data; and   (6)

o Government agencies that provide funds for research should be encouraged to give particular attention to the need for well-done studies of immigration.   (6)

In making its recommendations, the panel has been mindful of costs. Many of its recommendations fall within the scope and margin of administrative discretion, and, if they require additional funds, the amounts are relatively small. Two of the panel's major recommendations will require new funding, but in both cases implementation will be gradual, with expenditures spread over a number of years. The major recommendation for change in administrative structure concerns the establishment of a Division of Immigration Statistics within the INS, which will have increased authority, responsibility, and professional staff. We expect, however, that a period of 3-5 years will be required for the full development of such a division, in order to locate and integrate new staff and to acquire new responsibilities and demonstrate capability on a step-by-step basis. Thus, the initial cost implications are modest and the cost increments can be viewed in the light of some initial accomplishments. The major recommendation for a new data collection initiative, the longitudinal survey of immigrants, also requires new funding but, again, the estimated cost will be spread over a number of years and is amply justified in the view of the panel.

Glossary

The terms as well as the list of acronyms in this glossary are highly selective and include only some of the more commonly used terms and acronyms found in the report.

ACQUIRED CITIZENSHIP - Citizenship conferred at birth for children born abroad to a citizen parent(s).

ADJUSTMENT TO IMMIGRANT STATUS - Procedure allowing certain aliens already in the United States to apply for immigrant status. Aliens admitted to the United States in a nonimmigrant or other category may have their status changed to that of lawful permanent resident if they are eligible to receive an immigrant visa as a permanent resident and an immigrant visa is immediately available. In such cases, the alien is counted as an immigrant as of the date of adjustment, even though the alien may have been in the United States for an extended period of time.

ALIEN - Any person not a citizen or a national of the United States.

ALIEN ADDRESS REPORT PROGRAM - A now-defunct annual registration program for aliens. Until P.L. 97-116 (Act of 12/29/81) eliminated the stipulation, all aliens in the United States were required to register with the Immigration and Naturalization Service each January. Nationality and state of residence data were compiled annually on the alien population reporting under the program. The last year for which data are available is 1980.

APPREHENSION - The arrest of a deportable alien by the Immigration and Naturalization Service. Each apprehension of the same alien in a fiscal year is counted separately.

ASYLEE - An alien in the United States or at a port of entry unable or unwilling to return to his or her country of nationality, or to seek the protection of that country because of persecution or a well-founded fear of persecution. Persecution or the fear thereof may be based on the alien's race, religion, nationality, membership in a particular social group, or political opinion. For persons with no nationality, the country of nationality is considered to be the one in which the alien last habitually resided.

BENEFICIARIES - Those aliens who receive immigration benefits from petitions filed with the Immigration and Naturalization Service. Beneficiaries generally derive privilege or status as a result of their relationship (including that of employer-employee) to a U.S. citizen or lawful permanent resident.

BORDER CROSSER - An alien or citizen resident of the United States reentering the country across land borders after an absence of less than six months in Canada or Mexico, or a nonresident alien entering the United States across the Canadian border for stays of no more than six months or across the Mexican border for stays of no more than 72 hours, or a U.S. citizen residing in Canada or Mexico who enters the United States frequently for business or pleasure.

BORDER PATROL SECTOR - Any one of 21 geographic areas into which the United States is divided for the Immigration and Naturalization Service's Border Patrol activities. Of the 21 sectors, all but one are located along the northern and southern borders of the United States.

CERTIFICATE OF CITIZENSHIP - Identity document proving U.S. citizenship. Certificates of citizenship are issued to derivative citizens and to persons who acquired U.S. citizenship (see definitions for acquired and derivative citizenship).

COUNTRY OF FORMER ALLEGIANCE - The previous country of citizenship of a naturalized U.S. citizen or of a person who derived U.S. citizenship.

COUNTRY OF LAST RESIDENCE - The country in which an alien habitually resided prior to entering the United States.

CREWMAN - A foreign national serving in any capacity on board a vessel or aircraft. Crewmen are admitted for 29 days, with no extensions. Crewmen required to depart on the same vessel on which they arrived are classified as D-1s. Crewmen who depart on a vessel different than the one on which they arrived are classified D-2s.

CUBAN/HAITIAN ENTRANT - Status accorded: (1) Cubans who entered the United States illegally prior to June 19, 1980, and (2) Haitians who entered the country illegally before January 1, 1981.

DECLARATION OF INTENTION - Form once filed by a lawful permanent resident as the first step toward naturalization. After two years' residence as an immigrant, the alien could file an application for naturalization. A declaration of intention has not been required of all applicants for naturalization since 1952. However, an immigrant may need to file the form for employment purposes.

DEPORTABLE ALIEN - An alien in the United States subject to any of the 19 grounds of deportation specified in the Immigration and Nationality Act. This includes any alien illegally in the United States, regardless of whether the alien entered the country illegally or entered legally but subsequently violated the terms of his or her visa.

DEPORTATION - The formal removal of an alien from the United States when the presence of that alien is deemed inconsistent with the public welfare. Deportation is ordered by an immigration judge without any punishment being imposed or contemplated.

DERIVATIVE CITIZENSHIP - Citizenship conveyed to children through the naturalization of parents or, under certain circumstances, to spouses of citizens at marriage.

DISTRICT - Any one of 35 geographic areas into which the United States and its territories are divided for INS field operations or one of three overseas offices located in Rome, Hong Kong, or Mexico City. Operations are supervised by a district director located at a district office within the district's geographic boundaries.

EMIGRANT - A person who leaves one country to live in another country.

EXCLUSION - The formal denial of an alien's entry into the United States. The exclusion of the alien is made by an immigration judge after an exclusion hearing.

EXEMPT FROM NUMERICAL LIMITATIONS - Those aliens accorded lawful permanent residence who are exempt from the provisions of the preference system set forth in immigration law. Exempt categories include immediate relatives of U.S. citizens, refugees, special immigrants, and certain other immigrants.

EXPATRIATION - The loss of citizenship as a result of a formal transference of loyalties to another country.

FILES CONTROL OFFICE - An INS field office--either a district office (including INS overseas offices) or a suboffice of that district--in which alien case files are maintained and controlled.

FISCAL YEAR - The 12-month period beginning October 1 and running through September 30. Prior to fiscal 1977, the fiscal year ran from July 1 through June 30.

FOREIGN STATE OF CHARGEABILITY - The independent country to which an immigrant entering under the preference system is accredited. Independent countries cannot exceed 20,000 immigrants in a fiscal year. Dependencies of independent countries cannot exceed 600 of the 20,000 limit. Chargeability is usually determined by country of birth. Exceptions are made to prevent the separation of family members when the limitation for the country of birth has been met.

GENERAL NATURALIZATION PROVISIONS - The basic requirements for naturalization that every applicant must meet, unless a member of a special class. General provisions require an applicant to be at least 18 years of age, a lawful permanent resident with 5 years of continuous residence in the United States, and to have been physically present in the country for half that period.

GEOGRAPHIC AREA OF CHARGEABILITY - Any one of five regions--Africa, East Asia, Latin America and the Caribbean, the Near East, and South Asia, and the USSR and Eastern Europe--into which the world is divided for the initial admission of refugees to the United States. Annual consultations between the executive branch and the Congress determine the number of refugees that can be admitted to the United States from each area.

HEMISPHERIC CEILINGS - Statutory limits on immigration to the United States in effect from 1968 to October 1978. Mandated by the Immigration and Nationality Act Amendments of 1965, the ceiling on immigration from the Eastern Hemisphere was set at 170,000, with a per-country limit of 20,000. Immigration from the Western Hemisphere was held to 120,000, without a per-country limit until January 1, 1977. The Western Hemisphere was then subject to a 20,000 per-country limit.

ILLEGAL ALIEN - A person entering the United States without inspection by the INS, or with fraudulent documentation, or entering legally but subsequently violating the visa terms.

IMMEDIATE RELATIVES - Certain immigrants who because of their close relationship to U.S. citizens are exempt from the numerical limitations imposed on immigration to the United States. Immediate relatives are: spouses of citizens, children (under 21 years of age) of citizens, parents of citizens 21 years of age or older, and orphans adopted by U.S. citizens who are at least 21 years of age.

IMMIGRANT - An alien admitted to the United States as a lawful permanent resident. Immigrants are those persons lawfully accorded the privilege of residing permanently in the United States. They may be issued immigrant visas by the Department of State overseas or adjusted to permanent resident status by INS in the United States.

INTERNATIONAL MIGRATION - A change of residence across national boundaries.

LABOR CERTIFICATION - Requirement falling on (1) those persons whose immigration to the United States is based on job skills (third, sixth, and nonpreference immigrant categories) and (2) nonimmigrant temporary workers (H-2s) coming to perform services unavailable in the United States. Labor certification is awarded by the secretary of labor when there are insufficient numbers of U.S. workers available to undertake the employment sought by an applicant and when the alien's employment will not have an adverse effect on the wages and working conditions of U.S. workers similarly employed. Determination of U.S. labor availability is made at the time of a visa application and at the location in which the applicant wishes to work.

NATIONALITY - The country of a person's citizenship.

NATURALIZATION - The conferring, by any means, of citizenship upon a person after birth.

NATURALIZATION COURT - Any court authorized to award U.S. citizenship. Jurisdiction for naturalization has been conferred upon the following courts: U.S. District Courts in all states, the District of Columbia, and Puerto Rico; the District Courts of Guam and the Virgin Islands; and state courts. Generally, naturalization courts are authorized to award citizenship only to those persons who reside within their territorial jurisdiction.

NATURALIZATION PETITION - The form used by a lawful permanent resident to apply for U.S. citizenship. The petition is filed with a naturalization court through the Immigration and Naturalization Service.

NEW ARRIVAL - A lawful permanent resident alien who enters the United States at a port of entry. The alien is generally required to present an immigrant visa, issued outside the United States by a consular officer of the Department of State. Three classes of immigrants, however, need not have an immigrant visa to enter the United States--children born abroad to lawful permanent resident aliens, children born subsequent to the issuance of an immigrant visa to accompanying parents, and American Indians born in Canada.

NONIMMIGRANT - An alien who seeks temporary entry to the United States for a specific purpose. The alien must have a permanent residence abroad and qualify for the nonimmigrant classification sought. Nonimmigrants include: foreign government officials, officials and employees of international organizations, visitors for business and pleasure, crewmen, students, trainees, and temporary workers of distinguished merit and ability or who perform services unavailable in the United States. Refugees are also considered nonimmigrants when initially admitted.

NONPREFERENCE CATEGORY - Visa numbers not used in any of the first six categories of the preference system (see Figure 2-2). Nonpreference visas are available to any applicant not entitled to one under the other preferences. Nonpreference numbers have been unavailable since September 1978 because of high demand in the preference categories.

OCCUPATION - For an alien entering the United States or adjusting without a labor certification, occupation refers to the employment held in the country of last or legal residence or the United States. For an alien with a labor certification, occupation is the employment for which certification has been issued. Labor certification would be issued to immigrants in the third, sixth, and nonpreference categories or to nonimmigrant temporary workers (H-2) performing services unavailable in United States.

OCCUPATIONAL PREFERENCES - The third and sixth categories of the preference system. Third preference allows for the admission of members of the professions and scientists or artists of exceptional ability. Sixth preference covers skilled or unskilled occupations for which labor is in short supply in the United States.

PAROLEE - An alien allowed to enter the United States under emergency conditions or when that alien's entry is determined to be in the public interest. Parole is temporary and does not constitute a formal admission to the United States. Persons paroled into the United States are required to leave when the conditions supporting their parole cease to exist.

PER-COUNTRY LIMIT - The maximum number of immigrant visas that can be issued to any one country in a fiscal year. Independent countries can currently use no more than 20,000 visa numbers; their dependencies no more than 600 of that total. The per-country limit does not mean, however, that a country will be given 20,000 visa numbers each year, just that it cannot receive more than that number. Because of the combined workings of the preference system and per-country limits, most countries do not reach this level of visa issuance.

PERMANENT RESIDENT ALIEN - A person entering the country with an immigrant visa, or adjusting to this status after having entered on a nonimmigrant visa or as a refugee or asylee, and thus entitled to live and work in the United States.

PORT OF ENTRY - Any location in the United States or its territories which is designated as a point of entry for aliens and U.S. citizens. All district and files control offices are also considered ports since they become locations of entry for aliens adjusting to immigrant status.

PREFERENCE SYSTEM - The six categories among which 270,000 immigrant visa numbers are distributed each year: (1) unmarried sons and daughters (over 21 years of age) of U.S. citizens (20 percent); (2) spouses and unmarried sons and daughters of lawful permanent residents (26 percent); (3) members of the professions or persons of exceptional ability in the sciences and arts (10 percent); (4) married sons and daughters of U.S. citizens (10 percent); (5) brothers and sisters of U.S. citizens over 21 years of age (24 percent); and (6) needed skilled or unskilled workers (10 percent). A seventh nonpreference category, historically open to immigrants not entitled to a visa number under one of the six preferences just listed, has had no numbers available since September 1978.

PRINCIPAL ALIEN - The alien from whom another alien derives a privilege or status under immigration law or regulation.

REFUGEE - Any person who is outside his or her country of nationality and who is unable or unwilling to return to that country because of persecution or a well-founded fear of persecution. Persecution or the fear thereof may be based on the alien's race, religion, nationality, membership in a particular social group, or political opinion. People with no nationality must be outside their country of last habitual residence to qualify as a refugee.

REFUGEE APPROVALS - The number of refugees approved for admission to the United States during a fiscal year. Refugee approvals are made by INS officers in overseas offices.

REFUGEE AUTHORIZED ADMISSIONS - The maximum number of refugees allowed to enter the United States in a given fiscal year. As set forth in the Refugee Act of 1980, P.L. 96-212, the annual figure is determined by the President after consultations with Congress.

REFUGEE-CONDITIONAL ENTRANT - An alien who entered the United States or who adjusted to lawful permanent resident status under the seventh preference category of P.L. 89-236, the Act of October 3, 1965. Visa numbers for conditional entrants were limited to 6 percent of the total numerical limitation. The seventh preference was abolished by the Refugee Act of 1980 (P.L. 96-212) and the 6 percent limitation assigned to second preference. At the same time, the worldwide numerical limit was reduced from 290,000 to 270,000.

REFUGEE-PAROLEE - A qualified applicant for conditional entry, between February 1970 and April 1980, whose application for admission to the United States could not be approved because of inadequate numbers of seventh preference visas. As a result, the applicant was paroled into the United States.

REGION - Any one of four areas of the United States among which the Immigration and Naturalization Service's district offices are divided for administrative purposes--Eastern Region, Southern Region, Northern Region, and Western Region.

RELATIVE PREFERENCES - The first, second, fourth, and fifth categories of the preference system. The first preference allows the entry of unmarried sons and daughters (over 21 years of age) of U.S. citizens. Second preference covers spouses and unmarried sons and daughters of aliens lawfully admitted for permanent residence. Fourth preference allows for the entry of married sons and daughters of U.S. citizens. Fifth preference deals with the brothers and sisters of U.S. citizens, provided such citizens are at least 21 years of age.

REQUIRED DEPARTURE - The directed departure of an alien from the United States without an order of deportation. The departure may be voluntary or involuntary on the part of the alien and may or may not have been preceded by a hearing before an immigration judge.

SILVA IMMIGRANTS - Immigrants from independent Western Hemisphere countries and their spouses and children who were issued preference numbers under the Silva Program (1977-1981). The Silva Program was instituted by court order to provide for the recapture of 144,946 preference visa numbers originally used for Cuban refugee adjustments. Silva numbers, although subject to an overall numerical limitation, were assigned in addition to the annual worldwide ceiling.

SIMPSON-MAZZOLI - Shorthand reference to legislation sponsored by Senator Simpson (Wyoming) and Representative Mazzoli (Kentucky) to amend the Immigration and Nationality Act. Somewhat different versions of the legislation were approved by each House; passage of a reconciled version of the legislation was not accomplished before final adjournment of the 98th Congress.

SPECIAL IMMIGRANTS - Certain categories of immigrants exempt from numerical limitations on visa issuance--persons who lost citizenship by marriage; persons who lost citizenship by serving in foreign armed forces; ministers of religion, their spouses and children; certain employees or former employees of the U.S. government abroad, their spouses and children; and Panama Canal Act immigrants.

SPECIAL NATURALIZATION PROVISIONS - Provisions covering special classes of persons who may be naturalized even though they do not meet all the general requirements for naturalization. Such special provisions allow: (1) wives or husbands of U.S. citizens to be naturalized in 3 years instead of the prescribed 5 years; (2) a surviving spouse of a U.S. citizen who served in the armed forces to file in any naturalization court instead of where he or she resides; (3) children of U.S. citizen parents to be naturalized without meeting the literacy or government-knowledge requirements or taking the oath, if too young to understand its meaning. Other classes of persons who may qualify for special consideration are former U.S. citizens, servicemen, seamen, and employees of organizations promoting U.S. interests abroad.

STATELESS - Having no nationality.

SUBJECT TO NUMERICAL LIMITATIONS - Condition imposed on all immigration to the United States, except for the immediate relatives of U.S. citizens and certain special immigrants. The number of aliens accorded lawful permanent residence under the provisions of the preference system must not exceed 270,000 in any fiscal year. The preference system provides for the admission of relatives of citizens (other than immediate relatives), immediate relatives of lawful permanent resident aliens, aliens in specified occupations, as well as other immigrants.

SUSPENSION OF DEPORTATION - A discretionary benefit adjusting an alien's status from that of deportable alien to one lawfully admitted for permanent residence. Application for suspension of deportation is made during the course of a deportation hearing before an immigration judge.

TRANSITION QUARTER - The three-month period (July 1 through September 30, 1976) between fiscal 1976 and fiscal 1977. At that time, the fiscal year calendar shifted from July 1 - June 30 to October 1 - September 30.

WORLDWIDE CEILING - The numerical limit imposed on immigrant visa issuance worldwide beginning in fiscal 1979. The current ceiling totals 270,000 visa numbers. Prior to enactment of P.L. 96-212 on March 17, 1980, the worldwide ceiling was 290,000. The ceiling in fiscal 1980 was 280,000.

Selected Acronyms

ADP   - Automated data processing
CPS   - Current Population Survey
ICM   - Intergovernmental Committee on Migration
IMDAC - Immigrant Data Capture System

INA   - Immigration and Nationality Act
INS   - Immigration and Naturalization Service
MIRAC   - Master Index Remote Access Capability System
NCHS   - National Center for Health Statistics
NIDC   - Nonimmigrant Document Control System
NIIS   - Nonimmigrant Information System
OMB   - Office of Management and Budget
ORR   - Office of Refugee Resettlement
RPG   - Refugee Policy Group
SRS   - Statistical Reporting System
SSA   - Social Security Administration
TSC   - Transportation Systems Center

Appendix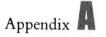

SELECTED FORMS

The forms that appear below include only those that are referred to in this report; they are used to collect a major portion of the available information about migration to the United States. Because of the very large number of forms used in connection with immigration, it was not possible to include a comprehensive array. The INS forms are listed in alphabetical and numeric order, followed by those used by other agencies.

Sponsoring Agency	Form Number	Form	Page
INS	G-23	Report of Field Operations: Selected pages	161
	G-325 C	Biographic Information--Applicant for Refugee Status	169
	G-540	Daily Record of Primary Inspections--CINSP-8	170
	G-541	Semiannual Report of Primary Inspection Activity--CINSP-8	171
	G-542	Semiannual Report of Hourly Workloads--CINSP-8	172
	I-53	Alien Address Report	173
	I-92	Aircraft/Vessel Report (Passenger manifest)	174
	I-94	Nonimmigrant Arrival/Departure Form	175
	I-213	Report of Deportable Alien	176
	I-485	Application for Status as Permanent Resident	177
	I-551	Alien Registration Receipt Card	180
	I-589	Request for Asylum in the United States	181
	I-590	Registration for Classification as Refugee	185
	I-591	Assurance by a United States Sponsor in Behalf of an Applicant for Refugee Status	187
	I-643	Statistical Data for Refugees. Collected by the INS for the Department of Health and Human Services	188
	N-400	Application to File Petition for Naturalization	189
	N-600	Application for Certificate of Citizenship	192
State Dept.	OF-155 A	Immigrant Visa and Alien Registration	195
Customs	5905	Customs workload form	196
Customs	6059 B	Customs Declaration Card	197
NCHS	HRA-161	Standard Birth Certificate--1978 revision	198
ACVA	ACVAFS Form #1	Refugee data form--American Council of Volunteer Agencies	199
SSA	SS-5	Application for a Social Security Number Card	200
ORR	ORR-6	ORR Quarterly Performance Reports, Schedules B and C.	201

U.S. Department of Justice
Immigration and Naturalization Service

Report of Field Operations
Period Covered:

Reporting Office:
RCS: CADM-3

I. EXAMINATIONS ACTIVITY (Cont'd)

PRIMARY INSPECTION (Cont'd)

106. **Aliens not admitted** (Total of lines 107 - 111)	- Total
(a)	- Sea
(b)	- Air
(c)	- Land
Prima facie inadm. aliens:	
107. **Crewmen**	- Total
(a)	- Sea
(b)	- Air
108. **Stowaways**	- Total
(a)	- Sea
(b)	- Air
109. **Border crossers**	- Total
(a)	- Sea
(b)	- Air
(c)	- Land
110. **Others**	- Total
(a)	- Sea
(b)	- Air
(c)	- Land
111. **Final exclusions**	- Total
(a)	- Sea
(b)	- Air
(c)	- Land
112. **Aliens paroled into U.S.** (Includes Line 119)	- Total
(a)	- Sea
(b)	- Air
(c)	- Land
114. **Fines relating to alien crewmen**	- Total
(a)	- Sea
(b)	- Air
(c) - Fines pending decision	*

*Do not include in Total Work Units on Form G-23.3

Form G-23.2 (Rev. 10-1-84)N

GPO 908-981

U.S. Department of Justice
Immigration and Naturalization Service

Report of Field Operations
Period Covered:

Reporting Office
RCS: CADM-3

I. EXAMINATIONS ACTIVITY (Cont'd)

PRIMARY INSPECTION (Cont'd)

115.	Fines - Other	- Total
	(a)	- Sea
	(b)	- Air
116.	Liquidated damages - TWOV's	- Total
	(a)	- Sea
	(b)	- Air
	(c)	- Land
117.	TOTAL WORK UNITS*	- Total
	(a)	- Sea
	(b)	- Air
	(c)	- Land
118.	Vessels - arrival	- Total
	(a)	- USMT
	(b)	- Commercial
	(c)	- Private
118a.	Airplane flights - arrival	- Total
	(a)	- USMT
	(b)	- Commercial
	(c)	- Private
118b.	Vessels - departure	- Total
118c.	Airplane flights - departure	- Total

ALIEN CREWMEN

119.	Alien crewmen paroled into U.S.	
119a.	Alien crewmen deserted or absconded	- Total
	(a) - Crew list (Form I-418) reports	
	(b) - Master or agents reports	
	(c) - Other	

*Total Lines 100-105, 106, 112 and 114-116.

Form G-23.3 (Rev. 10-1-84)N

GPO 908-960

U.S. Department of Justice
Immigration and Naturalization Service

Report of Field Operations

Reporting Office _____
Period Covered _____

II. DEPORTATION, CUSTODY, RECOGNIZANCE,
BOND, AND SUPERVISION

DEPORTATION AND REQUIRED DEPARTURE

226. Deportations effected
.1(a) – Mexican Deportations effected
(b) – Productive Hours
.2(a) – Non-Mexican Deportations effected
(b) – Productive Hours

227. Voluntary departures verified – Total (a) & (b)
(a) – Cases under docket control
(a)(1) Pre-hearing departures (Form I-161)
(a)(2) Productive hours (I-161)
(a)(3) Hours per unit (line 227(a)(2)÷227(a)(1)
(a)(4) Hearing (OSC) departures (Form I-154)
(a)(5) Productive hours (I-154)
(a)(6) Hours per unit (line 227(a)(5)÷227(a)(4)
(b) – Cases not under docket control
(b)(1) Alien crewmen
(b)(2) All other Mexican voluntary departures
(b)(3) All other non Mexican voluntary departures

127.1 Aliens processed for removal under safeguards – Total
(a) – Mexican aliens
(b) – Other than Mexican aliens
(c) – I-274/274A Program (Productive Hours)
(d) – Hours per unit (hours÷aliens)

228. Docket control index
(a) – Cases at beginning of period
(b) – Cases received during period
(c) – Cases processed out during period
(d) – Cases pending end of period (Total)

229. Total pre-hearing category 1 (I-161)
(a) – Subsection 1(a) unexpired/unverified
(b) – Subsection 1(b), Extended V/D etc.
(c) – Subsection 1(c), To INV to locate

Form G-23.8 (Rev. 10-1-80)N

GPO 874-102

UNITED STATES DEPARTMENT OF JUSTICE
Immigration and Naturalization Service

DEPORTABLE ALIENS LOCATED BY BORDER PATROL

Month: _____
Reporting office: _____

IV. BORDER PATROL (Contd.)

Operation	TOTAL (Columns 2-12) 1	Status at entry											Length of time illegally in U.S.				B.U.S.C. 1324, 1327, 1328				Fraudulent claim to USC		Fraudulent claim to legal status	
		Agricultural worker 2	Visitor 3	Student 4	Crewman D-1 Non-willful violator 5	Crewman D-1 Willful violator 6	Crewman D-2 Non-willful violator 7	Crewman D-2 Willful violator 8	Immigrant 9	Stowaway 10	E.W.I. 11	Other 12	At entry 13	Within 72 hours 14	4-30 days 15	Over 30 days 16	Principals 17	Alien By aircraft 18	Alien By watercraft 19	Alien By other means 20	Presented documents 21	Unsupported oral claims 22	Alien Registration Receipt Card (I-151) 23	Non-resident alien Mexican Border Crossing Card (I-186) 24	Other 25
1. TOTAL (Lines 2-10)........																									
2. Line watch																									
3. Patrol																									
4. Farm-ranch check																									
5. Traffic check																									
6. Transportation check - Total																									
(a) Bus																									
(b) Passenger train																									
(c) Freight train																									
(d) Aircraft																									
7. City patrol																									
8. Boat patrol																									
9. Crewman-stowaway																									
10. Turned over to BP by other agencies.																									
11. *Observation aircraft																									
12. *Electric eyes																									
13. *Ultraviolet light																									
14. *Other elec./mech. devices ..																									

* Included in appropriate activity, lines 2 through 10.

CREWMAN - Exclude crewmen on 29-day vessels.

E. W. I. - Place of entry - Station area

TOTAL	CHU	ECJ	CAO	ELC	CAX	YUM	TNA	GBN	TCA	NGL	DGL	LOB	DNM	EPT	YST	PMB	WRM	INF	FHT	SBT	VHT	MAR	PRC	AFT	SNN	COM	DRT	FGT	CAR	LRT	HFB	RGC	MCA	MLR	HHI	DRP
	BLW	LMD	ORV	COV	BON	RVL	WHF	SWG	BRN	HVM	MLT	WOL	PLB	PRT	BOT	PMB	WRM	INF	GMM	SMM	PHM	DTM	TRE									*\/				
	BUN	NIB	WAT	OGN	MNB	MLB	ROB	SWB	RIB	DBV	BVB	JMB	VMB	FFM	HLT	LMB	CMB																			

*/ Stations not included by Service location code.

** Land Border EWI's employed at time of apprehension
| Canadian | |
| Mexican | |

G-23.17 (Rev. 7-1-77)N

UNITED STATES DEPARTMENT OF JUSTICE
Immigration and Naturalization Service

MONTHLY REPORT OF DEPORTABLE ALIENS FOUND IN U.S. BY NATIONALITY, STATUS AT ENTRY, PLACE OF ENTRY, STATUS WHEN FOUND

RCS:CADM-3

Month _____ Reporting Office _____

Part I. Status at entry

Nationality	*Total	Agricultural Worker	Visitor	Student	Crewman D-1 Non-wilful violator Total	*On 29-day vessels	Other	D-1 Wilful violator	D-2 Non-wilful violator	D-2 Wilful violator	Immigrant	Stowaway	E.W.I. Canadian Border	E.W.I. Mexican Border	E.W.I. Other	Other
	(1)	(2)	(3)	(4)	(5)	(6)	(7)	(8)	(9)	(10)	(11)	(12)	(13)	(14a)	(14b)	(14c)	(15)

Line
1 Total
2 Canada
3 Mexico-adult males
4 Mexico-females and children
5 B.W.I. and Belize
6 Dominican Republic
7 El Salvador
8 Guatemala
9 Other North America
10 Colombia
11 Ecuador
12 Other South America
13 Chinese
14 Philippines
15 Other Asia
16 Greece
17 Italy
18 United Kingdom
19 Other Europe
20 Africa
21 Other nationalities

Part II. Length of time illegally in U.S.

At entry	Within 72 hours	4-30 days	1-6 months	7 months-1 year	Over 1 year
(16)	(17)	(18)	(19)	(20)	(21)

Part III. Status when found

In Agriculture	Employment Industry and other	Seeking Employment	In institutions	In travel
(22)	(23)	(24)	(25)	(26)

Part IV. Place of entry

Status at entry	Total	Land Borders Canadian Border**	From Atlantic thru Erie	From Erie thru Duluth	From Duluth to Pacific	Mexican Border** California and Arizona	New Mexico thru Del Rio, Texas	From Del Rio to Gulf	Sea Coasts	New England	New York Area	Delaware Bay	Chesapeake Bay	North and South Carolina & Georgia	Florida	Gulf except Florida	Lower Calif., No. 16	Upper Calif., No. 13	Washington & Oregon	Alaska	Hawaii	Territories
	(1)	(2)	(3)	(4)	(5)	(6)	(7)	(8)	(9)	(10)	(11)	(12)	(13)	(14)	(15)	(16)	(17)	(18)	(19)	(20)	(21)	(22)
20 Crewman-D-1(wilful violator)																						
21 Crewman-D-2(wilful violator)																						
22 Stowaway																						
23 E.W.I.**																						

23(2) Canadian Border ____ Mexican Border ____

Part V. Method of location

24. Total located
25. Masters or agents reports
26. Area control-illegal status
27. Other Investigative efforts
28. Border Patrol
29. Other

Land Border EWI's employed at time of apprehension

*The crewmen on 29-day vessels (col. 6 should not be included in total (col.1). (See instructions on other side)
**Enter total EWI'S by land border under 23(2) who were employed at time of apprehension.

FORM G-23.18(Rev. 10-1-76)N

U.S. Department of Justice
Immigration and Naturalization Service

Report of Field Operations
Period Covered:

Reporting Office
RCS: CADM-3

INVESTIGATIONS ACTIVITY

IMPACT LEVEL I

511 CRIMINAL ALIENS
A. Received
B. Cases in progress
C. Completed
D. Successfully completed
E. Hours

512 EMPLOYERS OF ILLEGAL ALIENS
A. Received
B. Cases in progress
C. Completed
D. Successfully completed
E. Hours
F. Apprehensions
   1. Wage Level 1
   2. Wage Level 2
   3. Wage Level 3
   4. Wage Level 4

513 IMMIGRATION FRAUD SCHEMES
A. Received
B. Cases in progress
C. Completed
D. Successfully completed
E. Hours
F. Aliens arrested
G. Prosecution accepted (Defendants)
H. Defendants convicted

514 ALIEN ENTITLEMENT FRAUD
A. Received
B. Cases in progress
C. Completed
D. Successfully completed
E. Hours
F. Unentitled aliens involved
G. Prosecution accepted (Defendants)
H. Defendants convicted
I. Dollar value of entitlement saved

FORM G—23 19 (Rev. 10–1–83) N

GPO 905-537

U.S. Department of Justice
Immigration and Naturalization Service

Report of Field Operations
Period Covered: _____

Reporting Office: _____
RCS: CADM-3

522 COINV DESIGNATED PROJECTS

A.															
B.															
C.															
D.															
E.															
F.															
G.															
H.															
I.															

523 ILLEGAL ALIEN EMPLOYMENT SUMMARY

CATEGORY OF EMPLOYMENT	1.	2.	3.	4.	TOTALS
HEAVY INDUSTRY (HI)					
LIGHT INDUSTRY (LI)					
AGRICULTURE (A)					
CONSTRUCTION (C)					
SERVICE (S)					
GRAND TOTALS					

Number of Employments Visited

In Agriculture _____

In Industry _____

TOTAL: _____

Number of Aliens Apprehended

_____

_____

_____

Public Assistance (aliens who are or have been receiving public assistance): _____

Form G-23.21.1 (10-1-83)

GPO 905-535

U.S. Department of Justice
Immigration and Naturalization Service

Reporting Office _____
RCS: CADM-3

Report of Field Operations
Period Covered: _____

ADMINISTRATION	FY:	FY:	FY:	FY:	OCT.	NOV.	DEC.	JAN.	FEB.	MAR.	Total Oct.-Mar.	APR.	MAY	JUN.	JUL.	AUG.	SEP.	Total Apr.-Sep.
700. A-FILES CREATED																		
(a) Pending beginning of period																		
(b) Received																		
(c) Completed																		
(d) Pending end of period																		
(e) Productive hours																		
701. OTHER FILES CREATED																		
(a) Pending beginning of period																		
(b) Received																		
(c) Completed																		
(d) Pending end of period																		
(e) Productive hours																		
702. FILES TRANSFERRED (FTI)																		
(a) Pending beginning of period																		
(b) Received																		
(c) Completed																		
(d) Pending end of period																		
(e) Productive hours																		
703. FILES FORWARDED ON LOAN																		
(a) Pending beginning of period																		
(b) Received																		
(c) Completed																		
(d) Pending end of period																		
(e) Productive hours																		
704. FILES CONSOLIDATION REQUESTS																		
(a) Pending beginning of period																		
(b) Received																		
(c) Completed																		
(d) Pending end of period																		
(e) Productive hours																		
705. FILES REQUESTED																		
Federal Record Center																		
(a) Pending beginning of period																		
(b) Received																		
(c) Completed																		
(d) Pending end of period																		
(e) Productive hours																		

Form G-23.24 (Rev. 3-1-84)N

GPO 905-644

U.S. Department of Justice

Immigration and Naturalization Service

FORM G-325C
BIOGRAPHIC INFORMATION

OMB No. 1115-0066

Approval expires 4-30-85

(FAMILY NAME)	(FIRST NAME)	(MIDDLE NAME)	☐ MALE ☐ FEMALE	BIRTHDATE (MO.-DAY-YR.)	NATIONALITY

ALL OTHER NAMES USED		CITY AND COUNTRY OF BIRTH	

	FAMILY NAME	FIRST NAME	DATE, CITY AND COUNTRY OF BIRTH (IF KNOWN)	CITY AND COUNTRY OF RESIDENCE
FATHER				
MOTHER (MAIDEN NAME)				

HUSBAND OR WIFE (IF NONE, SO STATE)	FAMILY NAME (FOR WIFE, GIVE MAIDEN NAME)	FIRST NAME	BIRTHDATE	CITY & COUNTRY OF BIRTH	DATE OF MARRIAGE	PLACE OF MARRIAGE

FORMER HUSBANDS OR WIVES (FILL IN THE BLOCKS BELOW. IF NONE, STATE "NONE".)

FAMILY NAME (FOR WIFE, GIVE MAIDEN NAME)	FIRST NAME	BIRTHDATE	DATE & PLACE OF MARRIAGE	DATE AND PLACE OF TERMINATION OF MARRIAGE

APPLICANT'S RESIDENCE LAST FIVE YEARS. LIST PRESENT ADDRESS FIRST.

STREET AND NUMBER	CITY	PROVINCE OR STATE	COUNTRY	FROM MONTH	FROM YEAR	TO MONTH	TO YEAR
						PRESENT TIME	

APPLICANT'S EMPLOYMENT LAST FIVE YEARS. (IF NONE, SO STATE) LIST PRESENT EMPLOYMENT FIRST.

FULL NAME AND ADDRESS OF EMPLOYER	OCCUPATION	FROM MONTH	FROM YEAR	TO MONTH	TO YEAR
				PRESENT TIME	

APPLICANT FOR REFUGEE STATUS	IF YOUR NATIVE ALPHABET IS IN OTHER THAN ROMAN LETTERS, WRITE YOUR NAME IN YOUR NATIVE ALPHABET BELOW:

	PENALTIES: SEVERE PENALTIES ARE PROVIDED BY LAW FOR KNOWINGLY AND WILLFULLY FALSIFYING OR CONCEALING A MATERIAL FACT.
DATE (SIGNATURE OF APPLICANT)	

APPLICANT: BE SURE TO PUT YOUR NAME IN THE BOX OUTLINED BY HEAVY BORDER BELOW.

COMPLETE THIS BOX (FAMILY NAME)	(GIVEN NAME)	(MIDDLE NAME)

FORM G-325C (Rev. 10-1-82)Y

CINSP-8

(Check one)
☐ VESSELS
☐ AIRCRAFT

DAILY RECORD OF PRIMARY INSPECTIONS

DISTRICT _____   LOCATION _____   DATE _____

Name of Vessel or Carrier and Flight Number	Time of Arrival	Time for which Inspection Requested	Total Passengers and Crewmen	TIME REQUIRED (Hours and Minutes)				NUMBER OF INSPECTORS ASSIGNED				Total Number of Inspectors On Duty	REMARKS
				Inspection Time	Waiting Time	Travel Time	Total Time	On Regular Tour of Duty	On 1931 Act Overtime	On 1945 Act Overtime	Total		
(1)	(2)	(3)	(4)	(5)	(6)	(7)	(8)	(9)	(10)	(11)	(12)	(13)	(14)

Form G-540 (Rev. 5-22-67)   United States Department of Justice Immigration and Naturalization Service

SEMIANNUAL REPORT OF PRIMARY INSPECTION ACTIVITY – CINSP-8

DISTRICT _____ LOCATION _____ MONTH AND YEAR _____

(Check One)
☐ VESSELS
☐ AIRCRAFT

PART A

Date	HOURS 0	1	2	3	4	5	6	7	8	9	10	11	12	13	14	15	16	17	18	19	20	21	22	23	24	TOTAL
TOTALS																										

PART B

	Total Auth. Processed	Total Hrs. on Auth.

PART C SCHEDULED ASSIGNMENTS

	12-8	8-4	4-12
Number Inspectors Regularly Scheduled			
Primary			
Authorizations			
Supervisory			
Other			
TOTAL			

Remarks

INSTRUCTIONS

This report is to be completed for a one week period during the months of February and August of each year.

PART A Post the entries daily from the data on Form G-540. Report vessels and planes separately. San Juan, P. R. will also maintain a separate form for preinspections. Hours for which there are no arrivals shall be left blank. Make Sunday and Holiday entries in red. For each hour show the total number of arriving persons and vessels or planes. For example, if 684 persons arrived on 6 vessels on the 3rd day of the month between 3:00 and 4:00 P.M., enter in the box between 15 and 16 on the third day "684" in the upper block and "6" in the lower block for that day. If the time of arrival is different from the time inspection is requested, the latter is controlling. Post horizontal totals daily. Post vertical totals at the end of the week.

PART B Post only those authorizations processed by inspectors at an airport or seaport facility. If the inspectors are not stationed at such facility show authorizations processed by inspectors in the primary inspection unit. In the absence of a facility and a unit show the authorizations processed by officers who normally perform the primary inspection work.

PART C Show scheduled assignments for all travel control officers on duty, excluding Assistant District Director.

Form G-541 (Rev. 5-22-67)   United States Department of Justice Immigration and Naturalization Service

GPO 924-495

CINSP-8

SEMIANNUAL REPORT OF HOURLY WORKLOADS

Port _____
Station _____

Date _____
Day of Week _____
On Duty Force _____

I PRIMARY SCREENING

	AM 12	1	2	3	4	5	6	7	8	9	10	11	PM 12	1	2	3	4	5	6	7	8	9	10	11	12	TOTAL
1. Autos																										
2. Passengers																										
3. Thru Buses																										
4. Passengers																										
5. Local Buses																										
6. Passengers																										
7. No. of Lanes																										
8. Referrals																										
9. Pedestrians																										
10. No. of Lanes																										
11. Referrals																										

II SECONDARY INSPECTION

12. Immigrants																										
13. NI for I-94																										
14. 212(d)(4)																										
15. Parole-Imm.																										
16. Parole-NI																										
17. False Claims																										
18. BCC Appl.																										
19. Other																										
20. Inspectors																										

III. TOURS OF DUTY - PRIMARY

	12-8	8-4	4-12
INS			
CUSTOMS			
USPHS			
PL. QUAR.			
TOTAL			

IV. FORCE DEPLOYMENT - INS

	12-8	8-4	4-12
PRIMARY			
SECONDARY			
SUPVRS.			
OTHER *			
TOTAL			

* Explain Under Remarks

V. REMARKS

FORM G-542 United States Department of Justice — Immigration and Naturalization Service
(Rev. 5-22-67)

ALIEN ADDRESS REPORT

COMPLETE ALL ITEMS—PRINT IN BLOCK LETTERS WITH BALL-POINT PEN OR USE TYPEWRITER. THIS CARD MUST BE MAILED. PLACE A TEN CENT U.S. POSTAGE STAMP ON REVERSE AND DROP IN MAIL BOX. THIS CARD IS REVISED ANNUALLY. ONLY SUBMIT A CURRENT YEAR CARD.

1. (LAST NAME) (FIRST) (MIDDLE)

2. ADDRESS IN THE U.S. (EXCEPT COMMUTERS—SHOW ADDRESS IN MEXICO OR CANADA. SEE ITEM 15)

| CITY OR TOWN | STATE | ZIP CODE | CHECK HERE IF ADDRESS IS CURRENT ☐ |

3. ALIEN NO. FROM ALIEN CARD A-   4. PLACE ENTERED THE U.S.   5. WHEN ENTERED U.S. (MO/DAY/YR)   6. SEX ☐ MALE ☐ FEMALE

7. COUNTRY OF BIRTH   8. DATE OF BIRTH (MO/DAY/YR)   9. COUNTRY OF CITIZENSHIP   10. ARE YOU NOW WORKING IN THE U.S.? ☐ YES ☐ NO

11. SOCIAL SECURITY NO. (IF ANY)   12. FOR GOVERNMENT USE ONLY

13. PRESENT OR MOST RECENT OCCUPATION IN U.S. (MAIN JOB)   14. TYPE OF FIRM OR BUSINESS OF PRESENT OR MOST RECENT EMPLOYMENT (MAIN JOB)

15. STATUS (CHECK APPROPRIATE BOX) WHEN DID YOU RECEIVE YOUR PRESENT IMMIGRATION STATUS? (MO/DAY/YR)_____

1 ☐ IMMIGRANT (PERMANENT RESIDENT)   3 ☐ VISITOR 4 ☐ CREWMAN 5 ☐ STUDENT
2 ☐ IMMIGRANT (COMMUTER WORKER-CHECK THIS BLOCK   6 ☐ EXCHANGE ALIEN 7 ☐ REFUGEE-PAROLEE
IF YOU ENTER THE U.S. DAILY OR AT LEAST TWICE A WEEK)   8 ☐ OTHER (SPECIFY)_____

16. I CERTIFY THAT THE STATEMENTS ON THIS CARD ARE TRUE TO THE BEST OF MY KNOWLEDGE

SIGNATURE (IF UNDER 14 YEARS OLD, SIGNATURE OF PARENT OR GUARDIAN)   DATE

Form I-53 (Rev. 1-1-81Y) U.S. DEPARTMENT OF JUSTICE—IMMIGRATION AND NATURALIZATION SERVICE FORM APPROVED OMB NO. 43--R0306

AIRCRAFT/VESSEL REPORT

Form Approved
OMB No. 43—RO497

☐ ARRIVAL
Last Foreign Port _____

☐ DEPARTURE
First Foreign Port _____

Airline/Vessel (Name and Nationality)	Flight Number	Port of Arr/Dep	Date of Arr/Dep

TYPE OF TRANSPORT—CHECK ONE

Total Passengers

1. ☐ U.S. military—including charters to military
2. ☐ Commercial—scheduled
3. ☐ Commercial—chartered
4. ☐ Foreign military

Do Not Write in These Blocks—For INS Use Only

Passengers Inspected	Passengers Deferred	Deferred Port

Attach CF 7507, ICAO Declaration, or I—418, or List Crew Below.

CREW: Name   Status

FOREIGN PORT AND COUNTRY	PASSENGERS		
	USC	ALIEN	TOTAL
TOTAL			

FORM I—92 (See instructions on reverse of form)
(Rev. 6—1—73)N

United States Department of Justice
Immigration and Naturalization Service

| I-94 | IMMIGRATION AND NATURALIZATION SERVICE ARRIVAL/DEPARTURE RECORD | Form Approved OMB No. 1115-077 Expires 8-31-85 |

WELCOME TO THE UNITED STATES

INSTRUCTIONS

- ALL PERSONS EXCEPT U.S. CITIZENS MUST COMPLETE THIS FORM. A SEPARATE FORM MUST BE COMPLETED FOR EACH PERSON IN YOUR GROUP.

- TYPE OR PRINT LEGIBLY WITH PEN IN ALL CAPITAL LETTERS. USE ENGLISH. DO NOT WRITE ON THE BACK OF THIS FORM.

- This form is in two parts, an ARRIVAL RECORD (Items 1 through 7), and a DEPARTURE RECORD (Items 8 through 10). You must complete both parts. Enter exactly the same information in spaces 8, 9, and 10 as you enter in spaces 1, 2, and 3.

  * Item 7. If you entered the United States by land, enter "LAND" in this space.

- WHEN YOU HAVE COMPLETED ALL REQUIRED ITEMS, PRESENT THIS FORM TO THE U.S. IMMIGRATION AND NATURALIZATION INSPECTOR.

THIS SIDE FOR GOVERNMENT USE ONLY

(DO NOT WRITE BELOW THIS LINE)

PRIMARY INSPECTION

NAME _____

II NUMBER _____ DATE/TIME REFERRED _____

REASON REFERRED _____

SECONDARY INSPECTION

II NUMBER _____ END TIME SECONDARY _____

DISPOSITION _____

ADMISSION NUMBER

995-01572478

I-94 ARRIVAL RECORD (Rev. 1-1-83)N

1. FAMILY NAME (SURNAME) (leave one space between names)

FIRST (GIVEN) NAME (do not enter middle name)

2. DATE OF BIRTH — DAY | MO. | YR.

3. COUNTRY OF CITIZENSHIP

4. COUNTRY OF RESIDENCE (country where you live)

5. ADDRESS WHILE IN THE UNITED STATES (Number and Street)

City _____ State

6. CITY WHERE VISA WAS ISSUED

7. AIRLINE & FLIGHT NO. OR SHIP NAME

THIS FORM IS REQUIRED BY THE IMMIGRATION AND NATURALIZATION SERVICE, UNITED STATES DEPARTMENT OF JUSTICE.

SAMPLE

11. OCCUPATION

12. SCHOOL

13. ITINERARY

14. PETITION NUMBER

15. INS FILE NO. A:

16. WAIVERS

WARNING
- A nonimmigrant who accepts unauthorized employment is subject to deportation.

IMPORTANT
- Retain this permit in your possession; you must surrender it when you leave the U.S. Failure to do so may delay your entry into the U.S. in the future.

ADMISSION NUMBER

995-01572478

8. FAMILY NAME (SURNAME) (same as Family Name in Item 1 above)

FIRST (GIVEN) NAME (same as First Name in Item 1 above)

9. DATE OF BIRTH (same as Item 2) — DAY | MO. | YR.

10. COUNTRY OF CITIZENSHIP (same as Item 3 above)

SEE REVERSE SIDE FOR OTHER IMPORTANT INFORMATION

| U.S. IMMIGRATION AND NATURALIZATION SERVICE | I-94 DEPARTURE RECORD (Rev. 1-1-83)N | STAPLE HERE |

IMPORTANT NOTICE

- You are authorized to stay in the U.S. only until the date written on this form. To remain past this date, without permission from immigration authorities, is a violation of law.

SURRENDER THIS PERMIT WHEN YOU LEAVE THE UNITED STATES

- By sea or air, to transportation line.
- Over Canadian border, to Canadian Official.
- Over Mexican border, at the designated location.

RECORD OF CHANGES

DEPARTURE RECORD

Port:

Date:

Carrier:

Flight No./Ship Name

For sale by the Superintendent of Documents, U.S. Government Printing Office Washington, D.C. 20402

RECORD OF DEPORTABLE ALIEN (See A.M. – 2790.31-.34 for Instructions)

Family Name (Capital Letters)	Given Name	Middle Name	Sex	Hair	Eyes	Complexion

Country of Citizenship	Passport Number and Country of Issue	File Number	Height	Weight	Occupation

U.S. Address	(Residence)	(Number)	(Street)	(City)	(State)	(Zip Code)

Scars or Marks

Date, Place, Time, Manner of Last Entry	Passenger Boarded At	F.B.I. No.	Marital Status

☐ Single ☐ Widow(er)
☐ Married
☐ Separated ☐ Divorced

Number, Street, City, Province (State) and Country of Permanent Residence

Method of Location/Apprehension

Birthdate	Date of Action	Location Code	(At/Near)	Date & Hour

City, Province (State) and Country of Birth	AR ☐	Form: (Type & No.)	☐ Lifted ☐ Not Lifted	By

Visa Issued At – NIV No.	Social Security Account Name	Status at Entry	Status When Found

Date Visa Issued	Social Security No.	Send C.O. Rec. Check To:	Length of Time Illegally in U.S.

Immigration Record	Criminal Record

Name, Address, and Nationality of Spouse (Maiden Name, if appropriate)	Number & Nationality of Minor Children

Father's Name, and Nationality and Address, if Known	Mother's Present and Maiden Names, Nationality, and Address, if Known

PLEASE TYPEWRITE OR PRINT IN BLOCK CAPITAL LETTERS

Monies Due/Property in U.S. Not in Immediate Possession ☐ None Claimed ☐ See Form I-43	Fingerprinted ☐ Yes ☐ No	Lookout Book Checked ☐ Not Listed ☐ Listed, Code___	Deportation Charge(s) (Code Words)

Name and Address of (Last) (Current) U.S. Employer	Type of Employment	Salary $___ ___hr.	From:	To:

Narrative (Outline particulars under which alien located/apprehended. Include details, not shown above, re time, place, manner of last entry, and elements which establish administrative and/or criminal violation. Indicate means and route of travel to interior.) Alien has been advised of communication privileges pursuant to 8 CFR 242.2(e).

Initial _____ . Date _____

(If space insufficient, show "continued" and continue on reverse, from bottom up).

_____
(Signature and Title)

DISTRIBUTION	Received (subject and documents) (report of interview) from

Officer: _____

_____ 19_____ at_____ ( ). M.

Disposition_____

(Receiving Officer)_____

Form 1-213 (Rev. 4-16-79)Y UNITED STATES DEPARTMENT OF JUSTICE Immigration and Naturalization Service

U.S. Department of Justice
Immigration and Naturalization Service

OMB No. 1115–0053
Approval Expires 8–85

APPLICATION FOR STATUS AS PERMANENT RESIDENT

FEE STAMP	File No.
	APPLICATION FOR THE BENEFITS OF SECTION:

☐ Sec. 209(b), I&N Act   ☐ Sec. 245, I&N Act

☐ Sec. 214(d), I&N Act   ☐ Sec. 249, I&N Act

☐ Sec. 13, Act of 9/11/57

(DO NOT WRITE ABOVE THIS LINE.) (SEE INSTRUCTIONS BEFORE FILLING IN APPLICATION. IF YOU NEED MORE SPACE TO ANSWER FULLY ANY QUESTION ON THIS FORM, USE A SEPARATE SHEET AND IDENTIFY EACH ANSWER WITH THE NUMBER OF THE CORRESPONDING QUESTION. FILL IN WITH TYPEWRITER OR PRINT IN BLOCK LETTERS IN INK.)

1. I hereby apply for the status of a lawful permanent resident alien on the following basis: (Check one of the boxes below.)

A. ☐ As a person granted asylum under Section 207(a) to whom an immigrant visa is immediately available (Section 209(b), I&N Act). (No fee required.)

B. ☐ As a person who entered the U.S. with a visa issued to me as the fiancee or fiance of a U.S. citizen whom I married within 90 days after my entry, or as a child of such fiancee or fiance (Sec. 214(d), I&N Act).

C. ☐ As a former government official, or as a member of the immediate family of such official (Section 13, Act of September 11, 1957).

D. ☐ As a person to whom an immigrant visa is immediately available, other than one described above (Section 245, I&N Act).

E. ☐ As a person who has resided in the United States continuously since prior to July 1, 1924 (Section 249, I&N Act).

F. ☐ As a person who has resided in the United States continuously since a date on or after July 1, 1924, but before June 30, 1948 (Section 249, I&N Act).

G. ☐ As a motion to reopen or to reconsider my case in deportation proceedings before an immigration judge. (The fee for this request is $50.00.)

2. My name is (family in capital letters)   (First Given)   (Middle)

3. Sex   ☐ Male   ☐ Female   Phone number

4. I reside in the United States at: (c/o) (Apt. No.) (No. and Street)

(City) (State) (ZIP Code)

5. Have you ever applied before for permanent resident status in the U.S.?   ☐ No   ☐ Yes
(If "Yes", give the date and place of filing and final disposition.)

6. My file number is
A-

7. I am a citizen of (Country)

8. Date of Birth (Month) (Day) (Year)

9. Place of Birth (City or Town)   (County, Province, or State)   (Country)

10. Name as appears on nonimmigrant document (Form I-94)

I last arrived in the United States at the port of (City and State)   on (Month) (Day) (Year)   by (Name of vessel or other means of travel)

as a (visitor, student, crewman, parolee, etc.)   I ☐ was   ☐ was not inspected.

11. My nonimmigrant visa, number _____ was issued by the United States Consul at (City) (Country)   on (Month) (Day) (Year)

12. I am   ☐ single   ☐ married   ☐ divorced   ☐ widowed

13. I have been married _____ times, including my present marriage, if now married. (If you are now married give the following:)

a. Number of times my husband or wife has been married

b. Name of husband or wife (Wife give maiden name)

c. My husband or wife resides ☐ with me ☐ apart from me at Address (Apt. No.) No. & Street) (Town or City) (Province or State) (Country)

14. a. I have _____ sons or daughters as follows: (Complete all columns as to each son or daughter; if living with you state "with me" in last column; otherwise give city and state or country of son's or daughter's residence).

Name	Sex	Place of Birth	Date of Birth	Now living at

b. The following members of my family are also applying for permanent resident status:

OVER

Form I-485 (Rev. 5-5-83) N

RECEIVED	TRANS IN	RET'D TRANS OUT	COMPLETED

15. I list below all organizations, societies, clubs, and associations, past or present, in which I have held membership in the United States or a foreign country, and the periods and places of such membership. *(If you have never been a member of any organization, state "None".)*

16. I ☐ have not ☐ have been treated for a mental disorder, drug addiction or alcoholism. (If you have been, explain.)

17. I ☐ have not ☐ have been arrested, convicted or confined in a prison. (If you have been, explain.)

18. I ☐ have not ☐ have been the beneficiary of a pardon, amnesty, rehabilitation decree, other act of clemency or similar action. (If you have been, explain.)

19. APPLICANTS FOR STATUS AS PERMANENT RESIDENTS MUST ESTABLISH THAT THEY ARE ADMISSIBLE TO THE UNITED STATES. EXCEPT AS OTHERWISE PROVIDED BY LAW, ALIENS WITHIN ANY OF THE FOLLOWING CLASSES ARE NOT ADMISSIBLE TO THE UNITED STATES AND ARE THEREFORE INELIGIBLE FOR STATUS AS PERMANENT RESIDENTS:

Aliens who have committed or who have been convicted of a crime involving moral turpitude (does not include minor traffic violations); aliens who have been engaged in or who intend to engage in any commercialized sexual activity; aliens who are or at any time have been, anarchists, or members of or affiliated with any Communist or other totalitarian party, including any subdivision or affiliate thereof; aliens who have advocated or taught, either by personal utterance, or by means of any written or printed matter, or through affiliation with an organization, (i) opposition to organized government, (ii) the overthrow of government by force or violence, (iii) the assaulting or killing of government officials because of their official character, (iv) the unlawful destruction of property, (v) sabotage, or (vi) the doctrines of world communism, or the establishment of a totalitarian dictatorship in the United States; aliens who intend to engage in prejudicial activities or unlawful activities of a subversive nature; aliens who have been convicted of violation of any law or regulation relating to narcotic drugs or marihuana, or who have been illicit traffickers in narcotic drugs or marihuana; aliens who have been involved in assisting any other aliens to enter the United States in violation of law; aliens who have applied for exemption or discharge from training or service in the Armed Forces of the United States on the ground of alienage and who have been relieved or discharged from such training or service; medical graduates (other than those for whom Relative petitions have been approved) coming principally to perform services as members of the medical profession, unless they have passed Parts I and II of the National Board of Medical Examiners Examination (or an equivalent examination as determined by the Secretary of the Department of Health and Human Services) and who are competent in oral and written English.

Do any of the foregoing classes apply to you? ☐ No ☐ Yes *(If answer is Yes, explain)*

20. *(COMPLETE THIS BLOCK ONLY IF YOU CHECKED BOX "A", "B", "C", or "D" OF BLOCK 1)*

APPLICANTS WHO CHECKED BOX "A" "B" "C" OR "D" OF BLOCK 1 IN ADDITION TO ESTABLISHING THAT THEY ARE NOT MEMBERS OF ANY OF THE INADMISSIBLE CLASSES DESCRIBED IN BLOCK 10 ABOVE MUST, EXCEPT AS OTHERWISE PROVIDED BY LAW, ALSO ESTABLISH THAT THEY ARE NOT WITHIN ANY OF THE FOLLOWING INADMISSIBLE CLASSES:

Aliens who are mentally retarded, insane, or have suffered one or more attacks of insanity; aliens afflicted with psychopathic personality, sexual deviation, mental defect, narcotic drug addiction, chronic alcoholism or any dangerous contagious disease; aliens who have a physical defect, disease or disability affecting their ability to earn a living; aliens who are paupers, professional beggars or vagrants; aliens who are polygamists or advocate polygamy; aliens who intend to perform skilled or unskilled labor and who have not been certified by the Secretary of Labor (see Instruction 10); aliens likely to become a public charge; aliens who have been excluded from the United States within the past year, or who at any time have been deported from the United States, or who at any time have been removed from the United States at Government expenses; aliens who have procured or have attempted to procure a visa by fraud or misrepresentation; aliens who have departed from or remained outside the United States to avoid military service in time of war or national emergency; aliens who are former exchange visitors who are subject to but have not complied with the two year foreign residence requirement.

Do any of the foregoing classes apply to you? ☐ No ☐ Yes *(If answer is Yes, explain)*

21. I ☐ do not ☐ do intend to seek gainful employment in the United States. If you intend to seek gainful employment in the United States, state the occupation you intend to follow.

22. *(Complete this block only if you checked box D of block 1)*

☐ a. I have a priority on the consular waiting list at the American Consulate at_____ as of _____
     (City)   (Date)

☐ b. A visa petition according me ☐ immediate relative ☐ preference status was approved by the district
     director at_____ on_____
     (City and State)   (Date)

☐ c. A visa petition has not been approved in my behalf but I claim eligibility for preference status because ☐ my spouse ☐ my parent is the beneficiary of a visa petition
     approved by the district director at_____ on_____
     (City and State)   (Date)

☐ d. A visa petition in my behalf accompanies this application.

☐ e. Other (Explain)

23. *(Complete this box only if you checked Box E or F of Block 1)*

A. I first arrived in the United States at (Port)_____on (Date)_____ by means of (Name of vessel or

other means of travel) _____

I ☐ was ☐ was not inspected by an immigration officer _____

B. I entered the U.S. under the name *(Name at time of entry)* _____

and I was destined to (City and State) _____

I was coming to join (Name and relationship) _____

C. Since my first entry I ☐ have not ☐ have been absent from the United States. *(If you have been absent, attach a separate statement listing the port, date and means of each departure from and return to the U.S.)*

24. ☐ Completed Form G-325A (Biographic Information) is attached as part of this application. | ☐ Completed Form G-325A (Biographic Information) is not attached as applicant is under 14 years of age.

25. IF YOUR NATIVE ALPHABET IS IN OTHER THAN ROMAN LETTERS, WRITE YOUR NAME IN YOUR NATIVE ALPHABET BELOW: | Signature of Applicant:

Date of Signature:

26. (SIGNATURE OF PERSON PREPARING FORM, IF OTHER THAN APPLICANT.) I declare that This document was prepared by me at the request of the applicant and is based on all information on which I have any knowledge. | Address of person preparing form, if other than applicant:

Date: | Occupation:

(Application not to be signed below until applicant appears before an officer of the Immigration and Naturalization Service for examination)

I, _____, do swear (affirm) that I know the contents of this application subscribed by me including the attached documents, that the same are true to the best of my knowledge, and that corrections numbered ( ) to ( ) were made by me or at my request, and that this application was signed by me with my full, true name:

_____
(Complete and true signature of applicant)

Subscribed and sworn to before me by the above-named applicant at_____ on_____
                                    (Month)   (Day)   (Year)

_____
(Signature and title of officer)

(Page:____)

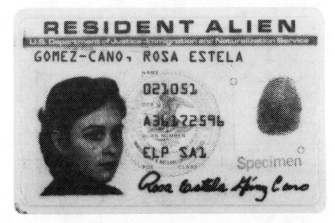

U.S. Department of Justice

Immigration and Naturalization Service

Form Approved
OMB No. 1115-0086

REQUEST FOR ASYLUM IN THE UNITED STATES

INS Office:

Date:

1. Family Name	First	Middle Name	2. A number (if any or known)

All other names used at any time (include maiden name if married)

3. Sex
□ Male
□ Female

4. Marital status
□ Single □ Divorced
□ Married □ Widowed

I was born: (Month) (Day) (Year) in (Town or City) (State or Province) (Country)

Nationality — at birth | At present | Other nationalities

5. If stateless, how did you become stateless?

6. Ethnic group | 7. Religion | 8. Languages spoken

9. Address in United States (In care of, C/O, if appropriate)
(Number and street) (Apt. No.) (City or town) (State) (Zip Code)

10. Telephone number (include area code)

11. Address abroad prior to coming to the United States
(Number and street) (City) (Province) (Country)

12. My last arrival in the U.S. occurred on: (Mo/Day/Yr)

As a □ Visitor □ Student □ Stowaway □ Crewman
□ Other (Specify)

At the port of (City/State)

Means of arrival (Name of vessel or airline and flight number, etc.)

I □ was □ was not inspected

Date authorized stay expires (Mo/Day/Yr)

13. My nonimmigrant visa number is _____, it was issued by the U.S. Consul on _____
(If none, state "none")
(Mo/Day/Yr)
at_____
(City, County)

14. Name and location of schools attended	Type of school	From Mo/Yr	To Mo/Yr	Highest grade completed	Title of degree or certification

15. What specific skills do you have?

16. Social Security No. (if any)

17. Name of husband or wife (wife's maiden name)

18. My husband or wife resides □ with me □ apart from me (if apart, explain why)

Address (Apt. No.) (No. and street) (Town or city) (Province or state) (Country)

Form I-589
(Rev. 3-1-81) N

(OVER)

RECEIVED	TRANS IN	RET'D TRANS OUT	COMPLETED

Page 1

19. If in the U.S. is your spouse included in your request for asylum? ☐ Yes ☐ No (If not, explain why)

20. If in the U.S. is spouse making separate application for asylum? ☐ Yes ☐ No (If not, explain why)

21. If in the U.S. are children included in your request for asylum? ☐ Yes ☐ No (If not, explain why)

22. I have ——— sons or daughters as follows: (Complete all columns as to each son or daughter. If living with you state "with me" in last column; otherwise give city and state or foreign country of son's or daughter's residence).

Name	Sex	Place of birth	Date of birth	Now living at

23. Relatives in U.S. other than immediate family

Name	Address	Relationship	Immigration status

24. Other relatives who are refugees but outside the U.S.

Name	Relationship	Country where presently located

25. List all travel or identity documents such as national passport, refugee convention travel document or national identity card

Document type	Document number	Issuing country or authority	Date of issue	Date of expiration	Cost	Obtained by whom

26. Why did you obtain a U.S. visa?

27. If you did not apply for a U.S. visa, explain why not?

28. Date of departure from your country of nationality (Mo/Day/Yr)	29. Was exit permission required to leave your country? ☐ Yes ☐ No (If so, did you obtain exit permission ☐ Yes ☐ No (If not, explain why)

30. Are you entitled to return to country of issuance of your passport ☐ Yes ☐ No Travel document ☐ Yes ☐ No Or other document ☐ Yes ☐ No (If not, explain why)

31. What do you think would happen to you if you returned? (Explain)

32. When you left your home country, to what country did you intend to go?

33. Would you return to your home country? ☐ Yes ☐ No (Explain)

34. Have you or any member of your immediate family ever belonged to any organization in your home country? ☐ Yes ☐ No. (If yes, provide the following information relating to each organization: Name of organization, dates of membership or affiliation, purpose of the organization, what, if any, were your official duties or responsibilities, and are you still an active member. (If not, explain)

35. Have you taken any action that you believe will result in persecution in your home country? ☐ Yes ☐ No (If yes, explain)

36. Have you ever been ☐ detained ☐ interrogated ☐ convicted and sentenced ☐ imprisoned in any country? ☐ Yes ☐ No (If yes, specify for each instance: what occurred and the circumstances, dates, location, duration of the detention or imprisonment, reason for the detention or conviction, what formal charges were placed against you, reason for the release, names and addresses of persons who could verify these statements. Attach documents referring to these incidents, if any).

37. If you base your claim for asylum on current conditions in your country, do these conditions affect your freedom more than the rest of that country's population? ☐ Yes ☐ No (If yes, explain)

38. Have you, or any member of your immediate family, ever been mistreated by the authorities of your home country/country of nationality ☐ Yes ☐ No. If yes, was it mistreatment because of ☐ Race ☐ Religion ☐ Nationality ☐ Political opinion or ☐ Membership of a particular social group? Specify for each instance: what occurred and the circumstances, date, exact location, who took such action against you and what was his/her position in the government, reason why the incident occurred, names and addresses of people who witnessed these actions and who could verify these statements. Attach documents referring to these incidents.

39. After leaving your home country, have you traveled through (other than in transit) or resided in any other country before entering the U.S.? ☐ Yes ☐ No (If yes, identify each country, length of stay, purpose of stay, address, and reason for leaving, and whether you are entitled to return to that country for residence purposes.

40. Why did you continue traveling to the U.S.?

41. Did you apply for asylum in any other country? ☐ Yes—Give details ☐ No—Explain why not

(over)

42. Have you been recognized as a refugee by another country or by the United Nations High Commissioner for Refugees? ☐ Yes ☐ No   (If yes, where and when)

43. Are you registered with a consulate or any other authority of your home country abroad?   ☐ Yes—Give details ☐ No—Explain why not

44. Is there any additional information not covered by the above questions?   (If yes, explain)

45. Under penalties of perjury, I declare that the above and all accompanying documents are true and correct to the best of my knowledge and belief.

_____
(Signature of Applicant)

_____
(Date)

_____
(Interviewing Officer)

ACTION BY ADJUDICATING OFFICER

_____
(Date of Interview)

☐ GRANTED   ☐ DENIED

_____
(Adjudicating Officer)

_____
(Date)

Advisory opinion requested ☐

_____
(Date)

(4)

GPO : 1981 O - 350-419

REGISTRATION FOR CLASSIFICATION AS REFUGEE
Section 207
Immigration and Nationality Act

Form Approved
Budget Bureau No. 43-R0408

UNITED STATES DEPARTMENT OF JUSTICE
IMMIGRATION AND NATURALIZATION SERVICE

File No.

A

REGISTRANT TO FURNISH THE FOLLOWING INFORMATION (READ INSTRUCTIONS ON REVERSE)

TYPE OR PRINT

1. My name is: First / Middle / Last

2. My present address is:

3. I was born on: (month)(day)(year) | Place of birth (city or town) | (Province) | (Country) | My present nationality is:

4. Height | Weight | Eyes | Hair | Complexion | Marks or Scars

5. I fled or was displaced from (Name of country) | On or about (month) (day) (year)

6. Reasons: (State in detail)

7. My present immigration status in _____ (Country in which residing) is: _____

The evidence of my immigration status in the country in which I am residing is:

(Describe)

8. My spouse's name is: | 9. (His)(Her) present address is: | 10. Spouse's nationality is:

11. My spouse ☐ will ☐ will not accompany me to the United States

12. Name of child(ren) | Date of birth | Place of birth | Present address

Place a mark (X) in front of name of each child who will accompany you to the United States

13. Schooling or Education

Name and location of school	Type	Dates attended	Title of Degree or Diploma

14. Military Service

Country	Branch and Organization	Dates	Serial No.	Rank Attained

Form I-590 (Rev. 5-1-80) N

15. I list below all organizations, societies, clubs, and associations, past or present, in which I have held membership, and the periods and places of such membership. (If you have never been a member of any organization, state "None") _____

_____

16. I ☐ have ☐ have not been charged with a violation of law. (If you have ever been charged with a violation of law, give date and place and nature of each charge and the final result) _____

17. I ☐ have ☐ have not been in the United States. (If you have ever been in the United States, show the dates of entry and departure and the purpose of your entry. Visitor, permanent resident, student, seaman, etc.) _____ File or Alien Registration number _____

18. I have the following close relatives in the United States:

Names	Relationship	Present address

19. I am being sponsored by (Give name and address of United States Sponsor)

Date	Signature of registrant

DO NOT WRITE BELOW THIS LINE

I, _____ , do swear (affirm) that I know the contents of this registration subscribed by me including the attached documents, that the same are true to the best of my knowledge, and that corrections, numbered ( ) to ( ), were made by me or at my request, and that this registration was signed by me with my full, true name:

_____
(Complete and true signature of registrant)

Subscribed and sworn to before me by the above-named registrant at _____ on _____
(month)(day)(year)

_____
(Signature and title of officer)

INTERVIEW DATE AT	APPROVED DATE	
Immigration Officer	Officer in Charge	

INSTRUCTIONS

This form should be executed, signed and submitted to the Officer-in-Charge of the nearest overseas office of the United States Immigration and Naturalization Service. When your name has been reached as a registrant you will be furnished additional instructions.

1. REGISTRATION - A separate Registration Form must be executed by each registrant and submitted in one copy. A Registration Form in behalf of a child under 14 years of age shall be executed by the parent or guardian.

2. ASSURANCES - Assurance Form I–591 executed by a United States sponsor will be required before your refugee status may be authorized but need not be submitted at this time.

UNITED STATES DEPARTMENT OF JUSTICE

IMMIGRATION AND NATURALIZATION SERVICE

Form Approved
OMB No. 43-R0407

ASSURANCE BY A UNITED STATES SPONSOR IN BEHALF OF
AN APPLICANT FOR REFUGEE STATUS
(Section 207 Immigration and Nationality Act)

(See Instructions on Reverse)

Name of Sponsor:

Present Address: (Number) (Street) (City) (State) (ZIP Code)

Date of Birth: (Month) (Day) (Year) Place of Birth:

I am a citizen of the United States by ☐ birth ☐ naturalization (If naturalized, show date, place naturalized and certificate number)

The refugee status into the United States of the applicant, his spouse and children, as described below, is herewith sponsored, and transportation from a port of entry in the United States to final destination in the United States is assured.

Principal applicant's name: (First) (Middle) (Last) Date of birth:

Place of birth: Present address:

Name of principal applicant's spouse is: (First) (Middle) (Last)

Date of birth: Place of birth:

Child(ren)	Name	Date of birth	Place and Country of birth

Assurances are herewith given that for one year, and without displacing any other person, the principal applicant will be employed and that he and all members of his family will be housed.

TO BE EXECUTED BY INDIVIDUAL SPONSOR

I ☐ am ☐ am not related to the applicant. (If related show exact relationship)

I have within the past five years sponsored the immigration of _____ persons into the United States
(state number)

I understand that the assurances given by me as stated above are my personal obligations. I certify that I am financially responsible and fully capable of entering into this undertaking:

Date: Place: Signature of assurer

TO BE EXECUTED BY VOLUNTARY AGENCY

Name of Agency:

Local Representative of Agency in United States in area where conditional entrant will be located.

Date: Place:

Name

Signature of authorized official of agency

Address (Number) (Street) (City) (State) (ZIP Code)

Form I-591
(Rev. 5-1-80) N

GPO 871 421

U.S. Department of Justice

Immigration and Naturalization Service

**Health and Human Services
Statistical Data**

OMB No. 1115-0104
Approval Expires 10/83

PLEASE PRINT OR TYPE – SEE INSTRUCTIONS ON REVERSE SIDE

1

Name _____ Date _____ A- _____
Last (Family)   First (Given)   Middle   Alien Registration Number

Country of Birth _____ Country of Citizenship _____
Social Security Number

Native Language _____
Date of Birth _____
Month/Day/Year

Current Address _____
Number and Street   Apartment No.   City   State   ZIP
( )
Telephone Number

2 My three (3) most recent cities of residence in the United States have been (list most recent first):

CITY OR TOWN	STATE	FROM month/year	TO month/year
			PRESENT

3 There are _____ members of my household, _____ of whom are employed. They are (please use another sheet if needed):
Number   Number

NAME	RELATIONSHIP TO ME	SEX M/F	DATE OF BIRTH mo/da/yr	COUNTRY OF BIRTH	ALIEN NUMBER	CURRENTLY EMPLOYED? yes no	ATTENDING SCHOOL? yes no
(SELF)	(SELF)					☐ ☐	☐ ☐
						☐ ☐	☐ ☐
						☐ ☐	☐ ☐
						☐ ☐	☐ ☐
						☐ ☐	☐ ☐

4 My employment since entering the United States has been (list most recent first):

COMPANY NAME	LOCATION CITY, STATE	DATES FROM mo/yr TO mo/yr	JOB TITLE	WAGE PER HOUR	CHECK ONE: PART TIME FULL TIME
					☐ ☐
					☐ ☐
					☐ ☐

My major occupation or profession before coming to the U.S. was:

5 My education before coming to the United States was (check all that apply):

☐ Grades 1-8   ☐ Technical school   ☐ Some university   ☐ Graduate studies
☐ Some high school   ☐ Technical school certificate   ☐ University diploma   ☐ Professional training
☐ High school diploma   ☐ Graduate degree

My knowledge of English was acquired by (check all that apply):

☐ Training in the U.S.   ☐ Training in another country   ☐ Training in refugee camp
☐ Use in the U.S.   ☐ Use in another country   ☐ Other (please explain):

6 I have had the following training or education in the U.S. (check all that apply):

TYPE OF SCHOOL	COURSE OF STUDY	CHECK IF STILL ATTENDING	CHECK IF COMPLETED
☐ High school		☐	☐
☐ College		☐	☐
☐ Technical/Vocational		☐	☐
☐ Other (specify):		☐	☐

7 My English ability is (check one):

☐ None
☐ A few words
☐ Fair
☐ Good

8 Since in the United States, I have received the following public assistance in my own name:

	FROM month/year	TO month/year
☐ Cash assistance (welfare)		
☐ Food stamps		
☐ SSI (gold check)		
☐ Medical assistance		
☐ Other (specify):		

Form I-643 (10-31-81)

189

UNITED STATES DEPARTMENT OF JUSTICE
IMMIGRATION AND NATURALIZATION SERVICE

OMB NO. 1115-0009
Approval Expires 1/31/84

APPLICATION TO FILE PETITION FOR NATURALIZATION

Mail or take to:
IMMIGRATION AND NATURALIZATION SERVICE

FEE STAMP

ALIEN REGISTRATION
(Show the exact spelling of your name as it appears on your alien registration receipt card, and the number of your card. If you did not register, so state.)
Name ....
No. ....

(See INSTRUCTIONS. BE SURE YOU UNDERSTAND EACH QUESTION BEFORE YOU ANSWER IT. PLEASE PRINT OR TYPE.)

Section of Law .... (Leave Blank)   Date: ....

(1) My full true and correct name is.. (Full true name without abbreviations)

(2) I now live at.. (Number and street.)
.... (City . county, state, zip code)

(3) I was born on........................ (Month) (Day) (Year) in........................ (City or town) (County, province, or state) (Country)

(4) I request that my name be changed to........................

(5) Other names I have used are: .... (Include maiden name)   Sex: ☐ Male   ☐ Female

(6) Was your father or mother ever a United States citizen?.................... ☐ Yes ☐ No
(If "Yes", explain fully)

(7) Can you read and write English?.................... ☐ Yes ☐ No

(8) Can you speak English?.................... ☐ Yes ☐ No

(9) Can you sign your name in English?.................... ☐ Yes ☐ No

(10) My lawful admission for permanent residence was on........................ under the name of
(Month) (Day) (Year)
.... at........................ (City) (State)

(11) (a) I have resided continuously in the United States since .... (Month) (Day) (Year)

(b) I have resided continuously in the State of .... since .... (Month) (Day) (Year)

(c) During the last five years I have been physically in the United States for a total of .... months.

FROM -	TO -	STREET ADDRESS	CITY AND STATE
(a) ......, 19......	PRESENT TIME		
(b) ......, 19......	......, 19......		
(c) ......, 19......	......, 19......		
(d) ......, 19......	......, 19......		

(14) (a) Have you been out of the United States since your lawful admission as a permanent resident?.................... ☐ Yes ☐ No
If "Yes" fill in the following information for every absence of *less than 6 months*, no matter how short it was.

DATE DEPARTED	DATE RETURNED	NAME OF SHIP, OR OF AIRLINE, RAILROAD COMPANY, BUS COMPANY, OR OTHER MEANS USED TO RETURN TO THE UNITED STATES	PLACE OR PORT OF ENTRY THROUGH WHICH YOU RETURNED TO THE UNITED STATES

(b) Since your lawful admission, have you been out of the United States for a period of *6 months or longer?*.......... ☐ Yes ☐ No
If "No", state "None"; If "Yes", fill in following information for every absence of more than 6 months.

DATE DEPARTED	DATE RETURNED	NAME OF SHIP OR OF AIRLINE, RAILROAD COMPANY, BUS COMPANY, OR OTHER MEANS USED TO RETURN TO THE UNITED STATES	PLACE OR PORT OF ENTRY THROUGH WHICH YOU RETURNED TO THE UNITED STATES

Form N-400 (Rev. 4-14-81)Y   (OVER)

(1)

(15) The law provides that you may not be regarded as qualified for naturalization, if you knowingly committed certain offenses or crimes, even though you may not have been arrested. Have you ever, in or outside the United States:

    (*a*) knowingly committed any crime for which you have not been arrested? .... ☐ Yes ☐ No

    (*b*) been arrested, cited, charged, indicted, convicted, fined or imprisoned for breaking or violating any law or ordinance,
         including traffic regulations? .... ☐ Yes ☐ No

If you answer "Yes" to (*a*) or (*b*), give the following information as to each incident.

	WHEN	WHERE	(City)	(State)	(Country)	NATURE OF OFFENSE	OUTCOME OF CASE, IF ANY
(*a*)							
(*b*)							
(*c*)							
(*d*)							
(*e*)							

(16) List your present and past membership in or affiliation with every organization, association, fund, foundation, party, club, society or similar group in the United States or in any other country or place, and your foreign military service. (If none, write "None.")

    (*a*) ...., 19........... to 19...........
    (*b*) ...., 19........... to 19...........
    (*c*) ...., 19........... to 19...........
    (*d*) ...., 19........... to 19...........
    (*e*) ...., 19........... to 19...........
    (*f*) ...., 19........... to 19...........
    (*g*) ...., 19........... to 19...........

(17) (*a*) Are you now, or have you ever, in the United States or in any other place, been a member of, or in any other way connected or associated with the Communist Party? (If "Yes", attach full explanation) .... ☐ Yes ☐ No

    (*b*) Have you ever knowingly aided or supported the Communist Party directly, or indirectly through another organization, group or person? (If "Yes", attach full explanation) .... ☐ Yes ☐ No

    (*c*) Do you now or have you ever advocated, taught, believed in, or knowingly supported or furthered the interests of Communism? (If "Yes", attach full explanation) .... ☐ Yes ☐ No

(18) During the period March 23, 1933 to May 8, 1945, did you serve in, or were you in any affiliated with, either directly or indirectly, any military unit, paramilitary unit, police unit, self-defense unit, vigilante unit, citizen unit, unit of the Nazi Party or SS, government agency or office, extermination camp, concentration camp, prisoner of war camp, prison, labor camp, detention camp or transit camp, under the control of or affiliated with:

    (a) the Nazi Government of Germany .... ☐ Yes ☐ No
    (b) any Government in any area occupied by, allied with, or established with the assistance or cooperation of, the Nazi Government of Germany? .... ☐ Yes ☐ No

(19) During the period March 23, 1933 to May 8, 1945, did you ever order, incite, assist, or otherwise participate in the persecution of any person because of race, religion, national origin, or political opinion? .... ☐ Yes ☐ No

(20) Have you borne any hereditary title or have you been of any order of nobility in any foreign state? .... ☐ Yes ☐ No

(21) **Have you ever been declared legally incompetent or have you ever been confined as a patient in a mental institution?** .... ☐ Yes ☐ No

(22) Are deportation proceedings pending against you, or have you ever been deported or ordered deported, or have you ever applied for suspension of deportation? .... ☐ Yes ☐ No

(23) (*a*) My last Federal income tax return was filed........................... (year) Do you owe any Federal taxes? ..... ☐ Yes ☐ No

    (*b*) Since becoming a permanent resident of the United States, have you:
        —filed an income tax return as a nonresident? .... ☐ Yes ☐ No
        —failed to file an income tax return because you regarded yourself as a nonresident? .... ☐ Yes ☐ No
    (If you answer "Yes" to (*a*) or (*b*) explain fully.)

(24) Have you ever claimed in writing, or in any other way, to be a United States citizen? .... ☐ Yes ☐ No

(25) (*a*) Have you ever deserted from the military, air, or naval forces of the United States? .... ☐ Yes ☐ No

    (*b*) If male, have you ever left the United States to avoid being drafted into the Armed Forces of the United States? ...... ☐ Yes ☐ No

(26) The law provides that you may not be regarded as qualified for naturalization if, at *any* time during the period for which you are required to prove good moral character, you have been a habitual drunkard; committed adultery; advocated or practiced polygamy; have been a prostitute or procured anyone for prostitution; have knowingly and for gain helped any alien to enter the United States illegally; have been an illicit trafficker in narcotic drugs or marijuana; have received your income mostly from illegal gambling, or have given false testimony for the purpose of obtaining any benefits under this Act. Have you ever, *anywhere*, been such a person or committed any of these acts? (If you answer yes to any of these, attach full explanation.) .... ☐ Yes ☐ No

(27) Do you believe in the Constitution and form of government of the United States? .... ☐ Yes ☐ No

(28) Are you willing to take the full oath of allegiance to the United States? (See Instructions) .... ☐ Yes ☐ No

(29) If the law requires it, are you willing:

    (*a*) to bear arms on behalf of the United States? (If "No", attach full explanation) .... ☐ Yes ☐ No
    (*b*) to perform noncombatant services in the Armed Forces of the United States? (If "No", attach full explanation) .... ☐ Yes ☐ No
    (*c*) to perform work of national importance under civilian direction? (If "No"', attach full explanation) .... ☐ Yes ☐ No

(30) (*a*) If male, did you ever register under United States Selective Service laws or draft laws? .... ☐ Yes ☐ No
    If "Yes" give date................; Selective Service No.....................; Local Board No.................; Present classification......................

    (*b*) Did you ever apply for exemption from military service because of alienage, conscientious objections, or other reasons? ☐ Yes ☐ No
    If "Yes," explain fully................ ....

(3)

(31) If serving or ever served in the Armed Forces of the United States, give branch...;

trom..............................., 19......., to ...., 19........, and from........................., 19....... to ...., 19........;

☐ inducted or ☐ enlisted at..   ....; Service No.....................................;

type of discharge..; ....; rank at discharge...;
                          (Honorable, Dishonorable, etc.)

reason for discharge..
                                     (alienage, conscientious objector, other)

☐ Reserve or ☐ National Guard from .... 19...... to ....

(32) My occupation is...

List the names, addresses, and occupations (or types of business) of your employers during the last 5 years.   (If none, write "None.")
List present employment FIRST.

From-	To-	Employer's Name	Address	Occupation or Type of Business
(a) ...., 19.....	Present Time			
(b) ...., 19.....	............., 19.....			
(c) ...., 19.....	............., 19.....			
(d) ...., 19.....	............., 19.....			

(33) Complete this block if you are or have been married.

I am......................................**1**.............................. The first name of my husband or wife is (was).....................................
      (Separated, married, divorced, widowed)

We were married on... at.. He or she was born at................................

.... on... He or she entered the United States at (place)................................

.... on (date)....................................... for permanent residence and now resides ☐ with me

☐ apart from me at ....
           (Show full address if not living with you.)

He or she was naturalized on.. at..................................; Certificate No....................................,

or became a citizen by .... His or her Alien Registration No. is ....

(34) How many times have you been married?............ How many times has your husband or wife been married?........... If either of you has
been married more than once, fill in the following information for each previous marriage.

Date Married	Date Marriage Ended	Name of Person to Whom Married	Sex	(Check One) Person Married Was Citizen ☐ Alien ☐	How Marriage Ended
(a)				☐ ☐	
(b)				☐ ☐	
(c)				☐ ☐	
(d)				☐ ☐	

(35) I have...............children: (Complete columns (a) to (h) as to each child. If child lives with you, state "with me" in column (h), other-
     (Number)   wise give city and State of child's residence.)

(a) Given Names	(b) Sex	(c) Place Born (Country)	(d) Date Born	(e) Date of Entry	(f) Port of Entry	(g) Alien Registration No.	(h) Now Living at-

(36) **READ INSTRUCTION NO. 6 BEFORE ANSWERING QUESTION (36)**

I..................................want certificates of citizenship for those of my children who are in the U.S. and are under age 18 years that are named below.
  (Do)   (Do Not)

(Enclose $15 for each child for whom you want certificates, otherwise, send no money with this application.)

....
         (Write names of children under age 18 years and who are in the U.S. for whom you want certificates)

If present spouse is not the parent of the children named above, give parent's name, date and place of naturalization, and number of marriages.

....

U.S. DEPARTMENT OF JUSTICE
IMMIGRATION AND NATURALIZATION SERVICE

APPLICATION FOR CERTIFICATE OF CITIZENSHIP

OMB No. 1115–0018
Approval Expires 7/31/85

FEE STAMP

Take or mail this application to:
IMMIGRATION AND NATURALIZATION SERVICE

Date ....

(*Print or type*) .... nee ....
(Full, True Name, without Abbreviations)   (Maiden name, if any)

....
(Apartment number, Street address, and, if appropriate, "in care of")

ALIEN REGISTRATION

....
(City)   (County)   (State)   (ZIP Code)

No. ....

....
(Telephone Number)

(SEE INSTRUCTIONS. BE SURE YOU UNDERSTAND EACH QUESTION BEFORE YOU ANSWER IT.)

I hereby apply to the Commissioner of Immigration and Naturalization for a certificate showing that I am a citizen of the United States of America.

(1) I was born in .... on ....
(City)   (State or country)   (Month)   (Day)   (Year)

(2) My personal description is: Sex ....; complexion ....; color of eyes ....; color of hair ....; height .... feet .... inches; weight .... pounds; visible distinctive marks ....

.... Marital status: ☐ Single; ☐ Married; ☐ Divorced; ☐ Widow(er).

(3) I arrived in the United States at .... on ....
(City and State)   (Month)   (Day)   (Year)

under the name .... by means of ....
(Name of ship or other means of arrival)

☐ on U.S. Passport No. .... issued to me at .... on ....;
(Month)   (Day)   (Year)

☐ on an Immigrant Visa. ☐ Other (specify) ....

---

(4) FILL IN THIS BLOCK ONLY IF YOU ARRIVED IN THE UNITED STATES BEFORE JULY 1, 1924.

(*a*) My last permanent foreign residence was ....
(City)   (Country)

(*b*) I took the ship or other conveyance to the United States at ....
(City)   (Country)

(*c*) I was coming to .... at ....
(Name of person in the United States)   (City and State where this person was living)

(*d*) I traveled to the United States with ....
(Names of passengers or relatives with whom you traveled, and their relationship to you, if any)

....

---

(5) Have you been out of the United States since you first arrived? ☐ Yes ☐ No. If "Yes" fill in the following information for every absence.

DATE DEPARTED	DATE RETURNED	NAME OF AIRLINE, OR OTHER MEANS USED TO RETURN TO THE UNITED STATES	PORT OF RETURN TO THE UNITED STATES
....	....	....	....
....	....	....	....
....	....	....	....
....	....	....	....

(6) I _____ filed a petition for naturalization.
(have)   (have not)

(*If "have", attach full explanation.*)

TO THE APPLICANT.—Do not write between the double lines below. Continue on next page.

ARRIVAL RECORDS EXAMINED	ARRIVAL RECORD FOUND
Card index	Place .... Date ....
Index books	Name ....
Manifests	
....	Manner ....
....	Marital status .... Age ....
....	
	(Signature of person making search)

Form N–600 (Rev. 5–5–83)N   (1)

(CONTINUE HERE)

(7) I claim United States citizenship through my *(check whichever applicable)* ☐ father; ☐ mother; ☐ both parents;

☐ adoptive parent(s) · ☐ husband

(8) My father's name is ....; he was born on ....
(Month) (Day) (Year)

at ....; and resides at ....
(City) (State or country) (Street address, city, and State or country. If dead, write

.... He became a citizen of the United States by ☐ birth; ☐ naturalization on ....
"dead" and date of death.) (Month) (Day) (Year)

in the .... Certificate of Naturalization No. ....;
(Name of court, city, and State)

☐ through his parent(s), and .... issued Certificate of Citizenship No. A or AA ....
(was) (was not)

(If known) His former Alien Registration No. was ....

He .... lost United States citizenship. *(If citizenship lost, attach full explanation.)*
(has) (has not)

He resided in the United States from .... to ....; from .... to ....; from .... to ....;
(Year) (Year) (Year) (Year) (Year) (Year)

from .... to ....; from .... to ....; I am the child of his .... marriage.
(Year) (Year) (Year) (Year) (1st, 2d, 3d, etc.)

(9) My mother's present name is ....; her maiden name was ....;

she was born on ....; at ....; she resides
(Month) (Day) (Year) (City) (State or country)

at .... She became a citizen of the United States
(Street address, city, and State or country. If dead, write "dead" and date of death.)

by ☐ birth; ☐ naturalization under the name of ....

on .... in the ....
(Month) (Day) (Year) (Name of court, city, and State)

Certificate of Naturalization No. ....; ☐ through her parent(s), and .... issued Certificate
(was) (was not)

of Citizenship No. A or AA .... (If known) Her former Alien Registration No. was ....

She .... lost United States citizenship. *(If citizenship lost, attach full explanation.)*
(has) (has not)

She resided in the United States from .... to ....; from .... to ....; from .... to ....; from ....
(Year) (Year) (Year) (Year) (Year) (Year) (Year)

to ....; from .... to ....; I am the child of her .... marriage.
(Year) (Year) (Year) (1st, 2d, 3d, etc.)

(10) My mother and my father were married to each other on .... at ....
(Month) (Day) (Year) (City) (State or country)

(11) If claim is through adoptive parent(s):

I was adopted on .... in the ....
(Month) (Day) (Year) (Name of Court)

at .... by my ....
(City or town) (State) (Country) (mother, father, parents)

who were not United States citizens at that time.

(12) My .... served in the Armed Forces of the United States from ....
(father) (mother) (Date)

to .... and .... honorably discharged.
(Date) (was) (was not)

(13) I .... lost my United States citizenship. *(If citizenship lost, attach full explanation.)*
(have) (have not)

(14) I submit the following documents with this application:

Nature of Document	*Names of Persons Concerned*
....	....
....	....
....	....
....	....
....	....

(15) Fill in this block if your brother, sister, mother or father ever applied to the Immigration Service for a certificate of citizenship.

NAME OF RELATIVE	RELATIONSHIP	Date of Birth	WHEN APPLICATION SUBMITTED	CERTIFICATE NO. AND FILE NO., IF KNOWN, AND LOCATION OF OFFICE

(16) Fill in this block only if you are now or ever have been a married woman. I have been married .... time(s), as follows: (1, 2, 3, etc.)

DATE MARRIED	NAME OF HUSBAND	CITIZENSHIP OF HUSBAND	IF MARRIAGE HAS BEEN TERMINATED:	
			Date Marriage Ended	How Marriage Ended (Death or divorce)

(17) Fill in this block only if you claim citizenship through a husband. (*Marriage must have occurred prior to September 22, 1922.*)

Name of citizen husband .... ; he was born on ....
(Give full and complete name) (Month) (Day) (Year)

at .... ; and resides at ....
(City) (State or country) (Street address, city, and State or country. If dead, write

.... He became a citizen of the United States by ☐ birth; ☐ naturalization on ....
"dead" and date of death.) (Month) (Day) (Year)

in the .... Certificate of Naturalization No. .... ;
(Name of court, city, and State)

☐ through his parent(s), and .... issued Certificate of Citizenship No. A or AA ....
(was) (was not)

He .... since lost United States citizenship. (*If citizenship lost, attach full explanation.*)
(has) (has not)

I am of the .... race. Before my marriage to him, he was married .... time(s), as follows:
(1, 2, 3, etc.)

DATE MARRIED	NAME OF WIFE	IF MARRIAGE HAS BEEN TERMINATED:	
		Date Marriage Ended	How Marriage Ended (*Death or divorce*)

(18) Fill in this block only if you claim citizenship through your stepfather. (*Applicable only if mother married U.S. Citizen prior to September 22, 1922.*)

The full name of my stepfather is .... ; he was born on ....
(Month) (Day) (Year)

at .... ; and resides at ....
(City) (State or country) (Street address, city, and State or country. If dead, write

.... He became a citizen of the United States by ☐ birth; ☐ naturalization on ....
"dead" and date of death.) (Month) (Day) (Year)

in the .... Certificate of Naturalization No. .... ;
(Name of court, city, and State)

☐ through his parent(s), and .... issued Certificate of Citizenship No. A or AA ....
(was) (was not)

He .... since lost United States citizenship. (*If citizenship lost, attach full explanation.*)
(has) (has not)

He and my mother were married to each other on .... at ....
(Month) (Day) (Year) (City and State or country)

My mother is of the .... race. She .... issued Certificate of Citizenship No. A ....
(was) (was not)

Before marrying my mother, my stepfather was married .... time(s), as follows:
(1, 2, 3, etc.)

DATE MARRIED	NAME OF WIFE	IF MARRIAGE HAS BEEN TERMINATED:	
		Date Marriage Ended	How Marriage Ended (*Death or divorce*)

(19) I .... previously applied for a certificate of citizenship on .... , at ....
(have) (have not) (Date) (Office)

(20) Signature of person preparing form, if other than applicant. I declare that this document was prepared by me at the request of the applicant and is based on all information of which I have any knowledge.

SIGNATURE:

ADDRESS: .... DATE:

(SIGN HERE) ....
(Signature of applicant or parent or guardian)

OPTIONAL FORM 155A (6-82)
(Formerly OF-155)
DEPT. OF STATE

NSN 7540-01-126-7762

50155-20

IMMIGRANT VISA AND ALIEN REGISTRATION

IV- , ,

☐ THE IMMIGRANT HAS BEEN PREVIOUSLY IN THE UNITED STATES

OF: (Family Name)   (First Name)   (Middle Name)

INS FILE #, IF KNOWN

ACTION BY IMMIGRATION INSPECTOR

THE IMMIGRANT NAMED ABOVE ARRIVED IN THE UNITED STATES VIA (Name of vessel or flight no. of arrival)

INELIGIBILITY FOR VISA WAIVED UNDER SECTION
☐ 212(e)   ☐ 212(h)
☐ 212(g)   ☐ 212(i)

CITY AND COUNTRY OF BIRTH

MO DAY YR OF BIRTH

CITY AND COUNTRY OF LAST RESIDENCE

NATIONALITY

MARITAL STATUS
[ ]M [ ]S [ ]W [ ]D [ ]SEP

MOTHER'S FIRST NAME

FATHER'S FIRST NAME

FINAL ADDRESS IN THE UNITED STATES

STREET ADDRESS, INCLUDE--IN CARE OF & APT# IF APPLICABLE

CITY, STATE, AND ZIP CODE, IF AVAILABLE

SEC. 212(a)(14)
LABOR CERTIFICATION ☐ NOT APPLICABLE ☐ NOT REQUIRED ☐ ATTACHED

OCCUPATION

This visa is issued under Section 221 of the Immigration and Nationality Act, and upon the basis of the facts stated in the application. Possession of a visa does not entitle the bearer to enter the United States if at the time he seeks to enter he is found to be inadmissible. Upon arrival in the United States, it must be surrendered to a United States Immigration Officer

IMMIGRANT CLASSIFICATION

CLASSIFICATION SYMBOL

AMERICAN _____

FOREIGN STATE OTHER AREA LIMITATION

AT _____

IMMIGRANT VISA NO.

ISSUED ON   (Day)   (Month)   (Year)

Consular Officer of the United States of America

THE VALIDITY OF THIS VISA EXPIRES MIDNIGHT AT THE END OF
(Day)   (Month)   (Year)

PASSPORT

NO.

OR OTHER TRAVEL DOCUMENTS (Describe)

ISSUED TO

BY

ON

Tariff No. 21
Fee Paid $75
Local Cy. Equiv.

EXPIRES

IV- , ,

ACTION OF I.J.

ACTION ON APPEAL

U.S.P.H.S.

AIR TRANSACTION LOG - ARRIVALS

DATE: 082879

AIRPORT: Chicago O'Hare

PORT (Region, District, and Port Code): 3906

MANIFEST NUMBER	AIRCRAFT ✓	AIRCRAFT DESIGNATION	FLIGHT NUMBER	AIRLINE	TIME	COMMERCIAL AIRCRAFT DIRECT FOREIGN PASSENGER	CREW	COMMERCIAL AIRCRAFT VIA U.S. PORT PASSENGER	CREW	MILITARY AIRCRAFT PASSENGER	CREW	PRIVATE AIRCRAFT PASSENGER	CREW	DECLARATIONS PASSENGER	CREW	MILITARY	BAGGAGE EXAMS
2051		N864	771	TWA	1400	396	18							210	18		225
2052		6Y-JME	051	JM	1600	252	13							185	13		180
2053		CF-119		Private	1630							5	2	5	2		3

Department of the Treasury
United States Customs Service

WELCOME
TO THE
UNITED STATES

DEPARTMENT OF THE TREASURY
UNITED STATES CUSTOMS SERVICE

CUSTOMS DECLARATION

FORM APPROVED
OMB NO. 1515-0041

Each arriving traveler or head of family must provide the following information (only **ONE** written declaration per family is required):

1. Name: ---
   Last   _First_   _Middle Initial_

2. Number of family members traveling with you ----------------------

3. Date of Birth: ----|----|----   4. Airline/Flight: -------------
   Month   _Day_   _Year_

5. U.S. Address: ---

   ----

6. I am a U.S. Citizen   YES   NO
   If No,
   Country: ----------------------------- □ □

7. I reside permanently in the U.S.   YES   NO
   If No,
   Expected Length of Stay: --------------- □ □

8. The purpose of my trip is or was
   □ BUSINESS   □ PLEASURE

9. I am/we are bringing fruits, plants, meats, food, soil,   YES   NO
   birds, snails, other live animals, farm products, or □ □
   I/we have been on a farm or ranch outside the U.S.

10. I am/we are carrying currency or monetary   YES   NO
    instruments over $10,000 U.S. or foreign □ □
    equivalent.

11. The total value of all goods I/we purchased
    or acquired abroad and am/are bringing
    to the U.S. is (see instructions under
    Merchandise on reverse side; visitors
    should report value of gifts only): $--------------------
    U.S. Dollars

SIGN ON REVERSE SIDE AFTER YOU READ WARNING.
(Do not write below this line.)

INSPECTOR'S NAME   STAMP AREA

BADGE NO.

Paperwork Reduction Act Notice: The Paperwork Reduction Act of 1980 says we must tell you why we are collecting this information, how we will use it and whether you have to give it to us. We ask for this information to carry out the Customs, Agriculture, and Currency laws of the United States. We need it to ensure that travelers are complying with these laws and to allow us to figure and collect the right amount of duties and taxes. Your response is mandatory

Customs Form 6059B (102584)

WARNING

AGRICULTURAL PRODUCTS

To prevent the entry of dangerous agricultural pests the following are restricted: Fruits, vegetables, plants, plant products, soil, meats, meat products, birds, snails, and other live animals or animal products. Failure to declare all such items to a Customs/Agriculture Officer can result in fines or other penalties.

CURRENCY AND MONETARY INSTRUMENTS

The transportation of currency or monetary instruments, regardless of the amount, is legal; however, if you take out of or bring into (or attempt to take out of or bring into) the United States more than $10,000 (U.S. or foreign equivalent, or a combination of the two) in coin, currency, travelers checks or bearer instruments such as money orders, checks, stocks or bonds, you are required by law to file a report on a Form 4790 with the U.S. Customs Service. If you have someone else carry the currency or instruments for you, you must also file the report. FAILURE TO FILE THE REQUIRED REPORT OR FALSE STATEMENTS ON THE REPORT MAY LEAD TO SEIZURE OF THE CURRENCY OR INSTRUMENTS AND TO CIVIL PENALTIES AND/OR CRIMINAL PROSECUTION.

MERCHANDISE

In Item 11, **U.S. residents** must declare the total value of ALL articles acquired abroad (whether new or used, whether dutiable or not, and whether obtained by purchase, as a gift, or otherwise) which are in their or their family's possession at the time of arrival. **Visitors** must declare in Item 11 only the total value of all gifts they are bringing with them.

The amount of duty to be paid will be determined by a Customs officer. U.S. residents are normally entitled to a duty free exemption of $400; non-residents are normally entitled to an exemption of $100. Both residents and non-residents will normally be required to pay a flat 10% rate of duty on the first $1,000 above their exemptions.

If the value of goods declared in Item 11 EXCEEDS $1,400 PER PERSON, then list the articles below and show price paid or, for gifts, fair retail value.

DESCRIPTION OF ARTICLES	PRICE	CUSTOMS USE
TOTAL		

IF YOU HAVE ANY QUESTIONS ABOUT WHAT MUST BE REPORTED OR DECLARED ASK A CUSTOMS OFFICER.

I have read the above statements and have made a truthful declaration.

SIGNATURE   _DATE (Month/Day/Year)_

Customs Form 6059B (102584) (Back)

GPO : 1984 O - 458-903

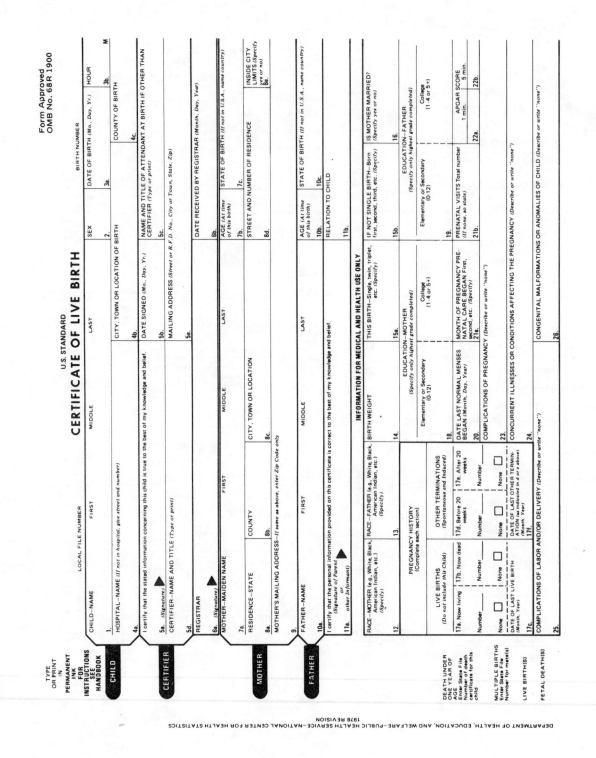

AMERICAN COUNCIL OF VOLUNTARY AGENCIES FOR FOREIGN SERVICE, INC.
200 Park Avenue South - New York, N.Y. 10003

Date:_____ File ID #_____ Present Location: _____

The following persons:

Name	A Number	Date of Birth	Sex	Place of Birth
1.				
2.				
3.				
4.				
5.				
6.				
7.				
8.				
9.				
10.				
11.				
12.				

have been accepted for resettlement under the auspices of:

Voluntary Agency (Principal Sponsor)   Local Sponsors

Tel: Tel:

Airport of Final Destination:

Special Instructions:

    This agency agrees to assist the principal refugee named above to obtain employment
and housing for him/herself and family, if any.

                                        Signature_____
                                        Authorized volag Representative

ACVAFS Form #1

DEPARTMENT OF HEALTH AND HUMAN SERVICES
SOCIAL SECURITY ADMINISTRATION

Form Approved
OMB No. 0960-0066

FORM SS-5 — APPLICATION FOR A SOCIAL SECURITY NUMBER CARD
(Original, Replacement or Correction)

MICROFILM REF. NO. (SSA USE ONLY)

Unless the requested information is provided, we may not be able to issue a Social Security Number (20 CFR 422-103(b))

INSTRUCTIONS TO APPLICANT ▶ Before completing this form, please read the instructions on the opposite page. You can type or print, using pen with dark blue or black ink. Do not use pencil.

NAA	NAME TO BE SHOWN ON CARD	First	Middle	Last

NAB	FULL NAME AT BIRTH (IF OTHER THAN ABOVE)	First	Middle	Last

1

ONA	OTHER NAME(S) USED

2

STT	MAILING ADDRESS	(Street/Apt. No., P.O. Box, Rural Route No.)

CTY	CITY	STE	STATE	ZIP	ZIP CODE

3

CSP CITIZENSHIP (Check one only)
- ☐ a. U.S. citizen
- ☐ b. Legal alien allowed to work
- ☐ c. Legal alien not allowed to work
- ☐ d. Other (See instructions on Page 2)

4

SEX / SEX
- ☐ MALE
- ☐ FEMALE

5

ETB RACE/ETHNIC DESCRIPTION (Check one only) (Voluntary)
- ☐ a. Asian, Asian-American or Pacific Islander (Includes persons of Chinese, Filipino, Japanese, Korean, Samoan, etc., ancestry or descent)
- ☐ b. Hispanic (Includes persons of Chicano, Cuban, Mexican or Mexican-American, Puerto Rican, South or Central American, or other Spanish ancestry or descent)
- ☐ c. Negro or Black (not Hispanic)
- ☐ d. Northern American Indian or Alaskan Native
- ☐ e. White (not Hispanic)

6 / **7** / **8**

DOB DATE OF BIRTH ▶	MONTH	DAY	YEAR	AGE PRESENT AGE	PLB PLACE OF BIRTH ▶	CITY	STATE OR FOREIGN COUNTRY	FCI ☐

9

MNA MOTHER'S NAME AT HER BIRTH	First	Middle	Last (Her maiden name)

FNA FATHER'S NAME	First	Middle	Last

10

PNO a. Has a Social Security number card ever been requested for the person listed in item 1? ☐ YES(2) ☐ NO(1) ☐ Don't know(1) If yes, when: ——▶ MONTH / YEAR

b. Was a card received for the person listed in item 1? ☐ YES(3) ☐ NO(1) ☐ Don't know(1) If you checked yes to a or b, complete Items c through e; otherwise go to item 11.

SSN c. Enter the Social Security number assigned to the person listed in item 1. ☐☐☐ — ☐☐ — ☐☐☐☐

NLC d. Enter the name shown on the most recent Social Security card issued for the person listed in item 1. | PDB | e. Date of birth correction (See Instruction 10 on page 2) ▶ | MONTH | DAY | YEAR

11 / **12**

DON TODAY'S DATE ▶	MONTH	DAY	YEAR		Telephone number where we can reach you during the day. Please include the area code. ▶	HOME	OTHER

ASD **WARNING: Deliberately furnishing (or causing to be furnished) false information on this application is a crime punishable by fine or imprisonment, or both.**

IMPORTANT REMINDER: SEE PAGE 1 FOR REQUIRED EVIDENTIARY DOCUMENTS.

13 YOUR SIGNATURE

14 YOUR RELATIONSHIP TO PERSON IN ITEM 1
- ☐ Self ☐ Other (Specify) _____

WITNESS (Needed only if signed by mark "X") | WITNESS (Needed only if signed by mark "X")

DO NOT WRITE BELOW THIS LINE (FOR SSA USE ONLY)	DTC SSA RECEIPT DATE

SSN ASSIGNED ☐☐☐ — ☐☐ — ☐☐☐☐ | NPN

BIC | SIGNATURE AND TITLE OF EMPLOYEE(S) REVIEWING EVIDENCE AND/OR CONDUCTING INTERVIEW

DOC	NTC	CAN

TYPE(S) OF EVIDENCE SUBMITTED

☐ MANDATORY IN PERSON INTERVIEW CONDUCTED

DATE

DATE

IDN | ITV | DCL

Form **SS-5** (5-84)   Destroy prior editions   3

SCHEDULE B

QUARTERLY CASELOAD STATUS REPORT

From _____ To _____

STATE: _____

	5/	C A S H				M E D I C A L 6/		
(For ALL time-eligible refugees/entrants)		AFDC	RCA	GA	SSI	MEDICAID	RMA	GA
A. Actual Number of Individual Recipients at the Beginning of the Quarter		----	----	----	·	----	----	----	a/
B. INCREASE DURING THE QUARTER		----	----	----	----	----	----	----	b/
1. Refugee Resettled in the State after the Beginning of FY (10/1)		----	----	----	----			
2. Secondary Migration 1/		----	----	----	----			
3. Old Cases Reactivated 1/		----	----	----	----			
4. Birth 1/		----	----	----	xxxx			
5. Other		----	----	----	----			
C. DECREASE DURING THE QUARTER		----	----	----	----			
1. Time Limitation 2/		----	----	----	----			
2. Out-of-State Migration 1/		----	----	----	----			
3. Economic Self-Sufficiency 3/		----	----	----	----			
4. Death 1/		----	----	----	----			
5. Sanctions 7/		----	----	----	----			
6. Other		----	----	----	----			
D. Number of Recipients at the End of the Quarter		----	----	----	----	----	----	----	c/
1. Recipients 18 Years of Age and above 4/		----	----	----	----			
2. Recipients under 18 Years of Age 4/		----	----	----	xxxx			

Form ORR-6 -- Revised 11/83

SCHEDULE C

QUARTERLY SUPPORT SERVICE CASELOAD REPORT

From: _ _ _ _ _ To: _ _ _ _ _ _ _

STATE: _ _ _ _ _ _ _

I. REFUGEE SUPPORT SERVICE PROGRAM

Location 1/	Number of Clients in Each Category during the Quarter				# of Client Outcomes in Each Category			# of Direct Job Placement Achieved 4/	# of Job Placements Reaching 90-Day Retention
	JOB	VOC 2/	ESL	OTHER	AA	BB 37	CC		

(Use additional sheets if necessary)

II. UNACCOMPANIED CHILDREN PROGRAM

(Number of Children Served in the Following Categories)

Location 1/	Income Maintenance	Medical Services	English Training	Vocational/Skills Training	Other 5/

(The State may use a separate form for each kind of placement, e.g., foster care, group home etc.)

III. HEALTH MONITORING PROGRAM 6/

Location 1/	Number of refugee recipients of health screening services	# of refugee recipients of health follow-up	# of refugee recipients of medical treatments

Form ORR-6 (6-82)

-4-

Appendix **B**

SOME METHODOLOGICAL ISSUES IN ANALYZING DATA ON IMMIGRATION

INTRODUCTION

The body of this report has been concerned largely with the process of collecting and disseminating data on immigration and the foreign-born. Analytical issues have been touched on, but no detailed examination of analytical procedures has been attempted. This appendix incorporates three papers concerning analysis, the first two by Kenneth Hill, of the panel staff, and the third by Kenneth Wachter, a member of the panel. Although the papers have benefited from the comments of a number of reviewers, they nonetheless represent the views of the authors rather than of the panel as a collective entity. They are included here because they concern issues central to the panel's charge and were prepared as a part of its overall work plan. We hope they will serve to stimulate both discussion and new research areas.

The first paper outlines three methodological procedures that could be applied to data that either are available or could be made available at little expense and with little change in current administrative practices. The methods outlined are aimed at measuring stocks or flows that are poorly documented by existing statistics: emigration of immigrants admitted for permanent residence (and, coincidentally, an estimate of average coverage of the Alien Address Report system), the size and growth of the population of illegally resident aliens, and net flows of U.S. citizens. These methods are intended to be illustrations of ways in which particular types of data might be used for analytical purposes and to indicate the potential analytical value of compiling or processing data that are already collected. The estimates obtained by these methods are also intended to be illustrative rather than substantive--for substantive applications, the necessary data must be available and the extensive assumptions underlying the methods must be evaluated in the light of the results obtained. The methods proposed do have some promise for producing useful new estimates, to complement rather than to replace existing ones, and it is hoped that, even if these methods in the form presented do not prove viable or prove to be excessively sensitive to critical and unsupportable assumptions, their presentation will stimulate discussion and the development of new approaches to the use of available or easily generated data.

The second piece is concerned with estimating the size of the illegally resident population of the United States. Estimating the size of this population, and still more its characteristics, poses serious and special measurement problems, since the population itself is, for obvious reasons, anxious to avoid any unnecessary contact with officialdom. As a result, the methods applied, though often ingenious, also often rely on extensive assumptions that are hard to justify. Hill reviews the major empirical studies that have been made of the size of the illegal population and examines their results in the context of their methodology and assumptions. Several of the methods have been reviewed elsewhere, and little new about these methods is presented here; however, some of the methods have not been subjected to detailed examination before, and it seemed useful to cover all the major methods and their results in one place and to pull together and evaluate all the available empirical estimates of the size of the illegal population. The paper is intended as an evaluation of the various estimates and thus concentrates on the negative rather than on the positive aspects of the methodologies used. The reader should bear in mind, however, that the measurement problems involved are particularly severe and that any methods used will inevitably involve assumptions and approximations that are hard to justify. It is an area in which new approaches or the use of different data are to be welcomed, and in which a wide margin of uncertainty in the estimates derived should not be interpreted as a criticism of the methodology or of the attempt.

The third piece discusses the issues of imputation and treatment of missing data with particular reference to procedures of the Immigration and Naturalization Service (INS) and the presentation of data in the INS statistical yearbooks. Wachter argues strongly that the procedures currently used by INS should be reviewed in terms of their statistical validity and should be carefully documented in the Statistical Yearbook so that users can be aware of how the necessary imputations have been made and be alerted to how such imputations might affect the data.

Indirect Approaches to Assessing Stocks and Flows of Migrants

Kenneth Hill

INTRODUCTION

Statistics for U.S. migrant groups are of very variable quality. The best data made available by the INS cover first arrivals of permanent immigrants, or those changing status to permanent immigrant, and those naturalizing to U.S. citizenship. These data seem to be fairly reliable, in general if not with regard to all the available detail, even though they have suffered from severe processing and publication delays in the last few years. Figures on first arrivals of refugees, published very promptly by the Office of Refugee Resettlement, also seem to be reliable. Some elements of inflow are thus adequately covered by existing statistics. Inflows of temporary visitors, returning citizens, and returning resident aliens are less satisfactory. Although total arrivals by air are reasonably well recorded by the INS, processing of arrival declarations for aliens has been sporadic in recent years, and permanent residents are no longer required to complete such declarations. The situation for the inflow through land border ports of entry is worse; in many cases no direct head count is made, the total flow being estimated as the product of numbers of cars and an average occupancy figure derived from semiannual surveys, also used to estimate citizen/noncitizen ratios (see Chapter 4 for a more complete description of these procedures). Since the gross inflow across land borders represents the great majority of total inflow, INS estimates of total inflow cannot be regarded as satisfactory and in any case exclude any inflow of undocumented aliens.

No systematic attempt is even made to record outflow; although temporary visitors are required to complete a declaration on departure, compliance is high only at airports. Departures of all passengers by air are recorded by the INS from airline reports, but coverage of charter flights appears to be incomplete (see Chapter 5). No attempt is made to record departures of citizens or permanent residents at land border points or even to estimate the number of vehicles crossing. There is thus no basis for estimating gross outflow from the United States and no basis for monitoring changes in population stock. Until 1981, the INS attempted to monitor the stock of resident aliens through the Alien Address Reporting system; however, reporting was widely felt to be incomplete and the system was scrapped, although resident aliens are still required to register changes of address with the INS. (This requirement is seldom observed, however, and the forms are not processed.) Information on the population stock and inflows is available from the decennial census, which collects country of birth, citizenship, period of arrival for the foreign-born, and residence one year and five years before the census. The accuracy of some of the information, which is self-reported, is open to question, and the coverage by the census of undocumented aliens is unknown.

There are thus major deficiencies in U.S. international migration statistics, the two most important being the size and structure of the undocumented population and emigration of both U.S. citizens and of noncitizens. Numerous ingenious approaches have been developed to obtain estimates of the stocks and flows involved. Siegel et al. (1980) provide a useful review of methods used to estimate illegal immigration, and methods of estimating emigration have been reviewed by Passel and Peck (1979) and Warren and Kraly (1985).

This paper describes three potentially useful new indirect approaches to the estimation of stocks and flows of U.S. migrants. Unfortunately, the approaches are based on data that are no longer collected, from the Alien Address Reporting system, on data that are collected but not processed, from records of deportable aliens located in the United States or on data that are difficult to compile, from foreign census counts of U.S. citizens or the U.S.-born living abroad. The immediate practical applicability of the methods described is thus severely limited, but the methods are described in order to indicate some directions that analysis could take if fairly simple procedures for data collection, processing, or compilation were instituted. They are not proposed as final solutions to the measurement problems with which they are concerned. Like all indirect methods, they too involve assumptions and approximations that will affect the results. Rather, these approaches illustrate how certain types of data could be used to obtain estimates of stocks and flows of people in, into, and out of the United States. We hope this illustration of the application of somewhat different approaches to the problem will generate further thinking, which may stimulate additional future research in this area.

The first method uses information on deportable aliens located by duration of illegal residence and other simple characteristics to estimate the size and structure of the nonlegal population of the United States. The second method combines information from the Alien Address Reporting system with information on numbers of new immigrants and naturalizations to estimate both the coverage of the address reporting program and the emigration of resident aliens. The third method uses census data from other countries on the U.S. citizen or U.S.-born population resident in those countries to scale information from an administrative data source--Internal Revenue Service tax filer records--on the U.S. population living abroad.

THE SIZE AND STRUCTURE OF THE NONLEGAL POPULATION OF THE UNITED STATES

Numerous methods have been described for estimating the number of nonlegal residents of the United States or major components of this population (see the second paper in this appendix) for a review of the more important studies). The approaches proposed here use information on locations of deportable aliens by duration of illegal residence to estimate the size and duration structure of the underlying population, first assuming the population to be demographically stable and second using duration-specific growth rates. The INS collects information on deportable aliens located on form I-213 (see Appendix A) but has not processed the data systematically, although Davidson (1981) has described the results of processing a sample of the forms completed in calendar 1978.

The use of I-213 data to estimate either numbers or characteristics of the nonlegal population is not straightforward for a number of reasons. First, the locations occur very largely at short durations of illegal stay; in fiscal 1982, for example, 75 percent of the 963,000 locations were of aliens with a duration of illegal stay of 30 days or less, and 50 percent occurred at entry; a high proportion of these locations may be of the same person located several times in the same year. Second, the located aliens cannot be regarded as a random sample of the underlying population, since probabilities of location are likely to vary by characteristics such as sex, nationality, and occupation. Third, the quality of the data on the I-213 is widely regarded as low, and although no thorough evaluation has been made, Davidson (1981) shows that employment and residence characteristics suffer from high levels of nonresponse. These shortcomings no doubt partly explain the INS's failure to process I-213 forms on a routine basis.

Before describing and illustrating the methods in detail, it is useful to provide a general explanation of why the methods might be expected to work at all. To make any analytical use of locations, it has to be assumed that the number of locations is related to the number of deportable aliens who can be located. If the number of locations is determined by INS targets, or the INS locates as many deportable aliens as it can given existing resources and manpower, there will be no systematic relationship between locations and population at risk, and locations will provide no basis for estimating the size of the population. No empirical basis exists for assuming a relationship between locations and population, but it does seem plausible that if the deportable alien population were doubled, the INS would locate at least some more deportable aliens without any increase in effort, although locations might increase by a factor of less than two. Even accepting this assumption of a positive elasticity of locations to population, it might appear at first sight that a series of numbers of locations by duration could only indicate relative, not absolute, rates of location by duration. Sets of location rates that are the same in duration pattern but different in level will produce the same numbers of locations at each duration when applied to populations that share a given distribution by duration but are appropriately scaled. It is not obvious, therefore, that recorded numbers of locations can tell us anything about the size of the underlying population. However, there is a link between the two because the number of locations affects the size of the population, in much the same way as deaths affect the size and age distribution of a closed population. If locations were the only source of attrition, the parallel with deaths would be exact, and methods for estimating population size from deaths by age for a stable population (that is, a population changing at a single, constant rate at all ages and thus maintaining a constant age structure though not a constant size), such as that proposed by Preston et al. (1980), or for a general population (Preston and Coale, 1982), could be applied to locations by duration. In practice, voluntary return migration, change of status, and deaths also contribute to the attrition of the population of illegal aliens, so estimates based on locations alone will underestimate the true size of the population unless allowance is made for other unobserved types of loss.

The first approach assumes that the illegal alien population is stable in the demographic sense of having a constant, unchanging rate of change at each duration of illegal residence. In such a stable population, the number reaching duration d in a year, N(d), can be expressed in terms of the number of entries in the year E, the stable rate of change r, and the probability of surviving from entry to d, p(d):

$$N(d) = E \ e^{-rd} p(d) \tag{1}$$

The average population at all durations, P, can be found by integrating equation 1:

$$P = \int_0^w N(d)dd = E \int_0^w e^{-rd} \ p(d)dd \tag{2}$$

where w is the highest duration attained. In any population, the rate of change r is equal to the entry rate, E/P, less the loss rate, L/P, where L is total losses; substituting rP + L for E in equation (2) and rearranging gives

$$P/L = \int_0^w e^{-rd} \ p(d)dd \ / \ [1 - r \int_0^w e^{-rd} \ p(d)dd] \tag{3}$$

Also in a stable population, survival to duration d can be expressed in terms of losses by duration, l(d), and r:

$$p(d) = \int_d^w l(d) \ e^{rd} \ dd \ / \int_0^w l(d) \ e^{rd} \ dd \tag{4}$$

If we now assume that losses from INS locations, D(d), form a constant proportion of all losses at all durations d, p(d) can be expressed in terms of D(d) and r, since the constant proportion will cancel out in equation 4.

We can now apply equations 3 and 4 to Davidson's data on locations by duration of illegal stay for 1978, assuming different growth rates, and limiting the analysis to locations at durations of one month or more. Equation 4 has been evaluated assuming that locations are distributed evenly over each duration group, applying a value of d for the midpoint of the interval, except for the open 7+ years interval, for which a value of 9.5 years was assumed. The integrals in equation 3 were then evaluated trapezoidally for each duration category. Calculations are shown in Table B-1. The ratio P/L, average population to average losses, increases from 1.655 for a zero growth rate to 1.882 for a growth rate of 5 percent to 2.168 for a growth rate of 10 percent; an annual growth rate of 10 percent implies a population doubling time of seven years. The estimated P/L is surprisingly insensitive to the assumed growth rate.

The estimates of P/L do not provide a basis for estimating P directly, since we do not know the value of L, average annual losses. However, we can obtain estimates of P for a range of assumptions about the value of L/D, total losses to location losses. Total locations at one month duration or more were 231,274 in 1978. If locations were 25 percent of total losses, the value of L would be 0.93 million, and the alien population present illegally in the United States for a month or more would then be 1.53 million for a growth rate of zero, 1.74 million for a growth rate of 5 percent, and 2.01 million for a growth rate of 10 percent. If locations were 50 percent of total losses, each estimate would be halved.

Locations data do not suggest a rapid growth rate of the population. In 1979, 245,118 deportable aliens illegally resident for a month or more were located, so if location rates remained constant the underlying population grew at 5.8 percent annually. A growth rate around 5 percent thus seems more likely than one of 10 percent. We have little guidance for a plausible figure for L/D, though Garcia y Griego (1980:Figure 3.3), using data from the Mexican CENIET border survey on migration histories of Mexicans returned by the INS, found that about 60 percent of returns to Mexico over the period 1970-1977 resulted from INS locations, and about 40 percent were voluntary. These results suggest that an L/D ratio of 2.0, allowing for deaths and legalizations in addition to voluntary returns, is more plausible than a ratio of 4.0, at least for Mexican illegal residents. Using these assumptions, the data suggest an illegal population resident one month or more that averaged around 0.9 million in 1978.

This procedure can also provide a number of other interesting results. For a growth rate of 5 percent, the ratio P/L is estimated at 1.882; this ratio is the inverse of the loss rate, which is therefore estimated as 0.531. The entry rate, E/P, is equal to the loss rate plus the growth rate, and is therefore estimated as 0.581. If the ratio L/D is taken to be 2.0, P is equal to 0.871 million, implying a value of E of 0.506 million. This value is the number of illegals achieving a month's residence in 1978; since locations under a month in 1978 totalled 0.817 million, and the value of E is estimated at 0.506 million reaching a month without being located, total entries are estimated (assuming all losses at durations less than a month result from locations) at 1.323 million, of which the Border Patrol located 62 percent at entry or during the first month of illegal residence.

We can also use the p(d) functions to calculate duration-specific annual location rates, dividing the life table losses $p(d) - p(d+1)$ by person-years lived by the life table population, approximated by $n(p(d) + p(d+1)) / 2$, where n is the length of the duration interval in years, and then dividing by 2.0 again to allow for the assumption that only half the losses resulted from locations. The resulting location rates $_n l_d$ are shown in the last column of Table B-1. One comforting feature of the rates is that those for the open interval, $_w l_d$, which are set at 0.200 by assuming a uniform distribution over 5 years, are more or less consistent with the rates for shorter durations. A discomforting feature is that the rates are lowest for the duration interval 1-2 years, whereas we might expect them to decline steadily with duration. A possible explanation would be that location losses represent a lower proportion of all losses at long durations than at short durations. This explanation is tested in Table B-2, in which locations numbers are inflated by variable duration-specific factors, averaging 2.0 overall, and then manipulated using a growth rate of 5 percent. Three models are presented, (a) with the location proportion of all losses rising with duration, (b) with it falling, and (c) with it starting high for duration 1-6 months, falling sharply to a minimum for duration 7-12 months, then rising steadily as duration increases. Model (b) does indeed produce location rates that are essentially constant at durations over one year.

More surprisingly, the results using these three models suggest that the procedure is not very sensitive even to substantial variations in the location to total loss ratios by duration, the estimated total population varying from 0.79 million for model (a) to 1.24 million for model (b).

The assumption of stability can be dropped if information is available on duration-specific growth rates. If duration-specific location rates were constant from year to year, population growth rates could be calculated directly from the numbers of locations in successive years, since the locations growth rates would be identical to the underlying population growth rates. Even if we wished not to assume constant rates, we could assume a constant duration pattern for the rates and an overall growth rate to which the duration-specific rates would be scaled. To apply this procedure, we need information on locations by duration for at least two consecutive years. Unfortunately, such useful data are not available, but we present the methodology required and illustrate the effects of departure from stability for two different cases.

Preston and Coale (1983) have shown that for a non-stable population,

$$N(a) = B\, e^{-\int_0^a r(x)dx}\, p(a) \tag{5}$$

where $N(a)$ is the population age a, B the number of births, $r(x)$ the growth rate at age x, and $p(a)$ the probability of surviving to age a, all at some particular time t. By integration, the total population P is given by:

$$P = \int_0^w N(a)da = B\int_0^w e^{-\int_0^a r(x)dx}\, p(a)da \tag{6}$$

In any population, the birth rate B/P is equal to the loss rate L/P plus the growth rate R, so equation 6 can be rewritten (replacing age by duration) as

$$P/L = \int_0^w e^{-\int_0^d r(x)dx}\, p(d)dd \,/\, [1 - R\int_0^w e^{-\int_0^d r(x)dx}\, p(d)dd] \tag{7}$$

we can estimate $p(d)$ and $r(x)$, we can then use this equation to estimate P/L. The variable growth rate version of equation 4 is

$$p(d) = \int_d^w l(d)\, e^{\int_0^d r(x)dx}\, dd \,/\, \int_0^w l(d)\, e^{\int_0^d r(x)dx}\, dd \tag{8}$$

Thus, given values of $l(d)$ (or $_nl_d$) and $r(d)$ (or $_nr_d$) we can obtain $p(d)$, the survival function needed in equation 7. Note that the values of $l(d)$ again do not need to be the correct level, as long as they have the true duration pattern, since a constant level factor will cancel out from the top and bottom of equation 8. Thus we can use locations $_nD_d$ in place of losses $_nl_d$ in equation 8 if we assume that locations make up a constant proportion of total losses for all durations.

We have no data to which to apply this more flexible approach, since Davidson's data on locations by duration are for 1978 only and provide no guidance concerning duration-specific changes in locations. However, we can test the sensitivity of the stable assumption estimates derived above to a non-stable underlying population by assuming different patterns of duration-specific growth rates. Using the basic model with an overall growth rate of 5 percent and a constant location to loss ratio of 0.5, we illustrate in Table B-3 the estimates obtained assuming first that duration-specific growth rates fall with duration and second that they rise. The P/L ratios obtained bracket the ratio for a stable population, lower for falling rates and higher for rising rates, but differ from it by only 4 or 5 percent. Thus it appears that the stable procedure is actually quite insensitive to departures from stability, at least for the range of growth rates tested, as it was to substantial differences in the stable growth rate used. This insensitivity arises from the heavy concentration of locations at short durations for which the growth rate has only a modest effect.

In conclusion, these methods make some strong assumptions, but the results are not very sensitive to many of them. Deviations from stability appear to be relatively unimportant, and the stability assumption can be relaxed if data are available for more than one year. Similarly, the results are not highly sensitive to the stable growth rate assumed in the stable method or to the overall growth rate in the non-stable method. The results are more sensitive to locations to losses ratios that change sharply with duration, although ratios that change by more than a factor of two affect the overall population to loss ratio by less than 50 percent. The assumption to which the final estimate is directly proportional is the overall location to loss ratio; a value of this ratio of 0.25 will produce an estimate of the illegal population exactly twice as large as will a value of 0.50. However, overall the methodology turns out to be surprisingly robust to deviations from the assumptions. It is likely to work best for groups with similar location and other loss probabilities, so it could usefully be applied to data on locations classified by sex and nationality groups, though not by age since age would introduce entries to and departures from the population considered as a result of birthdays. Data for consecutive years would also prove useful for relaxing the assumption of stability and for examining the consistency of the results.

Given the limited data available, the results using location to loss ratios that fall with duration appear most plausible; with an overall location to loss ratio of 0.5, they suggest an average illegal alien population resident a month or more of 1.2 million for 1978, a figure by no means inconsistent with other empirical estimates available. This figure of course excludes the contribution of illegal immigrants at durations of 30 days or less, but their contribution in terms of person-years lived must be fairly small, even if their number is large;

for 1978, it would increase the estimate of 1.2 million by less than 0.1 million. This estimate is of course only arrived at in order to illustrate how these methods work. More extensive data, permitting repeated applications, the relaxation of certain assumptions, and separate analyses for more homogenous subgroups, are necessary to establish the ultimate value of the methods for estimation purposes.

ESTIMATING EMIGRATION OF RESIDENT ALIENS

Until 1981, most aliens resident in the United States were required to report their address to the INS in January every year. Reporting was made by completing and mailing to the INS a special card (form I-53) available at post offices and elsewhere. The information collected is described in Chapter 4, and the form reproduced in Appendix A. Figures from the reporting system were published in the INS Statistical Yearbook by nationality and state of residence.

Reporting under the system was widely regarded as being incomplete, one of the reasons why the Alien Address Reporting (AAR) system was dropped after 1981, and year-to-year fluctuations in the numbers of reporting foreigners can only be explained plausibly in terms of varying coverage. However, the information available provides some basis for estimating the emigration of permanent resident aliens. If all recording is complete, the number of permanent residents reporting in year $t+1$, $PR(t+1)$, should be equal to the number who reported in year t, $PR(t)$, plus immigrants (both arriving and changing status), $_1I_t$, less naturalizations, $_1N_t$, emigration, $_1E_t$, and deaths in the United States of permanent immigrants, $_1D_t$. Thus

$$PR(t+1) = PR(t) + {}_1I_t - {}_1N_t - ({}_1E_t + {}_1D_t) \tag{9}$$

If reporting in years t and $t+1$ was $k(t)$ and $k(t+1)$ complete, and $PRR(t)$ and $PRR(t+1)$ are the numbers reporting, then

$$PRR(t+1)/k(t+1) = PRR(t)/k(t) + {}_1I_t - {}_1N_t - ({}_1E_t + {}_1D_t)$$

or

$$\frac{PRR(t+1)}{PRR(t)} = \frac{k(t+1)}{k(t)} - \frac{k(t+1)}{PRR(t)}({}_1E_t + {}_1D_t) + k(t+1)\frac{({}_1I_t - {}_1N_t)}{PRR(t)}$$

Since $PRR(t) = k(t)[PR(t)]$, we can write

$$\frac{PRR(t+1)}{PRR(t)} = \frac{k(t+1)}{k(t)} - \frac{k(t+1)}{k(t)}\frac{({}_1E_t + {}_1D_t)}{PR(t)} + k(t+1)\frac{({}_1I_t - {}_1N_t)}{PRR(t)}$$

$$= \frac{k(t+1)}{k(t)}[1 - R(t)] + k(t+1)\frac{{}_1I_t - {}_1N_t}{PRR(t)} \tag{10}$$

where R(t) is a loss ratio of deaths and emigrants divided by the initial population; if deaths and emigration are regarded as minimal for immigrants during their year of entry, R(t) can be regarded approximately as a loss rate equal to the sum of the death and emigration rates (note that the denominator of R(t) is the true, not the reported, population at time t). If over a number of years k(t) and R(t) are approximately constant, equation 10 becomes

$$\frac{PRR(t+1)}{PRR(t)} = (1 - \bar{R}) + \bar{k} \, \frac{{}_1I_t - {}_1N_t}{PRR(t)} \qquad (11)$$

where $\bar{R}$ is the loss rate, $\bar{k}$ is the average coverage completeness of the AAR system, and ${}_1I_t$, ${}_1N_t$, PRR(t) and PRR(t+1) can be obtained from INS statistics. $\bar{R}$ and $\bar{k}$ can thus be estimated by plotting the ratios in equation 11, and fitting a straight line of intercept $(1-\bar{R})$ and slope $\bar{k}$.

The estimated value $\bar{R}$ is not an emigration rate but rather a combined emigration and death rate. The emigration element could be obtained by subtracting a death rate calculated on the basis of the age distribution of the population being considered; this death rate would probably not exceed 10 per 1,000 for the immigrant populations from most countries of origin.

The derivation above suggests some practical implications for applying the method. Since R(t) and k(t) are assumed to be constant, the method should be applied to groups as homogenous as possible, such as country of origin by sex groups. It is also clear that the method will not work well if (a) the fluctuations in k(t) or R(t) are large, or (b) ${}_1I_t - {}_1N_t$ is small relative to PRR(t), or (c) $({}_1I_t - {}_1N_t)/PRR(t)$ varies little over time. Simulations suggest that the line should be fitted to the points using a group mean procedure, ordering the observations by the values of $({}_1I_t - {}_1N_t)/PRR(t)$; that the resulting estimate of $\bar{R}$ is reasonably robust to random fluctuations in R(t) and k(t); but that the resulting estimate of $\bar{k}$ is much more sensitive to such fluctuations.

It is also necessary to discuss in more detail the effects of the assumption that R(t) and k(t) can be summarized by average values $\bar{R}$ and $\bar{k}$ applying to the whole period. Simulations suggest that random variations around the average values will have little effect on $\bar{R}$ but will have a more pronounced effect on the estimate of $\bar{k}$, tending to reduce its value. Underlying trends in R(t) and k(t) might be expected to have more substantial effects, however. Limited simulations suggest that trends in R(t) result in overestimates in $\bar{R}$ and $\bar{k}$ if R(t) is increasing, and underestimates of $\bar{R}$ and $\bar{k}$ if R(t) is declining; the effect on $\bar{R}$ is small, the estimate not deviating much from the average value, but the effect on $\bar{k}$ is substantial, and the estimate might be in error by as much as plus or minus 5 percent for a trend in R(t) over a 15-year period of about 1 percent per annum. A trend over time in k(t) has relatively little effect on the estimate of $\bar{k}$, which works out close to the weighted average of k(t) regardless of the direction of the trend, but the estimate of $\bar{R}$ is biased upward by declining coverage and downward by increasing coverage. In general it can be concluded that the estimates of $\bar{R}$ and $\bar{k}$ are reasonably robust to trends in R(t) and k(t), so long as there is reasonable year-to-year fluctuation in PRR(t+1)/PRR(t) and $(_1I_t - _1N_t)$/PRR(t).

The method is applied for the period 1959-1979 to data on permanent immigrants from Colombia, Mexico, the Philippines, and the United Kingdom in Table B-4; Figure B-1 shows scatterplots of the basic ratios and the fitted straight lines.

These applications are quite interesting. For the United Kingdom, the independent variable $(_1I_t - _1N_t)$/PRR(t) is small and varies little, but considerable variation is found in the dependent variable PRR(t+1)/PRR(t), presumably arising from fluctuations in k(t). As a result, the points show no obvious linear trend, and estimation is impossible. Mexico is somewhat similar, though in this case neither variable shows much variation from year to year; though the fluctuations are small, the points appear to show some linearity, and the estimated loss rate is 4 percent, or about 40,000 a year on the reporting population of about 1 million. The estimated coverage of the AAR is 121 percent, however, and though the fit is by no means close, the points do seem to indicate overreporting by Mexicans; some nonpermanent residents such as those on educational or temporary worker visas, and possibly some illegals, may have reported themselves as permanent residents under the reporting system. For Colombia and the Philippines, the two ratios show much more variability and a more pronounced linear trend; for Colombia the loss rate is 2.6 percent and the coverage 85 percent, whereas for the Philippines the loss rate is higher, 7.8 percent, the coverage well over complete at 135 percent, and the fit quite respectable. Once again, overreporting may arise as a result of misreporting of residence status.

It may be concluded that this method will not work in all applications, as a result of fluctuations in R(t) and k(t) from year to year, but that in some applications it seems to produce reasonable estimates of both coverage and loss rates. The death of the AAR system in 1981 means that the method will not be of any use in the future, but it should be applied more widely to data for the 1960s and 1970s. Such applications should experiment with different fitting procedures, such as trimmed means, and with fitting to different time periods to assess the possible impact of trends in k(t) and R(t).

COMBINING ADMINISTRATIVE AND FOREIGN CENSUS DATA

Population censuses often collect, and sometimes tabulate, information on country of birth or country of citizenship. No systematic attempt has been made to estimate emigration from the United States on the basis of foreign census data on Americans abroad, for some very good reasons, among them difficulty of access to the data, lack of timeliness, variation in census dates, and variation in census content. However, the success of the IMILA project, coordinated by the U.N. Latin American Demographic Centre, which estimated migration flows in Latin America from birthplace data contained in samples from population censuses in the Americas, suggests that more could be done through international cooperation.

The issue of timeliness is important. Censuses are generally taken at best only every 10 years, and detailed results rarely become available until 3 or 4 years later. Thus even if the required data on the

American-born or American-nationality population by age and sex are
tabulated, the best that can be hoped for is a stock figure every 10
years and never less than 3 or 4 years out of date, or an intercensal
flow averaging at best almost 10 years out of date. This problem can be
alleviated by combining foreign census data, which suffer from timeliness
problems, with U.S. administrative data sources that are potentially much
more up to date. American citizens meeting residence requirements abroad
can claim tax benefits as a result of such residence; and the Internal
Revenue Service (IRS) has analyzed such returns for the tax years 1975
and 1979 and is currently processing returns for 1983. Unfortunately,
changes in tax law regarding foreign residence and in IRS tabulation
procedures invalidate a comparison of the 1975 and 1979 data; for
instance, the number of returns claiming residence in Canada declined
from 18,700 in 1975 to 2,500 in 1979. In addition, tax returns count
households rather than individuals, so adjustment is required on the
basis of foreign census data to obtain numbers of residents abroad from
numbers of tax returns. However, the use of foreign census data, and
possible combination with IRS information, can be illustrated for the
case of Japan.

The number of American citizens resident in Japan is available by age
and sex from the 1970, 1975, and 1980 censuses. Table B-5 shows the
reported numbers and the expected numbers in 1975 and 1980 derived by
projecting forward the populations from the 1970 and 1975 censuses
(survivorship ratios for the projection were taken arbitrarily from a
Coale-Demeny "West" model life table with a life expectancy at birth of
75 years for females and 71 years for males). For each age group except
that of 0-4, the difference between the reported and the expected numbers
is taken as net (surviving) emigration from the United States to Japan;
many of the 0-4 age group are likely to have been born in Japan and are
thus not emigrants from the United States. The resulting net emigration
figures are also shown in Table B-5. The age pattern of the estimates is
plausible: negative up to age 20, reflecting net return migration to the
United States, positive from 20-39, reflecting migration to Japan, and
negative above age 40, except for the odd blip in old age, again
reflecting return migration. Overall, the data suggest net return
migration of about 100 between 1970 and 1975 (nearly 400 male emigrants
being more than balanced by over 500 female returnees) and of nearly
1,200 between 1975 and 1980 (with only a slight preponderance of females).

The IRS recorded 5,100 tax returns filed for 1975 by U.S. citizen
residents of Japan (both those with bona fide residence and those under a
17-month foreign presence rule), compared with a 1975 Japanese census
figure of 18,755 U.S. citizens living in Japan. On this basis, later IRS
estimates of tax filers resident in Japan would have to be inflated by a
factor of 3.7 to estimate the U.S. citizen total. The IRS number of tax
filers from Japan in 1975 in fact looks quite reasonable given the age
and sex structure of the population, which shows 6,566 male and 4,920
female U.S. citizens aged 20-64 in the 1975 census of Japan given that
many of the tax returns will cover husband and wife joint returns.
Unfortunately, the IRS tables for 1979 tax returns do not classify Japan
separately, so the application of the 1975 inflation factor to filers
resident in Japan in 1979 cannot be tested by comparison with the 1980
Japanese census results.

The use of citizenship information in the above analysis is less than ideal because citizenship can change. U.S. immigrants who naturalize but then return permanently to their country of origin are likely to be missed because they are likely to assume their original citizenship, and births abroad to U.S. citizen parents appear in the gross figures as emigrants. Information by birthplace would be less ambiguous, though such information would still exclude emigration of U.S. immigrants.

The application of this procedure to all countries with resident U.S. emigrants would be tedious at best and impossible as a result of data unavailability at worst. However, it would not be impossible to focus on some 10 or 15 key countries covering a high proportion of U.S. emigrants, to obtain the necessary data either from published sources or by requesting special census tabulations from the statistical authorities involved and updating the estimates of the U.S. population living in each country on the basis of IRS tax returns claiming foreign residence exemptions. The IRS data could also be used to extend the coverage of the analysis from the key countries selected to the entire world by assuming constant inflation factors for regions or continents. The resulting estimates, though by no means perfect, would at least add to the weak existing empirical basis for estimating net flows of the U.S.-born or U.S. citizen population.

CONCLUSIONS

U.S. international migration statistics are particularly poor regarding the nonlegal immigrant population as well as emigration both of U.S. citizens and immigrants admitted for permanent residence. Fairly straightforward though indirect methods of analysis using data that are collected but not processed or compiled, or data that could be collected relatively simply, could provide complementary estimates of the size of these stocks and flows at a modest cost. The methods proposed in this paper require further empirical testing and theoretical refinement, but they illustrate how techniques developed in analytical demography can be usefully applied to migration statistics.

REFERENCES

Davidson, C.A.
  1981   Characteristics of Deportable Aliens Located in the Interior of
          the United States. Paper presented at the annual meetings of
          the Population Association of America, Washington, D.C.
Garcia y Griego, M.
  1980   El Volumen de la Migracion de Mexicanos no Documentados a los
          Estados Unidos (Nuevas Hipotesis). Secretaria del Trabajo y
          Prevision Social. Centro Nacional de Informacion y
          Estadisticas del Trabajo. Mexico City.
Passel, J.S., and Peck, J.M.
  1979   Estimating Emigration from the United States--A Review of Data
          and Methods. Paper presented at the annual meetings of the
          Population Association of America, Philadelphia.

Preston, S.H., Coale, A.J., Trussell, T.J., and Weinstein, M.
 1980   Estimating the completeness of reporting of adult deaths in
        populations that are approximately stable. Population Index
        46(2):179-202.
Preston, S.H., and Coale, A.J.
 1982   Age structure, growth, attrition, and accession: A new
        synthesis. Population Index 48(2):217-259.
Siegel, J.S., Passel, J.S., and Robinson, J.G.
 1980   Preliminary Review of Existing Studies of the Number of Illegal
        Residents in the United States. Mimeo. Bureau of the Census,
        U.S. Department of Commerce, Washington, D.C.
Warren, R., and Kraly, E.
 1985   The Elusive Exodus: Emigration from the United States.
        Population Trends and Public Policy, No. 8. Population
        Reference Bureau, Washington, D.C.

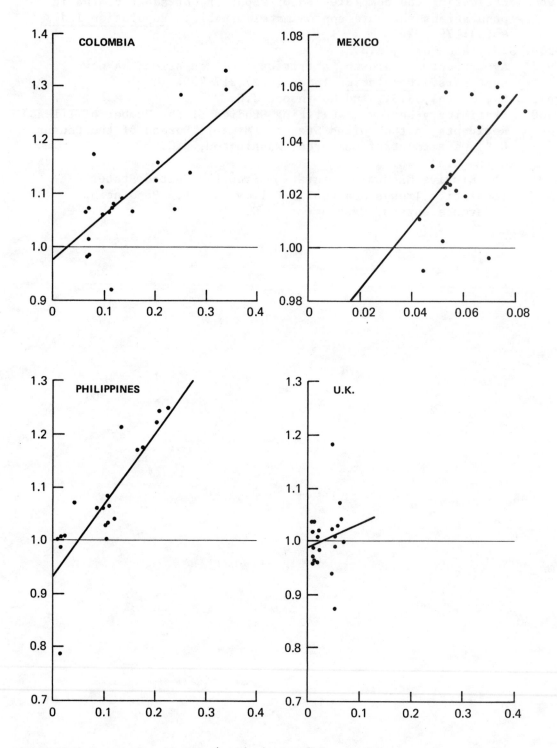

FIGURE B-1 Plots of PRR $(t+1)$ / PRR (t), vertical scale, against $({}_1I_t - {}_1N_t)$ / PRR (t), horizontal scale, for Colombia, Mexico, the Philippines, and the United Kingdom, 1959 to 1979.

TABLE B-1 Estimation of Population to Loss Ratios P/L From Locations by Duration Assuming Population to be Stable; Growth Rates of 0, 5, and 10 Percent; 1978

Duration d,d+n (Years)	Locations $_nD_d$	Midpoint d*	rd* $_nD_de$	p(d)	e^{-rd} p(d)	P/L	$_nl_d$
(a) r = 0.0							
0.0–0.416	1686	.208	1686	1.000	1.000		0.759
0.417–0.916	399	.667	399	.519	.519		0.247
0.917–2.916	698	1.917	698	.405	.405		0.164
2.917–4.916	408	3.917	408	.205	.205		0.197
4.917–6.916	196	5.917	196	.089	.089		0.230
6.917+	115	9.417	115	.033	.033		(0.200)
Total	3502		3502		1.655	1.655	
(b) r = 0.05							
0.0–0.416	1686	.208	1704	1.000	1.000		0.686
0.417–0.916	399	.667	413	.555	.544		0.216
0.917–2.916	698	1.917	768	.447	.427		0.144
2.917–4.916	408	3.917	496	.247	.213		0.179
4.917–6.916	196	5.917	263	.117	.091		0.209
6.917+	115	9.417	184	.048	.034		(0.200)
Total	3502		3828		1.720	1.882	
(c) r = 0.10							
0.0–0.416	1686	.208	1721	1.000	1.000		0.609
0.417–0.916	399	.667	427	.595	.571		0.185
0.917–2.916	698	1.917	845	.494	.451		0.126
2.917–4.916	408	3.917	604	.295	.220		0.158
4.917–6.916	196	5.917	354	.153	.094		0.189
6.917+	115	9.417	295	.069	.035		(0.200)
Total	3502		4246		1.782	2.168	

TABLE B-2 Estimates of Population to Loss Ratios from Locations by Duration Assuming Different Duration-Specific Location to Loss Ratios and a Growth Rate of 5 Percent

Duration	Locations nD_d	Location-Specific Loss Ratio, na_d	Losses nA_d	Midpoint $d*$	$rd*$ nA_de	$p(d)$	$e^{-rd}p(d)$	P/L	$n1_d$
(a) na_d Rising with duration									
0-0.416	1686	.413	4081	.208	4124	1.000	1.000		.740
0.417-0.916	399	.496	805	.667	832	.448	.439		.276
0.917-2.916	698	.590	1183	1.917	1302	.337	.322		.198
2.917-4.916	408	.708	576	3.917	701	.163	.141		.275
4.917-6.916	196	.826	237	5.917	319	.069	.054		.358
6.917+	115	.944	122	9.417	195	.026	.018		.336
Total	3502		7004		7473		1.565	1.698	
(b) na_d Falling with duration									
0-0.416	1686	.632	2669	.208	2697	1.000	1.000		.618
0.417-0.916	399	.553	722	.667	746	.660	.646		.169
0.917-2.916	698	.474	1473	1.917	1621	.566	.541		.103
2.917-4.916	408	.395	1033	3.917	1256	.362	.313		.109
4.917-6.916	196	.316	621	5.917	835	.203	.159		.108
6.917+	115	.237	485	9.417	777	.098	.069		.084
Total	3502		7004		7932		2.367	2.684	
(c) na_d Falling to 7-12 months, then rising with duration									
0-0.416	1686	.623	2707	.208	2735	1.000	1.000		.651
0.417-0.916	399	.312	1279	.667	1322	.641	.628		.195
0.917-2.916	698	.390	1790	1.917	1970	.468	.447		.146
2.917-4.916	408	.545	749	3.917	911	.209	.181		.213
4.917-6.916	196	.623	315	5.917	423	.090	.070		.273
6.917+	115	.701	164	9.417	263	.034	.024		.251
Total	3502		7004		7625		1.641	1.788	

TABLE B-3 Estimates of Population to Loss Ratios from Locations by Duration Assuming Variable Duration-Specific Growth Rates

Duration d,d+n	Locations $_nD_d$	Midpoint d*	Growth Rate $_nr_d$	$\int_0^{d*} {_nr_d}$	$e^{\int_0^{d*} {_nr_d}}$	$_nD_d e^{\int_0^{d*} {_nr_d}}$	p(d)	$e^{-\int_0^d {_nr_d}} p(d)$	P/L
(a) Growth rates falling with duration									
0-0.416	1686	.208	.061	.013	1.013	1708	1.000	1.000	
0.417-0.916	399	.667	.052	.038	1.039	415	.548	.534	
0.917-2.916	698	1.917	.043	.094	1.099	767	.438	.416	
2.917-4.916	408	3.917	.035	.172	1.188	485	.235	.205	
4.917-6.916	196	5.917	.026	.233	1.263	248	.107	.087	
6.917+	115	9.417	.017	.302	1.352	156	.041	.032	
Total	3502		(.05)			3779		1.669	1.821
(b) Growth rates rising with duration									
0-0.416	1686	.208	.035	.007	1.007	1698	1.000	1.000	
0.417-0.916	399	.667	.047	.026	1.027	410	.565	.557	
0.917-2.916	698	1.917	.059	.097	1.102	769	.460	.443	
2.917-4.916	408	3.917	.071	.227	1.255	512	.264	.226	
4.917-6.916	196	5.917	.082	.380	1.462	287	.133	.099	
6.917+	115	9.417	.094	.697	2.008	231	.059	.037	
Total	3502		(.05)			3907		1.797	1.975

TABLE B-4 Estimation of Emigration and Coverage of Alien Address Reporting System, 1959-1979: Colombia, Mexico, the Philippines, and the United Kingdom

Year t	Colombia		Mexico		Philippines		United Kingdom	
	$\frac{PRR(t+1)}{PRR(t)}$	$\frac{{}_1I_t-{}_1N_t}{PRR(t)}$	$\frac{PRR(t+1)}{PRR(t)}$	$\frac{{}_1I_t-{}_1N_t}{PRR(t)}$	$\frac{PRR(t+1)}{PRR(t)}$	$\frac{{}_1I_t-{}_1N_t}{PRR(t)}$	$\frac{PRR(t+1)}{PRR(t)}$	$\frac{{}_1I_t-{}_1N_t}{PRR(t)}$
1959	1.125	0.201	1.011	0.043	1.007	0.016	0.873	0.051
1960	1.158	0.208	1.022	0.057	0.999	0.010	1.180	0.047
1961	1.071	0.238	1.054	0.074	0.787	0.014	0.937	0.047
1962	1.140	0.268	1.052	0.084	0.966	0.026	0.988	0.053
1963	1.296	0.337	1.058	0.063	1.008	0.023	1.040	0.066
1964	1.331	0.337	1.031	0.048	0.985	0.014	0.997	0.072
1965	1.286	0.249	1.024	0.055	1.070	0.043	1.028	0.057
1966	1.066	0.155	1.033	0.056	1.063	0.110	1.010	0.053
1967	1.073	0.115	1.023	0.053	1.173	0.176	1.072	0.063
1968	1.091	0.134	1.025	0.054	1.221	0.203	1.022	0.046
1969	1.081	0.119	1.017	0.054	1.248	0.225	1.018	0.022
1970	0.919	0.113	1.028	0.055	1.243	0.207	0.958	0.018
1971	1.173	0.080	1.046	0.066	1.170	0.165	1.036	0.011
1972	1.065	0.064	1.070	0.074	1.211	0.135	0.987	0.010
1973	0.982	0.069	1.057	0.075	1.040	0.121	0.970	0.009
1974	1.072	0.070	0.997	0.070	1.059	0.097	1.017	0.008
1975	0.983	0.069	1.020	0.061	1.028	0.103	0.956	0.009
1976	1.014	0.070	1.059	0.053	1.081	0.106	1.036	0.009
1977	1.111	0.095	1.003	0.052	1.002	0.105	0.962	0.013
1978	1.065	0.108	1.061	0.073	1.060	0.086	1.007	0.019
1979	1.061	0.098	0.992	0.045	1.032	0.106	0.982	0.023
Slope, $\bar{k}$	0.850		1.212		1.347		0.464	
Intercept, $(1-\bar{R})$	0.974		0.960		0.932		0.988	

TABLE B-5 Estimating the Net Flow of U.S. Citizens to Japan, 1970-1980

Age Group in 1980	$_5P_a$[a]	1970 Census	1975 Population Expected	1975 Population Census	1975 Population Net Change	1980 Population Expected	1980 Population Census	1980 Population Net Change
Male U.S. Citizens								
0-4	.997	—	—	—	—	n.a.	731	n.a.
5-9	.998	—	n.a.	881	n.a.	878	727	-151
10-14	.997	878	875	848	-27	846	649	-197
15-19	.996	938	936	845	-91	842	807	-35
20-24	.995	1008	1005	814	-191	811	1325	514
25-29	.995	721	718	1257	539	1251	988	-263
30-34	.993	730	726	925	199	920	1021	101
35-39	.990	632	629	861	232	855	765	-90
40-44	.984	647	642	606	-36	600	579	-21
45-49	.973	710	703	687	-16	676	587	-89
50-54	.955	873	859	851	-8	828	731	-97
55-59	.927	752	732	667	-65	637	547	-90
60-64	.885	506	483	438	-45	406	355	-51
65-69	.820	343	318	274	-44	242	186	-56
70-74	.726	169	150	141	-9	116	95	-21
75-79	.481[b]	172	141	104	-37	76	69	-7
80-84		137	99	76	-23			
85-89		69	69	83	14	76	75	1
90+		75						
Total		9360		10358	391		10237	-555

TABLE B-5 (continued)

Age Group in 1980	$_5P_a$ [a]	1970 Census	1975 Population Expected	1975 Population Census	1975 Population Net Change	1980 Population Expected	1980 Population Census	1980 Population Net Change
Female U.S. Citizens								
0-4	.998	—	—	—	—	n.a.	706	n.a.
5-9	.999	—	n.a.	864	n.a.	862	766	-96
10-14	.999	855	853	809	-44	808	638	-170
15-19	.998	939	938	824	-114	823	668	-155
20-24	.997	991	990	777	-213	775	883	108
25-29	.996	690	689	815	126	813	991	178
30-34	.995	521	519	825	306	822	800	-22
35-39	.993	676	673	699	26	696	575	-121
40-44	.988	556	553	505	-48	501	434	-67
45-49	.981	661	656	583	-74	576	476	-100
50-54	.971	723	714	619	-95	607	554	-53
55-59	.953	605	594	472	-122	458	383	-75
60-64	.921	318	309	254	-55	242	210	-32
65-69	.865	210	200	148	-52	136	128	-8
70-74	.776	157	145	89	-56	77	59	-18
75-79	.520[b]	120	104	56	-48	43	39	-4
80-84		88	68	34	-34			
85-89		44	41	24	-17	30	43	13
90+		34						
Total		8188		8397	-513		8353	-624

aWest model life table, level 24.
bT(80)/T(75).

Illegal Aliens: An Assessment

Kenneth Hill

INTRODUCTION

Few population issues generate as much political heat as that of illegal immigration. Although limited legal immigration is generally accepted as a continuation of the American tradition and past immigration is associated with a halcyon period of dynamic growth, illegal immigration is almost universally viewed pejoratively, and numerous societal ills, from budget deficits and high unemployment to overcrowding and rising crime rates, are ascribed to it. Perhaps more than in any other area, however, the public debate on illegal immigration is founded on much smoke and little fire. It is argued, with some justification, that hard data on illegal aliens are difficult to obtain, so discussion has been based on soft data ranging from guesses or informed opinions to results of assumption-laden estimation procedures.

The Staff Report of the Interagency Task Force on Immigration Policy (1979:382) sums up the pervasive attitude concisely: "The lack of existing data [on illegal immigrants] points up the most vexing aspect of the issue--the dilemma of either waiting for more data to become available (with no guarantee that it ever will) while the problem worsens, or acting on the available scanty data with the corollary risk of a misguided policy choice." The pessimistic views that the illegal alien population, being a clandestine population, is essentially unsurveyable and that reasonable data on it may never become available have affected attitudes to data collection, data use, and data evaluation since illegal aliens reemerged as an issue in the early 1970s to the recent discussion of legalization and control provisions in the Simpson-Mazzoli legislation. Results of imaginative data collection and analysis projects carried out over the last few years have not been given the credence they deserve because of the belief that the uncountable cannot be counted. This paper reviews the more important of these projects and underexploited data sets to see what conclusions can be drawn about the numbers, trends, and characteristics of illegal aliens in the United States.

For our purposes, an illegal alien is defined as a noncitizen physically present in the United States who entered the country illegally and has not regularized his or her situation, or who has violated his or her terms of entry. This definition thus includes those who enter without inspection or with falsified documents, those who enter legally but overstay their visa period, those who enter legally but violate their terms of entry (for instance, by taking employment), and those who enter as permanent residents but break the law in such a way as to become deportable. There are thus a number of ways of entering the illegal population, not all coinciding with an entry into the country. There are also a number of ways of leaving the population: death, deportation, immediate "voluntary" departure after being located by the INS, genuinely voluntary emigration, and regularization of status. It is not clear either exactly what we mean by the illegal population; at a particular moment, there is some number of illegal aliens in the United States (although the status of a permanent resident alien who has committed but not been convicted of a deportable offense is ambiguous), but the number varies from day to day, as do the actual individuals. The illegal population for a given year could be the number present on some particular date, July 1 for example, or the maximum number present at any moment during the year, or the minimum number present, or the total number of individuals present illegally at any time during the year, or an average such as the person years of illegal residence during the year. This last measure is attractive, since it seems to reflect likely impact most closely, but it will not coincide with all measurement definitions--an estimate of the illegal population covered by the 1980 census, for example, has an April 1, 1980, reference date. In comparing estimates of the illegal population, it is most important to keep in mind the definitions of the population being estimated.

ESTIMATES OF NUMBERS OF ILLEGAL ALIENS

The reemergence of illegal immigration as an issue of public concern since the early 1970s has been accompanied by a number of attempts to estimate the size of the illegal population, or components of it. Some of the early attempts were little more than guesses, and we will not review them here, beyond suggesting that they could be aptly characterized as coming out of the blue (figures of 1 million given by INS Commissioner Farrell for March 1972 and 6-7 million for September 1974 given by INS Commissioner Chapman), cumulated out of the blue (figures of 5 million for April 1975 and 6 million for November 1976 obtained by adding up estimates from INS district directors), or averaged out of the blue (a figure of 8 million for September 1975 obtained by Lesko Associates using a Delphic technique). Unfortunately, the press continues to quote similarly conjectural estimates (for example, a range of 6-12 million quoted by Thornton and Sieghart in the Washington Post, June 26, 1984) despite the existence of a number of empirical studies that, though making numerous assumptions and often giving rise to estimates within a broad range of uncertainty, are at least based on some sort of evidence. By reviewing the major studies and their critical assumptions, we aim to define the limits of the size of the illegal population, and its trend over time, that are indicated by the available data, so that public debate can be put on a sounder footing. We do not attempt to arrive at a single figure regarded as a best estimate, however, because we do not believe that the existing data and methods are strong enough to support more than ranges within which the true figure is likely to lie.

A number of reviews of this sort have been prepared in the past, for example that by Siegel, Passel, and Robinson (1980), prepared as a working document for the Select Commission on Immigration and Refugee Policy. Because we do not wish to go over again the ground already adequately surveyed elsewhere, our review is limited to summarizing the main strengths and weaknesses of the approaches covered by the major

studies, clarifying and adding as necessary, to examining in more detail
the most recent approaches, and to examining some scraps of data that
apparently have not been utilized previously.

Empirical Estimates of the Size of the Illegal Alien Population

First, however, it is useful to summarize the main findings. Table B-6
shows the major empirical estimates of the size of the illegal
population, or components thereof, prepared since the early 1970s.
Several points can be made about these estimates: (a) for those studies
that produced estimates of upper and lower population limits, the range
between the limits is typically large; (b) variations from method to
method are large; (c) the estimates do not show a clear trend over time,
although no estimates are available for the period since 1980; (d) only
two estimates, the maxima of Lancaster and Scheuren for 1973 and Bean,
King, and Passel for 1980, are consistent with an illegal population in
the range of 6-12 million. However, before trying to draw any
conclusions, we briefly describe the methodologies and data used to
arrive at the various and varying estimates.

Goldberg (1974)

The population by age and sex recorded by the 1960 Mexican census was
projected forward to 1970 using a 1964 life table; differences by age and
sex between the 1970 census population and the 1970 projected population
were interpreted as emigration to the United States between 1960 and
1970, net of return migration and deaths of migrants in the United States
during the period; the total obtained was 1,866,000. Legal net migration
from Mexico was then estimated from data on the growth of the
Mexican-born population enumerated by the 1960 and 1970 U.S. censuses as
269,000. The balance, 1,597,000, was taken as net illegal migration from
Mexico to the United States between 1960 and 1970.

There is nothing wrong with the principle of this approach, except
its reliance on the critical assumption that census coverage did not
change between 1960 and 1970. The sensitivity of the results to this
assumption can readily be demonstrated; the enumerated population in 1970
was 48.2 million, so if coverage had been 1 percent less complete in 1970
than in 1960, the 1970 population comparable to the 1960 population would
have been about 48.7 million, and forward projection of the 1960
population would give an excess of 500,000 "emigrants" over the
enumerated 1970 population.

In practice, however, the application has two clear shortcomings.
First, the 1960 population (reference date June 8) was projected forward
for 10 years, to June 8, 1970; the reference date of the 1970 census was
January 18, so the survivorship ratios used were somewhat too low.
Goldberg argues that this difference in reference rates reduces the
expected 1970 population and thus the estimated emigration. This
argument is quite wrong, since the main influence on the size of
particular age groups, at least for young adults, is not mortality but
the underlying population growth rate. To take an example, if the
population aged 15-19 in mid-1960 is projected forward by 10 years, the

result is the expected population aged 25-29 in mid-1970. The survivors of this cohort at the beginning of 1970 would be somewhat more numerous, since some deaths would occur during the first half of 1970, but they would be aged 24.5-29.5, rather than 25.0-29.99 years. If the population were growing at 3 percent per year, the difference would be about 1.5 percent, who would appear as emigrants when the enumerated population aged 25-29 was subtracted. This error would inflate Goldberg's estimate of emigration above age 10 by about 500,000.

The second shortcoming is the estimation of the emigration of children. Registered births between 1960 and 1970 and the enumerated population aged 0-4 in 1960 are not used in the forward projection because they are viewed as inaccurate. Instead, emigrants aged 0-4 are estimated as one-quarter of the product of the observed child-woman ratio (children 0-4 divided by women aged 15-44) and the number of estimated emigrant women aged 15-44; the factor one-quarter allows for the fact that children aged 0-4 in 1970 are alive for only about one-quarter of the period 1960-1970. Emigrants aged 5-9 are estimated as three-quarters of the product of the observed child-woman ratio (children 5-9 divided by women 20-49) and the number of emigrant women aged 20-49, and the emigrants aged 10-14 as the product of the child-woman ratio and emigrant women for children aged 10-14 and women aged 25-54. This procedure assumes that emigrant women have the same number of children as nonemigrant women and that they emigrate with their children; these assumptions are not plausible for illegal female migrants, but they do produce large numbers of emigrant children under age 15, 368,000 females or 46 percent of total female emigrants, and 383,000 males or 36 percent of total male emigrants. These estimates would of course be reduced by about half by adjusting the emigrant female population for the effects of the dating error described above, but would remain much the same proportion of total emigration. Standard forward projection of registered births and the population aged 0-4 in 1960 indicate a net inflow of 327,000 males and 176,000 females between the 1960 and 1970 censuses. Underregistration of births and underenumeration of the population under age 5 affect these results, and the development of suitable adjustment factors would require a major analysis of Mexican census and vital registration data, but at face value these data do not support an outflow of children of the magnitude suggested by Goldberg.

However, the Mexican census data clearly represent a valuable source of data on the possible magnitude of flows to the United States. We have reanalyzed the 1960 and 1970 census age distributions and included the age distribution from the 1980 census, using a rather different analytical technique. Preston and Coale (1982) propose a method for estimating age-specific migration rates using age-specific growth rates and an intercensal life table. The estimating equation used here, starting at age 10, is

$$-5 \sum_{10}^{a-5} {}_5e_x = \ln \frac{N(a+5)l(10)}{N(10)l(a+5)} + 5 \sum_{10}^{a-5} {}_5r_x \qquad (1)$$

where ${}_5e_x$ is the emigration rate, and ${}_5r_x$ the recorded growth rate, for the age group x, $x+5$, $N(10)$ and $N(a+5)$ are the numbers having 10th and a+5th birthdays between the censuses, and $l(10)$ and $l(a+5)$ are life table survivors to ages 10 and a+5 respectively. $N(10)$ and $N(a+5)$

were calculated as the geometric means between censuses of the geometric means of the recorded populations aged a-5,a and a,a+5 at each census. The use of equation 1 has two advantages for the present applications: first, the method accommodates an intercensal interval that is not an exact multiple of five years very conveniently and, second, the analysis can start at age 10, as above, avoiding the uncertainties of enumeration completeness under age 10.

Table B-7 shows the details of the calculations for males for the period 1960-1970, and Table B-8 summarizes the results in terms of emigrants by age and sex for the periods 1960-1970 and 1970-1980. For the 1960-1970 period, emigration, net of returns but not of mortality, is estimated as some 420,000 males and 300,000 females aged 10-80. Over this period, some 350,000 permanent immigrants born in Mexico aged 10 and over were admitted to the United States, suggesting an illegal inflow to the United States of at least 370,000 over the period. Between 1970 and 1980, however, the method estimates a net outflow from Mexico of 78,000 males and a net inflow to Mexico of 381,000 females, despite the admission of some 530,000 Mexicans aged 10 and over to permanent residence status by the United States alone over the period. Clearly the method has not worked between 1970 and 1980, probably either because the 1980 enumeration was substantially more complete than that of 1970 or that of 1960 or because the results have been distorted by changes in age misreporting patterns between the two censuses. If we assume that legal emigration from Mexico was approximately evenly distributed by sex (an assumption supported by INS records) and that return migration of legal emigrants was also approximately evenly distributed by sex, the difference for the period 1970-1980 between the estimated male outflow from Mexico and the estimated female inflow to Mexico of 460,000 could be taken as an indicator of the balance of male over female illegal emigration during the period. If 85 percent of illegal emigrants were males, the total flow of illegal emigrants would be 652,000 males and 115,000 females, or 767,000 overall. However, this figure assumes no change in the sex differential of enumeration completeness and would be doubled by assuming that only 65 percent of illegal emigrants were males, so it cannot be taken in any way as a firm estimate.

In summary, data from recent Mexican censuses, although at first sight a promising source of estimates of emigration to the United States, prove to be of little value for this purpose, probably because of changes in enumeration completeness. However, it can be said that the data do not support a huge flood of Mexicans into the United States in the 1970s, nor the entry of 1.6 million illegal Mexicans in the 1960s. It should be pointed out that the Mexican censuses are conducted on a de jure basis, so short-term illegal migrants would often be included in the census counts, further clouding the conclusions that can be drawn from the data.

Lancaster and Scheuren (1978)

This study used a matching procedure to estimate the number of U.S. residents not included in the March 1973 Current Population Survey (CPS). Three administrative data sets, of IRS tax filers, workers covered by social security (SSA) contributions, and social security beneficiaries, were used to classify CPS households by whether they contained a tax filer, an SSA worker, or an SSA beneficiary. Individuals were then classified by whether they were part of a household containing a tax filer, an SSA worker, or an SSA beneficiary. Log-linear models were then used to estimate the number of people not covered by any of the three data systems, the missing cell in the 2x2x2 table. The total population was then found by adding all the cells together, and the nonlegal population obtained as the difference between this population and a presumed legal population based on the 1970 census adjusted for coverage and projected forward to March 1973 allowing for births, deaths, and legal immigration. The estimate arrived at is of 3.9 million nonlegal residents aged 18-44, with subjective 68 percent confidence intervals of 2.9 to 5.7 million.

This study was the first major attempt to estimate the size of the nonlegal population empirically and remains the only major application of record matching for this purpose. Lancaster and Scheuren make no exaggerated claims for their results, describing the study as exploratory and pointing out possible shortcomings, notably failures to match correctly nonindependent probabilities of omission from the various systems and problems in calculating the 1973 legal population. To these may be added the problem posed by the high degree of overlap between the tax filer and SSA employment variables and the low degree of overlap of SSA beneficiaries with either of the other two variables. Siegel et al. (1980) provide an effective review of the application and conclude that ". . . the assumptions required for the estimate of 3.9 million illegal residents to be valid are very strong indeed. Consequently, the subjective 68-percent confidence interval cited by the authors is probably too narrow, especially for the lower limit of the interval, and could be broadened to include the statistical possibility of much less than 2.9 million illegal aliens in the United States." Given the dependence of the results on the small number of households receiving social security benefits (only 2.5 percent of all households) and on the accuracy of the legal population estimate for 1973 based on adjusted 1970 census data, Lancaster and Scheuren's estimates should not be given undue weight.

Robinson (1980)

This study examines trends in age-specific death rates over the period 1950-1975, for the United States as a whole and for three groupings of states, a southwestern group (Texas, Colorado, New Mexico, Arizona, and California), an eastern group (New York, New Jersey, Illinois, Michigan, and Florida), and the remainder of the country. Trends for certain population groups (under age 20, aged 45-64, age 65+, white females aged 20-44 and black and other females aged 20-44) are similar for all three groups of states of residence; however, trends for white males aged 20-44 and black and other males aged 20-44 show different trends for the five-state groups than for the 40-state group. Specifically, death rates for white males aged 20-44 increase more rapidly (1960-1970) and fall more slowly (1970-1975) for the two five-state areas than for the 40-state area; death rates for black and other males aged 20-44 rise more

rapidly (1960-1970) and fall more slowly (1970-1975) for the eastern
five-state group than for the 40-state group, while for the southwestern
group they rise more slowly (1960-1970) and fall more slowly (1970-1975)
than for the 40-state group. The irregularities for the black and other
death rates for males aged 20-44 are assumed to reflect real changes in
mortality risks, since the increases between 1960 and 1970 are largely
accounted for by violent deaths, and the declines from 1970 to 1975 are
similar for all three state groups. The irregularities for death rate
trends of white males aged 20-44, on the other hand, are taken as
indicating an increase in the illegal population contributing to
registered deaths but not to census-based population denominators, on the
assumptions that deaths of illegal residents are likely to be registered,
whereas such residents may not be included in census enumerations. It
may be noted that the reasons for deciding that trends for black and
other males aged 20-44 are real, whereas rather similar trends for white
males result from illegal residents, seem rather thin.

Estimates of the illegal white male population aged 20-44 are then
obtained as follows. An estimate of deaths of illegal residents is found
as the number of excess deaths in the two five-state groups over the
number that would have occurred if death rates had changed at the same
rates as in the 40-state group. This number of excess deaths is the key
to the estimates of the illegal population, which are obtained from it by
assuming different death rates, different levels of death registration
completeness, and different levels of enumeration completeness for
illegal residents. The estimates vary widely, the lowest being obtained
by assuming that all deaths to illegal residents are registered, that no
illegal residents appear in the population denominators, and that illegal
residents experience the mortality rates of black and other males, while
the highest are obtained by assuming that 90 percent of deaths to illegal
residents are registered, that 50 percent of illegal residents are
included in the population denominators, and that illegals experience the
death rates of white males aged 20-44 in the United States from violent
causes only. The lowest and highest estimates vary by a factor of about
10, though they are all based on a single number of excess deaths, for
which no variability is allowed, though Robinson describes it as only a
rough estimate. This estimate itself must have a large margin of
possible error; the death rate may have been affected by the substantial
legal immigration into the two five-state groups, the observed
disproportionate effects on deaths from violent causes and deaths in
metropolitan areas being not inconsistent with this explanation, or by
differential underenumeration of the legal population of these states by
the 1970 census, an explanation not inconsistent with the metropolitan
area effect. Indeed, the fact that much of the death rate differential
in the two five-state groups arises from an increased death rate in
metropolitan areas argues against the presence of a substantial rural
illegal population. Thus the true range of the size of the illegal
population indicated by these data is wider even than that suggested by
Robinson, and the analysis cannot even be taken as conclusive evidence
that there was at least some increase in the illegal population not
included in the death rate denominators over the period 1960-1975,
although it is certainly suggestive of an increase.

Heer (1979)

This study examines the change in the population of Mexican origin
reported in the CPS between 1970 and 1975, interpreting the difference
between the reported change and expected change from natural increase and
legal immigration as net illegal immigration. Siegel et al. (1980) raise
serious questions about the results, pointing out, first, that the
sampling error of the difference in the CPS populations of Mexican origin
is quite large, in fact larger than Heer's lowest estimate of net illegal
inflow; second, that the results are sensitive to the choice of starting
and ending points, because the CPS estimate of the population of Mexican
origin fluctuated irregularly during the mid-1970s, such that the choice
of 1973-1977 as the period of study would have resulted in estimates of a
net outflow; and third, that the estimates depend heavily on inadequately
supported assumptions about levels of CPS coverage of the population in
question, particularly on the coverage of illegal residents. Using CPS
data on the Mexican-born population, Siegel et al. conclude that the
change from 1969 to 1975 can be entirely accounted for by natural
increase and legal immigration, suggesting two possible conclusions, one
that the net flow of illegal Mexicans balanced the return migration of
legal immigrants, and the other that the CPS covered negligible numbers
of illegal Mexicans. Heer's analysis should not be taken even as
confirming a small inflow of illegal Mexicans in the early 1970s, nor as
ruling out a substantial inflow during the period.

Garcia y Griego (1980)

In response to concerns about the political impact of migration to the
United States, the Mexican government established a research program in
the late 1970s aimed at measuring the flow and characteristics of Mexican
migrants seeking employment in the United States. One part of this study
was a series of surveys of illegal Mexican migrants returned by the INS
from the United States. Migration histories provided by the surveyed
returnees, in combination with INS data on locations by duration of
illegal stay in the United States and information on prior U.S. residence
of a sample of Mexican immigrants (Cue, 1976), are the basis for Garcia y
Griego's study.

The methodology is based on the fact that the illegal Mexican
population of a given entry cohort at any time is equal to the cohort
losses that will occur after that time. Thus if cohort losses after a
given date can be estimated, the population stock at that date for the
cohort is also estimated; by summing across cohorts, the total illegal
stock is then obtained. If the stock can be estimated in this way for
two dates, the rate of growth of the illegal population can be found.
The difficulty clearly lies in estimating cohort losses in the future.
Garcia y Griego defines four mutually exclusive and exhaustive ways in
which cohort losses can occur: return to Mexico by the INS, voluntary
return, legalization, and death.

The first element, return by the INS, is estimated using INS data on
locations by duration of illegal stay for the years 1972-1977, with
locations at one year or over being distributed according to the
distribution reported for each entry cohort by the illegal aliens

returned to Mexico by the INS in October-November 1977 and interviewed by the border survey. Since location may not result in loss, two alternative assumptions are used to estimate losses from locations: that all locations lead to losses, and that only 40 percent of locations lead to losses, at all durations of illegal stay. This step places heavy reliance on the accuracy of the migration histories reported by the returnees at the border survey; a comparison of the reported durations of stay ended by INS return to Mexico with INS locations by duration suggests the omission from the histories of short stays.

The second element, voluntary return to Mexico, is based on losses estimated from INS locations and ratios of voluntary to enforced return by year and entry cohort as obtained from the border survey migration histories. As with enforced returns, two alternative assumptions are used, the first using ratios as observed (the low hypothesis) and the second using ratios adjusted upward by a factor of 1.72 (the high hypothesis) to allow for possible selection bias, that enforced returnees may have had a higher than average probability of being located by the INS, and may therefore underestimate true voluntary returns in their migration histories.

The third element, legalization, is based on reports to a small survey conducted in 1973 of 822 Mexican males aged 18-60 at initial entry to the United States as permanent residents. Of these immigrants, 61.5 percent had lived in the United States before; the study assumes all such prior residence to have been illegal and uses the reported distribution by duration of residence applied to cohorts of legal Mexican immigrants to estimate period and cohort losses to the illegal population resulting from legalization. This step seems the most problematic of the four: since the data may not represent only periods of illegal residence, the distribution obtained will be affected by cohort effects and sampling errors, and there seems to be some possibility for overlap between voluntary return as estimated in step 2 and voluntary return followed by legal immigration as estimated in step 3.

Once the first three steps have been completed, losses are projected forward from 1977. For durations of stay up to 7 years, ratios of losses for successive durations by cohort obtained for the period 1972-1977 and averaged across the years available are used to project future losses; for durations from 8 to 40 years, a model of losses was used to project future losses. Stocks by date and cohort in the absence of mortality were then obtained by cumulating losses beyond the date, and mortality was then incorporated as the fourth type of loss by applying survivorship ratios to the estimated stocks of survivors. Once the dead are added in, all four elements of loss are accounted for, and entries, stocks, and loss rates can be calculated for each year from 1972 to 1977.

The above account is a very inadequate description of the extremely elaborate procedures used by Garcia y Griego, but it gives a broad idea of the bases and manipulations of data used in the estimation, if not of the detail given of the Lexis diagrams, separation factors, and justification of the hypotheses involved. Though some minor methodological changes would appear suitable--such as some smoothing of the ratios of voluntary to enforced returns across cohorts and the use of duration values other than the midpoint of the duration intervals for the highly convex to the origin distribution of INS locations by duration--the effects of such changes would be relatively minor.

The final estimates must be interpreted with caution, however, for the following reasons. First, the ratios of voluntary to enforced returns and distributions of enforced returns by duration of stay are based on migration histories of uncertain validity from a fairly small and possibly unrepresentative sample of 9,930 returnees. Second, the number of legalizations is based on data of uncertain relevance from a very small sample; although the number of losses from legalization is small, only 30,000 of an estimated 1.67 million losses in 1976, they are concentrated at high durations of illegal stay and thus have considerable weight in the forward projection process. Third and most important, the estimates at short durations for 1975 and 1976 depend heavily on forward projection of losses based mainly on histories for 1972-1977. Such projection is a hazardous process, especially given the very sharp increase in INS locations at durations of a year or more from 1975 (34,491) to 1977 (89,793). INS records show lower numbers of locations at a year or more for 1978 and 1979, although the application of Garcia y Griego's location rates for 1977 to the beginning 1978 population would imply a sharply higher number of locations for 1978. Fourth, the linking of voluntary to enforced returns implies that if INS locations rates rise, so do voluntary returns, the reverse of the effect one would expect.

In summary, the analysis is ingenious, but constructs rather large numbers from rather small ones in ways that are bound to be sensitive to data errors. The final estimates, of a stock between 482,000 and 1,224,000 at the beginning of 1977, net annual inflows ranging from 75,000 to 284,000 for 1975 and 1976, and a growth rate in 1976 of around 27 percent, cannot be regarded as solid limits on the size of the illegal Mexican population, although the stock estimates for the beginning of 1972, from 234,000 to 436,000, may be more robust since they are based more on data and less on projection than the stock estimates for later in the decade.

CENIET (1982)

Another part of the Mexican research program that collected the data on returnees used in the analysis by Garcia y Griego just described was a major national household survey conducted in December 1978 and January 1979 covering 62,500 households and focused on labor migration to the United States. This survey was carried out on a de jure basis, comparable to the Mexican censuses, and incorporated special questionnaires for persons with migration experience in the United States. Two migrant populations were identified: (1) those age 15 and over normally resident in the household but at the time of the survey working or looking for work in the United States and with a family member in the household to provide information about them and (2) those age 15 and over actually present in the household who had spent at least one day working or looking for work in the United States during the preceding five years. When inflated to the national level, the former population, of normal residents actually in the United States working or seeking work, was estimated as 519,000, and the latter population, of actual residents who had worked or looked for work in the United States in the preceding five years, was estimated as 471,000. In addition to numbers, the survey report provides a considerable amount of information on the characteristics of these two populations.

The problem with the results of this survey is how to interpret them in terms of illegal migration to the United States from Mexico. The report argues that both populations represent illegal migrants, and the age and sex compositions of the populations support this contention. However, the absent resident population is likely to include some recent legal migrants and to exclude both those illegal migrants who have been absent for a long period and those illegal migrants who left no family members behind to report on them or who were under age 15 or not working or looking for work. Thus the 519,000 can be taken, plus or minus some allowance for sampling error, as a minimum estimate of the illegal Mexican population in the United States at the end of 1978. The returned migrant population will include some returned legal migrants, but since about half these returnees had apparently worked or looked for work in the United States during 1978, and only 15 percent reported having entered the United States legally, a substantial proportion of them were probably illegal migrants who had entered the United States for seasonal summer work but had returned to Mexico for the winter.

Interpretation would be easier if the results had been published more fully. Particularly useful would be tabulations of both populations by age group and sex, by month and year of departure for the absent population, and by month and year of both most recent departure and return for the returned migrants. With the results given in the report and the hints dropped in the text, it is really not possible to do more than speculate about the relationship between the CENIET-defined populations and the population of interest to us, of Mexicans illegally in the United States. The figures could be taken to indicate a net annual flow of around 250,000, if the 500,000 or so absent residents had left in 1978 and half the returnees had returned in 1978. Alternatively, the figures could be taken to indicate a stock of 500,000 (those actually in the United States), or 600,000 illegal person years lived, if the 500,000 spent all 1978 in the United States and half the returnees had spent half a year each in the United States in 1978; to these stock estimates an unknown amount should be added for migrants not covered by the survey, namely those under 15, or not employed or seeking employment, or no longer regarded as normal Mexican residents, or with no household member still in Mexico to report on them. It can thus be regarded as unlikely that the illegal Mexican population in the United States at the beginning of 1979 was less than half a million, but upper limits of a million or more would not be inconsistent with the survey results. It might be noted for future reference that a household survey of this type would be an ideal vehicle for applying multiplicity-type questions concerning residence of children or siblings to estimate emigration (see for example IUSSP, 1981).

Warren and Passel (1983)

This study used data from the 1980 census and the INS to estimate the number of nonlegal aliens included in the 1980 census by age group, sex, period of entry, and country of birth. The basis of their methodology is to compare the recorded 1980 census population with a constructed legal population based on the INS Alien Address Registration system combined with data on new immigrants and naturalizations. Extensive adjustments were required to the data on both sides of this comparison. The number of people in the census reporting U.S. citizenship through naturalization by period of entry was higher than recorded INS naturalization figures, so the noncitizen foreign-born population was adjusted upward from close to 7 million to about 8 million on the basis of the reported INS data on naturalizations, by period. A further, though smaller, adjustment was incorporated for incorrectly reporting (or overstating) the United States as the place of birth. The legally present population was obtained by adjusting the 1980 alien registration data (reported on form I-53) for undercoverage averaging 11 percent overall, though the undercoverage was estimated separately for 40 countries or groups of countries of birth.

The procedure used to estimate I-53 coverage in 1980 is complex, but the principles may be summarized as follows. Annual change in the resident alien population can be represented as

$$P_2 + U_2 = P_1 + U_1 + I - N - D - E \tag{1}$$

where P_1 and P_2 are INS registration figures for permanent residents for two successive years; U_1 and U_2 represent underreporting for the respective years; I is the number of aliens admitted for permanent residence during the year; N is the number of aliens becoming naturalized citizens during the year; D is the estimated number of deaths;* and E represents emigration of resident aliens. No information is available for E, U_1 or U_2, but the net effect of all three can be approximated as follows:

$$E + (U_2 - U_1) = P_1 - P_2 + I - N - D \tag{2}$$

Application of equation 2 produces a series of figures for the net effects of emigration and change in coverage for each year. The next step was to derive an annual series of emigration estimates. First an estimate of total emigration for the 1965-1976 period was made by assuming equivalent proportional coverage in 1965 and 1977. The estimated total emigration for 1965-1976 was then allocated by year, two-thirds on the basis of annual immigrants and one-third on the basis of registering aliens. These ratios were also used to estimate emigration for 1977-1979. The estimates of emigration for each year were then subtracted from the annual series of combined emigration and change of coverage to obtain annual estimates of change of coverage. By cumulating the estimates of U_2-U_1 from 1965 onward, it is possible to identify the year with the lowest absolute "omission." Registration for this "best" year was adjusted upward by 2 percent and used along with the annual components of alien population change thereafter to calculate the adjusted legal resident population for 1980.

Warren and Passel conclude that some 2.1 million illegal aliens were recorded in the 1980 census, an estimate that is quite sensitive to the

---

* The annual numbers of deaths were estimated by applying crude death rates calculated from 1970 census data for aliens by age and sex and U.S. mortality rates for each country of origin to the registered, rather than true, alien populations.

numerous and sometimes substantial adjustments made to the basic data. In support of the estimate, the characteristics of the illegal population are plausible in terms of origin (over half born in Mexico), age and sex distribution (mainly young adult males), period of entry (largely 1975-1979) and state of residence (predominantly California, Texas, and Illinois for Mexicans). An analysis of November 1979 CPS data by Warren (1982) also provides support for this approach. In that study two separate estimates of the legally resident population were derived for comparison with CPS data. One estimate, based on I-53 data adjusted as described above, was compared with the CPS alien population (adjusted for overreporting of naturalizations). The other estimate, based on INS immigration figures and an allowance for emigration and mortality, was compared with the CPS foreign-born population entering during the 1970-1979 period. The two comparisons produced comparable estimates not only for the total for 1970-1979 (1.2 and 1.1 million, respectively) but also for the age-sex distribution of the estimated illegal population included in the CPS.

Uncertainties remain, however. First, the adjustments for false claims to naturalized citizenship and misreporting of country of birth more than double the number of illegals from under 1 million to over 2 million, and thus need powerful justification. The adjustment for naturalizations was based on comparisons of the number of naturalizations by country of birth and year of immigration from INS data, with some small allowance for emigration and mortality, and numbers of naturalized citizens by country of birth and period of entry from the census. If the latter exceeded the former, the balance was taken as representing false claimants to naturalized citizenship. INS data on naturalizations are regarded as very reliable, primarily because the administrative procedure is clearly defined, but the INS classification by year of immigration may not necessarily agree with the census classification by period of entry, which might be interpreted as most recent entry, or might precede year of immigration in the INS sense of legal status. Such an inconsistency between the two sources would affect the estimated distribution of illegals by period of entry. The total number of illegals would be directly affected by incorrect allowance for mortality and emigration of naturalized citizens and by any omission of naturalizations from INS data.

Second, the procedure used to estimate I-53 coverage is only approximate. Its most important area of uncertainty, from the point of view of the subsequent use of its results, is that the completeness estimates are relative to an arbitrarily assumed level of 98 percent completeness of registration in the "best" year. Using a figure of 90 percent, or 110 percent, neither of which can be ruled out from the data, would have a substantial effect on the final estimates of illegals of plus or minus half a million or so. Some other assumptions in the procedure are given little justification, although they probably have little effect on the final estimates. In summary, the estimates of coverage of the I-53 system have a substantial margin of error (the first paper in this appendix shows that, at least for the Philippines and possibly also for Mexico, overregistration of the legal alien population by the I-53 is consistent with the annual fluctuations in registration, immigration, and naturalization).

An additional source of uncertainty in the Warren-Passel study arises from the fact that the adjusted I-53 data estimate the actual number of aliens residing legally in the United States in April 1980. However, it is not the "true" legally resident population that is needed for comparison with the census data, but the legally resident population actually included in the census. Any undercount of legal residents by the 1980 census would reduce the number of illegal aliens estimated as included in the census by the same amount, whereas any overcount would inflate the estimate of illegals.

Warren and Passel's analysis clearly establishes that a substantial number of illegal aliens were included in the 1980 census population but does not establish the precise number because of the nature of the adjustments made to the underlying data. However, the range of uncertainty of the estimate is narrower than that of the estimates produced by other methods reviewed here, and the analysis represents a major advance in measuring the size of the illegal population.

Two final reflections are that the method should also be applied to the 1970 census, to get an idea of both the stability of the methodology and of the rate of growth of the illegal population over the 1970-1980 decade, and that a composite procedure might be used to estimate the coverage of the I-53 data, using Hill's approach (described in the first paper of this appendix), applied perhaps to the period 1964-1976, to estimate absolute coverage by country of origin, and then applying the Warren-Passel approach to carry this estimate forward to 1980.

Bean, King, and Passel (1983)

If emigration is age- and sex-selective, it will affect the sex ratios by age of the population of origin. This study analyzes the sex ratios of the Mexican population as reported by the provisional results of the 1980 census for the age range 15-39 to derive estimates of net Mexican emigration. The advantage of using sex ratios from one census over using intercensal residual methods is that sex ratios are not affected by overall census omission, although they are affected by sex differentials in enumeration completeness and by sex differentials in age misreporting.

Bean et al. assume that immigration and emigration between Mexico and countries other than the United States are either negligible or not sex-selective, and that a deficit of males aged 15-39 in the 1980 census is a function of differential undercount of such males in the census and differential emigration by sex to the United States. Surviving emigrants to the United States aged 15-39, E_{15-39} , can then be estimated as

$$E_{15-39} = \frac{PM_c \dfrac{M_{15-39}}{c_m} + \dfrac{F_{15-39}}{c_f} - \dfrac{M_{15-39}}{c_m}}{PM_e - PM_c} \qquad (1)$$

where PM_c is the proportion male of the population aged 15-39 in the absence of migration, M_{15-39} and F_{15-39} are the number of males and females respectively enumerated by the census, c_m and c_f are the male and female enumeration completenesses in 1980, and PM_e is the proportion of males among the surviving emigrants aged 15-39. For the unknowns, PM_c was estimated using assumed sex ratios at birth ranging from 103 to 105 males per 100 females, life table $_nL_a$ values by sex, and the enumerated female populations by age group as weights; PM_e was assumed to be 0.60 or 0.65; c_f was assumed to be 0.97; and c_m was assumed to range from 0.91 to 0.95. Total emigrants to the United States were then obtained from the estimates of E_{15-39} by assuming that either 60 or 65 percent of all emigrants were aged 15-39.

All possible combinations of assumptions produced 60 estimates of total Mexican emigrants to the United States. Each estimate was then evaluated by seeing whether it satisfied three additional constraints, namely that the proportion male among illegal Mexicans aged 15-39 not included in the 1979 CPS should fall between 0.65 and 0.85, that the proportion aged 15-39 among illegal Mexicans not included in the 1979 CPS should not fall below 0.65 nor exceed 1.0, and that the total number of Mexican emigrants should not be lower than the total legal and illegal number included in the 1979 CPS. These constraints eliminate 42 of the 60 estimates, no less than 30 by the last constraint alone.

The estimates of illegal emigrants are then obtained from the remaining estimates of total emigrants by subtracting legal emigrants, taken from INS I-53 data for 1980, adjusted for 9.2 percent underreporting, as 1.208 million. The highest estimate is 3.8 million, for a sex ratio at birth of 104 males per 100 females, a proportion male of all emigrants aged 15-39 of 0.6, and a proportion of all emigrants aged 15-39 of 0.65. The lowest estimate is zero, since many combinations of parameters fail to account even for legal immigration from Mexico.

To assess this range of possible estimates, we need to assess the parameter values assumed since the basic equation is clearly correct. The sex ratio at birth in Mexico is likely to be close to 105 males per 100 females, lower observed ratios probably arising from sex-selective underregistration or delayed registration of births; combined with a 1969-1971 Mexico life table developed by the United Nations (1982), this sex ratio at birth gives a value of PM_c of 0.5047, within the range of values used in the paper. The estimate of total emigration at ages 15-39 is highly sensitive to the value assumed however, the difference between 0.505 and 0.504 being over 10 percent in the estimate of emigration.

The assumed values of male and female undercount, c_m and c_f, and most critically the difference between them, are impossible to assess, the values in the paper being justified in terms of estimates of completeness of coverage of the Hispanic population by the 1970 U.S. census, a basis of doubtful validity and uncertain accuracy. The estimates of emigration are highly sensitive not to the absolute values assumed but to the sex differential; assuming female coverage of 97 percent, the use of a male coverage of 94 percent instead of 93 percent increases the estimated emigration by over 30 percent.

The proportion male among all emigrants aged 15-39, PM_e, is assumed to be 0.60 or 0.65, a range based on sex ratios among legal immigrants of 50.3 percent and an estimate derived by Warren (1982) of 55.2 percent among illegal Mexican immigrants included in the 1979 CPS. The estimates are again highly sensitive to the values used, the use of a value of 0.70 instead of 0.65 reducing the estimate of total emigration by 25 percent. The proportion male of counted illegals seems surprisingly low, given that most studies indicate a proportion around 0.80 or 0.85 (e.g. Reichert and Massey, 1979; CENIET, 1982), and the higher the proportion illegals make up of total emigrants, the higher would be the overall proportion male; the range assumed in the paper may thus be too low, at least for higher proportions illegal.

The final parameter introduced is the proportion of all emigrants who are aged 15-39; a range of 0.60 to 0.65 is used again, also based on INS statistics on legal immigrants (0.502) and Warren's (1982) estimate for illegals counted in the 1979 CPS (0.70). Estimates of total emigration are somewhat less sensitive to this assumption, but it might have been preferable to avoid it altogether by concentrating solely on the age range 15-39; it may also be noted that the higher the proportion illegal among total emigrants, the higher this parameter would be, thus reducing the upper limit on illegal emigration somewhat.

The same procedures applied to the provisional results of the 1980 Mexican census can also be applied to the 1960, 1970, and final 1980 census age distributions. Using common parameter values for all three (PM_c = 0.5061, c_m = 0.93, c_f = 0.97, PM_e = 0.65), total emigrants aged 15-39 are estimated as 0.838 million for 1960, 0.970 million for 1970, and 1.486 million for 1980 (the estimate for 1980 using the provisional census results was 1.743 million). Given the magnitude of legal immigration from Mexico from 1960 to 1970, the estimated increase from 1960 to 1970 looks low, whereas the increase from 1970 to 1980 is some 190,000 higher than legal immigration from Mexico at ages 15-39 over the period. The increases, though possibly affected by changes in relative underenumeration by sex from census to census, are certainly not consistent with a flood of Mexican illegal immigrants to the United States in the 1970s and do not seem to be consistent with the higher estimates of illegals given by Bean et al.

In summary, this method is particularly sensitive to its assumptions, and even the ranges used do not seem to encompass all plausible values, particularly in those cases leading to the highest estimates of numbers of illegal Mexican immigrants in the United States. The results certainly suggest that estimates of illegal Mexicans living in the United States in mid-1980 in excess of 4 million would be hard to reconcile with Mexican census data, though even this conclusion is weakened by the de jure nature of the 1980 census. Intercensal changes suggest an illegal flow between 1970 and 1980 that is unlikely to have greatly exceeded half a million. Once again, the sensitivity of the estimation procedure to uncertain assumptions about the underlying parameters and the nature of the data used indicate that the results must be viewed with great caution; they do, however, provide some additional empirical support for dismissing the more irresponsible and excessive guesses of the growth and size of the illegal Mexican population in the United States.

Further Indications of the Size and Growth of the Illegal Population

Apart from the procedures of Garcia y Griego described above, little analytic use has been made of INS data on locations of deportable aliens to draw inferences about the size and growth of the illegal immigrant population of the United States. Nonanalytic uses of total locations are quite common, however; for example, in a recent article in the Washington Post (10 September 1984) Representative Daniel Lungren noted that apprehensions by the Border Patrol in the last 2 years were nearly 2 million, and that this figure implied that at least 4 million illegal immigrants had successfully entered the United States over this period. The basis for this assumed 2:1 ratio is not given, and clearly such simple rule of thumb adjustment factors need to be examined carefully before it is concluded that high numbers of locations really indicate yet higher numbers of successful entries. The relationships between locations, successful entries, and the size of the illegal population are unlikely to be simple, since they will depend on the number of attempted entries, location rates at entry and thereafter, and voluntary return rates.

There are a number of possible explanations why INS data on locations have received little analytical attention. First, there is a definitional problem of the population covered; the same person may make several attempts to enter the United States illegally and may therefore show up several times in a year's locations data.

Second, INS data on locations are not tabulated or published in an optimal way for analytic purposes. The source of the data is the INS form I-213, Report of Deportable Alien, completed for all deportable aliens located, even at or immediately after entry, but these forms are not processed by machine; instead, such data as are available are hand extracted from the I-213 and summarized on the G-23 report (pages 18 and 19) and in some internal INS intelligence reports. The detail available from this hand extraction on the G-23 form is limited to 20 countries or country groups of nationality, classes of status at entry, grouped duration of illegal stay in the United States (the groups being at entry, within 72 hours, 4-30 days, 1-6 months, 7 months to 1 year, and over 1 year), and status when found. Limited additional detail is available from a study of a sample of I-213 forms for 1978 covering locations of deportable aliens in the United States illegally for at least 4 days (Davidson, 1981), giving the distribution of the aliens located for duration of illegal stay categories 4-30 days, 1-6 months, 7 months to 1 year, 1-2 years, 3-4 years, 5-6 years, and 7 or more years. The analytic value of the data would be greatly enhanced by regular tabulation by sex, broad age group, major nationality groups, and single-year durations of illegal stay, but it should be possible to draw some general inferences about the illegal population given just the limited detail currently available.

Third, locations of deportable aliens will be affected by INS enforcement practices and allocations of manpower. For instance, a concentration of resources on the Mexican border rather than on internal enforcement would produce a high concentration of locations at short durations, and a change in staffing levels would affect all location rates. These considerations provide one reason for analyzing locations data by country of origin, since more homogeneous groups would tend to be less affected by changes.

Table B-9 shows the number of deportable aliens located by duration of illegal residence for fiscal years 1977-1984 (data for fiscal 1984 are partially estimated, based on locations in the first 9 months of the year rated up to full year estimates using 9 month/1 year ratios from 1983); also shown is the percentage change for each duration category from one year to the next. Total locations remain remarkably consistent from year to year during the period, except for a drop of 15 percent in 1980 and a jump of 30 percent in 1983; locations in 1984 were 25 percent higher than in 1977. This aggregate consistency masks much more marked fluctuations by duration category, however. The drop in 1980 appears for all duration groups and may reflect shifts in resources to deal with the Mariel boatlift. Locations in 1981 and 1982 at durations of 30 days or less remain around their 1980 level, whereas locations for longer durations recover to their pre-1980 levels. The sharp increase in locations in 1983 is entirely accounted for by much higher locations at durations of 30 days or less, the numbers located at longer durations actually declining somewhat. Overall, locations at durations over 30 days fluctuate substantially but show no clear trend, whereas locations at durations of 30 days or less show no very marked trend until jumping substantially to high levels in 1983 and 1984.

How can we interpret these location numbers in terms of flows and stocks? One extreme assumption would be that locations are unrelated to the underlying flows and stocks, for example if INS enforcement activities were so overwhelmed by the volume of illegal migrants that location numbers represent physical ceilings of locations per officer-day. If this were the case, no interpretation would be possible since the location numbers would be determined by the level of enforcement activity alone. However, this assumption would fail to account for the drop in locations in the early 1980s and for the sharp rise in 1983; it is also hard to believe that the 90,000 or so illegal aliens located at durations of more than a year really represent the maximum number that the INS can possibly locate, and the decline in 1984 would be hard to explain.

An alternative assumption is that the location rates are essentially constant, in which case the numbers of locations directly reflect flows (locations at durations of 30 days or less, say) and stocks (the cases of longer duration). Under this assumption, the long-term illegal population has not changed substantially over the last eight years, whereas the number of attempted entries rose gradually in the late 1970s, fell some 10 percent in the early 1980s, and then increased sharply to high levels in 1983 and 1984. This assumption is not consistent with the data, however, since the sharply higher inflow in 1983 should, given constant location rates, have resulted in higher long-term locations in 1984, whereas these locations in fact fell. Other possible assumptions include that location rates have been rising, a possibility at least at short durations given the high-tech equipment introduced by the Border Patrol, in which case flows and stocks of illegals may have been constant or declining, or that rates have been falling, in which case flows and stocks may have been rising. However, the most tempting conclusions are that pressure of attempted entries has risen in 1983 and 1984 but the long-term illegal population has not increased much since the late 1970s; accepting the former conclusion further implies that the Border Patrol does a much better job of locating illegal aliens shortly after entry than it is generally given credit for; the latter conclusion has to be accepted unless it is believed that location rates at longer durations of illegal residence have declined at least as fast as the population has increased since the late 1970s, a belief hard to sustain since chance locations, for instance through police referrals, would be expected to reflect the underlying population size even if investigations activities did not.

Some further use of the locations data can be made by considering the person years lived illegally in the United States by located deportable aliens. The person years lived approach provides a measure of impact on U.S. society and also avoids the problem of multiple entries, since an individual making several entry attempts but being located shortly after each one will contribute only modestly to person years lived, though substantially to numbers of locations. Each duration category in Table B-9 has been assigned an average duration of illegal residence (zero for the at-entry category, .002 of a year for the less than 72 hours category, .035 of a year for 4-30 days, 0.26 for 1-6 months, 0.75 for 7-12 months, and 3.70 years, derived from Davidson's data, for over 1 year). The locations in each duration group and fiscal year of location can then be converted into person years of illegal residence, and these person years can be allocated to fiscal years of residence. Thus for example the 74,556 aliens located at durations of over a year in 1984 are assumed to have contributed half a year each to 1984, one year each for 1983, 1982, and 1981, and 0.2 of a year to 1980. The results are shown in Table B-10 by fiscal year of residence. Totals can only be obtained for years up to 1980, since the 1981 and subsequent totals will be affected by locations at durations over one year in 1985 and later. However, the totals obtained show little trend to 1980 (and the 1981 total is very unlikely to be substantially different), averaging around 360,000 per year. These totals represent the person years lived by, or average population of, deportable aliens who are subsequently located by the INS. They thus represent estimates of the lower limits for the average size of the deportable alien population each year, though clearly they do not define upper limits and are quite sensitive to the assumed average length of the open interval: increasing this average to 5 years would add over 100,000 to each estimate, while reducing it to 2.5 years would reduce each estimate by a similar amount.

CONCLUSIONS

As a result of this review of empirical estimates of the size of the illegal population of the United States, what can we conclude? First, the procedures that have been used, though often imaginative and sometimes elaborate, all invoke numerous assumptions that often cannot be adequately justified and to which the estimates obtained are sensitive. Second, even the commonly quoted range of 3-6 million illegals may be too high, though none of the procedures reviewed produces compelling upper or lower limits. The study by Warren and Passel suggests that it is unlikely that less than 1.5 million or more than 2.5 million illegal aliens were included in the 1980 census; locations data suggest that a figure under half a million is unlikely; Mexican census data fail to confirm the permanent absence in 1980 of more than half a million Mexicans who might be illegally resident in the United States, and the figure could be substantially lower. Though no range can be soundly defended, a population of 1.5 to 3.5 million illegal aliens in 1980 appears reasonably consistent with most of the studies. Third, there is no empirical basis at present for the widespread belief that the illegal alien population has increased sharply in the late 1970s and early 1980s; the only data available on recent trends, INS records of locations of deportable aliens, in fact suggest that the population has increased little if at all since 1977, although entry attempts may have increased,

possibly for no other reason than that the efficiency of the Border
Patrol has increased, causing more entries to fail early and thus to be
repeated. The size and growth of the illegal alien population may not be
problems of the magnitude sometimes suggested, although any substantial
number of illegal residents may cause social and economic problems,
particularly at the local level; these wider issues are not considered in
this discussion, which is limited to the size of the population only.

REFERENCES

Bean, F.D., King, A.G., and Passel, J.S.
   1983   The number of illegal migrants of Mexican origin in the United
          States: Sex ratio-based estimates for 1980. Demography
          20(1):99–110.
CENIET
   1981   Informe Final: Los Trabajadores Mexicanos en los Estados
          Unidos (Encuesta Nacional de Emigracion a la Frontera Norte del
          Pais y a los Estados Unidos--ENEFNEU--). Secretaria del
          Trabajo y Prevision Social. Centro Nacional de Informacion y
          Estadisticas del Trabajo. Mexico City.
Cue, R.A.
   1976   Men from an Underdeveloped Society: The Socioeconomic and
          Spatial Origins and Initial Destination of Documented Mexican
          Immigrants. Unpublished Doctoral Dissertation. University of
          Texas at Austin, Austin, Texas.
Davidson, C.A.
   1981   Characteristics of Deportable Aliens Located in the Interior of
          the United States. Paper presented at the annual meetings of
          the Population Association of America, Washington, D.C.
Garcia y Griego, M.
   1980   El Volumen de la Migracion de Mexicanos no Documentados a los
          Estados Unidos (Nuevas Hipotesis). Secretaria del Trabajo y
          Prevision Social. Centro Nacional de Informacion y
          Estadisticas del Trabajo. Mexico City.
Goldberg, H.
   1974   Estimates of Emigration from Mexico and Illegal Entry into the
          United States, 1960–1970, by the Residual Method. Unpublished
          graduate research paper. Center for Population Research.
          Georgetown University, Washington, D.C.
Heer, D.M.
   1979   What is the annual net flow of undocumented Mexican immigrants
          to the United States? Demography 16(3):417–423.
Interagency Task Force on Immigration Policy
   1979   Staff Report. Departments of Justice, Labor and State.
          Washington, D.C.
IUSSP
   1981   Indirect Procedures for Estimating Emigration. IUSSP Papers,
          No. 18. IUSSP, Liege, Belgium.

Lancaster, C., and Scheuren, F.J.
   1978   Counting the Uncountable Illegals: Some Initial Statistical
          Speculations Employing Capture-Recapture Techniques. 1977
          Proceedings of the Social Statistics Section. Part 1, pp.
          530-535. American Statistical Association.
Preston, S.H., and Coale, A.J.
   1982   Age structure, growth, attrition, and accession: A new
          synthesis. Population Index 48(2):217-259.
Reichert, J.S., and Massey, D.S.
   1979   Patterns of migration from a Mexican sending community: a
          comparison of legal and illegal migrants. International
          Migration Review 13:599-623.
Robinson, J.G.
   1980   Estimating the approximate size of the illegal alien population
          in the United States by the comparative trend analysis of
          age-specific death rates. Demography 17(2):159-176.
Siegel, J.S., Passel, J.S., and Robinson, J.G.
   1980   Preliminary Review of Existing Studies of the Number of Illegal
          Residents in the United States. Mimeo. Bureau of the Census,
          U.S. Department of Commerce, Washington, D.C.
Warren, R.
   1982   Estimation of the Size of the Illegal Population in the United
          States. Paper presented at the 1982 annual meetings of the
          Population Association of America, San Diego.
Warren, R., and Passel, J.S.
   1983   Estimates of Illegal Aliens from Mexico Counted in the 1980
          United States Census. Paper presented at the annual meeting of
          the Population Association of America, Pittsburgh.

TABLE B-6 Empirical Estimates of the Size of the Illegal Alien Population of the United States by Reference Date

Author	Reference Date or Period	Population Covered	Population Estimate (thousands)		
			Lower Limit	Point	Upper Limit
Goldberg (1974)	1960-1970	Net flow of illegal Mexicans to the U.S.	n.a.	1,600	n.a.
Lancaster and Scheuren (1978)	1973	Stock of illegal immigrants aged 18-44.	2,904	3,885	5,722
Robinson (1980)	1960-1970	Increase in the illegal white male population aged 20-44 in 10 eastern and south-western states.	177	n.a.	1,930
Robinson (1980)	1970-1975	Same as above.	400	n.a.	2,743
Heer (1979)	1970-1975	Average annual net flow of illegal Mexicans into the U.S.	80	n.a.	242
Garcia y Griego (1980)	1975	Stock of illegal Mexicans.	294	n.a.	684
Garcia y Griego (1980)	1977	Stock of illegal Mexicans.	482	n.a.	1,220
CENIET (1982)	1979	Usual residents of Mexico working or seeking work in the U.S.	n.a.	519	n.a.
Warren and Passel (1983)	1980	Illegal aliens included in 1980 U.S. census.	n.a.	2,047	n.a.
Bean, King, and Passel (1983)	1980	Stock of illegal Mexicans residing in the U.S.	n.a.	n.a.	n.a.
Hill (this study)	1980	Person years lived by illegal aliens, fiscal 1980.	0	n.a.	3,869
Hill (this study)	1970-1980	Net outflow from Mexico.	364	-303	n.a.
Hill (this study)	1960-1970	Net outflow from Mexico.	n.a.	731	n.a.

TABLE B-7 Estimation of Mexican Emigration Using Variable Growth Rate Procedure: Males, 1960-1970

Age Group a, a+5	Males (thousands) 1960	Males (thousands) 1970	$\dfrac{l(a+5)}{l(10)}$ [a]	$_5r_a$	N(a+5)	$\log\dfrac{N(a+5)l(10)}{N(10)l(a+5)}$	$5\sum\limits_{10}^{a-5}{}_5r_a$	$-5\sum\limits_{10}^{a-5}{}_5e_a$	$-{}_5e_a$	$-5E_a$
5-9	2,716	3,935			595					
10-14	2,243	3,271	.9922	.0391	475	-.2171	.1957	-.0214	-.0043	-112
15-19	1,745	2,491	.9809	.0369	371	-.4536	.3803	-.0733	-.0104	-209
20-24	1,410	1,930	.9641	.0326	301	-.6445	.5431	-.1014	-.0056	-89
25-29	1,200	1,575	.9450	.0282	250	-.8089	.6842	-.1247	-.0047	-62
30-34	1,013	1,285	.9236	.0247	223	-.9018	.8075	-.0942	.0061	67
35-39	963	1,235	.8978	.0258	187	-1.0473	.9366	-.1108	-.0033	-35
40-44	677	959	.8661	.0361	152	-1.2237	1.1172	-.1065	.0009	7
45-49	613	830	.8255	.0314	126	-1.3588	1.2744	-.0844	.0044	30
50-54	529	590	.7736	.0113	101	-1.5219	1.3310	-.1910	-.0213	-115
55-59	407	502	.7049	.0218	86	-1.5834	1.4398	-.1437	.0095	41
60-64	373	451	.6173	.0197	66	-1.7172	1.5383	-.1789	-.0070	-28
65-69	204	345	.5052	.0545	46	-1.8809	1.8108	-.0701	.0218	56
70-74	162	242	.3749	.0416	29	-2.0484	2.0190	-.0295	.0081	16
75-79	91	120	.2420	.0287	17	-2.1411	2.1624	.0213	.0102	10
80-84	58	81	.1264		14					
85+	63	71								
Total										-423

[a] Uses the United Nations (1982) model life table, Latin American Pattern, with an expectation of life at age 10 of 56.53 years.

TABLE B-8 Estimated Mexican Emigrants by Age Group and Sex, 1960-1970 and 1970-1980, Using Variable Growth Rate Procedure (in thousands)

Age Group	Males 1960-1970[a]	1970-1980[a]	Females 1960-1970[a]	1970-1980[a]
10-14	112	196	-67	-143
15-19	209	190	-48	-141
20-24	89	58	48	42
25-29	62	39	209	179
30-34	-67	-196	27	-163
35-39	35	-42	25	-28
40-44	-7	-12	27	45
45-49	-30	56	22	2
50-54	115	-52	137	-43
55-59	-41	-88	-38	-57
60-64	28	24	24	18
65-69	-56	-4	-43	4
70-74	-16	-17	4	-15
75-79	-10	-74	-19	-81
Total	423	78	308	-381

[a]The life tables used were from the United Nations model life tables (UN 1982) selected with an expectation of life at age 10 of 56.53 years (males 60-70), 58.21 years (males 70-80), 60.28 years (females 60-70) and 62.09 years (females 70-80).

TABLE B-9 Deportable Aliens Located by Duration of Illegal Residence: Fiscal Years 1977-1984

Fiscal Year	Duration of Illegal Residence						
	At Entry	72 Hours	4-30 Days	1-6 Months	7-12 Months	1 Year	Total
1977	460,413	202,134	96,219	110,959	36,621	127,081	1,033,427
1978	509,345 (+10.6)	210,749 (+4.3)	93,478 (-2.8)	104,098 (-6.2)	30,624 (-14.4)	99,493 (-21.7)	1,047,787 (+1.4)
1979	532,145 (+4.5)	202,578 (-3.9)	91,537 (-2.1)	125,197 (+20.3)	36,416 (+18.9)	81,527 (-18.1)	1,069,400 (+2.1)
1980	468,303 (-12.0)	179,912 (-11.2)	62,257 (-32.0)	97,029 (-22.5)	31,866 (-12.5)	63,550 (-22.1)	902,917 (-15.6)
1981	494,314 (+5.6)	180,597 (+0.4)	64,022 (+2.8)	101,984 (+5.1)	39,461 (+23.8)	73,047 (+14.9)	953,425 (+5.6)
1982	482,334 (-2.4)	176,089 (-2.5)	66,171 (+3.4)	103,263 (+1.3)	39,870 (+1.0)	94,960 (+30.0)	962,687 (+1.0)
1983	698,003 (+44.7)	236,858 (+34.5)	80,456 (+21.6)	100,818 (-2.4)	35,503 (-11.0)	94,853 (-0.1)	1,246,491 (+29.5)
1984a	710,140 (+1.7)	294,924 (+24.5)	84,903 (+5.5)	95,380 (-5.6)	31,495 (-11.3)	74,556 (-21.4)	1,291,398 (+3.6)

NOTE: Percentage change appears in parentheses.

aFigures for 1984 are based on 9 month totals rated up to annual estimates on basis of 1983 9 month/1 year ratios by duration category.

TABLE B-10 Distribution of Person-Years Lived by Located Deportable Aliens and Fiscal Year of Residence, 1977-1984

Duration Category	Fiscal Year of Location	Fiscal Year of Residence 1977	1978	1979	1980	1981	1982	1983	1984
4 days	1977	404	-	-	-	-	-	-	-
	1978	-	421	-	-	-	-	-	-
	1979	-	-	405	-	-	-	-	-
	1980	-	-	-	360	-	-	-	-
	1981	-	-	-	-	361	-	-	-
	1982	-	-	-	-	-	352	-	-
	1983	-	-	-	-	-	-	474	-
	1984	-	-	-	-	-	-	1	589
4-30 days	1977	3309	-	-	-	-	-	-	-
	1978	57	3215	-	-	-	-	-	-
	1979	-	56	3148	-	-	-	-	-
	1980	-	-	38	2141	-	-	-	-
	1981	-	-	-	39	2202	-	-	-
	1982	-	-	-	-	41	2275	-	-
	1983	-	-	-	-	-	49	2767	-
	1984	-	-	-	-	-	-	52	2920
1-6 months	1977	25099	-	-	-	-	-	-	-
	1978	3518	23547	-	-	-	-	-	-
	1979	-	4232	28319	-	-	-	-	-
	1980	-	-	3280	21948	-	-	-	-
	1981	-	-	-	3447	23069	-	-	-
	1982	-	-	-	-	3490	23358	-	-
	1983	-	-	-	-	-	3408	22805	-
	1984	-	-	-	-	-	-	3224	21575
7-12 months	1977	17166	-	-	-	-	-	-	-
	1978	8613	14355	-	-	-	-	-	-
	1979	-	10242	17070	-	-	-	-	-
	1980	-	-	8963	14938	-	-	-	-
	1981	-	-	-	11099	18498	-	-	-
	1982	-	-	-	-	11214	18689	-	-
	1983	-	-	-	-	-	9985	16642	-
	1984	-	-	-	-	-	-	8858	14763
1 year	1977	63541	-	-	-	-	-	-	-
	1978	99493	49747	-	-	-	-	-	-
	1979	81527	81527	40764	-	-	-	-	-
	1980	63550	63550	63550	31775	-	-	-	-
	1981	14609	73047	73047	73047	36524	-	-	-
	1982	-	18992	94960	94960	94960	47480	-	-
	1983	-	-	18971	94853	94853	94853	47427	-
	1984	-	-	-	14911	74556	74556	74556	37278
Total (thousands)		380.9	342.9	352.5	363.5	-	-	-	-

The Imputation and Treatment of Missing Data

Kenneth Wachter

Every statistical reporting system needs well-defined, routine procedures for the treatment of missing data. That data are missing does not in itself reflect badly on administrators who collect or report it; all good data collection involves missing values--they are an ordinary fact of life. What does reflect badly on those who report statistics is to fail to recognize the importance of obtaining as complete a response as possible, to deny that there were missing values, or to pretend that the reported values are free from gaps in coverage and free from nonresponse. Nothing undermines confidence in an administrative tabulation so badly as the absence of a column showing the number of offices that failed to report or whose reports could not be included in the tabulation, the number of forms submitted incomplete, and so forth. Reporting the extent of missing values builds confidence in a report, by showing that the agency seeks a realistic view of the completeness that its compilations achieve.

Of course, it is better when data are not missing, although no large reporting system comes close to 100 percent reporting. There is no statistical magic that can make up for information that is not there. There does now exist a large body of statistical know-how for minimizing the bad effects that missing data could otherwise have on reported totals and on inferences about patterns and trends. Some of these statistical methods are already routine and are in continual use by government agencies, including the Census Bureau. Others are at the stage of research development and testing. A good recent overall account can be found in the entry on "Incomplete Data" in the Encyclopedia of Statistical Sciences (Little and Rubin, 1982).

The first rule of treating missing data is that procedures must be as uniform, standardized, and well-documented as possible. It is more important to know what the numbers before one mean and how they were arrived at than to have them compiled by superior but unfathomable methods. It is better to have a run-of-the-mill but uniform reporting system than to have a system in which (unbeknownst to readers of its reports) certain district offices have pursued every last elusive case while others have misplaced whole bundles of forms. Even if star offices can be identified, they cannot be regarded as a random subset of all offices. A good approach to missing data is to target a random sample of offices for intensive follow-up of missing cases and then to present correction multipliers based on the sample follow-up. Sampling can be an efficient, cost-effective way to allocate resources for improvement in data quality.

Using the INS Statistical Yearbook as an example, these general considerations lead immediately to the observation that all tables in the yearbook should include a row or column enumerating cases with status unknown. If unknown or uncertain cases have been distributed among other rows or columns, the formula for distributing them should be stated in the table notes. For example, Table 10A in the <u>1979 Statistical Yearbook</u> on page 28 illustrates this point in having a row for "no occupation reported." In contrast, however, the row for "unknown marital status" in Table 10A contains zeroes for all years and both sexes. The zeroes suggest that ambiguous cases have been assigned by some rules that are not explained, since it is not credible that of some 2 million people not a single person failed to check a box; not a single coder accidentally punched a nonsense digit, and not a single error eluded the agents who accepted the forms. Furthermore, age must have been missing from some records, since age nonresponse is commonplace. A row showing the number of cases that lacked ages next to the median age row would be reassuring. For another example, consider Table 17C on page 54. A row showing numbers of temporary visitors whose region of last permanent residence was uncertain, or a formula showing how such cases have been allocated among regions would bolster confidence and enhance the value of this table.

A further observation to be noted is that the footnotes in each table in the <u>Statistical Yearbook</u> should include a statement of the basic data sources or sources from which the table is derived. For instance, Table 17C of the <u>1979 Statistical Yearbook</u> is probably derived from the I-94 Nonimmigrant Arrival/Departure Forms. But that cannot be determined from the yearbook itself. Such footnotes would aid both outside readers and those in the INS who trace errors and regenerate the tables in later years. Which tables derive from the same basic data and which from different sets of data? The yearbook should also contain a statement of the total numbers of I-94 forms accounted for in central office tabulations and the number of those that were incomplete, missing matching departure records, and so forth. In that way the information that would help in the interpretation of all the tables based on those particular forms would be assembled in one place.

It is very important in treating missing data to know whether the data are missing at random. For example, suppose that a border office typically fails to report at all when it is so busy with exceptional numbers of apprehensions that there is no time for statistical work. Or suppose that at border crossing points, fewer booths are staffed at peak weekends or peak hours, because of staff holidays or staff shortages. In such situations the data are not missing at random. There is a relationship between the values that would have been reported if they were not missing and the fact that those values are missing--a relationship that seriously undermines the statistics. Such situations can sometimes be prevented by astute staffing decisions, but they are bound to occur. The preface to the INS <u>Statistical Yearbook</u> should discuss the most salient such situations, on the basis of direct consultation with the officers in the field who know the realities firsthand.

Formalized statistical techniques that compensate for or diminish the bad effects of missing data come under the general heading of imputation. Missing information can be imputed or made up on the basis of information that is not missing. The first rule of imputation is information must never be imputed to records in a way that does not allow the imputed cases to be separated from the actually reported cases at every later stage of the analysis. For instance, values should never be imputed into the basic records, like I-94 forms, unless they are coded in such a way that the imputed values will be clearly distinguished from the real values whenever totals are assembled. When data are computerized, it is generally easy to add a code to each value indicating whether it is imputed. Then totals can be run off with and without the imputed values. In this way, the effects of imputation can be observed.

Of the various imputation strategies now in use, three are mentioned here: "hot deck imputation," generalized regression single or multiple imputation, and incomplete data likelihood maximization with algorithms like those of the "E-M" type. Good accounts of these methods can be found in the entry on incomplete data in the Encyclopedia of Statistical Sciences. For an account of hot deck imputation, see Ford (1983). This is the type of method in widest use among government agencies, especially in the Census Bureau. For regression-based imputation, a new variant that allows unbiased estimation of standard errors in cross-tabulations has been pioneered by Rubin and called "multiple imputation" (Rubin, 1980). It is not restricted to sample surveys alone. A large experiment using this method to insert 1980 occupational codes into the 1970 census public-use sample is now under way at the Census Bureau. For likelihood maximization methods, more formal statistical expertise in model building is required, although the results can repay the extra effort if the data are otherwise of high quality. A good entree to this extensive statistical literature is the cautionary article by Little and Rubin (1983).

The statistical virtues of these methods are not the only considerations in a decision about which to use. The simplicity of the methods and the feasibility of implementing them in practice under the difficult conditions that the INS often faces must be taken into account. When missing values on individual forms like the I-94 are at issue the simplest and most easily implemented formal imputation method is the hot deck method. When missing blocks of data in aggregate tables are at issue, for example if a computer tape or the transmissions from one district office should be garbled or misplaced, a likelihood maximization method would be efficient and appropriate.

The idea of hot deck imputation is to substitute for values missing on one record the values that occur on another record whose values have a high probability of agreeing with those that are not missing. As an example, consider I-94 forms that are missing entry 11, occupation. A person coding the I-94 forms, finding a missing occupation, would go back, either manually or by computer, to the last-processed I-94 form which showed, say, the same country of citizenship (entry 3) and decade of birth (entry 2). The value from that form would then be coded as occupation for the form with occupation missing, along with a code showing that this occupation value was an imputed value rather than a true value. The final tabulations of admissions by occupation would then show separate values for occupations without imputations and occupations including imputations.

It is essential that any hot deck imputation use a set of formal rules that state that if such and such entries are missing, then the donor form from whom the missing values are supplied shall be the first form that is similar in a number of prespecified variables. The selection of donor form should not be left to the judgment of the coder. It is also essential that the rules be simple, particularly if they are being implemented by hand, but also, in the interests of efficiency, if they are being implemented by computer. Thus the requirements for a match to a donor should not be overly rigid, yet appropriate for the variable to be imputed.

The use of likelihood maximization methods, especially those that employ E-M algorithms, demands the specification of a statistical model and therefore demands a trained statistician to formulate the model. In an example such as that of a missing tape, the need might be to estimate cells in a cross-tabulation, in which the total number of records with missing age and sex values might be known, but in which their distribution among the cells of the table might be uncertain. In such a case, a standard model for contingency tables could be used. It remains essential, however, to present the table without as well as with the entries adjusted for the missing data. The impact of the statistical adjustments needs to be visible, so that readers and administrators can assess their plausibility. Likelihood maximization methods would be recommended if fairly large quantities of data, numbering, say, into the thousands of records or 5 percent of the total sample, proved missing. For cases in which few values were missing, either in absolute amounts or relative to the size of the sample, it is generally not cost-effective to adjust.

Any statistical system has to deal with missing data. With a record-generating system as large and complex as that of the INS, what is simplest and most easily implemented is undoubtedly best. It is therefore right to advocate a pragmatic approach, rather than a fancy theoretical solution, and to encourage, above all, common sense, uniformity, and candor.

REFERENCES

Ford, B.L.
  1983   An overview of hot-deck procedures. Pp. 185-207 in W.G. Madow, I. Olkin, and D.B. Rubin, eds., Incomplete Data in Sample Surveys: Theories and Bibliographies. Vol. 2. New York: Academic Press.
Little, R.J., and Rubin, D.
  1982   Incomplete data. In S. Kotz and N.L. Johnson, eds., Encyclopedia of Statistical Science. New York: Wiley.
  1983   On jointly estimating parameters and missing data by maximizing the complete-data likelihood. American Statistician 37:218-220.
Rubin, D.B.
  1980   Pp. 1-9 in Bureau of the Census, Handling Nonresponse in Sample Surveys by Multiple Imputation. Washington, D.C.: U.S. Department of Commerce.

Appendix C

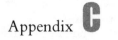

THE SETTLEMENT PROCESS AMONG MEXICAN MIGRANTS TO THE UNITED STATES:
NEW METHODS AND FINDINGS

Douglas S. Massey
Population Studies Center, University of Pennsylvania

This paper illustrates a new approach to gathering data on Mexico-United States migration. The approach is the ethnosurvey, which combines representative survey sampling with ethnography to generate data on social processes operating at the community level. These data indicate that as migrants accumulate experience in the United States, a variety of social and economic ties are formed that progressively increase the likelihood of U.S. settlement. Over time, migrants collect family members abroad, make new friends, establish formal and informal institutional ties, learn English, and obtain more stable, better-paid jobs. As a result, over time less money is remitted home to Mexico, and more is spent in the United States. These trends are reflected in a steady, cumulative increase in the probability of U.S. settlement. The number of Mexicans settling in the United States in years to come will undoubtedly increase because of the large number of people that began migrating during the 1970s. Of these, many will inevitably become recurrent seasonal migrants, and of them, a sizable share will ultimately settle.

INTRODUCTION

This paper is both methodological and substantive. On one hand, it describes and illustrates a new approach to gathering data on Mexican immigration to the United States. On the other hand, the example was chosen for more than its heuristic value. Indeed, it concerns a question of central importance in the immigration debate: whether Mexican migrants are sojourners or settlers. That is, are they seasonal laborers who enter the United States for only brief periods and have no interest in staying permanently, or are they immigrants seeking to establish a permanent residence in this country? This question is important because the two views portend very different futures of population growth, labor force expansion, and ethnic change for the United States.

This research was conducted under grant HD15166 from the National Institute of Child Health and Human Development, whose support is gratefully acknowledged.

Within the past decade, immigration has once again become a topic of absorbing interest in the United States. As in previous eras of public agitation about this topic, an intense demand for data has arisen, and the sorry state of knowledge in the field has again been exposed. Much of the public debate has focused on the "numbers game": how many immigrants are there, who are they, and where do they live? These are indeed important questions, and the immigration statistics system is ill-equipped to provide timely, reliable answers, especially with the growth of undocumented migration during the 1970s. Most professional attention has therefore focused on designing estimation methods and statistical systems to provide better data on U.S. immigration (Lancaster and Scheuren, 1978; Heer, 1979; Kraly, 1980; Robinson, 1980; Bean et al., 1983; Tienda and Sullivan, 1984; Hill, 1984; Kraly et al., 1984; Goodman, 1984).

However, there is more to our poor understanding of immigration than a lack of aggregate-level information. We also have a very limited comprehension of the basic social processes that underlie Mexico-United States migration. In a narrow sense, of course, migration between the two countries is strictly economic. Migrants are motivated primarily by their desire for higher wages and the things they buy. But these basic economic motivations are defined within a social context. Migration changes this social context in systematic ways that fundamentally alter the way its costs and benefits are perceived and that in turn change the nature of the migratory process itself. Migration has a way of feeding back upon itself through a complex social process that is very poorly understood. As the social context of migration gradually changes, so do important characteristics of the migrant stream: how many and what kind of migrants are involved, where they go, what they do, how long they stay, whether they migrate alone or with families. Until we understand the social foundations of migration, we have no basis for anticipating changes in these important parameters of the migration process.

This report represents part of a much larger study designed to describe, understand, and ultimately to model the social process of Mexico-United States migration. In undertaking such a study, government statistics are of little use. First, they are too general. Most are gathered through surveys or bureaucratic mechanisms that are not designed to measure international migration per se. They often do not include variables important in the migration process, especially those that operate primarily within the context of small, localized communities. Second, government data on migration are usually cross-sectional and therefore preclude the detailed study of migration as a developmental social process. Third, Mexico-United States migration transcends national boundaries, requiring data on communities of origin and destination as well as on the social networks that link the two. Government statistical bureaus do not provide this kind of information. Finally, in the case of Mexican migration, much of the movement is undocumented, and therefore excluded, or at least underrepresented, in official data.

In order to deal with these difficult problems, we developed the ethnosurvey. This method combines intensive ethnographic study of particular communities with representative survey sampling in order to generate ethnographically informed quantitative data on social processes operating at the local level. Strictly speaking, the ethnosurvey is

neither ethnography nor sample survey, but a marriage of these two
complementary approaches. Questionnaire design, sampling, and
interviewing are shaped by the ethnographic conventions of
anthropological research as well as by those of sociological survey
sampling. At the same time, the ethnographies are guided and illuminated
by quantitative data emanating from the representative sample survey. In
design as well as analysis the two approaches inform one another, so that
the weaknesses of one become the other's strengths. In the end, the data
that emerge have much greater validity than would be provided by either
method alone.

Obviously, the social process of Mexico-United States migration is a
very broad topic, much too broad to be considered comprehensively here.
This paper therefore uses ethnosurvey data to focus on one aspect of the
migration process that is of considerable interest to social scientists
and policy makers alike: the process of integration and settlement in
the United States. As mentioned at the outset, an important controversy
in the immigration debate is whether Mexican migrants are sojourners or
settlers. The prevailing wisdom seems to be that they are primarily
sojourners who come to work in the United States on a seasonal basis.
They have little or no interest in permanent settlement, and while they
may make frequent trips, these are enumerated in months rather than years
(Cornelius, 1978:24-28).

On the surface, the empirical evidence seems to bear out this
conclusion. Most studies show average trip lengths of between 6 and 12
months (North and Houstoun, 1976; Bustamante, 1978; Cornelius, 1978;
Reichert and Massey, 1979; Ranney and Kossoudji, 1983). However, the
theories of Bohning (1972) and Piore (1979) suggest a different
perspective: namely that the relative prevalence of sojourners versus
settlers is not a fixed characteristic of migrants. Rather it is a
variable that changes as the social context of migration changes. While
most migrants from Mexico may begin as sojourners, they are increasingly
likely to become settlers the more trips they make to the United States
and the greater the store of time they build up abroad. Although
migrants' interests initially are utilitarian--to achieve a target income
and return home as soon as possible--they inevitably acquire social and
economic ties binding them to U.S. society, ties that make permanent
settlement progressively more likely.

While the ideas of Bohning and Piore are provocative, there is little
hard empirical evidence to document such a process of integration and
settlement among Mexican migrants. On the contrary, the empirical
information that exists points to low average durations of stay in the
United States. However, to the author's knowledge, no studies have
adequately controlled for the cumulative amount of U.S. migrant
experience, the crucial factor in the settlement process. If social and
economic ties to the United States, and hence the propensity to settle,
develop slowly over time, and if there has been a recent and dramatic
upswing in Mexican migration, then a high rate of return migration today
would not be surprising, even given an underlying crescive settlement
process. Because of the recent upswing, most Mexicans migrating today
have only been migrants for a few years, so naturally their trips are
short and infrequent. However, as these recent migrants age, many will
become habitual seasonal migrants and accumulate U.S. experience, and of

these many will eventually settle in the United States. It is a classic period-cohort situation.

This paper uses ethnosurvey data to study the settlement process among migrants from four Mexican communities. It examines the formation of social and economic ties to the United States over time and explores how the social context of migration changes systematically with progressive exposure to U.S. society. Having considered the process of socioeconomic integration, probability models of out-migration and settlement are estimated to confirm basic hypotheses regarding the nature of the migration process and to draw inferences regarding future course of Mexican settlement within the United States.

STUDY DESIGN

Asking about migration to the United States, most of it undocumented, is a delicate matter that must be approached with care and deliberation (Reichert and Massey, 1979; Cornelius, 1982). The ethnosurvey provides a vehicle that is well-suited to the task. The basic rationale for the ethnosurvey is not, of course, original to this project. Many studies have conducted small-scale surveys within migrant sending communities (Wiest, 1973; Cornelius, 1978; Dinerman, 1978, 1982; Shadow, 1979; Reichert, 1981, 1982; Mines, 1981; Roberts, 1982; Pressar, 1982). However, the current study is different in being wholly designed and implemented by an interdisciplinary team of qualitatively trained anthropologists as well as a quantitatively trained sociologist/demographer. Thus both analytic perspectives were brought to bear in all phases of the study.

The questionnaire design represents a compromise between the exigencies of survey research and ethnography. On one hand, a highly structured survey instrument consisting of a battery of closed questions is inappropriate for studying undocumented migration among Mexican campesinos (Cornelius, 1982). On the other hand, some standardization is required in order to collect the same information on each household. Basically we sought a design that was informal, nonthreatening, and as unobtrusive as possible, one that allowed the interviewer some discretion about how and when to ask sensitive questions, but ultimately yielded a standard set of data.

The form we chose was a semistructured interview schedule. The instrument was laid out in a series of tables, or in Spanish cuadros, with household members listed down the side and variables across the top. The interviewer could then solicit the required information in ways that the situation seemed to demand, using his or her judgment as to timing and precise wording. Each cuadro corresponded to a different topic, and was at times separated by questions of a more specialized nature in order to elaborate the theme under examination. The questionnaire was designed in Spanish during August 1982, pretested and modified during September and October of that year, and finally put into the field beginning in November.

The questionnaires were applied to households selected in simple random samples of four communities located on the western edge of Mexico's central plateau, one of the most important source regions for Mexican migration to the United States (Samora, 1971; Dagodag, 1975;

North and Houstoun, 1976; Cornelius, 1978; Jones, 1982; Ranney and Kossoudji, 1983). Two criteria were employed in selecting the communities. First, we sought towns or cities in which a member of the anthropological research team had prior ethnographic experience. With an established unobtrusive presence in the community and an existing network of trusted informants, the potential level of threat from a study of out-migration could be considerably reduced and the validity of data much enhanced. Second, we wanted to pick four different kinds of communities in order to give the study a comparative focus. Prior studies of Mexican sending communities have mostly been of rural agricultural towns, and we sought to include urban industrial communities in order to broaden our base of generalization.

The first of the four communities we selected was the rural community of Altamira,[1] a town of roughly 6,100 located in a traditional agricultural region in southern Jalisco. The second was Chamitlan, a somewhat larger rural community of 9,900 located in a more modern commercialized agricultural area not far from the city of Zamora, Michoacan. The third community was Santiago, an industrial town of 9,400 located south of the metropolis of Guadalajara, in the state of Jalisco. Its main source of employment since the turn of the century has been a textile mill, and its population contains virtually no agricultural workers. The last community was San Marcos, an urban barrio of 4,800 people located in a working-class section of Guadalajara itself, Mexico's second largest city. These communities were not selected because they were thought to contain many migrants. Although we knew that all contained some U.S. migrants, with the exception of Chamitlan, which we knew had a long migrant tradition, we had no idea whether they contained many or few.

Within each of these four communities, a simple random sample of 200 households was drawn. This number was large enough to provide sufficient cases for analysis, yet small enough so that detailed, ethnographically informed interviews could be conducted. Detailed maps showing the location of households in each community were prepared during August 1982, and from these the sampling frames were constructed. Interviewing of sample households began in November 1982 and ended in February 1983, with most being conducted during the months of December and January, the months when most seasonal migrants have returned home from the United States. If a dwelling was unoccupied throughout the month of December, another was randomly selected. Strictly speaking, then, the sample is representative of dwelling units that were occupied during the month of December 1982 in each of the four communities.

The interviews were conducted by three Mexican anthropologists,[2] who comprised the field unit of the research team, and by assistants whom they trained especially for the project. In Santiago and San Marcos, the assistants were graduate students in sociology from a local university, and in the two rural communities they were local schoolteachers. Obviously, in using an ethnographic approach that does not rely on standardized question wordings, it is absolutely essential that interviewers understand clearly what information is being sought in each of the cuadros. The research team therefore spent long hours going over the questionnaire in painstaking detail, making sure that each person had the same understanding of what information was being sought and why. The anthropological field team in turn placed considerable emphasis on training their assistants, repeating the task of going over the questionnaire line by line. Finally, in each community, subsamples of the questionnaires were checked with informants to verify their accuracy and truthfulness, and additional checks for internal consistency were later performed with the aid of a computer.

The questionnaire was applied in two phases. In the first phase, basic social and demographic data were collected from people in the household. In the opening question, the head of household was identified, followed by his or her spouse and living children. If a son or daughter was a member of another sample household, this fact was ascertained and recorded. (A person was considered to be in a separate household if he or she was married, maintained a separate house or kitchen, and organized expenses separately.) Finally, other household members were identified and their relationship to the head clarified.

In Santiago, relatively few migrants turned up in early interviews conducted within sample households. In order to secure a number of migrants large enough for detailed analyses, an additional 25 migrant households were located and interviewed from outside the sample. In all, the total Mexican sample consists of 5,949 people enumerated in 825 households. Of these people, 4,953 were members of sample households and 1,352 were sons and daughters living in other households outside the sample.

The second phase of the questionnaire compiled a complete life history from household heads with migrant experience in the United States. The life history focused on lifetime processes of occupational mobility, migration, resource accumulation, and family formation. If the household head had never been a U.S. migrant but another household member (typically a son) had significant prior experience in the United States, an abbreviated life history (mainly a labor history) was taken. Both groups were also asked a detailed series of questions about their experiences as migrants in the United States.

Obviously, studies limited to returned migrants interviewed in their home communities underrepresent, if not exclude, migrants who have settled more permanently in the United States. Therefore, the four community samples were supplemented by an additional 60 interviews conducted among migrant households residing in California, with and without documents, during August and September 1983. Representative random sampling was impossible, so migrants were located using the chain-referral or "snowball" method (Goodman, 1961). Twenty households each were selected from among out-migrants from Altamira, Chamitlan, and Santiago, yielding a total sample of 367 California-based migrants in 60 households. Of these, 305 were members of sample households and 62 were members of others. A household was eligible for inclusion in the California sample if its head had been in the United States for three continuous years and was born in either Altamira, Chamitlan, or Santiago. Out-migrants from San Marcos were not sought owing to limited time and resources.

THE SOCIAL PROCESS OF INTEGRATION IN THE UNITED STATES

An important module of the ethnosurvey questionnaire asked migrants about experiences on their most recent trip to the United States. The results of this section are based on a special data file constructed from their responses to these questions. In all, 440 migrants provided information about their last U.S. trip (including 60 migrants from the California sample). Of these, 19 percent were documented, 65 percent were undocumented, and 17 percent were Braceros.[3] The median date of their last trip was 1975. Early work on the project indicated that rural/urban origin was an important factor that conditioned key parameters of the migration process (see Mullan, 1984). Therefore, all data presented in this paper are broken down by this variable. Migrants were considered to be of rural origin if they were from Altamira or Chamitlan or were out-migrants from these towns living in California. They were of urban origin if they were from Santiago or San Marcos or out-migrants from the former. By this definition, 66 percent of the 440 migrants were of rural origin and 34 percent were of urban origin.

A common view of Mexican migrants is that they are predominantly young men traveling to the United States without family dependents (Cornelius, 1978:30). This is clearly not the case for legal migrants, a majority of whom are women (Massey and Schnabel, 1983a); but perusing the available empirical evidence, it does seem to represent fairly the current status of undocumented Mexican migrants (Massey and Schnabel, 1983b; Passel and Warren, 1983).

However, some community studies suggest that while Mexican migration is indeed a male-led phenomenon, women and children tend eventually to become involved in the migration process (Reichert and Massey, 1980; Mines and Massey, 1985), a result that is consonant with Piore's (1979) theory. According to Piore's view, whether one migrates alone or with family dependents is a function of the years of migrant experience that have been accumulated. On the few first trips, migrants live a spartan existence, often sharing living quarters with other men and sleeping in shifts to save money. They are true homo economica, seeking to maximize short-term income before returning home to family and community. They work long hours and have little interest in social activities. According to Piore (1979:55) they are "a group of people divorced from a social setting, operating outside the constraints or inhibitions that it imposes, working totally and exclusively for money."

If a migrant makes only one or two trips, there is no particular problem with this way of life. The migrant knows it will end, and he does not define himself with respect to the foreign context. The labor may be menial and life unpleasant, but he will return home with a good deal of money, and with it he will be able to buy a certain amount of status and prestige. However, satisfaction of the wants that initially led to migration often only creates new wants. The levels of wealth and consumption that migration brings have a way of altering tastes and expectations in a way that lead to more trips (Piore, 1979; Reichert, 1981; Mines, 1981). As the migrant accumulates time in the United States, his anomic social life becomes increasingly problematic. People are intrinsically social beings, and inevitably homo economicus gives way to homo socibilis. Ultimately, the migrant becomes enmeshed in a web of social ties within the United States. As the migrant experience begins to lengthen and appear more open-ended, enforced separation from family and loved ones becomes more and more difficult to sustain. Over time, pressure to bring along wives and children grows.

Table C-1 shows the percentage of migrants with selected family and friendship ties in the United States classified by years of migrant experience. The latter variable refers to the total time a migrant has accumulated in the United States over a lifetime of trips, be they one or several. Looking at the marginals, we see the basis for the common generalization that Mexican migrants are predominantly males traveling without dependents. The vast majority (84 percent of rural migrants and 77 percent of urban migrants) have neither wife nor children with them in the United States. However, considering the marginal distributions alone does not give a true picture of what is going on and, indeed, can be quite misleading. The tendency for migrants to be accompanied by family members clearly increases with time spent in the United States. Consistent with expectations, the percentage with spouses, sons, and daughters rises smoothly, almost monotonically, with U.S. migrant experience, as does the average number of relatives reported to be living in the United States. Among both rural and urban migrants with at least 15 years of U.S. experience, around 43 percent report their spouse to be in the United States, and among rural migrants a majority (54 percent) report having their sons along (among urban migrants the figure is 36 percent). The average number of relatives living in the United States doubles from 10 or 11 among beginning migrants to 23 or 24 among the most experienced.

Another thing that naturally happens with the passage of time abroad is the formation of friendship ties with members of the host society. Table C-1 also clearly documents the gradual development of friendly relations between Mexican migrants and members of various U.S. ethnic groups. It is not surprising that, in general, the most prevalent social relations are with Chicanos (native Americans of Mexican descent) and other Latinos (who may themselves be Spanish-speaking immigrants; see the marginal distributions). However, as the amount of time spent in the United States grows, the percentage knowing Anglos (non-Hispanic white Americans) increases quite dramatically, from 11 percent to 63 percent among rural migrants and from 17 percent to 72 percent among urban migrants. Indeed, by the time rural migrants have accumulated 15 years in the United States, they are more likely to be friendly with Anglos than either Chicanos or Latinos. There is also a mild increase in the tendency to be friends with American blacks, in spite of the high degree of residential segregation between the two groups (Massey, 1979) and the apparent disinclination of Mexicans to live near blacks (Lieberson and Carter, 1983; Massey and Mullan, 1984). In short, if one were to look at the marginals alone, one would mistakenly conclude that there is little social intercourse between Mexican migrants and Americans; but allowing for the crucial role of U.S. experience we find clear evidence of growing social integration over time.

The last datum in Table C-1 is the average number of fellow townspeople, or paisanos, migrants reported being in touch with in the United States. Here we find a curious contrast. Among urban migrants the number rose with years of migrant experience, while among those of rural origin it fell slightly but steadily. In fact, this curious anomaly is explained by an important finding that emerges from Table C-2, which reports some other indicators of social integration in the United States.

An important dimension of the integration process is the movement from transitory seasonal employment to a steadier, more sedentary job in the United States. Among rural Mexican migrants, in particular, this trend involves moving from agricultural to nonagricultural employment. Table C-2 shows a very marked shift in rural migrants' sector of employment with increasing years of migrant experience. Among those with less than a year's experience on their latest U.S. job, 91 percent were farm workers; but after 15 years of migrant experience, this percentage fell to 38 percent. Thus, over time there is a transition from overwhelmingly agricultural to predominantly industrial or service employment. In contrast, urban migrant workers are predominantly nonagricultural no matter what their experience category. However, a sizable plurality of those in the lowest experience class, 40 percent, work in agriculture, even though almost all of these people come from nonagricultural backgrounds in Mexico. This fact suggests the strong tendency for Mexican migrants to be channeled into agriculture, regardless of their occupation (Mullan, 1984). However, in the next experience interval, there is a rapid shift back to a sector of employment more consonant with their Mexican occupational background.

These results help to explain contrasting rural-urban patterns in the number of paisanos that migrants report knowing in the United States. Migrant networks from rural communities feed primarily into areas of U.S. agricultural employment. Family and friendship connections are widely used to secure jobs with specific growers at specific times. There is therefore a disproportionate concentration of paisanos or kinsmen in certain farms and fields. When a migrant from a rural area opts for nonagricultural employment, he drifts away from a close connection with this network, leading to a decrease in the intensity of his relations with paisanos. Networks from Mexican urban areas, in contrast, lead directly into U.S. urban areas and associations with nonagricultural employers in particular factories and service establishments. The settlement process for urban migrants thus provides an opportunity to cement friendships with other paisanos living and working in the same U.S. communities, leading to an expansion of friendly relations with other townspeople.

A crucial step in the settlement process, particularly from the migrant's point of view, is the acquisition of legal papers. Most Mexican migrants to the United States began going north without documents or as Braceros, depending on the era in which they first left. However, if the accumulation of migrant experience leads to progressive integration and settlement in the United States, then a regularization of status at some point becomes indispensable. Indeed, the "green card" or mica,[4] as the migrants call it, is highly sought after, providing security and ready access to most classes of U.S. jobs (see Reichert and Massey, 1979). It is not surprising, therefore, to find a steady, sharp, virtually monotonic increase in the proportion of migrants having legal papers as the years of U.S. experience accumulate. Only about 2 percent of rural migrants and 14 percent of urban migrants with less than a year of U.S. experience have their green cards. Most of these people acquired documents through a legally resident relative (typically a parent), using the family reunification provisions of U.S. immigration law. However, after 15 years of migrating to the United States, the vast majority of migrants have regularized their status--69 percent of those from rural areas and 73 percent of those from urban areas.

English language ability is an obvious indicator of acculturation and integration in the United States. Overall, the English ability of the migrants in the sample is quite limited. The average rural migrant barely understands spoken English and cannot speak it at all, while the typical urban migrant's only improvement on this is that he understands it a little better. Nonetheless, there is an obvious improvement in English skills with increasing years of U.S. experience. Naturally, those with less than a year's time in the United States neither speak nor understand English; but after accumulating 15 years in this country, migrants from both areas report that, on average, they understand well and speak at some level of proficiency.

A natural concomitant of the accumulation of interpersonal and family ties in the United States is an increase in social ties of a more institutional nature. For example, we saw earlier how the accumulation of U.S. experience was accompanied by a growing presence of wives and children. Many of these children are minors and will therefore be enrolled in U.S. schools. Indeed, the percentage of migrants reporting a child in U.S. schools grows steadily over the years of U.S. experience, from 8 percent to 69 percent among rural migrants and from 13 percent to 53 percent among urban migrants. Another example is membership in informal organizations. The percentage who report an affiliation with a U.S. social club rises from 2 percent in the lowest experience category to 16 percent and 7 percent in the highest rural and urban experience categories, respectively.

A particularly important integrative mechanism for urban migrants involves participation in U.S.-based soccer clubs. The percentage reporting membership in an athletic club rises from 16 percent in the lowest to 64 percent in the highest class of U.S. migrant experience. As homo economicus gives way to homo socibilis, migrants become less obsessed with earning money and take more time for recreation and socializing. Among migrants from Santiago, in particular, this takes the form of playing in a hometown soccer league. Every week out-migrants from Santiago meet in a Los Angeles area park, where they field up to four teams. This institution provides a ready means of keeping in touch with friends and relatives and introducing new settlers to the Santiagueño out-migrant community. It is an important mechanism of social cohesion and community integration within the United States.

A topic of widespread interest to many in the United States is the use of social services by Mexican migrants. Without controlling for the duration of U.S. experience, studies generally show low rates of service utilization among immigrants (Avante Systems, 1978; Bustamante, 1977; 1978; Cornelius, 1976; North and Houstoun, 1976; Orange County Task Force, 1978; Van Arsdol et al., 1979; North, 1983). Among those services that are used by migrants, unemployment compensation and medical facilities seem to be the most common. But when studies have controlled for the length of time an immigrant has been in the United States, a pattern of increasing usage over time has been discovered (Blau, 1984; Simon, 1984).

The service usage data of Table C-2 is generally consistent with this prior research. Looking at the marginal distributions, we find that migrants from the sample communities are quite unlikely to draw on U.S.

social services. Only 2-6 percent of migrants have ever received food stamps, welfare, or social security. However, some 20 percent have used U.S. unemployment compensation, and roughly 45 percent have made use of U.S. medical facilities. When we break these figures down by accumulated years of migrant experience, we generally find a pattern of increasing use over the years. Food stamps, welfare, and social security show a low and somewhat erratic rate of service usage between 0 and 15 years of migrant experience, followed by a sharp jump for migrants with more than 15 years of experience. Nonetheless, even in this last interval the percentage of service users never exceeds 29 percent. The percentages of migrants who have ever received unemployment compensation and medical treatment display a more regular, crescive increase over the course of the migrant career. After 15 years of migrant experience, the vast majority have made use of U.S. medical facilities (80 percent of those from rural areas and 86 percent of those from urban areas), and around half have received U.S. unemployment compensation (56 percent of rural migrants and 50 percent of urban migrants).

Of course, migrants not only draw on the U.S. social service system, they also contribute to it, and another dimension of U.S. integration is the payment of taxes. Migrants tend to be employed within the secondary labor market, a class of unstable, marginal jobs in labor intensive enterprises subject to intense competitive pressures. Employers in these firms may try to maintain profits through a variety of tactics: by keeping some or all employees off official books, dealing strictly in cash, not paying taxes, or not conforming to minimum wage legislation. However, over time migrants should experience a formalization of their economic status in the United States, moving into more regularly taxed, better-paid, and more legitimate jobs.

Table C-3 presents selected measures of economic integration within the United States by U.S. experience and sector of employment. These data generally support the notion of a gradual regularization of migrants' economic status over time. Those with little U.S. experience are less likely to be paid by check or have taxes withheld from their pay and more likely to earn less than the minimum wage, compared with experienced migrants. But even among those with the least experience the vast majority seem to be in reasonably legitimate job situations: three-quarters report being paid by check and having taxes withheld, although a sizeable plurality, 40 percent, did report earning less than the minimum wage (42 percent in agriculture and 37 percent not in agriculture). After 15 years as U.S. migrants, however, all were paid by check and nearly all had taxes withheld from their pay. Moreover, among nonagricultural workers, the percentage earning less than the minimum wage had fallen to 12 percent.

Among agricultural workers, however, the percentage earning less than minimum wage falls with up to 15 years of experience but then increases, an apparently anomalous result that deserves special comment. It probably reflects a selection process operating among migrant farm workers. Over time there is a marked shift out of agriculture into service and industrial jobs, leaving a very small number of farm workers in the highest experience category. These workers may be negatively selected for productivity, with the most productive workers having long since moved into the better-paid nonagricultural sector. The result probably also reflects sampling variability stemming from the small number of workers involved. Farm workers were not covered by minimum wage laws until 1966, so migrants whose most recent trip was before this time were excluded. This exclusion plus the natural selection away from agriculture leaves only eight migrant farm workers in the highest experience interval.

The last two indicators of economic integration in Table C-3 measure connections between migrants and U.S. economic institutions, namely, banks. The more experience a migrant builds up in the United States, the more likely he is to have opened a U.S. bank account of one kind or another. The percentage of farm workers with a savings or a checking account rises from 0 initially to 15 percent after 15 years. Among nonagricultural workers, the percentage with a checking account rises from 11 percent to 15 percent, and the percentage with a savings account rises from 11 percent to 29 percent.

In recognition of the intense interest that has been displayed in the use of public services by undocumented migrants, we present Table C-4 as a short digression from the main theme of the paper. This table cross-classifies use of U.S. social services by legal status and years of migrant experience. Looking at the marginals, we see that, with the exception of medical services, undocumented migrants are quite unlikely to use public services. Only around 2 or 3 percent have ever used food stamps, welfare, or social security, 12 percent have had a child in U.S. schools, and 14 percent have received unemployment compensation. In contrast, 83 percent report taxes being withheld on their latest U.S. job.

When these figures are broken down by years of migrant experience, some interesting patterns emerge. The basic findings concerning the use of food stamps, welfare, and social security do not really change. No matter how much time undocumented migrants have accumulated in the United States, they are unlikely to use these services. Therefore the increases reported for migrants in Table C-3 mainly reflect the ongoing process of legalization. The use of unemployment compensation, however, triples, from 10 percent to 33 percent, as one moves from less than a year of migrant experience to more than 15. Over the same length of time, the proportion of migrants with children in U.S. schools quadruples, from 12 to 50 percent. There is also considerable variation in tax withholding across levels of migrant experience. Among undocumented migrants with less than a year of experience, only 68 percent had taxes withheld, but this percentage increases steadily to 100 percent in the highest experience category.

Medical services are different from the others in that they may be provided either publicly or privately. It is not surprising to find a marked increase, over time, in the percentage of migrants who report having received medical care in the United States. Sooner or later nearly everyone has need of a doctor. The figures range from 19 percent among those with less than a year in the United States to 78 percent among those with more than 15 years. Overall, the percentage having used medical facilities is 40 percent. However, use does not necessarily imply service at public expense. Our questionnaire also asked undocumented migrants how their U.S. medical bills were paid: 39 percent reported they paid the bills themselves, 34 percent said the service was covered by health insurance, 20 percent said their employer paid, 4 percent said a relative picked up the tab, and 3 percent reported some other arrangement. Of the 105 undocumented migrants who reported receiving medical attention in the United States, not one admitted to receiving treatment at public expense.

Our results, therefore, do not suggest the widespread abuse of publicly provided social services by undocumented migrants. The public service that is most likely to be used by migrants is, understandably, education, which increases monotonically as migrants become more integrated into U.S. society and accumulate family members here. The one public transfer that is illegitimately used by undocumented migrants to any degree at all is unemployment compensation, the usage level of which varies from 10 to 33 percent, depending on experience. But in each experience category, the percentage of tax withholding far exceeds the percentage of service use. Moreover, with respect to service use, the effect of increasing migrant experience tends to be overshadowed by the simultaneous effect of ongoing legalization. Thus a key step in making a more intense use of services is the acquisition of legal papers. But even while legal migrants use social services more intensively than undocumented migrants, in absolute terms the usage is relatively modest, compared with native service-dependent groups (see North, 1983).

In summary, this section has shown how the social context of Mexican migration changes with the accumulation of experience in the United States. As the amount of time spent as a migrant increases, a host of formal and informal social and economic ties to the United States are formed: family members congregate, friendships develop with U.S. natives, a facility with English is acquired, jobs become more stable, clubs are joined, children go to U.S. schools, and institutional connections with banks and government emerge. In short, people begin to think and act like U.S. residents rather than like seasonal commuters. Over time, therefore, we expect a growing probability of settlement within the United States.

THE SETTLEMENT PROCESS

In the early phases of migration to the United States, the migrant's main social frame of reference is the home community, and most of the money that is earned is sent home in the form of remittances or savings. There it is used to enhance the social and economic status of the migrant's family through the purchase of land, housing, businesses, or consumer goods (Reichert, 1981, 1982; Mines, 1981; Pressar, 1982). A sure sign that the settlement process is under way occurs when a migrant sends less of his earnings back to the home community and begins spending more in the United States. In order to get at this dimension of the settlement process, we asked migrants a detailed series of questions about income, expenses, and work in the United States. Table C-5 presents information on the components of annual U.S. income defined from their responses to these questions, broken down by years of migrant experience and U.S. sector of employment.

Each economic sector has two panels of information. The top panel shows the components of gross annual income during the respondent's most recent U.S. trip: hourly wage, hours worked per week, and months worked per year. The second panel shows the average yearly expenses for food and rent in the United States. These were ascertained from migrants' estimates of the amount spent each month, on average, for food and lodging in the United States. These estimates were then multiplied by the average months worked per year from the top panel to give the yearly totals. Disposable income is computed as gross annual income minus annual expenses and is shown underneath the two panels in each employment sector. Since the data refer to the most recent U.S. job, which could have been held in a variety of years, all figures are expressed in 1967 U.S. dollars.

Considering first the components of gross annual income, we see a rather steep rise in wages over the years of U.S. migrant experience. In both agricultural and nonagricultural jobs, wages roughly triple as one moves from those with under a year of experience to those with more than 15 years, although wages are consistently higher in the nonagricultural sector.

Among farm workers, hours worked per week increase up to a point and then fall abruptly, peaking at about 48 hours among those with 5-9 years of experience before falling to a more conventional 40-hour week thereafter. Months worked per year display exactly the same pattern, rising from 4.1 to 8.4 months between 0-1 and 5-9 years of experience, and falling to 7 months thereafter. Thus, for up to nine years of experience, utilitarian economic motives apparently predominate, as migrants work on maximizing income by working long hours and more months in their U.S. job. After this time they ease up, working fewer hours and months for higher wages. The higher wages are more than enough to offset the shorter work time, so that gross income is maintained or rises steadily as years of U.S. experience accumulate.

In the nonagricultural sector, hours worked per week are somewhat erratic. Starting high at 45.1, they fall to 40.8 in the experience interval of 5-9 years, rise to 46.2 years in the interval of 10-14, and then fall back again in the 15+ experience class. Months worked per year, however, are more regular, displaying a steady increase from 6.4 to 9.9 over the range of U.S. experience considered. The increase in months worked combines with a rising wage rate to almost quintuple the annual gross income of nonagricultural workers from the first to the last experience interval.

In every experience interval the gross income of nonagricultural workers is considerably larger than that of farm workers. Overall the former exceeds the latter by a factor of 2.8. However, the expenses of nonagricultural workers are also considerably higher, by a factor of 4 on average. Food and lodging for migrant farm workers are often provided or subsidized by growers, while in cities, nonagricultural workers must make their own arrangements. However, even though the latter's expenses are higher, the income differential is not significantly reduced. Instead of exceeding the income of farm workers by a factor of 2.8, taking account of expenses reduces it to 2.4.

In both groups, expenses rise steadily with years of accumulated migrant experience. As wives and children join the emigrants in the United States, household expenses naturally rise. Among farm workers, these added expenses produce a decline in disposable income between the experience intervals of 5-9 and 10-14, before recovering at a peak of about $3,000 in the highest interval. Among nonagricultural workers, disposable income does not decline, but it clearly stalls at the same point before peaking at $6,600 in the interval 15+ years.

The most important rows in the table, from the viewpoint of our model of settlement, give disposable income as a proportion of gross income. Obviously our measure of disposable income is very crude, since it does not include necessary expenses such as utilities and clothing. Nonetheless, among those just beginning a migrant career, over three-quarters of gross income is "disposable" in both agricultural and non-agricultural sectors. That is, the quantity of money that migrants potentially have available to remit back to their home communities amounts to 77 percent of their gross earnings. Farm workers maintain this level up through 9 years of migrant experience. Beyond this point, it falls to roughly 63 percent of gross pay as more and more of their earnings are spent on maintaining families resident in the United States. The share of nonagricultural workers' income potentially available for remittance home falls immediately and rapidly from 76 percent in the experience interval 0-1 to 50 percent in the experience interval 10-14, as the cost of maintaining families is much higher in urban areas and its growth over time exceeds the growth of migrants' wages. In the highest experience interval, the share of nonagricultural income that is disposable recovers somewhat, to 59 percent.

A more telling indicator of the settlement process is what happens to migrants' disposable incomes. The questionnaire asked migrants to estimate the average amounts they saved and remitted home each month. The residual of these two quantities from disposable income provides an estimate of the amount spent in the United States on things other than food and rent. The percentages of disposable income devoted to each of these three categories--savings, remittances, and spending--are presented in Table C-6.

Farm workers begin their careers remitting or saving all the disposable income they earn in the United States. As the years of U.S. experience add up, however, they save and remit less and less and spend more and more in the United States. After 15 years as a U.S. migrant, they are spending 65 percent of their U.S. income in the United States. Nonagricultural workers begin by spending 59 percent of their disposable income. Apparently much more spending is required to establish one's self in a city job, and of course there are many more inducements to spending for recreation and pleasure. However, after one is established in the city, the relative amount spent rather than saved or remitted falls by almost half. In the experience interval 1-4, nonagricultural workers spend only 34 percent of their disposable incomes. However, as with farm workers this quantity rises rapidly and steadily thereafter, to 76 percent in the highest experience interval.

These figures provide tangible evidence of a crescive settlement process operating over the course of migrants' careers. The more time spent in the United States, the more U.S.-based family members one acquires, the smaller the relative share of income is disposable, and the smaller the share of disposable income is remitted or saved for return to the home community. However, while this evidence is tangible, it is indirect. Can we produce a more direct measure of settlement propensities among Mexican migrants to the United States? The life histories collected from 421 male household heads with U.S. experience in phase two of the ethnosurvey questionnaire provide us with the data to measure directly the probability of settlement by years of U.S. migrant experience. This information is shown in Table C-7.

There are several technical problems underlying the calculations in this table that must be discussed. First, what is settlement? It is a notoriously slippery concept to define with respect to Mexican migrants. Even after many years of residence in the United States--complete with a house and car in California--families often make annual trips back to their home communities in Mexico. They may even own land and a house in the community and play a role in local affairs; and if asked, they will swear to their intention to return permanently some day. Many do, others don't.

For present purposes, I adopt an arbitrary, yet reasonable, criterion for defining settlement in the United States. A settler is a migrant who has been in the United States for three continuous years. This definition excludes seasonal migrants who work several months in the United States in successive years. It is a far more stringent criterion than most censuses use to define when someone has moved and settled. The number of migrants settling by this definition is classified by years of migrant experience in column 2 of Table C-7.

The amount of time continuously spent in the United States was determined from the labor history, which was enumerated in months. Migrants thus had to report a solid block of 36 contiguous months in the United States in order to be defined as settlers. It is possible that some of these settlers actually returned to Mexico for brief visits during this time, but unless the visits were reported in the labor history, the person would still be considered a settler. Obviously, visits of less than one month would not be reported.

A second problem concerns right-hand censoring of the data. In the top line of column 4, 123 migrants are listed as having been censored between the first and second experience interval. That is, 123 people began migrating, but did not accumulate more than 2 years of experience before the survey date. Of these people, some are retired migrants who made one or two trips many years ago and will probably never go again. Others are young migrants who migrated fairly recently but had not yet returned for additional trips at the survey date. Since retired migrants are not of interest in the present instance, we lump the two together as censored cases and consider it the second decrement in a double decrement table, given in the column 4 of the table.

The Q_x functions for a double decrement table defined by settlement and censoring are presented in columns 3 and 5 of Table C-7. Most censoring occurs in the first few experience intervals. The unadjusted probability of not going on to accumulate at least two years of U.S. experience is quite high, about 45 percent, reflecting the combination of censoring and retiring among migrants. The results of greatest interest here are presented in the last three columns of the table, which give the l_x, $_nd_x$, and $_nq_x$ functions for the associated single decrement life table of migrant settlement, computed using formulas given in Pollard et al. (1974). The $_nq_x$ column gives the probability of settlement within the interval between x and x+2 years of experience, and the l_x column gives the cumulative probability of not settling after x years of migrant experience. Therefore, the quantity $1-l_x$ gives the cumulative probability of settling after x years, and this value is plotted in Figure C-1.

The q_x of zero between 0 and 2 years of migrant experience is an artifact of the arbitrary definition of settlement employed. Among migrants of rural origin, the probability of settlement varies from .08 to .27 over the different exposure intervals, but the $_nq_x$ function displays no characteristic shape over time. Rather, settlement seems to be a steady incremental process occurring throughout the migrant career. Thus the cumulative probability of settling is roughly linear between 2 and 18 years of experience, during which time it rises from .10 to .76, after which it decelerates and begins to approach 1.0 asymptotically. After 30 years of U.S. experience, the probability that a rural migrant has settled is 93 percent.

While there are some differences between the rural and urban life tables, the settlement process is essentially the same. Settlement occurs at a somewhat more rapid pace among urban migrants. After 10 years of experience the cumulative probability of U.S. settlement is .53 for urban migrants, compared with .42 for rural migrants. However, from 10 to 24 years, the cumulative probabilities of settlement are quite close and do not depart again until the last experience intervals, when the few urban migrants who still have not settled experience a high probability of doing so. After 30 years in the United States, the chances are 98 percent an urban migrant will have settled.

These results provide direct evidence of a settlement process among Mexican migrants to the United States. As migrants accumulate U.S. experience and acquire an increasing number of social and economic ties in this country, the probability of settling becomes ever more likely. Settlement appears to be an incremental process that occurs at a steady, if irregular, pace throughout the migrant career. Over the course of years, the cumulative probability of settling becomes overwhelming. Seemingly the only way to preclude settlement is to stop migrating. However, as we see next, migration has a way of becoming a self-perpetuating enterprise.

IMPLICATIONS FOR THE UNITED STATES

What do all these findings mean for the future of Mexico-United States migration? We have shown that the length of migrants' U.S. experience is a crucial factor in determining whether they are sojourners or settlers. More to the point, the specification of the problem in terms of this simplistic dichotomy is misleading and inappropriate. Settlement is a part of a continuous social process occurring over the migrant career. As Mexican migrants accumulate time in the United States, social changes occur that make settlement progressively likely. Settlement is a cumulative stochastic process, not a fixed trait of the migrant population. The relative number of sojourners versus settlers at any point in time depends on the number of people who became migrants in the past and the number of those who have gone on to become repeat migrants. These quantities reflect, in turn, the probability of becoming a migrant in different periods, and the probability that those who became migrants went on to become repeat migrants.

In order to make discussion more tangible, we estimated the probability of becoming a U.S. migrant by period using an age-period-cohort analysis (Mason et al., 1973, 1976). Men were selected for analysis because community studies indicate they are leaders in the process of U.S. migration (Reichert and Massey, 1980; Mines, 1981; Mines and Massey, 1985). We employed a discrete-time approach that looked at person-years as units of observation (Fienberg and Mason, 1978; Allison, 1982, 1984). Beginning at birth, each year of a man's life was coded 0 if he had never migrated and 1 if he became a migrant for the first time in that year. All years subsequent to the one in which he became a migrant were excluded.

Migration probabilities were estimated by using a maximum likelihood logit procedure that regressed this 0-1 variable on dummy variables for age (in five-year intervals), period (measured in five-year intervals from 1940-1982, with the last interval truncated), and birth cohort (in five-year intervals). Unless one makes an a priori restriction on the parameters of this model, it will be underidentified (Fienberg and Mason, 1978). Since Rodgers (1982) has warned of biases that may result if the identification restriction is arbitrary, we first computed separate life tables for age, period, and cohort and examined them to see what restrictions might legitimately be made. The age life table indicated that the probability of out-migration was virtually constant below age 15 and above age 40, so the first model we estimated forced the coefficients in the intervals under 15 to equal one another, and likewise for those above 40. When this model was estimated separately for rural and urban areas, none of the cohort coefficients proved significant, so the model was further reduced to a simple age-period analysis.[5]

Three kinds of censoring are at issue in the estimation of this model. First, there is random censoring on the right-hand side, which means that censoring times vary across individuals. In this case, observation ends at approximately the same time for all people, but it begins at different times (i.e. their various birth dates). The estimation method assumes that censoring time is independent of the likelihood of migration (Allison, 1984). This assumption may be violated to the extent that people with short censoring times (those born recently) are more likely to migrate (because of recent upturns in the rate of out-migration), leading to underestimates of probabilities of out-migration in recent years. Given the very high migration probabilities estimated by the model for the 1970s (see Table C-8), this bias tends to be conservative, with the exception of the most recent post-1980 period, which displayed a suspicious downturn in the probability of U.S. migration.

A second censoring problem occurs because the data consist of retrospective life histories. People who died before the survey date cannot report their experiences for the period under consideration. The implicit assumption, therefore, is that migrants and nonmigrants are equally likely to die.

Finally, censoring results because some migrants leave the communities permanently to settle in the United States and are not around to report their experiences to the interviewers. We attempted to compensate for this bias by selecting a purposive sample of out-migrants who had established residences in California. This sample, of course, is not representative of all permanent out-migrants. To the extent that our California sample over- or underrepresents these out-migrants, the probabilities of out-migration will be biased. In general, we feel the sample underrepresents permanent out-migrants, but whether the California sample is included or excluded does not change the conclusions that follow. Excluding the sample puts a lower bound on the probabilities, producing figures slightly below those we report, but the age and period trends are exactly the same.

The age-period model predicts the yearly probability of becoming a U.S. migrant given an age and a period. These were converted into estimates of $_nq_x$'s for the age-period life table shown in Table C-8. The l_x functions in this table give the probability of remaining a nonmigrant by age x, given the prevailing period rates, so that $1-l_x$ represents the cumulative probability of becoming a migrant by age x. The value of $1-l_{60}$ can be taken as an indicator of the lifetime probability of becoming a U.S. migrant, and it is plotted by period in Figure C-2.

The pattern of out-migration probabilities is very different in rural and urban areas. The lifetime probability of migration in rural areas is quite high in all periods considered. Given the period rates prevailing between 1940 and 1982 in the communities under consideration, the probability is never less than .56 that a man will become a migrant at some point in his life (.51 if the California sample is excluded). In these rural communities, then, migration to the United States is a very common experience among men, one that became ever more common during the 1970s. After reaching an early peak of .70 during the height of the Bracero period in 1950-1954, the lifetime probability of migration falls during 1955-1959 (when Operation Wetback was in full swing to deport undocumented Mexican workers) and 1960-1964. Following the close of the Bracero Program in 1964, out-migration probabilities once again take off. By the late 1970s, the chances are 90 percent that a man will go to the United States at some point in his life (84 percent excluding the California sample). Thus, U.S. migration has become an almost universal experience for men in these rural communities. And compared to the communities studied by Reichert and Massey (1979, 1980) and Mines (1981), the prevalence of out-migration in these rural towns is relatively moderate. The apparent downturn during the early 1980s is probably an artifact of the truncated interval and censoring biases.

The urban areas display a completely different temporal pattern of out-migration. The underlying lifetime probability of U.S. migration in these communities seems to be about .30 to .35, substantially lower than in the rural areas. Superimposed on this underlying level are two peaks when the probability reached around .50: 1945-1954 and 1960-1964. These two periods correspond to eras of intensive capital investment in Mexico. In Santiago's textile factory, for example, labor-saving machinery was introduced that displaced a large number of workers, many of whom became U.S. migrants.

Thus the time trends, and probably the causes, of U.S. migration are quite different in Mexican rural and urban areas. In rural areas, the dramatic rise in out-migration from 1960 to the present probably reflects the growing acuteness of Mexico's agricultural land shortage (Hewitt de Alcantara, 1976; Russell, 1977); while in urban areas, periods of likely out-migration reflect labor dislocation brought about by capital substitution in industry. But no matter what the underlying cause, the fact remains that a majority of rural dwellers and a significant plurality of urban dwellers are likely to migrate to the United States at least once in their lives, and among rural areas this likelihood has grown rapidly over the last decade.

Given these facts, the obvious question is, how likely are these migrants to go on and become repeat migrants, thereby accumulating U.S. experience?

Table C-9 undertakes a double decrement life table analysis of migration progression probabilities, analogous to parity progression ratios in fertility analysis, in order to answer this question. The table begins with all migrants who ever made a trip to the United States. Between each successive trip, it then looks at the number who go on to make an additional trip and the number who do not. The decrement in the process therefore occurs when a migrant fails to make an additional trip. This decrement is subject to censoring biases, however. Many migrants have only recently gone to the United States and will probably do so again, but were observed before the next trip could take place. Other migrants may not have yet returned from their latest U.S. trip. If a migrant had not yet accumulated five years since his most recent U.S. trip, or if he had not yet returned from this trip, the observation was considered to be censored. Migrants who had not made another trip within five years of the last were considered to have "retired." Columns 3 and 5 give the Q_x functions associated with these two decrements, censoring and retirement. The associated single decrement table for retirement is given in the last three columns of the table. The $_nq_x$ column gives the independent probability of retirement between trips x and x+1, so $1-_nq_x$ gives the likelihood of going on to the next trip. The l_x function in this case represents the cumulative probability of making x trips. The l_x and $1-_nq_x$ functions are plotted in Figure C-3. Both functions assume one is a migrant in the first place and are therefore conditional probabilities.

The probability of making an additional U.S. trip is generally quite high. For those with one trip the likelihood of making a second is .77 in rural areas and .59 in urban areas. Moreover, the likelihood of making an additional trip rises with the number of trips. The more one migrates, the more likely one is to continue migrating. Migration is therefore a self-perpetuating kind of social phenomenon, as many observers have noted (Bohning, 1972; Griffiths, 1979; Piore, 1979; Rhoades, 1979; Wiest, 1979; Reichert 1981, 1982; Mines, 1981; Pressar, 1982). Specifying the mechanisms by which migration becomes self-feeding is beyond the scope of this paper. This topic will be thoroughly covered in the larger study of which this paper is only a part. For present purposes, it is sufficient to know that the probability of becoming a recurrent seasonal migrant increases the more trips that are taken. Thus the probability of making x trips falls rapidly over the first few trips, but then levels off asymptotically after seven or eight trips. The probability that a new migrant will go on to make 10 U.S. trips is .22 in rural areas and .08 in urban areas.

At this point, we have estimated life tables that summarize three steps in the developmental process of Mexico-United States migration. First is the out-migration step. It is obvious that a vast number of Mexicans, have made at least one U.S. trip over the past 40 years, and that this number grew very rapidly during the 1970s, especially in rural areas. Second is the continuation step. Of those that begin migrating, some proportion will inevitably become regular seasonal migrants, traveling to the United States for wage labor year after year. Third is the settlement step. Of those that become recurrent migrants, another proportion will ultimately develop social and economic ties leading to their permanent settlement in the United States. That most Mexican migrants are now sojourners and not settlers is not surprising given the rapid increase in Mexican migration to the United States during the 1970s. However, as these migrant cohorts age and the social process of migration takes its course through these three steps, a growing proportion will become settlers, deeply integrated into the social and economic fabric of U.S. society.

The ethnosurvey data thus provide a basis for making informed statements about the relative prevalence of sojourners and settlers among Mexican migrants in years to come. The figures in Table C-7 give probabilities of settlement by years of accumulated U.S. experience. We presented the data in this way in order to break the settlement process down into its component parts: initial out-migration, continuation, and settlement. However, life tables can just as easily be prepared to compute settlement probabilities by number of calendar years since migration began, combining the continuation and settlement steps into a single table. When this is done, we find that 32 percent of rural migrants and 41 percent of urban migrants settle in the United States within 10 years of their first U.S. trip (tables not shown). To place the issue in perspective, Passel and Warren (1983) estimate that a minimum of 756,000 undocumented Mexicans entered the United States during the 1970s. If we adopt the convenient fiction that all these people were first-time migrants, then the rural probability model predicts that 242,000 will settle in the United States over the next decade. The urban probability model predicts an even higher figure of 310,000. These numbers are not presented as estimates in any sense. They simply illustrate the magnitude of the phenomenon under consideration. The ultimate point is that because of the large number of Mexican migrants who began migrating during the 1970s, the United States must be prepared to integrate growing cohorts of settlers in years to come, even though rates of return migration may now appear to be high.

CONCLUSION

There are two important lessons to be gleaned from this study. The first is the utility of the ethnosurvey method for gathering data on sensitive topics not easily measured in standard social surveys and for understanding social processes that operate at the community level. The ethnosurvey is not a technique for aggregate statistical estimation. It will not help one estimate the number of undocumented migrants in the United States or the number that are enrolled in U.S. public schools. What the ethnosurvey does provide is a way of understanding and interpreting the social processes that underlie the aggregate statistics. Thus, the various numbers computed from the ethnosurvey data cannot be generalized to the rest of Mexico or even to the population of Mexican migrants. Probabilities of out-migration and settlement may be higher or lower in this or that Mexican community. But while the specific numbers may vary with the particular setting, the social processes they reify do not. In the six migrant communities with which the author has worked, there has been a remarkable consistency in the structure and processes of out-migration. The strength of the ethnosurvey is that it provides hard information so that these processes and structures can be described to others in a cogent and convincing way.

The second lesson concerns the nature of the migration process itself. This paper examined only one part of a larger social process, that of integration and settlement within the United States. The ethnosurvey unambiguously shows how socioeconomic connections to the United States are gradually formed by migrants over the years. The growing number of U.S. ties creates conditions favorable to permanent settlement in the United States. Over time there is a regular crescive settlement of migrants out of the seasonal migrant labor force into established U.S. residence. Thus the perceptive observations of Piore (1979) and Bohning (1972) are amply born out by a detailed examination of the data.

The settlement process is especially important in understanding migration between Mexico and the United States. Mexican migration clearly took a sharp upswing during the 1970s, a finding fully consonant with aggregate level estimates based on U.S. census data (Passel and Warren, 1983; Passel and Woodrow, 1984). It is also clear that migration is a self-feeding process. Putting the two findings together, the logic is inescapable. The more people who begin migrating, the more people who will continue to migrate; the more people who continue migrating, the more who will inevitably settle in the United States. Thus any temporary migrant program or inflow of short-term undocumented migrants can reasonably be expected to lead to ultimate settlement in significant proportions. And the more people who settle, the heavier use of social services such as schools and medical facilities, the higher the concentration of Hispanics in cities such as Los Angeles and Chicago, and the greater the institutional support for further migration.

A figure of 756,000 undocumented Mexican migrants entering the United States during the 1970s is probably too low for our purposes. First, it is a lower bound since it represents only undocumented Mexican migrants enumerated in the 1980 U.S. census. And even if there were no undercount, it is only an estimate of net Mexican immigration to the United States. The number of people who became U.S. migrants during the 1970s is probably much larger. Thus, the number of people to which our probabilities apply is probably much larger--in the millions. Any way you look at it, a large number of Mexicans will be establishing permanent ties in the United States in years to come, augmenting the already large Hispanic minority in this country.

NOTES

1. The community names are all fictitious.
2. The anthropologists are Mexican in the sense that they are affiliated with El Colegio de Michoacan in Zamora, Mexico. One is actually Peruvian.
3. The Bracero Program was established in 1942 by joint agreement of the governments of Mexico and the United States. It arranged for the important of agricultural workers into the United States for periods not to exceed six months. At its height in the mid 1950s, several hundred thousand Braceros entered the U.S. for work each year. The

program ended in 1964, by which time over 4 million Braceros had worked in the United States.

4. INS form I-551 is called a _mica_ in the slang of migrants. It is derived from the verb _enmicar_, to laminate or cover with plastic, which is what the INS does to the green card when it is issued. _Mica_ thus refers to a plastic coated card.

5. For a thorough review of age-period-cohort effects in demography see Hobcraft et al. (1982). One of the few examples of cohort effects in migration is Eldridge (1964).

REFERENCES

Allison, P.D.
  1982 Discrete-time methods for the analysis of event histories. In S. Leinhardt, ed., _Sociological Methodology 1982_. San Francisco: Jossey-Bass.
  1984 _Event History Analysis_. Sage University Paper Series, forthcoming. Beverly Hills, Calif.: Sage.

Avante Systems
  1978 _A Survey of the Undocumented Population in Two Texas Border Areas_. San Antonio, Tex.: U.S. Commission on Civil Rights.

Bean, F.D., King, A.G., and Passel, J.S.
  1983 The number of illegal migrants of Mexican origin in the United States: sex ratio-based estimates for 1980. _Demography_ 20:99-110.

Blau, F.D.
  1984 The use of transfer payments by immigrants. _Industrial and Labor Relations Review_ 37:222-239.

Bohning, W.R.
  1972 _The Migration of Workers in the United Kingdom and the European Community_. London: Oxford University Press.

Bustamante, J.A.
  1977 Undocumented migration from Mexico: research report. _International Migration Review_ 11:149-77.
  1978 Pp. 22-40 in _Proceedings of the Brookings-El Colegio de Mexico Symposium on Structural Factors in Mexican and Caribbean Basin Migration_. Washington, D.C.

Cornelius, W.A.
  1976 Outmigration from rural Mexican communities. _Interdisciplinary Communications Program Occasional Monograph Series_ 5(2):1-39. Washington, D.C.: Smithsonian Institute.
  1978 _Mexican Migration to the United States: Causes, Consequences, and U.S. Responses_. Migration and Development Monograph c/78-9. Cambridge, Mass.: MIT Center for International Studies.

Cornelius, W.A.
  1982 Interviewing undocumented immigrants: methodological reflections based on fieldwork in Mexico and the U.S. _International Migration Review_ 16:378-411.

Dagodag, W.T.
    1975   Source regions and composition of illegal Mexican immigration
            to California. International Migration Review 9:499-512.
Dinerman, I.R.
    1978   Patterns of adaptation among households of U.S.-bound migrants
            from Michoacan, Mexico. International Migration Review
            12:485-501.
    1982   Migrants and Stay-At-Homes: A Comparative Study of Rural
            Migration from Michoacan, Mexico. Monographs in U.S.-Mexican
            Studies No. 5. La Jolla: Program in United States-Mexican
            Studies, University of California at San Diego.
Eldridge, H.T.
    1964   A cohort approach to the analysis of migration differentials.
            Demography 1:212-219.
Fienberg, S.F., and Mason, W.M.
    1978   Identification and estimation of age-period-cohort models in
            the analysis of discrete archival data. In K.F. Schuessler,
            ed., Sociological Methodology 1979. San Francisco:
            Jossey-Bass.
Goodman, L.A.
    1961   Snowball sampling. Annals of Mathematical Statistics
            32:148-170.
Goodman, L.W.
    1984   The Data Collection and Research Program of the Office of
            Refugee Resettlement. Presented at the Annual Meetings of the
            Population Association of America, Minneapolis.
Griffiths, S.
    1979   Emigration and entrepreneurship in a Philippine peasant
            village. Papers in Anthropology 20(1):127-144.
Heer, D.M.
    1979   What is the annual net flow of undocumented Mexican immigrants
            to the United States? Demography 16:417-23.
Hewitt de Alcantara, C.
    1976   Modernizing Mexican Agriculture: Socioeconomic Implications of
            Technical Change, 1940-1970. Geneva: United Nations Research
            Institute for Social Development.
Hill, K.
    1984   Assessing Stocks and Flows of Migrants. Presented at the
            Annual Meetings of the Population Association of America,
            Minneapolis.
Hobcraft, J., Menken, J.A., and Preston, S.P.
    1982   Age, period, and cohort effects in demography: a review.
            Population Index 48:4-43.
Jones, R.C.
    1982   Undocumented migration from Mexico: some geographical
            questions. Annals of the Association of American Geographers
            72:77-87.
Kraly, E.P.
    1980   International Migration Statistics: Definition and Data.
            Presented at the Committee on National Statistics Conference on
            Immigration Statistics, National Academy of Sciences,
            Washington, D.C.

Kraly, E.P., Chervany, N., and Warren, B.
  1984   INS Data Sources: Their Strengths and Shortcomings. Presented
         at the Annual Meetings of the Population Association of
         America, Minneapolis.
Lancaster, C., and Scheuren, F.J.
  1977   Counting the uncountable illegals: some initial statistical
         speculations employing capture-recapture techniques. Pp.
         530-535 in Proceedings of the Annual Meetings of the American
         Statistical Association, Social Statistics Section.
Lieberson, S., and Carter, D.K.
  1983   A model for inferring the voluntary and involuntary causes of
         residential segregation. Demography 19:511-26.
Mason, K.O., Mason, W.M., Winsborough, H.H., and Poole, W.K.
  1973. Some methodological issues in cohort analysis of archival
         data. American Sociological Review 38:242-58.
Mason, W.M., Mason, K.O., and Winsborough, H.H.
  1976   Reply to Glenn. American Sociological Review 41:904-905.
Massey, D.S.
  1979   Residential segregation of Spanish Americans in U.S. urbanized
         areas. Demography 16:553-563.
Massey, D.S., and Mullan, B.P.
  1984   Processes of Hispanic and Black spatial assimilation. American
         Journal of Sociology 89:836-73.
Massey, D.S., and Schnabel, K.M.
  1983a Recent trends in Hispanic immigration to the U.S.
         International Migration Review 17:212-244.
  1983b Background and characteristics of undocumented Hispanic
         migrants to the United States. Migration Today 11(1):6-13.
Mines, R.
  1981   Developing a Community Tradition of Migration: A Field Study
         in Rural Zacatecas Mexico and California Settlement Areas.
         Monographs in U.S.-Mexican Studies No. 3. La Jolla: Program
         in United States-Mexican Studies, University of California at
         San Diego.
Mines, R., and Massey, D.S.
  1985   A comparison of patterns of U.S.-bound migration in two Mexican
         sending communities. Latin American Research Review
         20(January):forthcoming.
Mullan, B.P.
  1984   Occupational Mobility of Mexican Migrants to the United
         States. Presented at the Annual Meetings of the Population
         Association of America, Minneapolis.
North, D.S.
  1983   Impact of legal, illegal, and refugee migrations on U.S. social
         service programs. Pp. 269-286 in M.M. Kritz, ed., U.S.
         Immigration and Refugee Policy: Global and Domestic Issues.
         Lexington, Mass.: Heath.
North, D.S., and Houstoun, M.F.
  1976   The Characteristics and Role of Illegal Aliens in the U.S.
         Labor Market: An Exploratory Study. Washington, D.C.: Linton.

Orange County Task Force
  1978   The Economic Impact of Undocumented Immigrants on Medical
          Costs, Tax Contributions, and Health Needs of Undocumented
          Migrants. Report to the Orange County Board of Supervisors,
          Santa Ana, California.
Passel, J.S., and Warren, B.
  1983   Estimates of Illegal Aliens from Mexico Counted in the 1980
          United States Census. Presented at the Annual Meetings of the
          Population Association of America, Pittsburgh.
Passel, J.S., and Woodrow, K.A.
  1984   Settlement Patterns of Immigrants: Undocumented Aliens Counted
          in the 1980 Census by State. Presented at the Annual Meetings
          of the Population Association of America, Minneapolis.
Piore, M.J.
  1979   Birds of Passage: Migrant Labor and Industrial Societies. New
          York: Cambridge University Press.
Pollard, A.H., Yusuf, F., and Pollard, G.N.
  1974   Demographic Techniques. New York: Pergamon.
Pressar, P.R.
  1982   The role of households in international migration and the case
          of U.S.-bound migration from the Dominican Republic.
          International Migration Review 16:342-64.
Ranney, S., and Kossoudji, S.
  1983   Profiles of temporary Mexican labor migrants in the United
          States. Population and Development Review 9:475-93.
Reichert, J.S.
  1981   The migrant syndrome: seasonal U.S. wage labor and rural
          development in central Mexico. Human Organization 40:56-66.
  1982   Social stratification in a Mexican sending community: the
          effect of migration to the United States. Social Problems
          29:422-33.
Reichert, J.S., and Massey, D.S.
  1979   Patterns of migration from a Mexican sending community: a
          comparison of legal and illegal migrants. International
          Migration Review 13:599-623.
  1980   History and trends in U.S.-bound migration from a Mexican
          town. International Migration Review 14:475-91.
Rhoades, R.E.
  1979   From caves to Main Street: return migration and the
          transformation of a Spanish village. Papers in Anthropology
          20(1):57-74.
Roberts, K.D.
  1982   Agrarian structure and labor mobility in rural Mexico.
          Population and Development Review 8:299-323.
Robinson, J.G.
  1980   Estimating the approximate size of the illegal alien population
          in the United States by the comparative trend analysis of
          age-specific death statistics. Demography 17:159-76.
Rodgers, W.L.
  1982   Estimable functions of age, period, and cohort effects.
          American Sociological Review 47:774-786.
Russell, P.
  1977   Mexico in Transition. Austin, Tex.: Colorado River Press.

Samora, J.
   1971   Los Mojados: The Wetback Story. Notre Dame, Ind.: University
          of Notre Dame Press.
Shadow, R.D.
   1979   Differential out-migration: a comparison of internal and
          international migration from Villa Guerrero, Jalisco (Mexico).
          Pp. 67-84 in F. Camara and R. Van Kemper, eds., Migration
          Across Frontiers: Mexico and the United States. Albany,
          N.Y.: Institute for Mesoamerican Studies, State University of
          New York at Stony Brook.
Simon, J.L.
   1984   Immigrants, taxes, and welfare in the United States.
          Population and Development Review 10:55-70.
Tienda, M., and Sullivan, T.
   1984   Integration of Multiple Data Sources in Immigrant Studies.
          Presented at the Annual Meetings of the Population Association
          of America, Minneapolis.
Van Arsdol, M., Moore, J.W., and Heer, D.M.
   1979   Non-Apprehended and Apprehended Undocumented Residents in the
          Los Angeles Labor Market: An Exploratory Study. Washington,
          D.C.: U.S. Department of Labor, Manpower Administration.
Wiest, R.E.
   1973   Wage-labor migration and the household in a Mexican town.
          Journal of Anthropological Research 29:180-209.
   1979   Anthropological perspectives on return migration: a critical
          commentary. Papers in Anthropology 20(1):167-188.

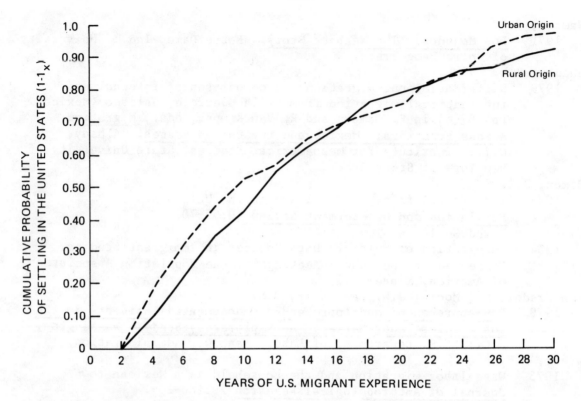

FIGURE C-1 Cumulative probability of settlement in the United States by total years of U.S. migrant experience and rural/urban origin.

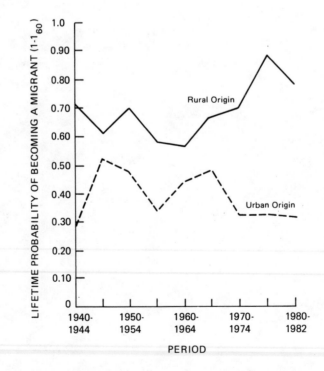

FIGURE C-2 Lifetime probability of becoming a migrant by period and rural/urban origin.

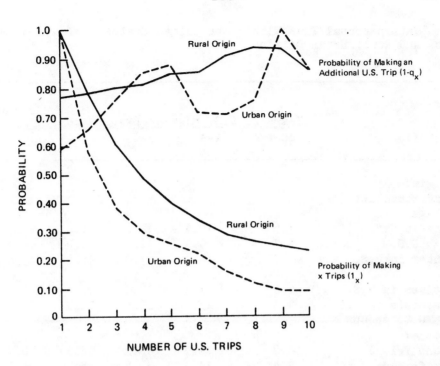

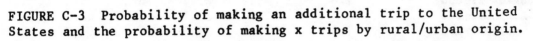

FIGURE C-3 Probability of making an additional trip to the United States and the probability of making x trips by rural/urban origin.

TABLE C-1 Interpersonal Ties Within the United States by Years of Migrant Experience and Rural/Urban Origin

Origin and Tie	Years of U.S. Migrant Experience					
	Under 1	1-4	5-9	10-14	15+	Total
Rural Origin:						
Family and Home Ties						
Percentage:						
Spouse in U.S.	3.6	10.4	18.6	26.0	44.0	16.3
Son in U.S.	1.7	6.3	11.6	40.0	54.2	14.3
Daughter in U.S.	1.7	5.3	7.0	36.0	45.8	11.8
Number:						
Relatives in U.S.	9.6	9.6	17.2	25.4	30.5	14.7
Townspeople in U.S.	29.1	23.6	23.3	22.5	22.5	24.6
Ties with U.S. groups						
Percentage:						
Chicano friend	14.8	28.9	45.2	58.3	58.3	34.6
Black friend	7.4	11.1	23.8	8.3	25.0	13.7
Anglo friend	11.1	20.0	38.1	33.3	62.5	26.9
Latino friend	7.4	27.8	31.0	20.8	54.2	25.6
Number of migrants	66	121	49	27	26	289
Urban Origin:						
Family and Home Ties						
Percentage:						
Spouse in U.S.	12.2	21.1	25.0	44.4	42.9	23.1
Son in U.S.	7.5	21.1	14.3	33.3	35.7	17.8
Daughter in U.S.	5.0	7.9	17.9	33.3	35.7	13.9
Number:						
Relatives in U.S.	11.2	8.9	16.0	14.8	24.9	13.3
Townspeople in U.S.	25.4	11.0	30.4	27.8	39.3	23.9
Ties with U.S. groups						
Percentage:						
Chicano friend	39.0	52.6	64.3	75.0	85.7	55.8
Black friend	4.9	18.4	10.7	12.5	35.7	13.9
Anglo friend	17.1	31.6	35.7	25.0	71.5	31.8
Latino friend	29.3	36.8	39.3	25.0	78.6	38.8
Number of migrants	45	47	32	12	15	151

TABLE C-2 Indicators of Social Integration Within the United States by
Years of Migrant Experience and Rural/Urban Origin

Origin and Indicator	Years of U.S. Migrant Experience					
	Under 1	1-4	5-9	10-14	15+	Total
Rural Origin:						
Percentage:						
Nonagricultural workers	9.1	30.6	46.9	44.4	61.5	32.5
With legal papers	1.5	5.0	10.2	44.4	69.2	14.6
English language ability[a]	0.1	0.2	1.2	2.0	2.4	0.8
Percentage:						
With child in U.S. schools	7.6	9.1	16.4	37.0	69.2	18.0
Member of athletic club	6.6	9.5	20.8	23.1	16.0	12.7
Member of social club	1.6	3.4	8.3	7.7	16.0	5.4
Percentage ever receiving:						
Unemployment	12.7	8.6	24.4	40.0	56.0	20.5
Food stamps	0.0	2.2	0.0	12.0	16.0	3.8
Welfare	0.0	2.2	0.0	4.0	12.0	2.5
Social security	0.0	3.2	0.0	4.0	28.0	4.6
Medical services	22.2	35.5	69.0	64.0	80.0	46.0
Number of migrants	66	121	49	27	26	289
Urban Origin:						
Percentage:						
Nonagricultural workers	60.0	80.9	65.6	100.0	80.0	72.9
With legal papers	13.6	25.5	25.0	41.7	73.3	28.0
English language ability[a]	0.5	1.2	1.4	1.9	2.6	1.2
Percentage:						
With child in U.S. schools	13.3	10.6	21.9	33.3	53.3	19.9
Member of athletic club	15.9	25.5	40.6	33.3	64.3	30.2
Member of social club	2.3	4.3	3.1	0.0	7.1	3.4
Percentage ever receiving:						
Unemployment	4.9	15.8	25.0	50.0	50.0	20.2
Food stamps	7.3	2.4	7.1	0.0	14.3	6.2
Welfare	2.4	0.0	3.6	0.0	28.6	4.7
Social security	0.0	5.3	7.1	0.0	7.1	3.9
Medical services	24.2	34.2	60.7	66.7	85.7	44.6
Number of migrants	45	47	32	12	15	151

[a]English language ability: 0=Doesn't speak or understand English; 1=Doesn't speak
but understands some; 2=Doesn't speak but understands well; 3=Speaks and understands
some; 4=Speaks and understands well.

TABLE C-3 Indicators of Economic Integration Within the United States by Sector of U.S. Employment

Sector & Indicator	Years of U.S. Migrant Experience					
	Under 1	1-4	5-9	10-14	15+	Total
Agricultural workers:						
Percentage:						
Below minimum wage[a]	41.7	28.6	25.8	15.4	37.5	30.6
Paid by check	77.0	93.2	94.3	93.3	100.0	88.4
With taxes withheld	74.3	91.0	88.9	93.3	84.6	85.0
With checking account	0.0	11.6	0.0	0.0	15.4	5.1
With savings account	0.0	14.3	11.8	20.0	15.4	9.5
Number of migrants	78	93	37	15	13	236
Nonagricultural workers:						
Percentage:						
Below minimum wage[a]	37.0	22.2	10.3	16.7	12.5	20.3
Paid by check	75.9	88.4	95.3	86.9	100.0	89.5
With taxes withheld	78.6	82.9	90.7	86.4	100.0	86.8
With checking account	10.7	6.8	11.8	22.2	37.5	14.7
With savings account	10.7	8.5	21.2	17.6	29.2	15.5
Number of migrants	33	75	44	24	28	204

[a]Includes only jobs held since 1965, reducing the n's for the experience categories as follows: for agricultural workers from left to right the n's are 36, 56, 31, 13, 8, and 144. For nonagricultural workers the respective numbers are 27, 54, 39, 18, 16, and 154.

TABLE C-4 Use of U.S. Social Services by Years of Migrant Experience and Legal Status

Legal Status and Service Usage	Years of U.S. Migrant Experience					
	Under 1	1-4	5-9	10-14	15+	Total
Documented Migrants:						
Percentage:						
With taxes withheld	83.3	93.3	92.3	88.2	96.4	92.4
With child in U.S. schools	28.6	38.9	38.5	64.7	72.4	54.8
Percentage ever receiving:						
Unemployment	50.0	31.3	40.0	75.0	64.3	55.3
Food stamps	16.7	6.3	0.0	18.8	17.9	13.1
Welfare	0.0	6.3	0.0	6.3	21.4	10.5
Social security	0.0	6.3	10.0	6.3	28.6	14.5
Medical services	66.7	50.0	70.0	93.8	82.1	75.0
Number of Migrants	7	18	13	17	29	84
Undocumented Migrants:						
Percentage:						
With taxes withheld	68.2	85.0	91.8	94.4	100.0	83.5
With child in U.S. schools	12.2	6.8	15.9	15.0	50.0	12.3
Percentage ever receiving:						
Unemployment	9.5	9.5	24.1	13.3	33.3	14.2
Food stamps	3.2	2.4	3.7	0.0	11.1	3.1
Welfare	1.6	1.2	1.9	0.0	11.1	1.8
Social security	0.0	3.6	1.9	0.0	0.0	1.8
Medical services	19.4	35.7	65.4	37.5	77.8	40.3
Number of migrants	74	118	63	20	10	285

TABLE C-5 Components of Annual U.S. Income by Years of U.S. Migrant Experience and Sector of U.S. Employment

Sector and Component of Income	Years of U.S. Migrant Experience					
	Under 1	1-4	5-9	10-14	15-19	Total
Agricultural Workers:						
Annual U.S. income	$ 935	$1,609	$3,309	$3,185	$4,647	$1,821
Hourly wage	$ 1.39	$ 1.63	$ 2.06	$ 2.97	$ 4.17	$ 1.87
Hours worked/week	41.0	43.3	47.8	38.3	39.8	42.7
Months worked/year	4.1	5.7	8.4	7.0	7.0	5.7
Annual U.S. expenses	$ 211	$ 356	$ 716	$1,194	$ 1,720	$ 461
Food	$ 147	$ 241	$ 518	$ 740	$ 1,389	$ 325
Rent	$ 64	$ 115	$ 198	$ 454	$ 331	$ 136
Disposable income	$ 724	$1,253	$2,593	$1,991	$ 2,927	$1,360
As percentage of total	77.4	77.9	78.4	62.5	63.0	74.7
Number of Migrants	78	93	37	15	13	236
Nonagricultural Workers:						
Annual U.S. income	$2,425	$3,375	$5,296	$7,260	$11,256	$5,101
Hourly wage	$ 2.10	$ 2.24	$ 3.38	$ 4.00	$ 6.95	$ 3.34
Hours worked/week	45.1	42.8	40.8	46.3	40.9	42.9
Months worked/year	6.4	8.8	9.6	9.8	9.9	8.9
Annual U.S. expenses	$ 579	$1,053	$1,965	$3,635	$ 4,672	$1,835
Food	$ 381	$ 612	$1,181	$2,581	$ 3,216	$1,186
Rent	$ 198	$ 441	$ 784	$1,054	$ 1,456	$ 649
Disposable income	$1,846	$2,322	$3,331	$3,625	$ 6,584	$3,266
As percentage of total	76.1	68.8	62.9	49.9	58.5	64.0
Number of Migrants	33	75	44	24	28	204

Note: All prices in 1967 U.S. dollars.

TABLE C-6 Disposition of U.S. Income by Years of Migrant Experience and Sector of U.S. Employment

Sector and Disposition	Years of U.S. Migrant Experience					
	Under 1	1-4	5-9	10-14	15+	Total
Agricultural Workers:						
Percentage:						
Remitted	59.3	38.8	29.6	18.4	25.8	39.4
Saved	40.7	31.4	24.3	10.9	8.9	28.8
Spent	0.0	29.8	46.1	70.6	65.3	31.7
Disposable income	$724	$1,253	$2,593	$1,991	$2,927	$1,360
Nonagricultural Workers:						
Percentage:						
Remitted	21.4	41.6	17.6	17.8	6.0	20.9
Saved	19.8	25.0	25.8	13.8	17.8	20.4
Spent	58.8	33.5	56.6	68.4	76.3	58.7
Disposable income	$1,846	$2,322	$3,331	$3,625	$6,584	$3,266

Note: Income given in 1967 dollars.

TABLE C-7   Life Table Analysis of Settlement Probabilities by Rural/Urban Origin

Origin and Years of U.S. Experience	Number of Migrants	Double Decrement Life Table				Associated Single Decrement Table for Settlement		
		Settled Migrants		Censored Migrants[a]				
		N	Q_x	N	Q_x	l_x	d_x	q_x
Rural Origin:								
0	271	0	.000	123	.454	1.00	.000	.000
2	148	13	.088	36	.243	1.00	.100	.100
4	99	13	.131	9	.091	.900	.124	.138
6	77	12	.156	8	.104	.776	.128	.164
8	57	6	.105	1	.018	.649	.069	.106
10	50	11	.220	0	.000	.580	.128	.220
12	39	6	.154	1	.026	.452	.070	.156
14	32	5	.156	0	.000	.382	.060	.156
16	27	7	.259	0	.000	.322	.083	.259
18	20	2	.100	0	.000	.239	.024	.100
20	18	3	.167	0	.000	.215	.036	.167
22	15	3	.200	0	.000	.179	.036	.200
24	12	1	.083	0	.000	.143	.012	.083
26	11	3	.273	0	.000	.131	.036	.273
28	8	2	.250	0	.000	.095	.024	.250
30	6					.071		
Urban Origin:								
0	150	0	.000	71	.473	1.00	.000	.000
2	79	14	.177	4	.051	1.00	.182	.182
4	61	10	.164	3	.049	.818	.138	.168
6	48	8	.167	2	.042	.681	.116	.170
8	38	6	.158	1	.026	.565	.090	.160
10	31	3	.097	0	.000	.474	.036	.097
12	28	5	.179	0	.000	.429	.077	.179
14	23	3	.130	0	.000	.352	.046	.130
16	20	2	.100	0	.000	.306	.031	.100
18	18	2	.111	0	.000	.275	.031	.111
20	16	5	.313	0	.000	.245	.077	.313
22	11	1	.091	0	.000	.168	.015	.091
24	10	6	.600	0	.000	.153	.092	.600
26	4	2	.500	0	.000	.061	.031	.500
28	2	1	.500	0	.000	.031	.015	.500
30	1					.016		

[a]Observation occurred before migrant accumulated additional migrant experience.

TABLE C-8 Probability of Becoming a Migrant (q_x) and Probability of Remaining a Nonmigrant (1_x) by Age, Period, and Rural/Urban Origin

Origin and Age	1940-1944 nq_x	1940-1944 1_x	1945-1949 nq_x	1945-1949 1_x	1950-1954 nq_x	1950-1954 1_x	1955-1959 nq_x	1955-1959 1_x	1960-1964 nq_x	1960-1964 1_x	1965-1969 nq_x	1965-1969 1_x	1970-1974 nq_x	1970-1974 1_x	1975-1979 nq_x	1975-1979 1_x	1980-1982 nq_x	1980-1982 1_x
Rural Areas:																		
0	.047	1.00	.036	1.00	.045	1.00	.033	1.00	.032	1.00	.042	1.00	.046	1.00	.080	1.00	.056	1.00
15	.180	.953	.141	.964	.176	.955	.132	.967	.126	.968	.166	.958	.177	.954	.285	.920	.213	.944
20	.225	.782	.179	.828	.221	.787	.168	.839	.160	.846	.208	.799	.222	.786	.349	.658	.265	.743
25	.150	.606	.117	.680	.147	.613	.110	.698	.105	.711	.138	.633	.148	.612	.242	.428	.179	.546
30	.130	.515	.101	.600	.127	.523	.094	.622	.090	.636	.119	.545	.127	.521	.211	.324	.155	.448
35	.242	.448	.193	.540	.237	.456	.181	.563	.173	.579	.224	.480	.238	.455	.372	.256	.284	.379
40	.132	.340	.103	.436	.129	.348	.096	.461	.091	.479	.121	.373	.130	.347	.218	.161	.159	.271
60		.295		.391		.303		.417		.436		.328		.302		.125		.228
Urban Areas:																		
0	.014	1.00	.030	1.00	.025	1.00	.017	1.00	.023	1.00	.026	1.00	.015	1.00	.015	1.00	.015	1.00
15	.045	.986	.096	.970	.082	.975	.056	.983	.075	.977	.084	.974	.051	.985	.050	.985	.049	.985
20	.054	.942	.115	.878	.099	.894	.067	.928	.090	.904	.101	.892	.062	.934	.061	.935	.059	.937
25	.058	.891	.121	.777	.105	.805	.071	.866	.095	.823	.108	.801	.065	.877	.065	.878	.063	.881
30	.037	.840	.080	.683	.069	.721	.046	.804	.062	.745	.070	.715	.042	.819	.042	.821	.041	.825
35	.048	.809	.102	.628	.088	.671	.059	.767	.079	.698	.090	.665	.054	.785	.054	.787	.052	.792
40	.074	.770	.157	.564	.136	.612	.092	.721	.123	.643	.139	.605	.085	.742	.084	.744	.082	.750
60		.713		.476		.529		.655		.564		.521		.679		.682		.689

TABLE C-9 Life Table Analysis of Migration Progression Probabilities

Origin and Number of Trips	Number of Migrants	Retired Migrants[a]		Censored Migrants[b]		Associated Single Decrement Table		
		N	Q_x	N	Q_x	l_x	d_x	nq_x
Rural Origin:								
1	564	73	.129	187	.332	1.00	.229	.229
2	304	37	.122	76	.250	.771	.167	.217
3	191	21	.110	47	.246	.604	.120	.198
4	123	13	.106	24	.195	.484	.093	.191
5	86	7	.081	19	.221	.391	.059	.151
6	60	5	.083	14	.233	.333	.051	.154
7	41	2	.149	6	.046	.281	.026	.093
8	33	1	.030	4	.121	.255	.015	.059
9	28	1	.036	2	.071	.240	.017	.069
10	25	2	.080	7	.280	.224	.033	.148
Urban Origin:								
1	216	56	.259	70	.324	1.00	.412	.412
2	90	19	.211	20	.222	.588	.205	.349
3	51	7	.137	8	.157	.383	.093	.241
4	36	3	.083	2	.057	.291	.045	.154
5	31	2	.065	5	.161	.246	.030	.121
6	24	4	.167	3	.125	.216	.062	.286
7	17	3	.177	0	.000	.154	.046	.300
8	14	2	.143	0	.000	.108	.027	.250
9	12	0	.000	0	.000	.081	.000	.000
10	12	1	.083	4	.333	.081	.013	.154

[a]Has been more than five years since last U.S. trip.
[b]Has been less than five years since last trip, or migrant still in U.S.

Appendix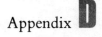

A REVIEW OF STATISTICAL ASPECTS CONTAINED WITHIN
PENDING IMMIGRATION LEGISLATION:
A LETTER REPORT TO THE INS, MAY 1983

NATIONAL RESEARCH COUNCIL

COMMISSION ON BEHAVIORAL AND SOCIAL SCIENCES AND EDUCATION

2101 Constitution Avenue   Washington, D.C. 20418

COMMITTEE ON NATIONAL STATISTICS
PANEL ON IMMIGRATION STATISTICS

May 26, 1983

TELEPHONE (202) 334-3086

Mr. Alan C. Nelson
Commissioner
Immigration and Naturalization Service
Department of Justice
Washington, D. C.   20536

Dear Mr. Nelson:

The Panel on Immigration Statistics of the Committee on National
Statistics was established by the National Academy of Sciences in late
1982, with funding support from the Immigration and Naturalization
Service, to review and determine data needs in the area of international
migration to and from the United States. Attachment 1 gives the names
and affiliations of Panel members. Although the work of the Panel is
still at an early stage, major provisions in legislation currently before
Congress (S. 529 and H.R. 1510) to revise and reform the Immigration and
Nationality Act have prompted the Panel to consider immediately two
issues of a statistical nature raised by the bills.

The Panel has concluded that from a statistical point of view the
legislation can be strengthened in two areas. The major points of our
recommendations are summarized below. Attachment 2 provides a more
detailed explanation and justification of them.

1. <u>Visa waiver for certain visitors</u>. The first recommendation
concerns the provision to institute a pilot program to waive visa
requirements for temporary visitors who are citizens of certain
qualifying countries. Criteria are set forth both for a country to
qualify as a pilot country in the first place and for a country so
selected to continue as a pilot country after the first year. The Panel
finds that the criteria established for permitting continued country
participation in the visa waiver experiment fail to recognize the extent
of the problems, difficulties, and errors inherent in the statistical
system generating the measures to be used. It is our judgment that
enactment of the 2-percent threshold as defined at present in the
legislation would result in few, if any, countries continuing to qualify
for the program after their first year. As a long-run solution, we
propose that INS explore and research the issues and problems involved in
producing the data required for threshold determination and provide
Congress with its findings and recommendations concerning a statistically
appropriate threshold level within one year. As part of its activities,
the Panel would be pleased to assist in this undertaking. In the
interim, we propose the use of a violation ratio based on the number of

Mr. Alan C. Nelson
May 26, 1983
Page Two

deportable aliens who had entered the United States under the visa waiver
system and were identified by INS in a fiscal year plus those refused
entry or withdrawing their applications for admission, and that the
threshold be adjusted accordingly.

2. Data collection aspects of legalization of certain qualifying
aliens. The proposed legalization process presents a unique opportunity
to obtain much needed information concerning a group about which virtually nothing is known. The Panel recommends, accordingly, the inclusion
of a specific provision in the legislation authorizing the collection of
demographic and socioeconomic data over a five-year period, to provide
important insights into the adjustment process of this unique group.
Such information should prove invaluable in evaluating and assessing the
impact of this legislation and in providing a reliable basis for future
debate.

We hope that it may yet be possible to effect the recommended changes
to strengthen the statistical aspects of the legislation.

Sincerely yours,

Burton H. Singer
Chair
Panel on Immigration
  Statistics

Attachments

cc: Lisa Roney
     Doris Meissner

Attachment 1

Panel on Immigration Statistics

BURTON H. SINGER (Chair), Department of Mathematical Statistics, Columbia
   University
SAM BERNSEN, Fragomen, Del Rey and Bernsen, Washington, D. C.
GEORGE BORJAS, Department of Economics, University of California, Santa
   Barbara
NORMAN CHERVANY, Management Sciences, University of Minnesota
CHARLES KEELY, Population Council, New York City
ELLEN KRALY, Department of Sociology, Hamilton College
MILTON MORRIS, Joint Center for Political Studies, Washington, D. C.
ALEJANDRO PORTES, Department of Sociology, Johns Hopkins University
JACK ROSENTHAL, The New York Times, New York City
MARK ROSENZWEIG, Department of Economics, University of Minnesota
TERESA SULLIVAN, Department of Sociology, University of Texas
MARTA TIENDA, Department of Rural Sociology, University of Wisconsin,
   Madison
JAMES TRUSSELL, Office of Population Research, Princeton University
KENNETH WACHTER, Department of Statistics, University of California,
   Berkeley

DANIEL B. LEVINE, Study Director
KENNETH H. HILL, Associate Study Director
ROBERT WARREN, Research Associate
ROBERTA PIROSKO, Administrative Secretary/Research Aide

Attachment 2

Rationale for Modifications to the
Immigration Reform and Control Act of 1983

1. <u>Visa waiver for certain visitors</u>. Both S. 529 and H.R. 1510
contain provisions for instituting a pilot program of waiving visa
requirements for nonimmigrant visitors for citizens of certain
countries. The language in the two bills differs in only very minor
respects. Essentially, a country cannot qualify as a pilot country
unless the number of refusals to grant nonimmigrant visitor visas in the
preceding fiscal year to citizens of that country is less than 2 percent
of the number of nonimmigrant visitor visas granted or refused to such
citizens. In order to continue to qualify as a pilot country, the number
of violators from that country in the preceding fiscal year must be less
than 2 percent of total applications for admission under the visa waiver
scheme; for this purpose, violators are taken to include people who are
excluded, those who withdraw their applications for admission, and those
who violate their terms of entry under the scheme, largely by overstaying.

Given the nature of the statistical system on which the test of
eligibility will be based, the Panel views these requirements for
continuation as a pilot country to be unreasonably restrictive. The
Nonimmigrant Information System (NIIS) recently introduced by INS is
based upon a new form (I-94), one part of which is completed upon
arrival, the other part being completed on departure; for departures by
air, the airline is required to collect the form. Each part of the form
contains the same unique identifying number, which permits matching the
arrival and departure portions. Thus, length of stay can be determined
from dates of arrival and departure, allowing in theory the identification of those who violated the length of stay condition of admission.
Arrival portions for which no matching departure portions are available
also may be interpreted as violations.

No such strict interpretation is valid, however, because of the
problems, difficulties, and errors inherent in the system that produces
the data and specifically with the matching of arrival and departure
portions of the I-94 form. The new NIIS system has not yet generated
enough data for an empirical assessment of its error level to be
possible. It will no doubt represent a substantial improvement over its
predecessor, but the Panel, based on its experience with similar systems,
doubts whether the 2-percent threshold can be meaningfully measured. The
weak points are as follows.

o First, the collection of departure portions of the forms is not
controlled directly by INS, and the possibility of loss is substantial.
For example, for visitors leaving by air, the departure portions may
either not be collected by the carrier or not forwarded to INS, particularly for nonscheduled flights. For persons leaving to Canada, all the
forms may not be collected and duly returned to INS from Canada; for
those departing to Mexico by land, the forms may not be surrendered
voluntarily on departure.

o   Second, a temporary visitor may lose the departure portion, in which case a replacement with no identification number is to be completed. The enforcement of such completion is quite limited for all types of departure, so some arrival portions will not have corresponding departure portions. A further problem with such a loss is the matching that, in the absence of an identification number, has to be based on name, date of birth, and citizenship: name is a notoriously unreliable basis for matching as a result of spelling variations and different forms of presenting the same name, and a fairly high incidence of false non-matches could therefore be expected in the case of such replacement departure portions.

o   The third problem is that of the not insignificant error associated with entering an 11-digit identification number into a data processing system; an error in the identification number of either the arrival or departure portion would result in a failure to match.

Errors in the NIIS process tend to produce false non-matches that appear as violations by visitors who in fact have not violated the terms of their admission. Further, important sources of error arise from parts of the system that are not under the direct control of INS, the responsibility being on individual visitors or carriers who are difficult if not impossible to monitor. Currently, measures of the extent and variability over time of such errors are not known, but in our judgment if the proposed requirements are put into effect, the 2-percent threshold is likely to defeat the object of the proposed visa waiver legislation, removing from eligibility countries with very low true violation rates, and indeed probably removing all countries from eligibility. The Panel believes that tests of eligibility of this sort should be based upon measures that can be reliably evaluated, with probable error levels that are small in comparison with trigger levels.

Accordingly, the following courses of action are recommended:

o   That INS explore and research the issues, problems, and errors involved in producing the data elements necessary for threshold determination and provide the Congress with its findings and recommendations as to a statistically appropriate threshold level within one year. The Panel would be pleased to assist the INS in this undertaking.

o   In the interim, that the threshold computation use information on persons positively identified by INS as being in violation of the terms of admission. Included as "violators" would be those overstaying, working unlawfully, or engaging in criminal activities, and those excluded from admission or withdrawing applications. "Violators" thus would represent the number of deportable aliens who had entered the country under the visa waiver system and who were identified as violators by INS in the fiscal year plus the number of exclusions and withdrawals in the year. Data for 1979, the most recent year for which information is available, indicate a violation ratio defined in this way of 0.5 percent for all temporary visitors. The Panel therefore recommends the adoption of a threshold of 0.5 percent pending completion of the study recommended above. The violation ratio as described here involves no matching, and the likely error in both numerator and denominator is small.

2. Data collection aspects of legalization of certain qualifying aliens. The provisions of S. 529 and H.R. 1510 for legalizing the status of certain unlawfully resident aliens represent an important opportunity for obtaining much needed information concerning a group about which virtually nothing is known. The Senate bill, S. 529, already recognizes in Section 401(e) the importance of obtaining information, for those aliens legalized under the act, on their demographic characteristics, employment, and participation in social service programs. In the spirit of this provision, the bill should also recognize, first, the need for this information to be collected in a statistically sound and reliable manner, and, second, the need for information to be collected concerning changes that occur over time among those legalized under the proposed legislation. It is such changes over time that will reflect the impact of the new law on the American economy and society and on the legalized population itself. Only information collected during the time when the effects of the law are felt, not before they are felt, can provide a sound basis for continuing responsible administration of the programs initiated by the law.

Objective findings on the progress of assimilation of the legalized population following enactment of the law would provide the basis for developing a consensus in regard to facts, bringing closer together the groups with highly diverse perspectives that have joined in the debate about proper immigration policy. Furthermore, the periodic updating of geographical and employment information on at least one group of former unlawfully resident aliens would be essential in realizing the potential value for law enforcement of statistical information acquired as part of the legalization program; this potential value was emphasized by the Select Commission on Immigration and Refugee Policy in its report. Modern statistical panel survey methods, using a sampling design, provide a way to obtain information on changes over time at a fraction of the cost of a routine reporting system. They also permit estimates of the reliability of the findings to accompany the resulting tabulations so that the quality of the conclusions can be assessed.

The Panel therefore recommends the inclusion in the legislation of a specific provision mandating the collection of demographic and socio-economic information over a five-year period from a sample of aliens coming forward for legalization. The group to be designated for this study could be selected in two stages. First, a sample could be drawn of aliens coming forward for legalization, and information additional to that normally obtained from applicants for permanent residence could be collected from the sampled aliens, particularly concerning their entry into, and employment history in, the United States. A subsample of these aliens could then be drawn to participate in the continuing survey. It is further recommended that a workshop be convened in the near future to discuss the design, methodology, content, and cost of the proposed surveys; that Section 401 of S. 529 be amended to provide explicitly for such data collection; and that a section similar to Section 401 of S. 529 be added to H.R. 1510.

It should be recognized that the proposed study will not provide information for undocumented aliens who do not come forward for legalization. Efforts to obtain information about this even more inaccessible group through other approaches should continue. The value of information about aliens seeking legalization also would be greatly enhanced by parallel studies of legal immigrants and refugees. It is recommended, therefore, that consideration be given to undertaking similar studies over a five-year period for these groups, though this recommendation is beyond the scope of the legislation currently before the Congress.

Appendix

A SUMMARY OF PANEL ACTIVITIES

In addition to the regular panel meetings, members and staff participated in a variety of activities structured to permit a more intensive examination of specific issues. These activities are described in more detail below.

WORKSHOP ON ESTIMATING ILLEGAL IMMIGRATION

A workshop was organized to review methodological approaches to estimating the growth and characteristics of the illegal alien population in the United States and explore suggestions for new research. Participants included representatives from the Census Bureau, the Department of Labor, the Immigration and Naturalization Service, the Social Security Administration, the National Research Council, the United Nations, and other researchers.
Major topics included:

o Methods of estimating the number of illegal aliens included in censuses and surveys;
o Analysis of data from INS form I-213, Record of Deportable Alien Located;
o Estimating emigration from Mexico by collecting data in Mexico on the place of residence of close relatives;
o Matching administrative records, such as records from the Social Security Administration and the Census Bureau's Current Population Survey;
o A survey of recently admitted immigrants to determine the extent of previous illegal residence;
o Ethnographic studies of the social processes related to legal and illegal migration;
o Analysis of regional trends in age-specific death rates and comparison of alternative measures of aggregate income; and
o Demographic analysis of Mexican census data.

Participants did not believe it likely that major advances could be made in the accuracy or detail of the estimates, regardless of the effort devoted to the task. The most promising techniques appeared to be those that have already been used with varying degrees of success.

Periodically updating the empirical estimates, even if the range of plausible estimates were to be fairly broad, was considered to be important for developing immigration policy.

SOCIAL SECURITY AND RELATED DATA: RESEARCH RESOURCES ON IMMIGRATION

The technical workshop was sponsored jointly by the Panel on Immigration Statistics and the Center for Population Research, National Institute of Child Health and Human Development, and attended by persons engaged in research on immigration. The objective of the workshop was to bring together providers and users of social security data for a discussion of the application of social security data to immigration research.

A major theme involved the need to improve accessibility of these data to the research community. The group proposed that strategies for increasing the availability of social security data be the subject of a future meeting to be convened by the Center for Population Research.

A SYMPOSIUM ON IMMIGRATION STATISTICS: WHERE DO WE GO FROM HERE?

Members of the panel and staff organized and participated in a session on immigration statistics at the annual meeting of the Population Association of America in May 1984. Papers were presented on: (1) INS Data Sources: Their Strengths and Shortcomings; (2) The Data Collection and Research Program of the Office of Refugee Resettlement; (3) Integration of Multiple Data Sources in Immigrant Studies; and (4) Assessing Stocks and Flows of Migrants.

OTHER ACTIVITIES

Numerous visits were made to selected field offices of the INS in order to observe the collection and use of statistics in INS activities. These included visits to the Burlington Regional Office and district offices in New York, Buffalo, Washington, D.C., Baltimore, Chicago, Los Angeles, and San Diego. Other activities included visits to Border Patrol sectors, ports of entry and detention centers, a briefing on INS automation activities, and a tour of the facilities of the contractor processing immigrant visas and adjustment of status forms. Within the central office in Washington meetings were held with INS officials in the following sections: adjudications, inspections, field inspections, refugee and parolee, enforcement, Border Patrol, detention and deportation, investigations, intelligence, legal counsel, information systems, plans and analysis, statistics, policy directives, project inform, and evaluation.

Meetings were held with officials of the Department of Labor; the visa office of the State Department; the Office of Refugee Resettlement in the Department of Health and Human Services; the Center for Population Research in the National Institute of Child Health and Human Development; the U.N. Statistical Office and Population Division; the Transportation Service Center in the Department of Transportation; the Congressional Research Service in the Library of Congress; the U.S. Consulate in

Toronto, Ontario; and with the staffs of the judiciary committees of both the House and Senate.

Members of the staff provided public information about the panel's work in a variety of forums. These included the presentation of a paper at the 1984 Conference on Asia-Pacific Immigration to the United States, East-West Center, Honolulu, Hawaii; and presentations to the Association of Federal Economists, the Washington Area Group of Immigration Researchers, the Population Reference Bureau, and the Southern Regional Demographic Group.

BIBLIOGRAPHIC SOURCES OF INFORMATION

Studies related to immigration are carried out by a wide assortment of researchers and analysts, including those in government, universities, and the private sector. Because the sources of information on U.S. immigration are so diverse, it is often difficult even for experienced investigators to locate studies about refugees, undocumented workers, resident aliens, naturalized citizens, temporary entrants, or other groups of interest. A thorough compilation and review of the literature on U.S. immigration would be a valuable contribution to the work of researchers and policy makers. Such a comprehensive effort was outside the scope of the panel's mandate; however, the following brief guide to sources of data, along with selected references to recent studies, was compiled to provide assistance in locating information about international migration involving the United States.

This appendix includes a description of an annotated bibliography published by the Immigration and Naturalization Service in 1979; an overview of a guide to sources of information on immigration and refugee policy issued in 1982 by the Congressional Research Service of the Library of Congress; and selected abstracts of immigration literature drawn from the National Technical Information Service (NTIS) data base along with other references provided by the Congressional Research Service. The INS bibliography includes references to many of the studies and reports that helped to shape U.S. immigration policy during the 1970s. The guide to sources of information prepared by the Library of Congress describes printed indexes, on-line data bases, and other tools for conducting research in the area of immigration to the United States. The selected references drawn from the NTIS data base are provided to illustrate the utility of the on-line data bases and to provide a limited update of immigration literature for the period following the publication of the INS bibliography.

The panel expresses its appreciation to Rosalyn Leiderman, information services librarian, and James Olsen, librarian, at the National Academy of Sciences-National Academy of Engineering Library, for their assistance and guidance in preparing the information presented in this appendix.

THE INS BIBLIOGRAPHY

In 1979 the Office of Planning, Evaluation and Budgeting of the INS published an annotated bibliography, Immigration Literature: Abstracts of Demographic, Economic, and Policy Studies (available from the U.S. Government Printing Office). The bibliography, prepared by Jeannette H. North and Susan J. Grodsky, was published in response to widespread and growing interest in immigration issues. Its scope is described in the introductory material: "The documents in [the] bibliography are generally concerned with immigration to the United States from 1965 to [1979]. The subject matter falls primarily within the following categories: (1) demographic studies of recent immigration, including methodological studies, descriptive statistical reports, and essays on migration theory, (2) economic studies pertaining to recent immigration, including works on both the economic impacts and the economic experiences of aliens in the United States, (3) "Brain Drain" studies, including the descriptive and analytic studies of the migration of foreign students and professionals, and (4) immigration policy studies, including sections on political refugees, undocumented aliens, and the enforcement and administration of the 1965 Immigration and Nationality Act. . . . The bibliography contains a variety of types of literature including books, pamphlets, reports, periodical articles, and government publications. The latter category encompasses Federal, State, and local government publications; Congressional Hearings and Committee prints as well as executive Branch reports are included."

THE LIBRARY OF CONGRESS GUIDE TO SOURCES OF INFORMATION

In 1982 the Congressional Research Service of the Library of Congress published a guide to information on immigration to the United States, U.S. Immigration and Refugee Policy: A Guide to Sources of Information. The guide, prepared by Marsha K. Cerny, provides information to assist researchers in locating bibliographic information on four major topics: immigration law and policy, alien labor, illegal aliens, and refugees. It also provides appropriate search terms for locating information in printed indexes and on-line data bases. The guide lists nearly 150 citations, including books, journal articles, legal resources, legislative information, executive department publications, statistical sources, and bibliographies. The last two categories, statistical sources and bibliographies, shown on pages 30 and 31 of the guide, are reproduced below because of their relevance to this report and to illustrate the utility of the guide.

Statistical Sources

Printed Indexes

The AMERICAN STATISTICS INDEX (ASI) aims to be a master guide and index to all the statistical publications of the U.S. Government, including periodicals, annual, biennial, semiannual, and special publications. The Index is divided into two

sections: an abstract volume which contains full descriptions
of the content and the format of each publication and an index
volume. ASI is published monthly and cumulated annually.
Access is provided by subject, name, issuing source, and title.
    Subject terms to be used in this index to locate
immigration materials include:

IMMIGRATION:	Immigration
	Immigration and Naturalization Service
	Aliens
	Citizenship
	Mexicans in the U.S.
ALIEN LABOR:	Alien workers
ILLEGAL ALIENS:	Aliens
REFUGEES:	Refugees

Selected statistical publications from non-Federal sources
are indexed in the STATISTICAL REFERENCE INDEX. It presents
data on business, industry, finance, economic and social
conditions, government and politics, the environment, and
population. The Index includes the publications of trade,
professional and other nonprofit associations and institutes,
business organizations, commercial publishers, university and
independent research centers, and state governments. Access is
provided by subject, name, categories, issuing source, and
title. Indexes are published monthly and annually.
    The subject terms that can be searched in the Index to find
material on immigration are listed here:

IMMIGRATION:	Immigration
	Aliens
	Citizenship
ALIEN LABOR:	Alien workers
	Aliens
ILLEGAL ALIENS:	Aliens
REFUGEES:	Refugees
	Cuban refugee program
	Indo-Chinese refugee programs

The PUBLIC AFFAIRS INFORMATION SERVICE BULLETIN (PAIS)
subdivides many of its subject categories with a statistical
section. For a longer description of this source and a list of
the subject terms that can be searched, see page 4 of this guide.

Online Data Bases

The CRS BIBLIOGRAPHIC DATA BASE (CITN or BIBL) also contains
Federal and private statistical material. Immigration
statistical material can be located by combining the search
terms listed in the journal article section of this guide (page
6) with the subdivisions "Statistics" or "Graphs and charts".

The online file for the PUBLIC AFFAIRS INFORMATION SERVICE BULLETIN (PAIS), available through Lockheed, can also be searched for statistical material. The subject terms listed in the journal article section of the guide (page 4) can be combined with the term "Statistics" to locate immigration material.

Other Source

The STATISTICAL ABSTRACT OF THE UNITED STATES is an annual publication of the Census Bureau. It contains a standard summary of statistics on the social, political, and economic makeup of the country. Immigration material is in the section entitled Immigration and Naturalization. . . .

Bibliographies

Fox, James W., and Mary Anne Fox. Illegal immigration: a bibliography, 1968-1978. Monticello, Ill., Vance Bibliographies, 1978. 32 p. (Public administration series: bibliography P-94)   Z7165.U5F67

Sharma, Prakash C. Refugee migration: a selected international research bibliography. Monticello, Ill., Council of Planning Librarians, 1975. 15 p. (Council of Planning Librarians. Exchange bibliography 801)   Z5942.C68 no. 801

----- A selected research bibliography on Mexican immigration to the United States. Monticello, Ill., Council of Planning Librarians, 1974. 18 p. (Council of Planning librarians. Exchange bibliography 672)   Z5942.C68 no. 672

U.S. Library of Congress. Congressional Research Service. Illegal aliens: selected references, 1978-1981, by Marsha Cerny. [Washington] 1981. 4 p. (Bibliography in brief L0063)

SELECTED ABSTRACTS OF IMMIGRATION LITERATURE, 1978-1983

Most of the abstracts below were selected from a search of the NTIS data base in June 1983 and reproduced here. The NTIS data base includes over 900,000 citations, most with abstracts, to technical reports resulting from U.S. and other government-sponsored research. The unpublished U.S. reports are prepared by federal, state, and local agencies and their contractors and grantees. Major areas covered include the biological, social, and physical sciences, mathematics, engineering, and business information (Chadra Associates, 1984, Directory of Online Data Bases 5(3)Spring).

The NTIS data base was searched by Rosalyn Leiderman of the National Academy of Sciences-National Academy of Engineering Library in mid-1983, and a list of annotated references was generated. The abstracts that appear below were selected from the original list to partially update the 1979 INS bibliography and to provide a brief list of abstracts of publications that illuminate many of the issues described in this report. The abstracts are loosely arranged into the following categories: bibliographies, employment and labor market impact, federal statistics, illegal aliens, assimilation/adaptation, and miscellaneous references.

A final section lists additional abstracts for the 1979-1982 period. These references, prepared by Marsha Cerny of the Congressional Research Service, Library of Congress, are divided into two categories: general sources and illegal aliens.

Selected References from the NTIS Data Base

Bibliographies

Department of Housing and Urban Development. Hispanic Americans in the United States: A Selective Bibliography, 1975-1980. Washington, D.C. 1981.

This is the second edition of a bibliography devoted to literature on the Hispanic minority in the United States. It reflects the growth of both the Hispanic population and the awareness of its importance since 1974. The bibliography consists of a selected list of studies, newspaper and periodical articles, and government publications which are arranged topically, beginning with general background on Chicanos, Puerto Ricans, and Cubans; followed by immigration, migration and settlement patterns, ethnicity and assimilation, and housing. Additional topics are the family, women, the elderly, education, employment, health, crime and law enforcement, political participation, civil rights, and race relations. Bibliographies are listed separately. Altogether 429 bibliographic entries are contained in this compilation. Most citations date from the late 1970s; a few are dated 1980. An author index is provided.

A Review and Analysis of the Literature on Asian/Pacific and Hispanic Aging and Mental Health Programs, and on Indochinese Refugee Mental Health Programs. CONSAD Research Corp., Vienna, VA. February 1981.

This literature review and analysis summarizes recent research, examines the issues on evaluation raised (and not raised) in the literature, and assesses the adequacy of available data for evaluation and for evaluability assessment. The task involved a broad search of the mental health and aging literature on Hispanic and Asian/Pacific Americans.

Foreign Medical Graduates. 1975-July, 1982 (Citations from the NTIS Data Base). National Technical Information Service, Springfield, VA. July 1982.

A compilation of research reports is presented on the following issues regarding the immigration of foreign trained medical personnel to the United States: (1) Immigration policies; (2) demographic and professional characteristics; (3) performance on examinations, licensing tests, and specialty certification; (4) clinical performance; and (5) information on location and professional activities. The impact of foreign medical graduates on health manpower planning is discussed. (This updated bibliography contains 96 citations, 7 of which are new entries to the previous edition.)

Employment and Labor Market Impact

Bailey, Thomas, and Marcia Freedman. Immigrant and Native-Born Workers in the Restaurant Industry. Columbia University, New York. Conservation of Human Resources Project. January 1982.

Each of four industry sectors, defined according to labor process, depends mainly on one particular category of worker: full-service restaurants on attached workers, intermediate restaurants on the quasi-attached, and fast-food on the unattached. . . . A large alien labor force supports the proliferation of full-service restaurants. Hiring networks are well developed; paternalistic management puts a premium on insider acceptance. As the stay of unskilled immigrants lengthens, they accumulate knowledge and capital, thus constituting a pool from which skilled workers and entrepreneurs are produced. The informality and uncertainty of the training process reduces the attractiveness of the industry for native-born workers seeking attachment. The most likely adjustment to immigration restriction would be a shift to fast-food production rather than a significant increase in wages or career-type jobs.

Borjas, George J. Economic Status of Male Hispanic Migrants and Natives in the U.S.: A Human Capital Approach. California University, Santa Barbara. Community and Organization Research Institute. 1981.

This research presents a theoretical and empirical analysis of the economic status of Hispanic natives and immigrants in the United States labor market. The empirical findings include results on the heterogeneity of the Hispanic population, the earnings growth of Hispanic immigrants, the labor supply behavior of Hispanic men, and the impact of Hispanics in the labor market. The empirical analysis is based on the Survey of Income and Education.

Chiswick, Barry R. Effects of Immigration on Earnings and Employment in the United States. Phase 1. Illinois University at Chicago Circle. Survey Research Lab. November 1981.

Part I is an analysis of the employment (weeks worked), unemployment and earnings among adult foreign-born men, and in comparison with the native-born. The analyses of employment and unemployment are done for the 1970 Census of Population and the 1976 Survey of Income and Education (SIE). Part II analyzes the impact of immigrants on the earnings and employment of native-born men using the 1970 census. The earnings of the native-born are higher the greater the proportion of immigrants in their labor market, and the higher the skill level of these immigrants.

Chiswick, Barry R. An Analysis of the Economic Progress and Impact of Immigrants. Illinois University at Chicago Circle, Survey Research Lab.

The theoretical analysis of earnings and occupational mobility is based on the international transferability of skills and the favorable self-selection of immigrants. Detailed analyses are performed by race/ethnic group and sex (1970 Census). Immigrants initially have lower earnings than the native born but their earnings rise rapidly with the duration of residence, reach equality after 11 to 25 years and then they have higher earnings. The children of immigrants earn 5 to 10 percent more than those with native-born parents. Using aggregate production function analysis, it is shown that an increase in supply of either low-skilled or high-skilled immigrants decreases the wage of that type of labor, and increases the return to both capital and the other type of labor. The immigration tends to increase the aggregate income of the native population, unless the immigrants are substantial net beneficiaries of income transfers. A bibliography is included.

Conroy, Michael E., Mario Coria Salas, Felipe Vila-Gonzalez. Socioeconomic Incentives for Migration from Mexico to the United States: Magnitude, Recent Changes, and Policy Implications. Texas University at Austin. Dept. of Economics. July 1980.

The purpose of the report is to present new evidence of the magnitude of recent estimated real wage differentials for low-skill laborers across regions within Mexico and through the Southwestern United States; to show the trend in those wage differentials across recent years, with specific attention to the effect of recent devaluations of the Mexican peso; to broaden the analysis of socioeconomic incentives to a series of measures beyond real wages alone; and to suggest policy implications with respect to migration which emerge from this analysis of changing incentives in the context of broader interrelationships between the two countries. (Prepared in cooperation with Instituto Politecnico Nacional, Mexico City, MX.)

Emerson, Robert D. Seasonal Agricultural Labor Markets in the United States. Florida University, Gainesville. Department of Food and Resource Economics. March 1981.

The report is a series of papers devoted to seasonal agricultural labor markets. The titles of the papers are as follows: Introduction to the Seasonal Farm Labor Problem; Some Analytical Approaches for Human Resource Issues of Seasonal Farm Labor; Seasonality of Farm Labor Use Patterns in the United States; Migration in Farm Labor Markets; The Off-Farm Work of

Hired Farmworkers; Nonimmigrant Aliens in American Agriculture;
Labor Supply Uncertainty and Technology Adoption; An
Intertemporal Approach to Seasonal Agricultural Labor Markets;
Unstructured Labor Markets and Alternative Labor Market Forms;
Occupational Structure and the Industrialization of Agriculture;
The California Agricultural Labor Relations Act and National
Agricultural Labor Relations Legislation; Impact of Labor Laws
and Regulations on Agricultural Labor Markets; Farmworker
Service and Employment Programs; Seasonal Farm Labor and U.S.
Farm Policy; and a Summary. The orientation of the document is
toward the consideration of policy alternatives, data needs, and
research needs.

Glover, Robert W. Attempting to Rationalize Agricultural
Labor Markets: A Review of Experiences with Citrus Harvesting
in the Lower Rio Grande Valley. Texas University at Austin.
Center for the Study of Human Resources. July 1981.
This report provides an overview of efforts to improve the
labor market for farm workers in the citrus industry of the
Lower Rio Grande Valley of Texas under the Citrus Labor Market
Demonstration Project from 1974 to 1977. A primary aim of the
effort was to increase productivity and incentives for workers
to remain in citrus harvest work on a more stable basis.
Meeting this objective would enable the industry to utilize
legal U.S. workers rather than relying on undocumented foreign
workers. Researchers worked with five packinghouses who agreed
to cooperate with the project in varying degrees. Efforts were
conducted in four areas: (1) improvements in fruit handling
methods, (2) development of company crews hired directly by the
packinghouse, (3) development of a variable piece rate system
that adjusted to the amount of effort put to picking and (4)
finding alternative employment during the off-season. For a
variety of reasons discussed in this report, none of the
attempts could be declared successful.

Johnson, Kyle, and James Orr. Labor Shortages and
Immigration: A Survey and Taxonomy. Bureau of International
Labor Affairs, Washington, D.C. Office of Foreign Economic
Research. February 1981.
The paper contributes to the debate on immigration by
analyzing recent discussions of the effects of immigration on
economic growth, income distribution and productivity and the
relationship of these effects to projected labor shortages. The
paper also provides a discussion of the principal economic
effects of immigration and briefly discusses the experience of
Europe and Japan in meeting labor shortages.

McLaughlin, Steven D. English Language Proficiency,
Occupational Characteristics and the Employment Outcomes of
Mexican-American Men. Battelle Human Affairs Research Centers,
Seattle, WA. June 17, 1982.

Several models of the employment outcomes process are
estimated in order to determine the effects of human capital,
immigrant status, English language proficiency and a set of
occupational characteristics on the employment and earnings of
Mexican-American males. A comparison is also made between
native-born, English proficient Mexican-Americans and a sample
of white, native-born English proficient non-Hispanics. The
results indicate that the employment outcomes of
Mexican-Americans is largely determined by human capital and
occupational characteristics.

North, David S. Seven Years Later: The Experiences of the
1970 Cohort of Immigrants in the U.S. Labor Market. Linton and
Co., Inc., Washington, D.C. June 15, 1978.

Each year about 400,000 legal immigrants enter the U.S.,
and each year about 222,000 immigrants (net) enter the labor
market. The demographic profile of the legal immigrants is
close to that of the population at large, and is thus different
from that of illegal immigrants (who tend to be young, single
males). In the U.S., immigrants earn more money and work fewer
hours per week than they did in their homeland, and, in the case
of women, quickly earn as much as their peers; the men appeared
to be on their way to earnings equity with their peers. There
are substantial occupational group movements, many of which
initially at least are downwards. The study is based on
published and unpublished government statistics and on a survey
of the 1970 cohort of immigrants.

Pollack, Susan L., Robert Coltrane, and William R. Jackson,
Jr. Farm Labor Wage Issues. Economic Research Service,
Washington, D.C. Economic Development Div. June 1982.

Proposed immigration reforms would make the hiring of
undocumented workers illegal. It would also establish a worker
program to permit agricultural employers to bring legal foreign
workers into the United States to replace illegal workers, but
only when domestic workers are unavailable for farmwork. The
proposed worker program would be a revision of the current H-2
temporary foreign worker program operated by the Departments of
Labor and Justice. The procedures adopted for establishing wage
rates and non-wage benefits of temporary foreign agricultural
workers could significantly affect farm labor expenditures and
the willingness of U.S. farmers to participate in the program.
This analysis of 1980 H-2 adverse effect wage rates provides new
information which policy-makers may use when they consider
changes in current H-2 wage determination procedures.

Roberts, Kenneth David, and Gustavo Trevino Elizondo.
Agrarian Structure and Labor Migration in Rural Mexico: The
Case of Circular Migration of Undocumented Workers to the U.S.
Department of State, Washington, D.C. Office of External
Research. July 1980.

The purpose of this study is to determine the specific
agricultural conditions in Mexico which cause off-farm wage

labor to take the form of undocumented migration to the U.S. The report reviews economic and anthropological migration literature and develops a migration model which is applied to 4 rural areas of Mexico. The principal conclusion to emerge from this research is that regional agricultural development will not necessarily stem the flow of migratory wage labor to the U.S. The Bajio, which contributed most heavily to the U.S. migration stream, was the most developed of the 4 zones studied, and within this zone there were no significant differences between migrant and non-migrant households with respect to most economic indicators. Migrant households were found to be significantly larger through the incorportion of more adult members into the extended family. Higher farm incomes in that zone permit more individuals to claim a share of farm production, while lower farm labor requirements and higher cash outlays dictate that the majority of labor by these members will be in off-farm occupations. This household structure encourages U.S. migration by partially off-setting through occupational diversification the higher level of risk associated with this activity.

Sullivan, Teresa A., and Silvia Pedraza-Bailey. Differential Success Among Cuban-American and Mexican-American Immigrants: The Role of Policy and Community. National Opinion Research Center, New York. June 1979.
The report analyzes the Cuban-Mexican differential in labor market success as a function of the differentials between economic and political immigrants. Cubans had higher initial social class and received a comprehensive program of government services; Mexicans were economic immigrants and received few services. The report uses multiple regression models with 1970 Census Public Use Sample data to show Cuban advantage in earnings and occupational prestige even when personal characteristics are statistically controlled. There is a detailed description of U.S. policy toward Cuban refugees.

General Accounting Office, General Government Div. Information on the Enforcement of Laws Regarding Employment of Aliens in Selected Countries. Washington, D.C. August 31, 1982.
This study provides information on legal and illegal alien workers in 19 countries and Hong Kong. Specifically, GAO compiled information on the countries' laws and policies concerning guest workers, national identification documents, employer responsibilities, illegal alien workers, and law enforcement. The information was obtained by questionnaire. Because of the subcommittee's specific interest, followup visits were made to four countries--Canada, France, Switzerland, and the Federal Republic of Germany--to obtain more detailed responses. The discussion of each country's situation contains characterizations of its laws, legal requirements, and sanctions. In most cases, GAO did not independently examine the countries' laws, regulations, and case law, but rather based its characterizations on information furnished by the countries in response to the questionnaire or in interviews.

Waldinger, Roger. Immigration and Industrial Change: A Case Study of Immigrants in the New York City Garment Industry. Harvard-MIT Joint Center for Urban Studies, Cambridge, MA. May 1982.

This report is a case study of immigrants in New York women's garment industry. The major purpose of this report is to examine the relationship between immigration and industrial change. The principal focus is on the transformation of New York from an industry center to a spot market and on the effect of this change on the incorporation of new immigrants and on the functioning of key labor market institutions. The study is based on a variety of data sources, the most important of which are interviews with the owners of apparel firms that directly produce in New York City. The literature on the labor market impact of immigrants is discussed in the introduction. A bibliography is included.

Federal Statistics

North, David S., and Jennifer R. Wagner. Government Records: What They Tell Us About the Role of Illegal Immigrants in the Labor Market and in Income Transfer Programs. New TransCentury Foundation, Washington, D.C. April 1981.

It has become obvious that illegal immigrants are making substantial impacts on U.S. society, its population, its economy, and particularly on its labor market; and, while it is clear that the impacts are occurring, no consensus has been reached about the nature of those impacts nor what to do about them. It is important to try to secure incremental data from whatever sources are available on the numbers, roles, and activities of illegal migrants.

North, David S. Analyzing the Apprehension Statistics of the Immigration and Naturalization Service. New TransCentury Foundation, Center for Labor and Migration Studies. Washington, D.C. November 1979.

This report is an exploratory study of the apprehension statistics of the Immigration and Naturalization Service (INS). The objective was to review these statistics on illegal migrants--which are gathered for law enforcement management purposes--to determine if they contained demographic and labor market data of utility to policymakers. The study found that all indices of migration to the U.S., legal and illegal, have increased markedly during the eight years studied, and that the indices of illegal migration appear to be rising more sharply than those of legal migration. Apprehensions of illegal aliens, for example, increased 213% between 1970 and 1977. Despite these trends, the amount of resources devoted to enforcement apparently has not kept pace with the increased flow; the number of officer hours spent on apprehensions increased only 31% during the studied period. Further, INS does not allocate its resources in such a way so as to maximize apprehensions,

particularly as they relate to removing undocumented workers
from jobs which could be filled by legal residents. The study
also examined a number of other migration control systems, such
as issuances of visas and inspections of arriving aliens.

Bureau of the Census. Census of Population and Housing:
1970. Evaluation and Research Program. Accuracy of Data for
Selected Population Characteristics as Measured by
Reinterviews. Washington, D.C. August 1974.

The report presents data on the accuracy of reporting for
selected population characteristics as measured in a large-scale
reinterview program, carried out shortly after the 1970 census
field work was completed. Response error data are presented for
three population characteristics which were collected for the
first time in the 1970 census: Spanish origin or descent,
mother tongue, and vocational training. In addition, response
error data are presented for six population characteristics
which had been collected in previous decennial censuses:
Nativity, citizenship, year of immigration, country of birth of
parents, year moved into present house, and number of children
ever born.

Illegal Aliens

Chiswick, Barry R., and Francis A. Fullam. Feasibility
Study for a Survey of the Employers of Undocumented Aliens.
Illinois Univ. at Chicago Circle, Survey Research Lab. June
1980.

A non-probability sample of Chicago employers was selected
from the Records of Deportable Alien (I-213) to determine
whether employers would participate in a survey on potentially
sensitive hiring practices, e.g., undocumented aliens. The
sample was stratified by the alien's ethnicity (Mexican,
non-Mexican) and industry (manufacturing, restaurant, other
service). The interviews were face-to-face, preceded by a
telephone appointment. The survey instrument was indirect, with
specific questions regarding hiring youths, older workers,
women, and migrants, including undocumented aliens. There were
31 completed interviews, 2 ineligible firms, and 9
refusals/unavailable, for a 78 percent completion rate among
eligible employers. Employer's procedures generally indicated
they check applicant's legal status which they incorrectly
perceived to be a legal obligation. Questions on practices
suggested they knew they were hiring undocumented aliens.

Maram, Sheldon, and Stewart Long. The Labor Market Impact
of Hispanic Undocumented Workers: An Exploratory Case Study of
the Garment Industry in Los Angeles County. California State
Univ., Fullerton. October 1981.

The study seeks to determine whether Hispanic undocumented
workers are occupying jobs in the garment industry in Los
Angeles County that might otherwise be held by unemployed Black

and Hispanic U.S. citizens and legal immigrants. The data
gathered suggest that the majority of the garment workers in Los
Angeles are Hispanic undocumented and that the prevailing wage
level for sewing machine operative jobs, the main production job
in the industry, is the minimum wage or below. The data also
indicate that very few unemployed Blacks and Hispanics would be
willing to work as sewing machine operatives at the prevailing
wage level, and that employers prefer to hire Hispanics over
Blacks as sewing machine operators. Thus, data from the supply
as well as the demand sides of the labor market indicate that
there is very little displacement of unemployed Blacks and
Hispanics by Hispanic undocumented workers at prevailing wages.
The authors were unable to obtain sufficient empirical data on
which to reach conclusions about the extent of indirect
displacement--that is, displacement that may be occurring if the
presence of the undocumented depresses wages and thus makes
these jobs unattractive to unemployed Blacks and Hispanics who
otherwise would accept them.

Morris, Milton D., and Albert Mayio. Illegal Immigration
and United States Foreign Policy. Brookings Institution,
Washington, D.C. October 1980.
The study examines how illegal immigration affects U.S.
foreign relations. It reviews the level and sources of illegal
immigration, the conditions that contribute to it, the actions
that might be taken to curtail it, the effects of these actions
on the principal source countries, on the United States, and on
relations between these countries and the U.S.

Van Arsdol, Maurice D., Jr., Joan W. Moore, David M. Heer,
and Susan Paulvir Haynie. Non-Apprehended and Apprehended
Undocumented Residents in the Los Angeles Labor Market: An
Exploratory Study. University of Southern California, Los
Angeles. Population Research Lab. May 1979.
The study presents for the first time detailed information
concerning the economic assimilation, demographic
characteristics, and social adjustment of a large sample of
undocumented Mexican residents of the United States who were not
apprehended by the U.S. Immigration and Naturalization Service
at the time they were interviewed. These persons were then
residing in Los Angeles, California. The purpose of the
research is to analyze previously unavailable data concerning
the social histories and assimilation of such migrants, and to
compare their characteristics with those of apprehended
undocumented migrants.

General Accounting Office, Program Analysis Div. Illegal
Aliens: Estimating Their Impact on the United States. March
14, 1980.
While the number of immigrants legally admitted to the
United States has remained fairly constant, the estimated number
of people entering illegally has been increasing. There are
conflicting points of view as to the illegal alien's role in the

United States. This report addresses the issues relating to the impact of illegal aliens and develops a framework for analyzing these issues.

General Accounting Office, Human Resources Div. Administrative Changes Needed to Reduce Employment of Illegal Aliens. January 30, 1981.
    The report examines the impact that the Department of Labor's program for reducing the employment of illegal aliens has had in six States. The report also describes the problems associated with a program that lacks penalties for use against nonagricultural employers who knowingly employ illegal aliens.

General Accounting Office, General Government Div. Number of Undocumented Aliens Residing in the United States Unknown. Washington, D.C. April 6, 1981.
    While various estimates on the size of the undocumented alien population residing in the United States have been made, none are considered reliable. Congress, therefore, in considering important immigration issues, may wish to weigh the desirability and feasibility of any proposed actions on both a best and worst case basis. What may seem right premised on an undocumented alien population of 1 or 2 million could be inappropriate if this population was actually 10 million or more.

General Accounting Office, Inst. for Program Evaluation. Problems and Options in Estimating the Size of the Illegal Alien Population. Washington, D.C. September 24, 1982.
    Illegal aliens are of concern to the Congress not only because of their illegal status but also because they may aggravate employment and community resource problems. As the Congress considers its response to the presence of illegal aliens in this country, accurate estimates of the size and growth of this population would be useful for deciding on policy options and for evaluating policy effectiveness. However, presently available estimates are imprecise and insufficiently reliable. GAO presents for congressional consideration three alternative ways of acquiring information relevant to policymaking on illegal aliens. In assessing the merit of these alternatives, the Congress should weigh the extent of its concern for reliable narrow-ranged estimates against the significant expenditure of resources that would be required.

Flores, Grace. Unpaid Medical Costs and Undocumented Aliens. Office of the Assistant Secretary for Planning and Evaluation, Office of Special Concerns. Washington, D.C. March 1979.
    The report presents the field materials collected under a contract commissioned by the Division of Spanish Surnamed Americans to examine the costs of medical services for undocumented persons. The findings of this study revealed that hospitals do not have systematic methods for determining the alienage status of their patients. As a result none of the

hospitals had exact figures on the amount of money lost due to the treatment of undocumented persons.

Assimilation/Adaptation

Dunning, Bruce B., and Joshua Greenbaum. Survey of the Social, Psychological and Economic Adaptation of Vietnamese Refugees in the U.S., 1975-1979. Bureau of Social Science Research, Inc. Washington, D.C. April 1982.

This document reports the principal findings of a survey of 555 adult Vietnamese refugees who entered the U.S. from 1975 through 1979 and were living as of Jan. 1980 in the areas of Orange and Los Angeles counties, California, Galveston/Houston or New Orleans. Data gathered in December 1980 include background, demographic and household characteristics, economic and employment status, social participation, religious identification, migration patterns, sponsorship and use of refugee services, and perceptions of problems and of socioeconomic status.

Hurh, Won Moo, and Kwang Chung Kim. Korean Immigrants in America: A Structural Analysis of Ethnic Confinement and Adhesive Adaptation. Western Illinois Univ., Macomb. December 1980.

Korean immigrants' adaptation in terms of their historical background, demographic characteristics, and various patterns of adaptation in cultural, social, economic, and psychological dimensions were studied. In addition to the historical overview of the Korean immigrants in the United States, their demographic and socioeconomic backgrounds, geographic adaptation patterns such as concentration, streaming and scattering ecological processes, and their general patterns of cultural and social adaptation are analyzed. Adhesive adaptation of Korean immigrants reflects multiple realities involved in intergroup relations, such as acculturation, assimilation, separatism, and pluralism. It also reveals the most salient aspect of an American dilemma--the idea of ethnic pluralism versus the reality of ethnic confinement.

Li, Angelina H. Labor Utilization and the Assimilation of Asian-Americans. Chicago Univ., IL. June 1980.

The research addresses the topic of underemployment as measured by the extent of unemployment, involuntary part-time work, inadequate income, and mismatch between education and occupation. The first part of the study critiques a number of conventional measures of economic well-being and compares them with Hauser's Labor Utilization Framework (LUF) in terms of operationalization and comprehensiveness. The second part of the study uses 1970 Census data and measures the degree of labor utilization of Asian-Americans in terms of the LUF. In this section, Asians are classified by ethnicity and immigration generation and comparisons are made with White Americans.

Portes, Alejandro. Latin American Immigrant Minorities in the United States. Duke Univ., Durham, NC. November 1981.

Immigration and immigrant adaptation among Cubans and Mexican immigrants to the U.S. was studied. Structural, social, and cultural adaptation were analyzed, as were the immigrants' views of the host society and their perceptions of discrimination against their ethnic group. Occupational and economic mobility and exposure to outside society appear to retard, rather than promote, cultural adaptation. Predominant ethnicity of community of residence and place of employment are more important predictors of social adaptation than race, class of origin, or religion.

Shifflett, Crandall A., and Richard J. Harris. Occupational Mobility and the Process of Assimilation of Mexican Immigrants to San Antonio, Texas: A Longitudinal Analysis. Texas Univ. at San Antonio, Div. of Social Sciences. June 1979.

The study examines the career patterns of 132 Mexican American male heads of household whose names were chosen at random from the San Antonio City Directory of 1977. Each person was contacted for a 45 minute interview, and information was collected on the head, his parents, and his grandparents to get a three generation perspective. The results were compared with a National Opinion Research Center sample of Anglo males from southern S.M.S.A.'s.

Miscellaneous References

Demographic and Socioeconomic Characteristics of the Hispanic Population in the United States: 1950-1980. Development Associates, Inc. Arlington, VA. January 1982.

The Hispanic population is the second largest and fastest growing minority in the country. While the total U.S. population is expected to double between 1950 and 2000, the Hispanic population, it is estimated, will increase approximately five times. Between 1950 and 1980, the group tripled in size, growing from about 4 million to over 14 million. By 1990 it is expected to reach over 19 million; by the end of the century, it is likely to number close to 24 million. Eighty percent of the Hispanics now live in 9 states: Cal., Tex., NY, Fla., Ill., NJ, New Mex., Ariz., and Col. The following groups have been identified with the Hispanic population: the Mexican Americans; the Puerto Ricans; the Cubans; and those from Central and South America and from Spain. In 1950, the Hispanic population was primarily of Mexican origin, concentrated then, as now, in the Southwestern U.S. Since the 1950s, there have been growing concentrations of Puerto Ricans in the NY area; Cubans in Florida; and other Hispanics dispersed over several states. Various factors, such as fertility, age distribution, immigration and mortality, are likely to result in differential growth patterns for each of these groups.

North, David S., and Jennifer R. Wagner. <u>Nonimmigrant Workers in the U.S.: Current Trends and Future Implications.</u> New TransCentury Foundation. Center for Labor and Migration Studies. Washington, D.C. May 1980.

The report describes one class of alien workers, nonimmigrants, who may work in the U.S. legally, but only temporarily and under other prescribed conditions. The numbers, occupations, wages, and working conditions of five subclasses of such workers are analyzed: foreign students, temporary workers of distinguished merit and ability, other temporary workers, exchange visitors, and intracompany transferees (multinational employees). Many of these workers are roughly comparable to the guestworkers of Europe, while the rural workers are comparable to the braceros (Mexican Nationals working in agriculture) of the period 1942-1964. The impacts of these workers on the micro labor markets they affect is discussed, as are their demographic impacts.

Reubens, Edwin P. <u>Temporary Admission of Foreign Workers: Dimensions and Policies.</u> City Univ. of New York. March 1979.

The report examines the policy dimensions of the H-2 Program (Temporary admission of foreign workers) in terms of legal and administrative provisions; numbers and trends of H-2 workers; functions of H-2 workers; the need for foreign workers; the capacity to absorb foreign workers; and the available policy options.

General Accounting Office. Human Resources Div. <u>Greater Emphasis on Early Employment and Better Monitoring Needed in Indochinese Refugee Resettlement Program.</u> Washington, D.C. March 1, 1983.

Although the Refugee Act of 1980 establishes the goal of quick self-sufficiency for refugees, its achievement has been impeded by problems in the Indochinese refugee resettlement program including (1) continued placement of most refugees in a few areas of the United States; (2) lack of employment assistance given to refugees soon after their arrival, coupled with the large number receiving public assistance; (3) limited monitoring by voluntary agencies to assure that refugees receive services needed to help them become self-sufficient; and (4) fragmented Federal management of the resettlement program and poor program direction and oversight. Much corrective action has been taken through recent reauthorizing legislation and administrative action. GAO is making additional recommendations to the Secretaries of the Departments of Health and Human Services and State that would (1) place program emphasis on quick employment for refugees and (2) improve direction and oversight of the refugee program by key offices involved in resettlement activities.

General Accounting Office. Human Resources Div. Issues
Concerning Social Security Benefits Paid to Aliens. Washington,
D.C. March 24, 1983.

There has long been congressional concern about aliens who
work only long enough to become eligible for social security
benefits and then return to their native countries to collect
the benefits for themselves and their dependents. In 1981, the
Social Security Administration paid nearly $1 billion to 313,000
beneficiaries living abroad, more than 60 percent of whom were
aliens. Alien retirees abroad generally have worked less time
in covered employment, have paid less taxes to social security,
and have more dependents than the average retiree, frequently
adding such dependents after retirement. GAO's study also
identified an inconsistency between the Social Security Act and
the Immigration and Nationality Act--aliens are allowed to earn
social security credits under the former act while violating the
latter. Accumulation of credits by and the payment of benefits
to aliens who worked illegally in the United States could be
costly to the trust funds.

General Accounting Office. International Div. Indochinese
Refugees: Protection, Care, and Processing Can Be Improved.
Washington, D.C. August 19, 1980.

The continuous exodus of refugees from Communist Indochina
in 1979 strained the willingness and the ability of Asian asylum
countries to accept refugees and to assist in providing
protection and temporary care. GAO reported in 1979 that
because of political restraints and the humanitarian plight of
these people, the Department of State should seek more active
participation of international and voluntary agencies in refugee
resettlement. In the past year, conditions at the transit
centers and resettlement camps have improved somewhat. GAO
makes additional recommendations to alleviate the continuing
problems associated with refugee protection, care, and
resettlement.

General Accounting Office. General Government Div.
Information on Immigration in 17 Countries. Washington, D.C.
January 12, 1979.

The immigration policies and trends in selected developed
and developing countries were reviewed. The following countries
were selected for review: Argentina, Australia, Canada,
Colombia, Dominican Republic, Federal Republic of Germany,
France, Great Britain, Guatemala, Haiti, Jamaica, Mexico, New
Zealand, Philippines, Sweden, Thailand, and Venezuela. From
each country specific data was requested concerning visitors,
foreign students, guest workers, refugees, permanent resident
aliens, citizenship, and immigration problems. The data
furnished varied by country. The data provided are incorporated
in a summary for each country. Included is information from
countries' representatives familiar with local immigration,
policies and trends, and the local U.S. embassy or consulate.

Data on immigration to the United States from these countries are also included.

Selected References Prepared by
Congressional Research Service: 1979-1982

General Sources

Martin, Philip L. Select commission suggests changes in immigration policy--a review essay. Monthly Labor Review, v. 105, Feb. 1982: 31-37.
Describes the recommendations of the Select Commission on Immigration and Refugee Policy for reforming the immigration system. These recommendations include "tougher enforcement, higher quotas, amnesty for most current illegal aliens," and a reliable means for checking the legal status of workers.

Reimers, David M. Post-World War II immigration to the United States: America's latest newcomers. In America as a multicultural society. Philadelphia, American Academy of Political and Social Science, 1981. (Annals, v. 454, Mar. 1981) p. 1-12.
Reviews changes that have occurred in U.S. immigration policy since the 1940s. Also looks at the shifts in country of origin of the immigrants--from northern and western European countries to Third World nations.

Schroeder, Richard C. Refugee policy. [Washington Congressional Quarterly] 1980. 387-404 p. (Editorial research reports, 1980, v. 1, no. 20).
Contents.--Spotlight on the Caribbean.--Global efforts to aid refugees.--Implications of policy reforms.

Teitelbaum, Michael S. Right versus right: immigration and refugee policy in the United States. Foreign affairs, v. 59, fall 1980: 21-59.
Concludes that, in the long term, the only humane and sustainable policy regarding immigration and refugees must be one that accurately reflects American national interest and humanitarian values, protects the civil liberties and rights of citizens and immigrants alike, and recognizes the importance of trade and foreign assistance policies for developing countries. Advocates the development of legislation to embody such an immigration policy.

U.S. Select Commission on Immigration and Refugee Policy. U.S. immigration policy and national interest; the final report and recommendations . . . with supplemental views by commissioners. [Washington] 1981. 453 p.

Partial contents.--Undocumented/illegal aliens.--The admission of immigrants.--Refugee and mass asylum issues.--Nonimmigrant aliens.--Administrative issues.--Legal issues.--Language requirement for naturalization.

Walter, Jacob. Lack of cash and poor coordination plague U.S. refugee policies. National journal, v. 12, July 26, 1980: 1234-1237.
     "If you count Cubans and Haitians, some 364,000 refugees are flocking to the United States this year, only to be greeted by a patchwork of government and voluntary agencies that have little in common except a shortage of money that many feel is necessary to cope with the problem."

Illegal Aliens

Abrams, Elliott. The myth of the illegal alien crisis. Journal of the Institute for Socioeconomic Studies, v. 4, spring 1979: 27-35.
     Examines the illegal alien problem from the viewpoint of its basis in American economic history.

Burnett, Richard. Illegal aliens come cheap. Progressive, v. 43, Oct. 1979: 44-46.
     Compares U.S. immigration policy with the employment of Mediterranean "guest workers" in northern Europe and the "homelands" policy of South Africa. Concludes that all of these policies ensure a supply of unskilled labor which, because it lacks a permanent right of residence, remains docile and relatively cheap.

Cornelius, Wayne A. Mexican migration to the United States. In Mexico-United States relations. New York, Academy of Political Science, 1980. (Proceedings, v. 34, no. 1, 1981) p. 67-77.
     Questions the view that illegal Mexican immigration could be reduced significantly by government action and concentrates instead on the limits to government intervention on the United States side of the border.

Keely, Charles B. Illegal migration. Scientific American, v. 246, Mar. 1982: 41-47.
     Focuses on the questions of how many illegal residents there are in the U.S., how fast the number of illegal aliens is growing, the effect of illegal immigration on U.S. society, and how this problem might be solved.

Keely, Charles B. The shadows of invisible people. American demographics, v. 2, Mar. 1980: 24, 26-29.
     Looks at the estimated number of illegal aliens in the United States. States that what has emerged from this analysis is a picture of a resident illegal migrant population that is

smaller than has been believed to be the case. "The more recent analyses, using demographic methods, conclude the number of illegal migrants around 1973-75 to be in the lower end of the 4 to 12 million range."

Martin, Philip L. Illegal immigration: the guestworker option, by Philip L. Martin and Ellen B. Sehgal. Public policy, v. 28, spring 1980: 207-229.

As a solution to the problem of illegal immigration into the United States, analyzes the effect of converting illegal aliens to the status of guest workers. Argues that a U.S. guest worker program is discouraged on conceptual and empirical grounds. Contends that "the availability of foreign workers does not solve 'labor shortage' problems; further, it only postpones debate and decision on the kinds of jobs and job structure the United States should have."

Appendix G

BIOGRAPHICAL SKETCHES OF PANEL MEMBERS AND STAFF

BURTON SINGER, chair of the Panel on Immigration Statistics, is professor and chair of the Department of Statistics at Columbia University and adjunct professor, Laboratory of Populations at Rockefeller University. He also is a member of the Committee on National Statistics. He received a Ph.D. in statistics from Stanford University. His interests include medical epidemiology, economics, demography, and the theory of stochastic processes.

SAM BERNSEN is a practicing immigration attorney in Washington, D.C., with the firm of Fragomen, Del Rey & Bernsen, P.C. He also teaches immigration law at the law schools of American University and Catholic University. From 1974 to 1977 he served as general counsel of the Immigration and Naturalization Service. Previously he served in that agency as an assistant commissioner and as a district director. He has an LL.B. from Brooklyn Law School.

GEORGE J. BORJAS is professor of economics at the University of California, Santa Barbara; he is also a research associate at the National Bureau of Economic Research. His present work examines the extent of quality changes among the immigrant cohorts admitted to the United States in the postwar period. He received a B.S. in economics and mathematics from St. Peter's College and a Ph.D. in economics from Columbia University.

NORMAN L. CHERVANY is a professor of management sciences and director of professional management programs in the Graduate School of Management at the University of Minnesota. His major work is in the area of applied decision-information systems and in organizational strategy. He is past president and a fellow of the American Institute for Decision Sciences. He has a B.S. in mathematics from Mount Union College and M.B.A. and D.B.A. degrees in quantitative business analysis from Indiana University.

KENNETH HILL, associate study director for the Panel on Immigration Statistics, has been on the staff of the Commission on Behavioral and Social Sciences and Education of the National Research Council since 1977. His previous work experience has been mainly in the field of demographic statistics for developing countries, working for the

Statistics Division of the government of Uganda, the Centre for
Population Studies of the London School of Hygiene and Tropical Medicine,
the U.N. Latin American Demographic Centre, and the Committee on
Population and Demography of the National Research Council. He has a
Ph.D. from the London School of Hygiene and Tropical Medicine. He has
authored or coauthored numerous articles and texts concerning the
estimation of fertility, mortality and migration for developing countries.

CHARLES B. KEELY is senior associate at the Population Council in New
York. He received a Ph.D. in sociology from Fordham University. His
research interests include labor migration, especially in the Middle
East, international policy and programs on refugees, and U.S. immigration
policy and its demographic impacts.

ELLEN PERCY KRALY is assistant professor of geography at Colgate
University. She received an M.S. degree in demography from Johns Hopkins
University and a Ph.D. in sociology from Fordham University. Her
research focuses on federal and international statistics on immigration
and emigration, the relationship between immigration and population
growth, and trends in emigration from the United States. She is also
directing a research project involving issues in infant nutrition.

DANIEL B. LEVINE, study director for the Panel on Immigration Statistics,
was formerly with the Bureau of the Census; he was deputy director
between 1979 and 1982 and also served as acting director. His interests
are in the management of statistical systems and in the collection,
processing, and presentation of statistical information, particularly
through the conduct of large-scale surveys and censuses. He is a fellow
of the American Statistical Association and a member of the International
Statistical Institute. He received an M.A. in economics from Columbia
University.

MILTON D. MORRIS is director of research at the Joint Center for
Political Studies. Previously he was associate professor of political
science at Southern Illinois University, a research fellow at the Joint
Center, and a senior fellow at the Brookings Institution. His research
interests are in political behavior, race and ethnic relations,
immigration, and urban policy. He received M.A. and Ph.D. degrees in
political science from the University of Maryland.

ALEJANDRO PORTES is professor of sociology at the Johns Hopkins
University and a member of the faculty of the Hopkins School of Advanced
International Studies in Washington. Previously he taught at Duke
University, the University of Brasilia, the University of Texas at
Austin, and the University of Illinois. He has served as chair of the
Latin American and Caribbean Dissertation Fellowship Committee of the
Social Science Research Council, program adviser for social sciences for
the Ford Foundation in Brazil, and associate director of the Institute of
Latin American Studies, University of Texas at Austin. His principal
research interests are comparative urbanization and international
migration. He is currently conducting a longitudinal study of 1980 Cuban
(Mariel) refugees and Haitian boat people in South Florida and a

comparative project on the urban informal sector in two South American capital cities.

JACK ROSENTHAL is deputy editorial page editor of The New York Times. He graduated from Harvard College, served as a senior aide in the Department of Justice and the Department of State, spent a year at Harvard's Institute of Politics as a fellow, served as principal author of the Kerner Commission report on urban disorders, and won the Pulitzer Prize for editorial writing in 1982. He has written about immigration since college, inside and outside the government. He is an immigrant.

MARK R. ROSENZWEIG is professor of economics at the University of Minnesota. He received a Ph.D. in economics from Columbia University. During 1979-1980 he was a research director of the Select Commission on Immigration and Refugee Policy. He is currently working on a monograph on U.S. immigration using Census Bureau, INS, and World Bank data and on studies of the determinants and consequences of child health, fertility, family structure, and public health programs in developed and developing countries.

TERESA A. SULLIVAN is associate professor of sociology and training director of the Population Research Center at the University of Texas at Austin. She received a Ph.D. in sociology from the University of Chicago. She is a demographer with interests in labor force, immigration, and minority groups. She is also a member of the National Research Council's Panel on Technology and Women's Employment.

MARTA TIENDA is professor of rural sociology and affiliate of the Center for Demography and Ecology and the Institute for Research on Poverty at the University of Wisconsin. She is principal investigator of a research project on the labor market and program participation of Hispanic immigrants and Southeast Asian refugees. Her expertise is in economic sociology, demography, international development and immigration. She is a member of the board of directors of the Population Association of America and the Census Advisory Committee on Population Statistics (1979-1985). She received a B.A. in Spanish literature from Michigan State University and M.A. and Ph.D. degrees in sociology from the University of Texas at Austin.

JAMES TRUSSELL is professor of economics and public affairs and faculty associate in the Office of Population Research at Princeton University. His principal research interests are demographic methods, fertility, and family planning, and he has published research papers in all three areas. He is a member of the Population Association of America and the International Union for the Scientific Study of Population. He received a B.S. in mathematics from Davidson College, a B.Phil. from Oxford University in economics, and a Ph.D. in economics from Princeton University.

KENNETH W. WACHTER is associate professor of demography and statistics at the University of California, Berkeley. Author of a major work on statistical studies of historical social structure, he also works in the areas of multivariate statistical analysis, mathematical population studies, demographic simulation, and kinship forecasting. An expert witness in the suit over the 1980 U.S. census, he serves as a member of the National Science Foundation's Review Panel on Measurement Methods and Data Improvement, as a member of the Scientific Committee on Family and Life Cycle Demography of the International Union for the Scientific Study of Population, and as research associate of the National Bureau for Economic Research. He has a Ph.D. in statistics from Cambridge University.

ROBERT WARREN, who served as research associate for the study, is now a demographer with the Statistical Analysis Branch of the Immigration and Naturalization Service. At the time of the study, he was on leave to the panel from the Bureau of the Census. His research interests have focused on the evaluation of decennial census coverage and the development of methodology to estimate emigration and undocumented immigration. He is the coauthor of a pathfinding report on estimating the number of illegal aliens counted in the 1980 decennial census. He has an M.S. from Indiana University.